*The Revised
and Enhanced*

HISTORY OF
JOSEPH SMITH
BY HIS MOTHER

*The Revised
and Enhanced*

HISTORY OF
JOSEPH SMITH
BY HIS MOTHER

Edited by Scot Facer Proctor
and Maurine Jensen Proctor

BOOKCRAFT
Salt Lake City, Utah

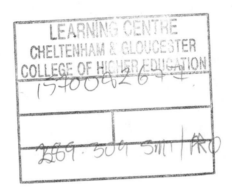
Copyright © 1996 by Bookcraft, Inc.

Library of Congress Catalog Card Number: 96-85700
ISBN 1-57008-267-7

Fifth Printing, 1998

Printed in the United States of America

Contents

Part I
Mack Ancestry

PART 2
The New England Years

PART 3

New York / Pennsylvania
Beginnings of the Restoration

PART 4

The Gathering in Ohio

PART 5
The Missouri Persecutions

PART 6
Nauvoo and the Martyrdom

ABBREVIATIONS USED IN NOTES

Anderson, *Heritage*

Anderson, Richard Lloyd. *Joseph Smith's New England Heritage.* Salt Lake City: Deseret Book Co., 1971.

Backman, *Eyewitness Accounts*

Backman, Milton V., Jr. *Eyewitness Accounts of the Restoration.* Salt Lake City: Deseret Book Co., 1986.

Biographical Sketches

Smith, Lucy Mack. *Biographical Sketches of Joseph Smith, the Prophet, and His Progenitors for Many Generations.* Liverpool: Published for Orson Pratt by S. W. Richards, 1853; photomechanical reproduction, Orem, Utah: Grandin Book Co., 1995.

Bushman, *Beginnings*

Bushman, Richard L. *Joseph Smith and the Beginnings of Mormonism.* Urbana and Chicago: University of Illinois Press, 1984.

Cook, *Revelations*

Cook, Lyndon W. *The Revelations of the Prophet Joseph Smith: A Historical and Biographical Commentary of the Doctrine and Covenants.* Salt Lake City: Deseret Book Co., 1985.

Cook, *Whitmer Interviews*

Cook, Lyndon W., ed. *David Whitmer Interviews: A Restoration Witness.* Orem, Utah: Grandin Book Co., 1991.

Early Notebook

Smith, Lucy Mack. Unpublished Early Notebook. 1844–45. Special Collections, Harold B. Lee Library, Brigham Young University.

George A. Smith, Edited 1853

Smith, Lucy Mack. *Biographical Sketches of Joseph Smith, the Prophet, and His Progenitors for Many Generations.* Liverpool: Published for Orson Pratt by S. W. Richards, 1853. Personal copy with pencil and ink mark edits and notes by George A. Smith.

History of the Church

Smith, Joseph. *History of The Church of Jesus Christ of Latter-day Saints.* Edited by Brigham H. Roberts. 7 vols. Salt Lake City: The Church of Jesus Christ of Latter-day Saints, 1932–51.

JD

Journal of Discourses. 26 vols. Liverpool, England: Printed and published by Albert Carrington [and others], 1853–1886.

Narrative

Mack, Solomon. *A Narrative of the Life of Solomon Mack. . . .* Windsor, Vt.: Printed at the expense of the author, 1811.

Papers

Smith, Joseph. *The Papers of Joseph Smith, Volume 1: Autobiographical and Historical Writings.* Edited by Dean C. Jessee. Salt Lake City: Deseret Book Co., 1989.

Porter, "Origins"

Porter, Larry C. "A Study of the Origins of the Church of Jesus Christ of Latter-day Saints in the States of New York and Pennsylvania, 1816–1831." Ph.D. diss., Brigham Young University, 1971.

Pratt, *Autobiography*

Pratt, Parley P. *Autobiography of Parley P. Pratt.* Edited by Parley P. Pratt Jr. Classics in Mormon Literature. Salt Lake City: Deseret Book Co., 1985.

Preliminary Manuscript

Smith, Lucy Mack. Unpublished Preliminary Manuscript. 1845. LDS Church Archives. (*Note:* All references to the Preliminary Manuscript are without page numbers.)

EDITORS' INTRODUCTION

❧

It was the bleak midwinter of 1844–45, only months since her sons Joseph and Hyrum had been murdered by a gloating mob at Carthage Jail, when Lucy Mack Smith sat down to tell her life story to a twenty-three-year-old scribe named Martha Jane Knowlton Coray. Lucy was sixty-nine years old, afflicted, as she said, "by a complication of disease and infirmities" and still aching with loss. In the fall of 1840 she thought she had experienced the most misery she would ever know. She recalled: "I then thought that there was no evil for me to fear upon the earth more than what I had experienced in the death of my beloved husband. It was all the grief which my nature was able to bear, and I thought that I could never again be called to suffer so great an affliction as this." But time had proven her wrong. Her nature would be called upon to bear more. On a June night in 1844, word had come to Nauvoo that her two sons had been murdered, and thirty-three days later another son, Samuel, would languish and die of complications arising from being chased on horseback by the mob. Of her six sons who had lived to maturity, five were gone, and with the exception of some sons-in-law, Lucy's family was reduced to widows and fatherless children.

These weren't her only losses. Once her son Joseph had received a heavenly vision and had learned that he was the prophet to restore the gospel in the latter days, trial had plagued Lucy. She had lost her farm in New York; she had seen her husband imprisoned; she had trudged through an incessant rain on the way to Missouri that reduced her to near death; she had seen soldiers whoop and holler as they dragged her sons to jail with a death sentence on their heads. Of the endless grief, she said: "I often wonder to hear brethren and sisters murmur at the trifling inconveniences which they have to encounter . . . , and I think to myself, salvation is worth as much now as it was in the beginning of the work. But I find that 'all like the purchase, few the price will pay.'"

It was a woman who not only was willing to pay the price for her religious convictions, but already had, who sat down with the scribe that winter in Nauvoo. Thus, her history rings with sincerity and deeply felt emotion. However much others may have doubted and harangued her son Joseph, Lucy had no doubt that he was exactly what he claimed to be—a prophet. She had a remarkable story to tell and she told it remarkably—with passion, candor, and fluency. Apart from anything else, it would be a wonderful story for generations of readers, but beyond that, it gives a personal glimpse of Joseph Smith seen nowhere else. Here is Joseph dealing with excruciating pain during a crude operation on his leg, sick with misery at Martin Harris's loss of the 116 pages, laying a cloak down on the hard floor night after night to give someone else his bed in Kirtland. Through Lucy's recollections, we enter the Smith family home, hear their conversations, watch a young boy beginning to understand that he has a profound destiny. It is a rare thing to have a sustained narrative from the mother of a man who has had such a significant impact on the world.

What's more, we come to know Joseph better in these pages because we come to know Lucy. To understand the mother is to understand something more about the son. They share the same native flair for expression, the same courage in the face of opposition. They are both high-spirited, deeply loyal to their beliefs, hardworking, and intelligent. Most of all, they share a passion to understand who God is and what he expects of them. When Lucy was a young married woman, sick and apparently dying, she made a covenant with God: "I covenanted with God that if he would let me live, I would endeavor to get that religion that would enable me to serve him right, whether it was in the Bible or wherever it might be found." For Lucy, this began an intense search for the true religion that is echoed in her son's similar yearnings. Joseph is certainly a product of the mother and home from which he came.

The Preliminary Manuscript

It is not entirely clear who motivated the creation of Lucy Mack Smith's history. In January 1845, she wrote to her son William that she

BRIEF LOOK AT THE LUCY MACK SMITH DICTATIONS AND HISTORY

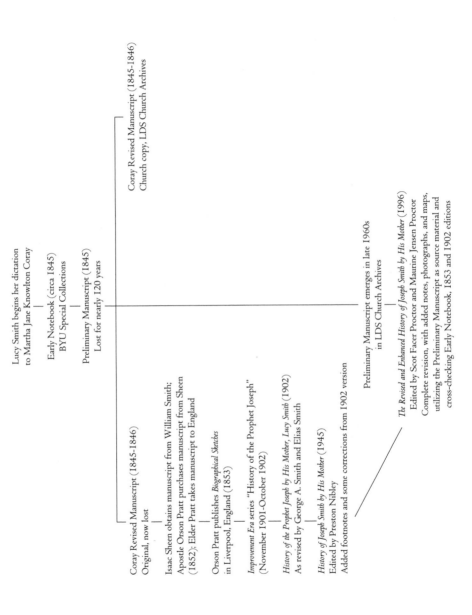

Lucy Smith begins her dictation
to Martha Jane Knowlton Coray

Early Notebook (circa 1845)
BYU Special Collections

Preliminary Manuscript (1845)
Lost for nearly 120 years

Coray Revised Manuscript (1845-1846)
Church copy, LDS Church Archives

Coray Revised Manuscript (1845-1846)
Original, now lost

Isaac Sheen obtains manuscript from William Smith;
Apostle Orson Pratt purchases manuscript from Sheen
(1852); Elder Pratt takes manuscript to England

Orson Pratt publishes *Biographical Sketches*
in Liverpool, England (1853)

Improvement Era series "History of the Prophet Joseph"
(November 1901–October 1902)

History of the Prophet Joseph by His Mother, Lucy Smith (1902)
As revised by George A. Smith and Elias Smith

History of Joseph Smith by His Mother (1945)
Edited by Preston Nibley
Added footnotes and some corrections from 1902 version

Preliminary Manuscript emerges in late 1960s
in LDS Church Archives

The Revised and Enhanced History of Joseph Smith by His Mother (1996)
Edited by Scot Facer Proctor and Maurine Jensen Proctor
Complete revision, with added notes, photographs, and maps,
utilizing the Preliminary Manuscript as source material and
cross-checking Early Notebook, 1853 and 1902 editions

was constantly answering questions on "the particulars of Joseph's getting the plates, seeing the angels at first, and many other things which Joseph never wrote or published," and she had "almost destroyed her lungs giving recitals about these things." She "now concluded to write down every particular."[1] In her rough preface to the work she also states that she has been induced to write because "none on earth is so thoroughly acquainted as myself with the entire history of those of whom I speak." But it is also evident that at the same period Church historian Willard Richards and his staff were working on the Church history up to Joseph's death, and they gave encouragement to Lucy to supply the background only she could give. In that same letter to William, she said, "I have by the council of the 12 undertaken a history of the family that is my father's family and my own."[2]

At any rate, sometime in the early winter, Mother Smith approached Martha Jane Knowlton Coray to be her scribe. Martha Jane's husband, Howard, remembered the event: "In the fall of 1844, I procured the Music Hall for a school room: it was large enough to accommodate 150 students; and I succeeded in filling the room. . . . Sometime in the winter following, Mother Smith came to see my wife, about getting her to help write the history of Joseph; to act in the matter, only as her, Mother Smith's, amanuensis. This my wife was persuaded to do; and so dropped the school."[3]

Martha Jane's background suited her for the job. She had developed the habit of recording and preserving Joseph Smith's speeches in Nauvoo. In fact, her daughter Martha Jane Coray Lewis later noted that Wilford Woodruff "consulted her notes, when he was Church Historian, for items not to be obtained elsewhere."[4] This superior note-taking ability was a great help to Lucy, who could write but was, during the production of the work, according to Martha Jane, "in a very low state of health, at times suffering great pains with rheumatism, and often suffocated with an affection of the chest."[5]

Ailing or not, Lucy wanted to get this history down, and it appears that she dictated her story to Martha through that winter, who wrote it with clear penmanship, excellent spelling, and little punctuation. Of course, whenever a second person is involved in a work the question arises: What part of the product reflects the personality and style of the author and what part the influence of the scribe? Martha Jane supplies the answer to this. She wrote Brigham Young that because of her practice at note taking, "this made it an easy task for me to transmit to paper what the old lady said, and prompted me in undertaking to secure all the information possible for myself and children. . . . Hyrum and Joseph were dead, and thus without their aid, she attempted to prosecute the work, relying chiefly upon her memory, having little recourse to authentic statements whose corresponding dates might have assisted her."[6] Martha Jane's husband, Howard, seconds his wife's description of her role in the project. As quoted earlier, he said she served "only as her, Mother Smith's, amanuensis."[7]

Thus, what Martha wrote down appears to be the raw, unedited Lucy, a reflection of her intellect and heart. What she expressed was her life as she saw it and the part that her family had played in bringing forth the Book of Mormon and the restored religion. It was not originally what it has long been titled, *History of Joseph Smith by His Mother, Lucy Mack Smith.* It was instead "The History of Mother Smith, by Herself," a family history, a story of drama, spiritual adventure, and pathos, but most of all a personal story. Thus, without hesitation, she shared intimate details, probed feelings and made assessments, felt free to soliloquize. She was frank, for instance, to say that she looked forward to standing at the bar of God, where, after a lifetime of persecution, justice will finally reign and her persecutors will be brought to task. And though she shared her suffering, she was not full of self-pity, but rather grateful to be the mother of a prophet and part of a transcendent work.

The material that was dictated to Martha is found in two major places. First, there is an early notebook, a sixty-four-page manuscript that contains a number of jottings: notes on the early Christian martyrs (and it is clear to see why Lucy would be interested in these), notes on Samuel Smith's mission, an account of her journey to Missouri, excerpts from John Smith's diary, and some chronological data. Second is the Preliminary Manuscript, which includes approximately 210 pages of foolscap paper as well as several fragments and torn sheets. Though there are some major gaps, this material is mostly chronological, with an occasional correction and sometimes additional notes added between the lines. Observing this, it appears that Martha wrote down Lucy's dictation and then read it back to her for correction. This Preliminary Manuscript only surfaced in the 1960s in the LDS church archives.

During 1845, Howard Coray turned over his school to others and joined his wife, Martha Jane, in a labor to revise the Preliminary Manuscript. Howard had been one of Joseph Smith's clerks, whose assignment included compiling the official historical record of the Church. Together they substantially revised the Preliminary Manuscript. This was not merely a job of correcting grammar or changing and clarifying confusing chronologies. It has been suggested that "about one-fourth of the revised manuscript is not in the preliminary draft, while approximately ten percent of the earlier manuscript is omitted from the revised manuscript."[8] What was added in the revision was information designed to make it a more balanced and complete history, as well as expand the information on Joseph and the formation of the Church: for instance, Joseph Smith's own version of the First Vision and Moroni's first visit were included. Additional information was added from "The History of Joseph Smith" published earlier in the *Times and Seasons*. Gaps were filled, necessary explanations added. While Mother Smith was probably frequently consulted during the entire composition, and she clearly gave her approval to the final version, certainly her biggest contribution had already passed.

It is not surprising, then, to observe that while the revised version had strengths lacking in the Preliminary Manuscript, it is also further from Lucy's own voice. The Corays deleted many of her soliloquies, they axed intimate details of family life and affections, they sometimes avoided emotion, they polished her phrases. Unfortunately, comparing the Preliminary Manuscript with the revised version, it is clear that this is not always a favor. The Corays' edits led to a more fussy, formal speech pattern than Lucy is given to. Ironically, their changes sound old-fashioned to the modern ear, as opposed to Lucy's more direct speech. But it is the moving from Lucy's perceptions and feelings that is the greater loss.

The work of revision appears to have been finished by the end of 1845, for on the afternoon of November 19, 1845, the Twelve discussed the need to "settle with Brother Howard Coray for his labor in compiling"[9] Lucy's history, and a settlement was made in January 1846. The Twelve's financial support and long interest in the project certainly made them feel that the Church had a vested interest in it.

Though Lucy was anxious that the manuscript be published, the end of 1845 found the Church with two other projects that consumed the energies and resources of the Saints. Their enemies had never let off the persecution. They had formed "wolf packs" to hunt the Saints; they had burned homes beyond Nauvoo, sending a flood of refugees into the city; they had harassed the Twelve with lawsuits; and now Nauvoo had been turned into a workshop to build wagons to flee the city. Packing to leave everything they owned while they continued to build a temple absorbed the Saints that winter, and Lucy's manuscript naturally took a backseat.

The Corays had created two handwritten copies of the revised manuscript. One was given to Mother Smith and the other retained by the Church and taken west.

The Controversy over the 1853 Publication

For eight years the manuscript remained unpublished, pushed aside by other priorities. President Joseph F. Smith, Lucy's grandson, summarizes its history: "Lucy Smith died near Nauvoo, May 5, 1855;[10] but years prior to this date, some of her effects were left in the hands of her son, William Smith, among them being the manuscript copy of this history. From William (who was the last surviving brother of the Prophet . . .) the document fell (surreptitiously it is declared by George A. Smith) into the hands of Isaac Sheen, who was at one time a member of the Church, in Michigan. When, in September, 1852, Apostle Orson Pratt went on a mission to England, he called on Mr. Sheen on his way East, and being shown the manuscript copy, he purchased it for a certain sum of money, took it to Liverpool with him, where, without revision and without the consent or knowledge of President Young or any of the Twelve, it was published under his direction in 1853."[11]

Martha Jane's account of what happened to the manuscript includes at least two other people. She wrote: "The first copy fell into the hands of Mr. Arthur Milliken, Mother Smith's son-in-law, and went from him, I hear, to A.W. Babbitt, Esq., and afterwards came into possession of an Editor named Sheen, and was sold by him to Elder Orson Pratt who took it to England and published it in its crude state."[12]

The 1853 edition of Lucy Smith's history was called *Biographical Sketches of Joseph Smith, the Prophet, and His Progenitors for Many Generations* and quite faithfully followed the Corays' revised manuscript. It was a popular book among the British Saints, and in 1854 became available in Great Salt Lake City to the applause of the *Deseret News:* "This new and highly interesting work should be possessed by all Saints who feel in the least degree interested with the history of the latter-day work."[13]

But George A. Smith, Lucy's nephew and the Church historian, had some major reservations about the book. In an 1859 letter to another nephew of Lucy's, Solomon Mack, he raised his concerns, suggesting that the "shocking massacre" of her two sons had affected her mind. "Although she endured this privation in a manner truly astonishing to her friends, yet we could not conceal from ourselves, that these terrible blows had made visible inroads upon her mind, as well as upon the bodily strength. . . . In the last fifteen years she got events considerably mixed up. . . . I would be pleased to learn your opinion of Mother Smith's history of her family, as far as you are acquainted with it."[14] Brigham Young and his counselors expressed a similar reservation, saying that when the history was written, "Mother Smith was seventy years old, and very forgetful." They suggested that "her mind had suffered many severe shocks" and that "she could, therefore, scarcely recollect anything correctly that had transpired."[15]

As George A. Smith continued to study the book and compared it to other sources, he began to feel there were factual mistakes, or at least the need to double-check stories for accuracy. For instance, in Lucy's history she tells a story about how three strangers showed up unexpectedly and spread David Whitmer's fields with plaster of paris, thus allowing him to leave for Harmony to meet Joseph Smith for the first time. George A. wrote to David Whitmer to verify the story, but received no response.[16] In the early months of 1859, George A. and assistant historian Wilford Woodruff continued to write inquiries to check the details of the book for accuracy.

Thus, questions about the book had been simmering in the minds of the Brethren for several years before 1865, when Brigham Young decided to recall it. In a rather dramatic gesture the First Presidency said, "We wish those who have these books to either hand them to their Bishops for them to be conveyed to the President's or Historian's Office or send them themselves, that they may be disposed of."[17] The First Presidency's worry seemed to be over perpetuating inaccuracies that they were certain dotted Lucy's history. "We do not wish incorrect and unsound doctrines to be handed down to posterity under the sanction of great names," they wrote, "to be received and valued by future generations as authentic and reliable."[18] Brigham Young did not wish to suppress the book permanently, but to revise it and reissue it in what he hoped would be a more correct form.

In a journal entry, Wilford Woodruff detailed what President Young's intent was: "He said he wished us to take up that work and revise it, correct it; that it belonged to the Historian to attend to it; that there was many false statements made in it, and he wished them to be left out, and all other statements which we did not know to be true, and give the reason why they are left out."[19] Though it is not entirely clear what "false statements" leaped out at Brigham Young, many of his concerns clearly came from doubting Lucy's capacity at her advanced age and given her ill health to get the story straight.

Time and scholarship would show that this assessment was refutable. Those who visited Lucy in Nauvoo during the last years of her life often reported her to be alert and mentally acute. Artist Frederick H. Piercy, who drew scenes of the Mormon trail still in use today, stopped by the Mansion House, and carefully observed Lucy. "I could not fail to regard the old lady with great interest. Considering her age and afflictions, she, at that time, retained her faculties to a remarkable degree. She spoke very freely of her sons, and, with tears in her eyes, and every other symptom of earnestness, vindicated their reputations for virtue and truth."[20]

Enoch Bartlett Tripp, visiting her in November 1855 in one of the last months of her life, also commented on her memory: "I called upon the Prophet's Mother and found her in a lonely room in the eastern part of the house in her bed and very feeble. Upon approaching her bedside and informing her who I was, she arose in her bed and placing her arms around my neck kissed me exclaiming, 'I can now die in peace since I have beheld your face from the valleys of the mountains.' She made many inquiries after the Saints and remarked that she took much comfort in riding out with me and my wife in the days that I taught school here."[21]

Far more significant than the anecdotal reports, however, are the modern studies conducted by Richard Lloyd Anderson on Mother Smith's history. Checking other journals, newspaper accounts, non-Mormon church records, vital records, and independent recollections for verification, he found that the great majority of what Lucy states tests very well. He noted: "The preliminary and finished manuscripts give about 200 names. With the exception of a small percentage of indefinite names, nearly all can be verified, including some spectacular memories clear from her New England childhood. Her percentage on dates is not as good, probably reflecting her interest in people more than calendar years—yet when mistaken, she is typically within a year or two of the precise time. Obviously an event itself was more vivid in her mind than the exact point of its occurrence. So Lucy's history is reliable but not an infallible source. How to tell? To reiterate a critical point, she will be a prime source when speaking from personal observation and only secondary when relaying what others have told her."[22]

Beyond accuracy, other factors influenced the 1865 recall of the book. Living in a time as we do today when succession in the Church Presidency is calm and orderly, the death of a prophet signaling a predictable change, it may be difficult to imagine the splintering, confusion, and emotion that followed the death of Joseph Smith for the everyday Saint. Claims and counter-claims to the Presidency divided parts of the Church, and though the vast bulk of the members followed Brigham Young, fragmented groups congregated around others like Sidney Rigdon, James Strang, and Lyman Wight.

Since William Smith, Joseph's brother, had made his own rival claim to be Joseph's successor, Lucy Smith's positive portrayal of him in her history probably concerned Brigham, and stood as just another evidence to him that the book contained distortions. Through Lucy's eyes we see William as a valiant missionary, a fighter for the restored gospel, and a recipient of revelation in a dire moment in Missouri. In reality, William was volatile, unstable, and controversial. He had a checkered past, having often been at odds with his prophet brother. Disagreeing with Joseph during a meeting in Kirtland, enraged William attempted to throw him out and inflicted him with an injury that Joseph felt occasionally the rest of his life. During the dark days at Far West when

Joseph was taken to Liberty Jail, William exclaimed, "Damn him, Joseph Smith ought to have been hung up by the neck years ago and damn him, he will get it now anyhow."[23] In his last encounter with Joseph in spring 1844, William asked him to give him a city lot in Nauvoo near the temple. Joseph said he would do it with great pleasure if he would build a house and live upon it there, but he would not give him this lot, worth one thousand dollars, to sell. William agreed to the terms, and within hours an application was made by a Mr. Ivins to the recorder to know if that lot was clear and belonged to William, for the Prophet's brother had sold it to him for five hundred dollars. Joseph, hearing this, directed the clerk not to make the transfer, and William's last words to Joseph were threatening.

After the death of his brothers, a somewhat humbled William petitioned to be ordained the Presiding Patriarch of the Church, a position he had legitimate claim to as the oldest lineal descendant of the Smith family. He was ordained to that position on May 25, 1845, but within a few days he claimed this gave him the right to succeed Joseph as the leader of the entire Church, and by October 1845, he was excommunicated. An aspiring man has to find a home for his aspirations, and William went looking. Expelled from the Church, he temporarily became a leader with James Strang's group. Excommunicated there, by 1850 he began teaching that legitimate leadership for the Church had to come from within the Prophet's immediate family. Since Joseph Smith III was too young, he suggested he should be sustained as president pro tem, "guardian of the seed of Joseph," until the boy came of age. By 1854 he was seeking to be restored to his former position as an Apostle in the Church, and then after 1860, when Joseph Smith III was sustained as president of the Reorganized Church in Plano, Illinois, he hoped to find a high office in the new organization.

Given this background, no wonder the First Presidency's 1865 recall of Lucy's book was so strong in singling out William: "Those who have read the history of William Smith, and who knew him, know the statements made in that book respecting him, when he came out of Missouri, to be utterly false."[24] The timing of the recall was probably also significant, coming so soon after Joseph's sons had newly organized a church and were advancing succession claims. Brigham didn't want

Lucy's book to bolster their effort. He may have felt the same way about the book's rosy portrayal of Emma, who supported her sons in the Reorganized Church.

Finally, the book was recalled because the printing by Orson Pratt was seen as unauthorized by the Church, which had some claim to the material, having paid the scribes. The Church leaders felt that they should be able to control its editing and publication, an idea underscored by an error that appeared in Orson Pratt's preface to the 1853 edition. He believed and said that "the following pages, embracing biographical sketches and the genealogy of Joseph Smith, the Prophet, and his Progenitors, were mostly written previous to the death of the Prophet, and under his personal inspection."[25] Since this was not the case, the Brethren saw this as an example of the inaccuracies that blighted the work, the laxness of Orson Pratt for publishing it without permission, and a justification for why the work needed to be carefully verified and checked before it was republished.

Revising the 1853 Edition

After the recall, President Young appointed a revision committee consisting of George A. Smith and Judge Elias Smith, both cousins of the Prophet and men who were thoroughly knowledgeable in Church history. George A. had been studying the book for years, and Elias had been an editor of the *Deseret News.* They poured over the book, consulted with others, made deletions and corrections right in the text and in the margins of copies of the book, and completed the work to the satisfaction of President Young. Ironically, after the storm that had whirled around Lucy's history, only a small amount of the material was changed, and then not significantly. She had not been in the great error previously assumed.

According to Howard Searle these changes primarily included the following: "(1) Several favorable references to William Smith were deleted or changed. (2) Six out of eighteen references to Emma Smith were omitted, although the deletions appear rather incidental. A glowing eulogy of Emma . . . was left intact. (3) Many corrections were made in dates and names, especially in the genealogical data of chapter nine. (4) Some misstatements and misconceptions of Mother Smith were corrected. Her exaggerated role in the construction of the Kirtland schoolhouse . . . was revised in both copies of the history which were used by the revision committee. (5) Some profanity and gross statements [made by the Missouri persecutors and reported by Hyrum to a court of law] were edited out of the history. (6) Words were changed to clarify meaning and improve the grammar. (7) A few additions were made to expand parts of the narrative. . . . (8) Statements that seemed unfavorable to the image of Joseph Smith or the Church were omitted. (9) Some references of purely family interest were left out."[26]

The version containing George A. and Elias Smith's revisions lay essentially forgotten until 1901, when the General Board of the Young Men's Mutual Improvement Association sought to publish it in their monthly magazine, the *Improvement Era*. President Lorenzo Snow gave his permission as Church President just before he died in October 1901, and the series began in the November 1901 magazine and continued through the next year. Lucy's grandson Joseph F. Smith, who had become the prophet, wrote a preface for the history: "By the presentation of this work to the public, a worthy record is preserved, and the testimony of a noble and faithful woman—a mother indeed, and heroine in Israel—is perpetuated."[27] A new generation, who did not face the pressures and dissensions of the old, brought a new outlook to the history.

Finally, in order to give Mother Smith's history a wider audience, it was published again as a book in 1945, edited by Preston Nibley, assistant Church historian, who made very few changes but added a few footnotes for the sake of context. Today's reader can find both the 1853 and 1945 editions in libraries and bookstores.

When Lucy sat down with Martha Jane, she certainly had no idea of the controversy that would sizzle around the simple recounting of her life's story, and the sets of hands it would pass through before it was enjoyed by a large audience. But it may not have surprised her either. Life had taught her that good things always come with a cost.

Why This Edition?

From the time the Corays first took the Preliminary Manuscript and edited it into what became the 1853 edition, the history has been moving farther away from Lucy's own voice. This 1996 edition is an attempt to lessen the distance, while adding photographs, extensive endnotes to provide texture and context, easy chapter headings, appendices, and an index for quick reference. In this edition, Lucy's voice is heard more clearly, her sentiments and perceptions explored more openly than ever before, because the Preliminary Manuscript is the foundation of the text. While the 1853 version was used in this book to supply structure, chapter divisions, and some transitions, as well as to fill in missing gaps not available in the Preliminary Manuscript, the flow of language is essentially Lucy's own. Sometimes this means very little change from the 1853 edition; sometimes the change is vast.

The 1853 edition often changes her voice, not allowing the full expression of her feelings about matters important to her. For instance, when Lucy was a young married woman searching for the truth, she went to the Presbyterian church and came away disappointed. In the 1853 edition it is recorded:

> I heard that a very devout man was to preach the next Sabbath in the Presbyterian Church; I therefore went to meeting, in the full expectation of hearing that which my soul desired—the Word of Life. When the minister commenced speaking, I fixed my mind with deep attention upon the spirit and matter of his discourse; but, after hearing him through, I returned home, convinced that he neither understood nor appreciated the subject upon which he spoke, and I said in my heart that there was not then upon earth the religion which I sought.[28]

The Preliminary Manuscript reads with more passion and intimacy:

> At last I heard that one noted for his piety would preach the ensuing Sabbath in the Presbyterian church. Thither I went in expectation of obtaining that which alone could satisfy my soul—the bread of eternal life. When the minister commenced, I fixed my mind with breathless attention upon the spirit and matter of the discourse, but all was emptiness, vanity, vexation of spirit, and fell upon my heart like the chill, untimely blast upon the starting ear ripening in a summer sun. It did not fill the aching void within nor

satisfy the craving hunger of my soul. I was almost in total despair, and with a grieved and troubled spirit I returned home, saying in my heart, there is not on earth the religion which I seek.

The 1853 edition sometimes ignores emotion as if it were somehow embarrassing, editing out valuable detail about the feelings of the Smith family as they cope with their challenges. In the Preliminary Manuscript Lucy describes the exhaustion and anxiety of her husband when the doctors come to operate on little Joseph, after the boy has suffered weeks of anguish from a pain in his leg. This paragraph is entirely deleted from the 1853 edition:

> My husband, who was constantly with the child, seemed to contemplate for an instant my countenance; then, turning his eyes upon his boy, at once all his sufferings together with my intense anxiety rushed upon his mind. He burst into a flood of tears and sobbed like a child.

Also missing from the 1853 edition is the expression of affection from Joseph Smith Sr. toward his children when they are reunited in Palmyra after some months' separation. The 1853 edition tells of Lucy and her children arriving in Palmyra

> with a small portion of our effects, and barely two cents in cash.
> When I again met my husband at Palmyra, we were much reduced—not from indolence, but on account of many reverses of fortune, with which our lives had been rather singularly marked.[29]

She gives us a more personal picture in the Preliminary Manuscript:

> I then proceeded on my way, and in a short time I arrived in Palmyra with a small portion of my effects, my babes, and two cents in money, but perfectly happy in the society of my family.
> The joy I felt in throwing myself and my children upon the care and affection of a tender husband and father doubly paid me for all I had suffered. The children surrounded their father, clinging to his neck, covering his face with tears and kisses that were heartily reciprocated by him.

We all now sat down and maturely counseled together as to
what course it was best to take, and how we should proceed to business in our then destitute circumstances.

In the Preliminary Manuscript Lucy periodically stops her narrative
to give us a soliloquy. For the most part these were deleted, shortened,
or severely edited for the 1853 edition until her voice in these is sometimes hardly recognizable. For example, one night during the printing
of the Book of Mormon, Lucy hid the manuscript in a chest under her
bed to keep it from the clutches of conspiring men who had determined to steal and destroy it. Lying there upon the record, the important scenes of Lucy's life began to play before her eyes. Cut from the
1853 edition is this insight into Lucy's spirituality:

At last, as if led by an invisible spirit, I came to the time when
the messenger from Waterloo informed me that the translation was
actually completed. My soul swelled with a joy that could scarcely
be heightened, except by the reflection that the record which had
cost so much labor, suffering, and anxiety was now, in reality, lying
beneath my own head—that this identical work had not only been
the object which we as a family had pursued so eagerly, but that
prophets of ancient days, angels, and even the great God had had
his eye upon it. "And," said I to myself, "shall I fear what man can
do? Will not the angels watch over the precious relic of the worthy
dead and the hope of the living? And am I indeed the mother of a
prophet of the God of heaven, the honored instrument in performing so great a work?" I felt that I was in the purview of angels, and
my heart bounded at the thought of the great condescension of the
Almighty.
Thus I spent the night surrounded by enemies and yet in an ecstasy of happiness.

Finally, the 1853 edition occasionally deletes an incident or description that completes the picture Lucy is painting. For instance,
Lucy tells of the pitiful conditions of the refugees who fled to Far West

when the militia had driven them from their homes in outlying areas. In the 1853 edition she says:

> It was enough to make the heart ache to see the children, sick with colds, and crying around their mothers for food, whilst their parents were destitute of the means of making them comfortable.[30]

This is a poignant scene by itself, but the Preliminary Manuscript adds a heartrending note.

> It was enough to make the heart ache to see children in the open sun and wind, sick with colds and very hungry, crying around their mothers for food and their parents destitute of the means of making them comfortable, while their houses, which lay a short distance from the city, were pillaged of everything, their fields thrown open for the horses belonging to the mob to lay waste and destroy, and their fat cattle shot down and turning to carrion before their eyes, while a strong guard, which was set over us for the purpose, prevented us from making use of a particle of the stock that was killed on every side of us.

Thus, using the Preliminary Manuscript as the major source of text, this edition gives us a fresher, keener view of Lucy and her response to the momentous events of the Restoration. At the same time, using the structure and chronology of the 1853 edition allows the history to transcend the limitations of an occasionally confusing, occasionally spotty oral history (as oral histories tend to be). Where Lucy is incorrect in dates or names, corrections have been made in the text and the changes often footnoted. No attempt has been made to restate her sentences in more polished prose or improve her vocabulary. She stands well on her own and thus the edits are light. Where transitions or explanations are necessary and not available in the Preliminary Manuscript, the 1853 text has been used. However, to save the text from becoming tedious, every shift between the Preliminary Manuscript and the 1853 edition has not been noted. The motivation was to find Lucy buried in the material, be true to her voice, and at the same time create a book that was accessible and inviting to a wide audience.

A Note on the Notes and Other Features

The endnotes in this book have been designed to add context, color, and texture to Lucy's story as well as to note significant differences between the Preliminary Manuscript and the various editions. They will add so much to a reader's understanding of the events Lucy describes, it is tempting to attach a sign that says "Read Me" to each one. The notes include anecdotes that expand with detail or with another point of view the event she describes. For instance, Lucy gives us a tragic picture of Joseph being dragged by the militia from his family at Far West, and in the notes Parley P. Pratt relates his personal heartrending experience, side by side with Joseph. The notes also include facts that make the background clearer. For instance, when Lucy and her family make their desperate journey from Kirtland to Missouri, the notes give a vivid picture of how many little children were in tow, a detail that adds pathos to their miserable circumstance. (For quotations that appear in the notes, spelling and punctuation have sometimes been standardized to facilitate readability.)

The photographs in this edition are pictures of the places Lucy describes as they appear today. They are included to add a visual dimension to the story. The maps have been added to give the reader a sense of location and proximity.

In the 1853 edition, chapter 9 was a genealogy of the Smith and Mack families. In this edition, the corrected contents of chapter 9 have been included in an appendix; a second appendix containing a simplified genealogy chart has been added for quick and easy reference. A third appendix presents a chronology of key events in the Joseph and Lucy Smith family, with emphasis on Joseph Smith Jr.

If Lucy Mack Smith's history is one of the priceless treasures of Church history, it is not just because her son Joseph was a prophet who restored the ancient gospel. It is also because her own life teaches us new dimensions of faith and courage. Her fervent outreach for the Lord was continually answered with blessings on her head. If her sons in Missouri are ailing with cholera, she prays them well. If at Far West she is tormented with worry about her sons' being murdered, she receives divine assurance that drives the anguish away. Her statement at Buffalo Harbor captures it all. When she and eighty Saints are blocked from leaving the harbor by ice that is twenty-feet thick, she tells the Saints that the Lord can make the way open for them. She asks them, "Where is your confidence in God? Do you not know that all things are in his hands, that he made all things and overrules them? . . . Now, brethren and sisters, if you will all of you raise your desires to heaven that the ice may be broken before us, and we be set at liberty to go on our way, *as sure as the Lord lives, it shall be done.*" That instant, the ice burst like thunder, and it was done. It was the kind of faith and super-faith that makes her story timeless, and vital for all generations of the Church.

Scot Facer Proctor
Maurine Jensen Proctor
Editors

Salt Lake City, Utah
Tuesday, May 14, 1996
Commemorating the 140th Anniversary
of the Death of Lucy Mack Smith, May 14, 1856

Notes

1. Lucy Smith to William Smith, Nauvoo, Illinois, January 23, 1845.
2. Ibid.
3. Howard Coray Autobiography, p. 16, Archives Division, Church Historical Department, The Church of Jesus Christ of Latter-day Saints, Salt Lake City, Utah (hereafter cited as LDS Church Archives).
4. Martha J. C. Lewis, "Martha Jane Knowlton Coray," *Improvement Era* 5 (April 1902): 440.
5. Martha Jane Coray to Brigham Young, June 13, 1865, Brigham Young Papers, LDS Church Archives.
6. Ibid.
7. Howard Coray Autobiography, p. 16, LDS Church Archives.
8. Howard Clair Searle, "Early Mormon Historiography: Writing the History of the Mormons 1830–1858" (Ph.D. diss., University of California, Los Angeles, 1979), p. 385.

9. *History of the Church* 7:519.

10. Lucy actually died May 14, 1856.

11. Joseph F. Smith, Introduction to "History of the Prophet Joseph, by His Mother, Lucy Smith," *Improvement Era* 5 (November 1901): 1–2.

12. Martha Jane Coray to Brigham Young, June 13, 1865, Brigham Young Papers, LDS Church Archives.

13. *Deseret News*, November 16, 1854.

14. George A. Smith to Solomon Mack, in *Manuscript History of Brigham Young*, February 23, 1859, p. 204.

15. *Millennial Star* 27 (October 21, 1865): 658.

16. The Whitmer story has been included in all editions of Lucy's history. Even though he didn't answer George A. Smith's letter to him, David Whitmer did later give a version of the story, as reported by Orson Pratt and Joseph F. Smith (see Cook, *Whitmer Interviews*, pp. 26–27, 41, 51).

17. *Millennial Star* 27 (October 21, 1865): 658.

18. Ibid., p. 659.

19. Wilford Woodruff Journal, February 13, 1859, LDS Church Archives.

20. Frederick H. Piercy, *Route from Liverpool to Great Salt Lake Valley* (1855; reprint, Cambridge, Mass.: Harvard University Press, 1962), p. 94.

21. Enoch Bartlett Tripp's Journal, vol. I to December 31, 1855, BYU Special Collections.

22. Richard Lloyd Anderson, "His Mother's Manuscript: An Intimate View of Joseph Smith," Brigham Young University Forum address, January 27, 1976.

23. Wilford Woodruff Journal, February 13, 1859, LDS Church Archives.

24. *Millennial Star* 27 (October 21, 1865): 658.

25. Orson Pratt, Preface in Lucy Smith, *Biographical Sketches of Joseph Smith, the Prophet, and His Progenitors for Many Generations* (Liverpool: Published for Orson Pratt by S. W. Richards, 1853), p. 12.

26. Searle, "Early Mormon Historiography," pp. 420, 422.

27. Smith, Introduction to "History of the Prophet Joseph," p. 3.

28. *Biographical Sketches*, p. 48.

29. *Biographical Sketches*, p. 70.

30. *Biographical Sketches*, p. 252.

Lucy Mack Smith's Introduction

Having attained my 67th year, and being afflicted with a complication of diseases and infirmities, many of which have been brought upon me by the cruelty of an ungodly and hard-hearted world and do many times threaten to put a period to my earthly existence, I feel it a privilege as well as my duty to give (as my last testimony to a world from whence I must soon take my departure) an account, not exclusively of my own manner of life from my youth up, but after saying somewhat concerning my ancestors, as well as myself, to trace carefully up, even from the cradle to the grave, the footsteps of some whose life and death have been such as are calculated to excite an intense curiosity in the minds of all who ever knew them personally or shall hear of them hereafter. And inasmuch as none on earth is so thoroughly acquainted as myself with the entire history of those of whom I speak, I have been induced by these and other considerations to assume the task of not only tracing them during their windings and vicissitudes of a life checkered with many ills, but likewise to give a sketch of their forefathers and the dealing of God with them also.

PART I

*Mack
Ancestry*

CHAPTER I

A brief sketch is given of the life of Solomon Mack, father of Lucy Mack, from his own writings. His early military service. His marriage to Lydia Gates and service in the Revolutionary War. His final devotion to God and family.

September 15, 1732 to fall 1788

My father, Solomon Mack, was born in the town of Lyme, New London County, state of Connecticut, September 26, 1735.[1] His father, Ebenezer Mack, was a man of considerable property and lived in good style, commanding all the attention and respect which are ever shown to those who live in fine circumstances and strict habits of morality. For some length of time, my grandparents lived in peace and plenty, fully enjoying the fruits of their industry, but at length a series of misfortunes visited them, occasioned in most instances by the perfidy of their fellowmen, which reduced them by degrees till at last they came to penury and want. A once happy and flourishing family was compelled to disperse, and throw themselves upon the charity of a cold, unfeeling world.

My father was taken into the family of a neighboring farmer, where he remained until he was nearly twenty-one years of age. I have here a sketch of my father's life, written by himself, from which I extract the following:[2]

"I was bound out to a farmer in the neighborhood. As is too commonly the case, I was considered rather a slave than a member of the family, and instead of allowing me the privilege of common hospitality,

*Solomon Mack was born and raised near the mouth of the
Connecticut River in Lyme, Connecticut.*

that kind of protection due to helpless and indigent children, I was
treated by my master as his property and not as his fellow mortal.

"At the age of twenty-one years, I left my master.[3] Shortly after
which I enlisted in the services of my country under the command of
Captain Harris,[4] and was annexed to the regiment commanded by
Colonel Whiting.

"From Connecticut, we marched to Fort Edward, in the state of
New York. We were in a severe battle, fought at Halfway Brook in
1755.[5] During this expedition I caught a heavy cold which rendered me
unfit for business until the return of warm weather. I was carried the
ensuing spring to Albany.

"In the year 1757, I had two teams in the King's service, which were
employed in carrying the general's baggage. While thus engaged, I went
one morning to yoke my team, but three of my oxen were missing.
When this knowledge came to the officer, he was very angry, and drawing his sword, threatened to run it through me. He then ordered me to

get three other oxen, which I accordingly did, and proceeded with the baggage to Fort Edward, and the next day I returned in order to find my missing oxen.

"While I was performing this trip, the following circumstance occurred. About halfway from Stillwater to Fort Edward, I espied four Indians nearly thirty rods distant, coming out of the woods. They were armed with scalping knives, tomahawks, and guns. I was alone, but about twenty rods behind me was a man by the name of Webster. I saw my danger, and that there was no way to escape unless I could do it by stratagem; so I rushed upon them, calling in the meantime at the top of my voice, 'Rush on! rush on, my boys! We'll have the devils.' The only weapon I had was a walking staff, yet I ran toward them, and as the other man appeared just at that instant, it gave them a terrible fright, and I saw no more of them.

Old fort house at Fort Edward.
George Washington would dine here twenty-six years after Solomon Mack.

"I hastened to Stillwater the next day, as aforementioned, and finding my oxen soon after I arrived there, I returned the same night to Fort Edward, a distance of seven miles, the whole of which was a dense forest.

"In 1758, I enlisted under Major Spencer and went immediately over Lake George with a company who crossed in boats to the western side, where we had a bloody and hot engagement with the enemy in which Lord Howe fell at the onset of the battle. His bowels were taken out and buried, but his body was embalmed and carried to England.

"The next day we marched to the breastworks, but were unsuccessful, being compelled to retreat with a loss of five hundred men killed and as many more wounded.

"In this contest I narrowly escaped—a musket ball passed under my chin within half an inch of my neck. The army then returned to Lake George, and, on its way thither, a large scouting party of the enemy came round by Skenesborough and, at Halfway Brook, destroyed a large number of both men and teams. Upon this, one thousand of our men were detached to repair immediately to Skenesborough in pursuit of them; but when we arrived at South Bay, the enemy was entirely out of our reach.

"The enemy then marched to Ticonderoga, New York, in order to procure supplies, after which they immediately pursued us, but we eluded them by hastening to Wood Creek, and thence to Fort Anne, where we arrived on the 13th day of the month. We had just reached this place, when the sentry gave information that the enemy was all around us, in consequence of which we were suddenly called to arms. Major Putnam led the company, and Major Rogers brought up the rear. We marched but three-quarters of a mile, when we came suddenly upon a company of Indians that were lying in ambush. Major Putnam marched his men through their ranks, whereupon the Indians fired, which threw our men into some confusion. Major Putnam was captured by them, and would have been killed by an Indian had he not been rescued by a French lieutenant.

"The enemy rose like a cloud and fired a whole volley upon us, and as I was in the foremost rank, the retreat of my company brought me in the rear, and the tomahawks and bullets flew around me like hailstones. As I was running, I saw not far before me a windfall which was so high that it appeared to me insurmountable; however, by making great exertion, I succeeded in getting over it. Running a little farther, I observed a man who had in this last conflict been badly wounded, and the Indians were close upon him; nevertheless I turned aside for the purpose of assisting him, and succeeded in getting him into the midst of our army in safety.

"In this encounter, a man named Gersham Rowley had nine bullets shot through his clothes but received no personal injury. Ensign Worcester received nine wounds, was scalped and tomahawked, notwithstanding which he lived and finally recovered.

"The above engagement commenced early in the morning and continued until about three o'clock p.m., in which half of our men were either killed, wounded, or taken prisoners. In consequence of this tremendous slaughter, we were compelled to send to Fort Edward for men in order to assist in carrying our wounded, which were about eighty in number.

"The distance we had to carry them was nearly fourteen miles. To carry so many thus far was truly very fatiguing, insomuch that when we arrived at the place of destination, my strength was about exhausted.

"I proceeded immediately to Albany for the purpose of getting supplies, and returned again to the army as soon as circumstances would admit.

"Autumn having now arrived, I went home, where I tarried the ensuing winter.[6]

"In the spring of 1759, the army marched to Crown Point, where I received my discharge. About this time I became acquainted with an amiable and accomplished young woman, a schoolteacher by the name of Lydia Gates, the daughter of Daniel Gates, a man living in ease and affluence in the town of East Haddam, state of Connecticut.[7] To this young woman I was shortly united in the bands of matrimony; and a most worthy and invaluable companion did she prove to be, for I soon discovered that she was not only pleasant and agreeable by reason of the polish of education, but also possessed that inestimable jewel which in a wife and mother of a family is truly a pearl of great price, namely, a pious and devotional character.

"Having received a large amount of money for my services in the army, and deeming it prudent to make an investment of the same in real estate, I contracted for the whole town of Granville in the state of New

York.[8] On the execution of the deed, I paid all the money that was required in the stipulation, which also called for the building of a number
of log houses. I accordingly went to work to fulfill this part of the contract, but after laboring a short time, I had the misfortune to cut my leg,
which subjected me, during that season, to the care of the physician. I
hired a man to do the work and paid him in advance, in order to fulfill
my part of the contract; but he ran away with the money without performing the labor, and the consequence was, I lost the land altogether.

"In 1761, we moved into the town of Marlow,[9] where we remained
until we had four children.[10] At that time Marlow was a desolate wilderness. There were but four families in forty miles. Then it was I learned
to prize the talents and virtues of my wife. As our children were wholly
deprived of the privilege of schools, she took the charge of their education, which task she performed as none but a mother can do. Debarred
in their earliest years and in their first experience in some measure from
intercourse with the world, the mother's precepts and example took
deeper root in their infant minds and had a more lasting influence upon
their future character than all the flowery eloquence of the pulpit surrounded with its ordinary disadvantages.

"Thus, my older children became confirmed in habits of gentle-
ness, piety, and reflection, which were under these circumstances more
easily impressed upon the minds of those who came after them. And I
often thought it would have been more difficult to have brought them
into the channel they were reared in had they not inherited much of the
disposition of their excellent mother, whose prayers and alms came up
daily before that all-seeing eye that rests upon all his works.

"She, besides instructing them in the various branches of an ordinary education, was in the habit of calling them together both morning
and evening and teaching them to pray, meanwhile urging upon them
the necessity of love toward each other, as well as devotional feelings towards Him who made them.

"In 1776 I enlisted in the service of my country and was for a considerable length of time in the land forces, after which I went with my
two sons, Jason and Stephen, on a privateering expedition commanded
by Captain Havens. Soon after we set sail, we were driven upon
Horseneck. We succeeded, however, in getting some of our guns on
shore and bringing them to bear upon the enemy so as to exchange

Solomon and Lydia Mack had four of their children here in the town of Marlow, New Hampshire.

many shots with them; yet they cut away our rigging and left our vessel much shattered.

"We then hauled off and cast anchor, but in a short time we espied two row-galleys, two sloops, and two schooners. We quickly weighed anchor and hauled to shore again, and had barely time to post four cannon in a position in which they could be used before a sanguinary contest commenced. The balls from the enemy's guns tore up the ground, cutting asunder the saplings in every direction. One of the row-galleys went round a point of land with the view of hemming us in, but we killed forty of their men with our small arms, which caused the enemy to abandon their purpose.

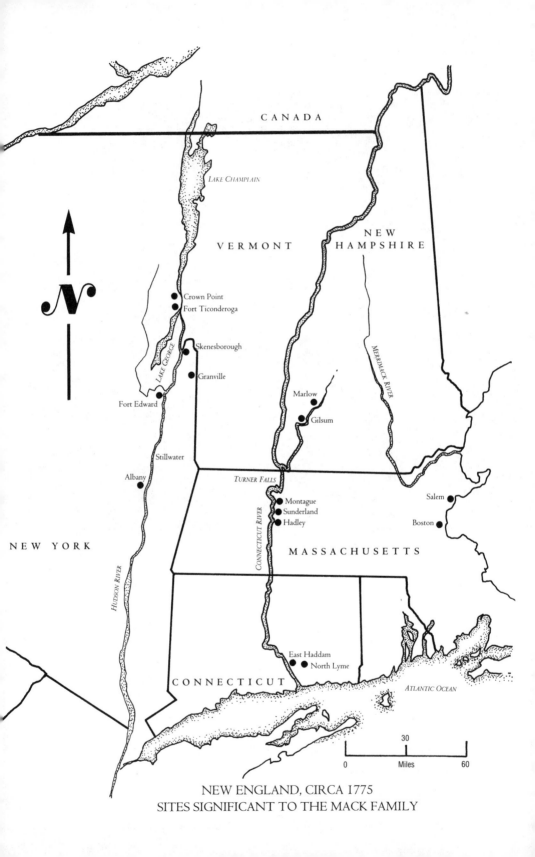

CANADA

Lake Champlain

VERMONT

NEW
HAMPSHIRE

Merrimack River

● Crown Point
● Fort Ticonderoga

Lake George

● Skenesborough

● Granville

● Marlow

Fort Edward ●

● Gilsum

Stillwater

Albany ●

Turner Falls

Salem ●

Connecticut River

● Montague
● Sunderland
● Hadley

Boston ●

NEW YORK

MASSACHUSETTS

Hudson River

● East Haddam
● North Lyme

CONNECTICUT

Atlantic Ocean

30

0   Miles   60

NEW ENGLAND, CIRCA 1775
SITES SIGNIFICANT TO THE MACK FAMILY

"My son Stephen, in company with the cabin boys, was sent to a house, not far from the shore, with a wounded man. Just as they entered the house, an eighteen-pounder followed them. A woman was engaged in frying cakes at the time, and being somewhat alarmed, she concluded to retire into the cellar, saying, as she left, that the boys might have the cakes, as she was going below.

"The boys were highly delighted at this, and they went to work cooking and feasting upon the lady's sweet cakes, while the artillery of the contending armies was thundering in their ears, dealing out death and destruction on every hand. At the head of this party of boys was Stephen Mack, my second son, a bold and fearless stripling of fourteen.[11]

"In this contest, the enemy was far superior to us in point of numbers, yet we maintained our ground with such valor that they thought it better to leave us and accordingly did so. Soon after this, we hoisted sail and made for New London.

"When hostilities ceased and peace and tranquility were again restored, we[12] freighted a vessel for Liverpool.[13] Selling both ship and cargo in this place, we embarked on Captain Foster's vessel, which I afterwards purchased; but, in consequence of storms and wrecks, I was compelled to sell her, and was left completely destitute.

"I struggled a little longer to obtain property in making adventures, then returned to my family after an absence of four years about penniless. After this I determined to follow phantoms no longer, but devote the rest of my life to the service of God and my family."[14]

I shall now lay aside my father's journal, as I have made such extracts as are adapted to my purpose, and take up the history of his children.

NOTES

1. The vital records of Lyme, Connecticut, give Solomon's birth as September 15, 1732. Solomon's master may have misrepresented his age to the young child to prolong his service. (See Anderson, *Heritage*, p. 162.)

2. Solomon Mack published a brief account of his life in 1811 in which the title page declared the work as *A Narrative of the Life of Solomon Mack, Containing an Account of the Many Severe Accidents He Met with During a Long Series of Years, Together with the Extraordinary Manner in Which He Was Converted to the Christian Faith. . . . Windsor. Printed at the expense of the author.* This forty-eight page pamphlet, published thirty-four years before Mother Smith dictated her own history, may very well have been an influence in Lucy's decision to record in detail her own life and dealings with God.

3. Solomon indicates in his *Narrative* that he left his master when he was "21 years of age lacking 2 months." This means that, according to when Solomon thought he was born, he would have left his master in July 1756. He did return and reluctantly fill the last short period of his indenture. The record, however, is somewhat contradictory, as he was fighting in battles in his military service in 1755.

4. Colonial records indicate Solomon enlisted under Capt. James Harris on September 10, 1755; was discharged on November 24, 1755; reenlisted under Capt. Israel Putnam on November 24, 1755; and stayed until his discharge on May 29, 1756 (see Anderson, *Heritage,* pp. 162–63).

5. This battle was part of the French and Indian War, which lasted from 1754 to 1763.

6. This was the fall of 1758 and through the winter of 1759. It was during this period of time that Solomon became acquainted with Lydia Gates and married her January 4, 1759 (see Anderson, *Heritage,* p. 164). Lydia was born in East Haddam, Connecticut, September 3, 1732. At the time of their marriage, both Solomon and Lydia were twenty-six years old.

7. East Haddam is located about sixteen miles north of Lyme, Connecticut.

8. Granville is located just sixteen miles east and south from Fort Anne at the extreme eastern border of New York. Solomon contracted for 1,600 acres (see Anderson, *Heritage,* p. 10).

9. Marlow is a small village just six miles north of Gilsum, New Hampshire.

10. These four children were Lovina, Lydia, Stephen, and Daniel. Two other children, Jason and Lovisa, had likely been born prior to the move to Marlow.

11. Stephen Mack was born in Marlow, Connecticut, June 15, 1766, and was almost thirteen at the time of these battles in March 1779.

12. The "we" here refers to Solomon and his eldest son, Jason.

13. This is Liverpool, Nova Scotia.

14. After being four years at sea, Solomon Mack returned to his family in western Massachusetts around 1788, and they spent subsequent years in various locations in New England. Solomon had not taken the opportunity for religion but turned to the Lord in the last part of his life. He was afflicted with a terrible siege of rheumatism in the winter of 1810–11, and of his experience during this time he reported: "I prayed to the Lord, if he was with me, that I might know it by this token—that my pains might all be eased for that night. And blessed be the Lord, I was entirely free from pain that night. And I rejoiced in the God of my salvation—and found Christ's promises verified. . . . Everything appeared new and beautiful. Oh how I loved my

neighbors. How I loved my enemies—I could pray for them. . . . The love of Christ is beautiful. There is more satisfaction to be taken in the enjoyment of Christ one day, than in half a century serving our master, the devil." (*Narrative*, pp. 23–24.) Solomon Mack spent his last years, though crippled through an accident, in the service of his fellowmen. Near the end of his record he wrote: "My friends, when you read this journal, remember your unfortunate friend Solomon Mack, who worried and toiled until an old age to try to lay up treasures in this world, but the Lord would not suffer me to have it. But now I trust I have treasures laid up that no man can take away—but by the goodness of God through the blood of a bleeding Savior." (*Narrative*, p. 44.)

CHAPTER 2

The tragic history of Jason Mack and his courtship and engagement to Esther Bruce. Jason sails with his father to the Maritime Provinces. Another man deceives Esther Bruce and takes her to wife. Jason's return and terrible disappointment.

1775 *to* 1790

My oldest brother, Jason, was a studious and manly boy.[1] Before he attained his sixteenth year, he became what is termed a seeker, a believer in the power of God manifest through the medium of prayer and faith.[2] He held that there was no church in existence which contained the pure principles of the gospel enjoyed by the ancient disciples of Christ, and he labored incessantly to convince the people that, by an exercise of prayer, the blessings and privileges of the ancient disciples of Jesus might be and eventually would be obtained.

At the age of twenty he became a minister of the gospel.[3] Shortly after this, he became enamored with a beautiful and wealthy young woman by the name of Esther Bruce of the state of New Hampshire. She was the pride of the place in which she resided, not so much on account of her splendid appearance as the soundness of her mind and her stately deportment, joined with an unaffected mildness of disposition and a condescension of manners which were admirably suited to the taste and principles of my brother. He was passionately fond of her, and she seemed also to have the most fervent attachment for him. It would have been as easy to have convinced Jason that he could exist without his head as that he could live and enjoy life without being united with her in marriage.

They were engaged to be married and every preparation was being made for their approaching nuptials, when my father received a letter from Liverpool[4] stating that a heavy debt that had been due him for a long time was collected and ready for him. Thus, it was agreed that the marriage of Jason should be deferred, and he should accompany my father to Liverpool. He left his betrothed with a heavy heart but with this arrangement—that he was to write to her and his sisters conjointly once every three months. In due time, according to their agreement, a letter arrived which Esther received most joyfully, but it was never followed by another from him. A young man who kept the office where she received her letters formed in his heart a design to thwart my brother in his intentions and obtain the hand of Esther Bruce himself. He used every art to dissuade her from marrying Jason, meantime detaining his letters in order that she might not hear from him, and he might the more easily accomplish his fiendish purposes.

Unforeseen circumstances detained my father and Jason beyond the time appointed for their return. Meanwhile, the postmaster continued to importune Miss Bruce upon the subject of my brother's neglect, until at last she received two or three epistles stating that Jason Mack was dead, that she and his relatives might cease to look for his return. This was two years after Jason had left the shores of America.[5] Esther gave no credence to the first message, till the tale was so confirmed that she could no longer doubt; but still she rejected the young man from the post office until within four months of Jason's arrival at home, three years and ten months from the time they had embarked for Liverpool.[6]

Jason went immediately to her father's house. She was absent with her husband. He seated himself in the same room where he had wooed her and obtained her consent to be his. He waited for her arrival with a beating heart, not knowing the perfidious game his rival had played him, until she entered. She was attired in a complete suit of mourning, as she had lost a brother recently by death, and beyond this there was a bitter disappointment preying like a cankerworm upon her very vitals, occasioned by the supposed death of him who now stood before her.

She bowed in gloomy silence as she entered the splendid apartment where he sat, fitted up as it had been in earlier, happier days to please the man now doomed to drink the bitter cup of sorrow to the dregs. She walked to the other side of the room and thrust aside her bonnet and shawl, but as she turned again to the stranger and beheld his distracted and inquiring look, she recognized to her amazement this person. She clasped her hands in agony and, with a piercing shriek, fell lifeless to the floor. My brother took the motionless form of her that should have been his own and, placing her on a sofa, resigned her into the hands of her cowering, conscience-smitten husband and left her with those pungent feelings which some few are fated to experience but none can tell nor imagine correctly.

By the active exertions of those who attended her, she at last revived to realize her lamentable situation more fully. Jason returned home, and hearing an explanation of the whole matter, which simply was that the man detained his letters and gave the intelligence of his death, he went immediately to sea. Jason lived single to his fiftieth year.[7]

From this time forward, Esther never recovered her health but, lingering for two years, died the victim of disappointment.[8]

NOTES

1. Jason's birth year can be reasonably estimated as 1760. He was therefore fifteen years older than his youngest sibling, Lucy.

2. He became a seeker about the time that Lucy was born.

3. This was in the year 1780, apparently just after Jason's service in the Revolutionary War.

4. Liverpool, Nova Scotia.

5. Solomon and Jason Mack had likely set sail for the Maritime Provinces in 1784, so this would have been about 1786.

6. The approximate period is late fall 1788.

7. Jason was single until about 1809.

8. Esther Bruce likely died in late 1790.

Chapter 3

The sicknesses of Lovisa and Lovina. Miraculous healing of Lovisa. She preaches to and exhorts the people for three years. Lucy cares for Lovina. Deaths of Lovina and Lovisa.

January 1780 to 1794

The history of Lovisa and Lovina, my two oldest sisters, is so connected and interwoven that I shall not attempt to separate it.[1]

They were one in faith, in love, in action, and in hope of eternal life. They were always together, and when they were old enough to understand the duties of a Christian, they united their voices in prayer and songs of praise to God. This sisterly affection increased with their years and continued steadfast until death. One might say as did one of old, "Let me die the death of the righteous, and let my last end be like theirs." The pathway of their lives was never clouded with a gloomy shadow until Lovisa's marriage and removal from home, which left Lovina very lonely.[2]

In about two years after Lovisa's marriage, she was taken violently sick with a disease so singular in its nature that her attendant physicians had seen no precedent and could give it no name. Suffice it to say she was nigh unto death and sorely afflicted for the space of two years. She revived a little about this time and showed some symptoms of recovery, but a malignant reattack soon brought her back in intense agony upon a bed of pain and languor. She grew worse and worse until she became utterly speechless, and was so for several days. Those who attended her were not allowed to move her. She ate not; she drank not, with the exception of a few drops of rice water which they were able to pour into her mouth with a teaspoon by prying her teeth apart. Thus she lay for three days and two nights. On the night of the third day at about two o'clock, she feebly pronounced the name of her sister Lovina, who had hovered indefatigably all the while around her pillow night and day like an attendant angel, watching every change with thrilling anxiety. Lovina now bent with deep emotion over the emaciated form of the invalid and said, "My sister!" but no more; her feelings choked her utterance.

Lovisa said emphatically, "The Lord has healed me, soul and body. Raise me up and give me my clothes. I want to get up."

Her husband told those present to gratify her, as this was probably a revival before death, and he would not have her crossed in her last moments. They raised her in bed and handed her clothing to her and assisted her to dress, but when she was lifted to her feet both of her ankles were instantly dislocated by her weight resting upon them. She said, "Put me in a chair and pull my feet gently, and I shall soon be sound again."

She then ordered her husband to bring her nourishment, and when she had taken some stimulance, she desired them to assist her to cross the street to her father-in-law's, who was then sick. They did so, and when she entered the house, he cried out in amazement, "Lovisa is dead and her spirit has come to admonish me of my final exit."

"No, Father, no," she said. "God has raised me up, and I have come to tell you to prepare for death." She then sat down and conversed with him some time, and afterwards, with the assistance of her husband and those who had attended upon her that night, she returned home.

When news of this excitement and her miraculous recovery was noised abroad, the inhabitants began to gather from all quarters, both to hear and see concerning the strange and marvelous circumstance which had taken place. She talked to them a short time, sang a hymn with angelic harmony, and then told them she would meet them at the village church on Thursday, where she would tell them all about the strange manner in which she had been healed.[3]

The next day, according to promise, she proceeded to the meeting-house, and when she arrived there a large congregation had collected.

The interior of the Sunderland, Massachusetts, village church where Lovisa preached may have been like this one.[4]

Soon after she entered, the minister arose and remarked that, as many of the congregation had doubtless come to hear a recital of the strange circumstance which had taken place in the neighborhood, and as he himself felt more interested in it than in hearing a gospel discourse, he would open the meeting and then give place to Mrs. Tuttle.

The minister then requested her to sing a hymn; she accordingly did so, and her voice was as high and clear as it had ever been. Having sung, she arose and addressed the audience as follows: "I seemed to be borne away to the world of spirits, where I saw the Savior as through a veil, which appeared to me about as thick as a spider's web, and he told me that I must return again to warn the people to prepare for death; that I must exhort them to be watchful as well as prayerful; that I must declare faithfully unto them their accountability before God and the certainty of their being called to stand before the judgment seat of Christ; and that if I would do this my life should be prolonged." After this she spoke much to the people upon the uncertainty of life.

When she sat down, her husband and sister, also those who were with her during the last night of her sickness, arose and testified to her appearance just before her sudden recovery.

Of these things she continued to speak boldly, and her house was always crowded for the space of three years, at the end of which time she was seized with the consumption.[5]

A short time before Lovisa was healed in the miraculous manner before stated, Lovina was taken with the consumption, when I was sixteen, and languished three years with this fatal disease.

Two years before sister Lovina's death, I visited sister Tuttle, who was then sick at South Hadley. Here lived one Colonel Woodbridge, who bought a large church bell about this time which was hung while I was there and I understand remains till this day.[6]

Lovina's character was that of a true follower of Christ, and she lived contemplating her final change with that peaceful serenity which characterizes those who fear God and walk uprightly. She spoke calmly of her approaching dissolution and conjured her young friends to remember that life on this earth could not be eternal, that they might see, therefore, the necessity of looking beyond this veil of tears to a far more glorious inheritance "where neither moth nor rust doth corrupt, and where thieves do not break through nor steal."[7]

The care of Lovina during her illness devolved chiefly upon myself.[8] The task, though a melancholy one, I cheerfully performed and, although she had much other attention, I never allowed myself to go an hour at a time beyond the sound of her voice while she was sick. Finally, she called to me one night (who am the youngest daughter of my father's family) and said, "Lucy, tell Mother and Father to come to me." When Mother came she said, "Mother, I am going now, and I wish you to call my young mates that I may speak to them again before I die." While my mother was giving the necessary directions, my sister bade me take her up and place her in a chair. When Mother and our associates with the family were seated, she commenced speaking, and finding that her strength failed her, she desired Mother to prepare her some food, saying, "'Tis the last you will ever get for me." She took the food, and after eating with seeming appetite a small quantity, she then gave back the dish to Mother and said, "There, Mother. You will never get me anything to eat again."

She then proceeded, "I do not know when I received my material change of heart, unless it was when I was ten years old.[9] God, at that time, heard my prayers and forgave my sins. Since then I have, according to my best ability, endeavored to serve him continually. I have called you here to give you my last warning and bid you all farewell and beseech you to endeavor to meet me where parting shall be no more."

Then, holding up her hands and looking upon them as one would mark a trifling thing which she had not observed before, she said, smiling, "See, the blood is now settling under my nails." As she contemplated the gradual change in her appearance, she again remarked how slowly death crept on there. Placing the fingers of her left hand across the right, she said, "'Tis cold to there. Soon this mortal flesh will be food for worms." Then, turning to me, she said, "Now, sister Lucy. Help me back to the bed."

I did as she desired, but as I moved my hand from beneath her side, she shouted, crying, "Oh sister, that hurt me." She moaned plaintively. As this was the last sad office I could ever perform for my sister, it wounded me to think that in laying her upon her deathbed I should cause her pain.

My sister now laid herself calmly back upon her pillow and said, "My nose is now quite cold." Then, slightly turning and straightening herself in bed, she continued, "Father, Mother, brother, sister, and dear companions, all farewell, I am going to rest—prepare to follow me." She then sang the hymn:

> Death! 'tis a melancholy day
> To those that have no God,
> When the poor soul is forced away
> To seek her last abode.
>
> In vain to heaven she lifts her eyes;
> But guilt, a heavy chain,
> Still drags her downwards from the skies,
> To darkness, fire, and pain.
>
> Awake and mourn, ye heirs of hell,
> Let stubborn sinners fear;
> You must be driven from earth, and dwell
> A long Forever there!
>
> See how the pit gapes wide for you,
> And flashes in your face;
> And thou, my soul, look downward too,
> And sing recovering grace.
>
> He is a God of sov'reign love,
> Who promised heaven to me,
> And taught my thoughts to soar above,
> Where happy spirits be.
>
> Prepare me, Lord, for thy right hand,
> Then come the joyful day,
> Come, death, and some celestial band,
> To bear my soul away.

After repeating this hymn, she folded her hands across her breast and closed her eyes to open them no more in this world.[10]

Having led my readers to the close of Lovina's life, I shall return to Lovisa, of whom there only remains the closing scene of her earthly career.

In the course of a few months subsequent to the death of sister Lovina, my father received a letter from South Hadley, stating that Lovisa was very low of the consumption and that she earnestly desired him to come and see her as soon as possible, as she expected to live but a short time.

My father set out immediately, and when he arrived there, he found her in rather better health than he expected. In a few days after he got there she resolved in her heart to return with him at all hazards. To this her father unwillingly consented, and, after making the requisite preparations, they started for Gilsum.

They traveled about four miles and came to an inn kept by a man by the name of Taff. Here her father halted and asked her if she did not wish to tarry a short time to rest herself. She replied in the affirmative. By the assistance of the landlord, she was presently seated in an easy chair. My father then stepped into the next room to procure a little water and wine for her. He was absent but a moment; however, when he returned it was too late, her spirit had fled from its earthly tabernacle to return no more until recalled by the trump of the archangel.

My father immediately addressed a letter to Mother, informing her of Lovisa's death, lest the shock of seeing the corpse unexpectedly should overcome her. As soon as he could get a coffin he proceeded on his journey for Gilsum, a distance of fifty miles.[11]

She was buried by the side of her sister Lovina, according to her own request.[12]

The following is part of a hymn composed by herself a few days previous to her decease:

> Lord, may my thoughts be turned to thee;
> Lift thou my heavy soul on high;
> Wilt thou, O Lord, return to me
> In mercy, Father, ere I die!
> My soaring thoughts now arise above—
> Oh, fill my soul with heavenly love.
>
> Father and Mother, now farewell;
> And husband, partner of my life,
> Go to my father's children, tell

That lives no more on earth thy wife,
That while she dwelt in cumbrous clay,
For them she prayed both night and day.

My friends, I bid you all adieu;
The Lord hath called, and I must go—
And all the joys of this vain earth
Are now to me of little worth;
'Twill be the same with you as me,
When brought as near eternity.

Thus closes this mournful recital, and when I pass with my readers into the next chapter, with them probably may end the sympathy aroused by this rehearsal, but with me it must last while life endures.[13]

Notes

1. The approximate birth year of Lovisa, Lucy's oldest sister, is 1761 and for Lovina, 1762.

2. Lovisa's marriage was to Joseph Tuttle, and its date is given as January 31, 1780 (see Anderson, *Heritage*, p. 68).

3. The healing took place sometime in 1791.

4. The church in the photograph dates to 1836 and belongs to the same congregation that owned the building where Lovisa told the people of her miraculous healing; but the church where she preached has long since been destroyed and was situated just a few hundred feet from this current meetinghouse.

5. Lovisa died in 1794, fourteen years after her marriage to Joseph Tuttle (see Anderson, *Heritage*, p. 69).

6. Money was appropriated for the belfry at South Hadley in 1792 and thus marks the time of Lucy's stay here. In her Preliminary Manuscript, Lucy gives an interesting personal note about the bell: "A company of young folks went to see it when it was first hung. I was one of the number and was the first who ever rang the bell. This Colonel Woodbridge afterwards built a large establishment for the education of poor children."

7. See Matthew 6:19–21.

8. Lucy's age was sixteen through nineteen during Lovina's illness.

9. In the year 1772.

10. It appears that Lovina was sick from 1791 to 1794, and she died just a few months before Lovisa.

11. Adding four to the fifty remaining miles to Gilsum gives a total of fifty-four miles, the exact distance from South Hadley to Gilsum. This gives the reader an idea of the remarkable memory of Mother Smith.

12. Lovina Mack and Lovisa Mack Tuttle are buried in the old Bond Cemetery on the hill above Gilsum, New Hampshire.

13. Lovisa died sometime in the year 1794, a few months after Lovina.

CHAPTER 4

The remarkable life of Stephen Mack. Young Revolutionary War soldier; successful businessman of Tunbridge, Vermont; pioneer developer of Detroit and Pontiac, Michigan.

June 15, 1766 to November 14, 1826

My brother Stephen, who was next in age to Jason, was born in the town of Marlow, June 15, 1766.[1]

I shall pass his childhood in silence and say nothing about him until he attained the age of fourteen, at which time he enlisted in the army, the circumstances of which were as follows:[2]

A recruiting officer came into the neighborhood to draft soldiers for the Revolutionary War, and he called out a company of militia to which my brother belonged in order to take therefrom such as were best qualified to do military duty. My brother, being very anxious to go into the army at this time, was so fearful that he would be passed by on account of his age that the sweat stood in large drops on his face and he shook like an aspen leaf. Fortunately the officer made choice of him among others, and he entered the army and continued in the service of his country until he was seventeen.[3] During this time he was in many battles, both on land and sea, traveling through cold, hunger, and fatigue and enduring every species of hardship that human nature could endure. Several times he narrowly escaped death by famine; but, according to his own account, whenever he was brought into a situation to fully realize his entire dependence upon God, the hand of Providence was always manifested in his deliverance.

Not long ago I met with an intimate acquaintance of my brother Stephen, and requested him to furnish me such facts as were in his possession in relation to him; and he wrote the following brief yet comprehensive account for the gratification of my readers:

"I, Horace Stanly, was born in Tunbridge, Orange County, Vermont, August 21, 1798. I have been personally acquainted with Major Mack and his family ever since I can remember, as I lived in the same township, within one mile and a half of the Major's farm, and two miles from his store, and eight miles from Chelsea, the county seat of Orange County, where he conducted the mercantile and tinning business.

"My eldest brother went to learn the tinning business of the Major's workmen. The Major, being a man of great enterprise, energetic in business, and possessed of a high degree of patriotism, launched forth on the frontiers of Detroit in the year 1800 (if I recollect rightly), where he immediately commenced trading with the Indians.

"He left his family in Tunbridge, on his farm, and while he was engaged in business at Detroit he visited them—sometimes once in a year, in eighteen months, or in two years, just as it happened.

"I visited Detroit, November 1, 1820, where I found the Major merchandising upon quite an extensive scale, having six clerks in one store; besides this, he had many other stores in the territory of Michigan, as well as in various parts of Ohio.

"His business at Pontiac was principally farming and building, but in order to facilitate these two branches of business, he set in operation a saw and flour mill, and afterwards added different branches of mechanism. He made the turnpike road from Detroit to Pontiac at his own expense. He also did considerable other public work, for the purpose of giving employment to the poor.

"He never encouraged idleness, or the man above his business. In 1828, having been absent from Detroit a short time, I returned. The Major was then a member of the council of the territory, and had acted a very conspicuous part in enhancing its prosperity and enlarging its settlement; and it was a common saying, that he had done much more for the territory than any other individual.

"In short, the Major was a man of talents of the first order. He was energetic and untiring. He always encouraged industry, and was very cautious how he applied his acts of charity."

My brother was in the city of Detroit in 1812, the year in which Hull surrendered the territory to the British crown. My brother, being somewhat celebrated for his prowess, was selected by General Hull to take the command of a company as captain. After a short service in this office, he was ordered to surrender. At this his indignation was roused to the highest pitch. He broke his sword across his knee and, throwing it into the lake, exclaimed that he would never submit to such a disgraceful compromise while the blood of an American continued to run through his veins.

This drew the especial vengeance of the army upon his head; and his property doubtless would have been sacrificed to their resentment had they known the situation of his affairs. But this they did not know, as his housekeeper deceived them by a stratagem related by Mr. Stanly as follows:

"At the surrender of Detroit, not having as yet moved his family hither, Major Mack had an elderly lady, by the name of Trotwine, keeping house for him. The old lady took in some of the most distinguished British officers as boarders. She justified them in their course of conduct towards the Yankees, and, by her shrewdness and tact, she gained the esteem of the officers, and thus secured through them the goodwill of the soldiery, so far as to prevent their burning (what they supposed to be) her store and dwelling, both of which were splendid buildings.

"The Major never forgot this service done him by the old lady, for he ever afterwards supported her handsomely."

Thus was a great amount of goods and money saved from the hands of his enemies. But this is not all: the news came to her ears that they were about to burn another trading establishment belonging to the Major, and without waiting to consult him, she went immediately to the store and took from the counting room several thousand dollars, which she secreted until the British left the city. The building and goods were burned.

As soon as the English left the territory, he recommenced business and removed his family from Tunbridge to Detroit. Here they remained but a short time, when he took them to Pontiac; and as soon as they were well established or settled in this place, he himself went to the city of Rochester, where he built a sawmill.

But in the midst of his prosperity, he was called away to experience another state of existence with barely a moment's warning, for he was sick only four days from the time he was first taken ill until he died, and even on the fourth day, and in the last hour of his illness, it was not supposed to be at all dangerous until his son, who sat by his bedside, discovered he was dying.[4]

He left his family with an estate of fifty thousand dollars, clear of encumbrance. He was a moral man, a man of business, and a man of the most intrepid courage, which last was shown in the defense of his country which was ever the interest that lay nearest to his heart.

NOTES

1. Mother Smith means the next *brother* in age to Jason. The birth order of Solomon and Lydia Mack's children is as follows: Jason, Lovisa, Lovina, Lydia, Stephen, Daniel, Solomon, and Lucy.

2. This was actually Stephen's reenlistment. He and his brother Jason had enlisted on July 25, 1779, and served until August 31, 1779. The enlistment mentioned here by Lucy was for a three-year term that began on April 2, 1781. (See Archibald F. Bennett, "Solomon Mack and His Family," *Improvement Era* 58 [December 1955]: 906, 907.)

3. Stephen served from 1781 until 1783.

4. It is insightful to note Stephen Mack's obituary, which appeared in the *Detroit Gazette,* November 14, 1826, and read, in part, as follows: "Col. Stephen Mack, a soldier of the Revolution, and enterprising and industrious citizen, and a kind and provident father, departed this life last Saturday morning at Pontiac, in the seventy-second year of his age. Col. M. has for nearly twenty years resided in this territory, and has been distinguished from the mass of his fellow-citizens for his enterprise and the great utility of his views. It is owing to his exertions more than to any other man's, that the first settlers of Oakland County were so soon accommodated with mills and other useful works. His sacrifices and his exertions in promoting the best interests of the new county, which he had been so eminently useful in settling and organizing, endeared him to his fellow-citizens. . . . The loss of such a man is truly that of the public—and many are those who share the grief of the numerous family which he has left." (Quoted in Anderson, *Heritage,* p. 180.)

CHAPTER 5

Brief look at Lydia Mack, third daughter of Solomon Mack.

1764 to January 8, 1826

O f my sister Lydia[1] I shall say but little; not that I loved her less, or that she was less deserving of honorable mention, but she seemed to float more with the stream of common events than those who have occupied the foregoing pages; hence fewer incidents of striking character are furnished for the mind to dwell upon.

She sought riches and obtained them, but in the day of prosperity she remembered the poor, for she dealt out her substance to the needy with a liberal hand through life and died the object of their affection. As she was beloved in life, so she was bewailed in death.[2]

NOTES

1. Lydia was born in 1764 and married prominent citizen Samuel Bill from Gilsum in 1786.

2. Lydia died at Gilsum and is buried in the cemetery with two of her sisters; her youngest brother, Solomon; and her father. Lydia's gravestone reads: "Lydia Mack Bill died Jan. 8, 1826, Ae. 62" (see Anderson, *Heritage*, p. 179). Her epitaph indicates her spiritual inclinations: "Now she's gone to realms above/Where saints and angels meet/ To realize her Savior's love/And worship at his feet" (see Anderson, *Heritage*, p. 29).

CHAPTER 6

Daniel Mack's courage in saving the lives of three men in Miller's River by Montague, Massachusetts.

1790s

Daniel comes next in order.[1] He was a man of the world, but with one peculiarity—he was, as many can testify, in many scenes of danger where lives were exposed, and he was always the first to the rescue, and thus was the means of saving many a helpless victim from the jaws of death.

One circumstance of this kind took place in the town of Montague on Miller's River, when one of the number proposed taking a swim.[2] Daniel objected, saying it was a dangerous place to swim in, yet they were determined and three went in; but, going out into the stream rather too far, they were overpowered by the current and a kind of eddy which they fell into, and they sank immediately.

At this Daniel said, "Now, gentlemen, these men are drowning; who will assist them at the risk of his life?" No one answered. At this he sprang into the water and, diving to the bottom, found one of them fastened to some small roots. Daniel took hold of him and tore up the roots to which he was clinging and brought him out, and then told the bystanders to get a barrel for the purpose of rolling him on it in order to make him disgorge the water which he had taken. He then went in again and found the other two in the same situation as the first and saved them in like manner.

Daniel Gates Mack saved three men from drowning in Miller's River near this spot.

After rolling them a short time on the barrel, he took them to a house and gave them every possible attention until they had so far recovered as to be able to speak. As soon as they could talk, one of them, fixing his eyes upon Daniel, said, "Mr. Mack, we have reason to look upon you as our savior, for you have delivered us from a watery tomb; and I would that I could always live near you. We are now assured that you have not only wisdom to counsel, but when men have spurned your advice, you still have that greatness of soul which leads you to risk your own life to save your fellowman. No, I will never leave you as long as I live, for I wish to convince you that I ever remember you, and that I will never slight your counsel again."

In this they were all agreed, and they carried out the same in their future lives.[3]

NOTES

1. Daniel was named after his mother's father and was the third son and sixth child of Solomon and Lydia Mack. His birth is estimated to be in 1770.

2. Miller's River, which flows by and through the town of Montague, Franklin County, Massachusetts, can be very dangerous, especially in the high waters of spring and early summer, because of the boulder-strewn course.

3. Daniel later lived in Royalton, Vermont. His mother, Lydia Mack, passed away in his home there.

CHAPTER 7

Brief account of Solomon Mack, youngest son of Solomon Mack.

January 28, 1773 to fall 1845

Solomon, the youngest son of my father, was born[1] and brought up, married, and still lives in the town of Gilsum, and although sixty-four years old,[2] he has never traveled farther than Boston, where his business leads him twice a year to purchase goods.

He has gathered to himself in that rocky region fields, flocks, and herds, which multiply and increase upon the mountains. He has been known these twenty years as Captain Solomon Mack of Gilsum; but as he lives to speak for himself, and as I have to do chiefly with the dead,[3] and not the living, I shall leave him, hoping that, as he has lived peaceably with all men, so he may die happily.

I have now given a brief account of all my father's family, save myself; and what I have written has been done with the view of discharging an obligation which I considered resting upon me inasmuch as they have all passed off this stage of action except myself and youngest brother. And seldom do I meet with an individual with whom I was even acquainted in my early years, and I am constrained to exclaim— "The friends of my youth! where are they?" The tomb replies, "Here are they!" But, through my instrumentality,

> Safely truth to urge her claims, presumes
> On names now found alone on books and tombs.

Solomon Mack Jr. died at Gilsum, New Hampshire,
October 12, 1851, at age seventy-eight.

NOTES

1. Solomon was born January 28, 1773.

2. At the time of Mother Smith's dictation, her brother Solomon was seventy-two years old.

3. When Lucy Mack Smith dictated her history in 1845, her parents and all of her brothers and sisters, save Solomon Jr., were dead.

PART 2

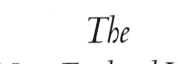

*The
New England Years*

Chapter 8

An introduction to the early life of Lucy Mack, her visits to Tunbridge, Vermont, and subsequent marriage to Joseph Smith.

July 8, 1775 to January 24, 1796

Now, my dear readers, I shall introduce myself to your attention. I was born in Gilsum,[1] Cheshire County, state of New Hampshire, July 8, 1776.[2]

When I arrived at the age of eight years, my mother had a severe fit of sickness. She was so low that she, as well as her friends, entirely despaired of her recovery. During this sickness, she called her children around her bed, and, after exhorting them always to remember the instructions which she had given them—to fear God and walk uprightly before him—she gave me to my brother Stephen, requesting him to take care of me and bring me up as his own child, then bade each of us farewell.

This my brother promised to do; but, as my mother shortly recovered, it was not necessary, and I consequently remained at my father's house until my sister Lovisa was married.[3] Some time after this event I went to South Hadley where Lovisa lived to pay her a visit.

I returned home to my parents in about six months, and remained with them in Gilsum until the death of Lovina.[4] Shortly after this, my brother Stephen Mack came from Tunbridge on a visit. He persuaded my parents to let him take me to Tunbridge in order to divert my mind from the death of my sister, as the grief of it was preying upon my health and was likely to be a serious injury to me.[5]

Gilsum, New Hampshire, is located in a dense forest,
ten miles east of the Connecticut River.

For months after this I did not feel as though life was worth seeking after, and in my reflections I determined to obtain that which was
spoken of so frequently from the pulpit, namely a change of heart.

In order to accomplish this, I perused the Bible and prayed incessantly; but one thought interposed itself into all my meditations: If I
remain out of any church, all religious people will say I am of the
world. If I join any one church, the rest will all declare that I am in the

Modern interior of Tunbridge, Vermont, town store.
Tradition says Lucy and Joseph met here.

This May certify that Joseph Smith was Married to Lucy Mack on the 24 of January AD 1796 by me attest A true record H Hutchinson &c Seth Austin Justice Peace

*Original marriage entry of Joseph Smith and Lucy Mack
in Tunbridge town clerk's office.*

wrong. No church will say I am right unless I unite with them, and this makes them witnesses against each other. How shall I decide, inasmuch as the Church of Christ in former days was not like any of them?

While I was in Tunbridge, my brother frequently spoke to me of one Mr. Asael Smith, an intimate acquaintance of his whose family I afterwards came to know.[6] Their names were Jesse, Joseph, Asael, John, Samuel, Silas, Stephen, Priscilla, Mary, Susan, and Sarah—a worthy, respectable, amiable, and intelligent family. It was the second son of this family to whom I was afterwards married.

I remained with my brother one year, then went home to visit my parents in Gilsum and my uncles and aunts in Marlow. After a short time, my brother came, and upon his urgent request I went again to Tunbridge, and was with him until the ensuing January when I was married.[7]

NOTES

1. At the time of Lucy's birth, Gilsum claimed 178 inhabitants, mostly made up of from twenty to thirty young to middle-aged families (see Bushman, *Beginnings*, p. 14).

2. Although Lucy gives 1776 as the year of her birth, the Gilsum, New Hampshire, town record cites her birth as July 8, 1775. This latter, and presumably more accurate, date will be used throughout the book to mark the age of Mother Smith. (See Anderson, *Heritage*, p. 182.) In the Preliminary Manuscript, Mother Smith gives a list of friends from her youth who she knows would be familiar with her history. They include "the children of one Mr. Harmon; John Toriah; Martha (called Fatty by her mates); also the daughters of Colonel Ebenezer Bill (whose brother mar-

ried my sister Lydia)"; further, "the family of Captain Gunn [of Montague]: Thankful, Eunice, Abel, Martin; also the Harveys' children. I mention these as I shall also others as I pass along in hopes that this may reach their ears and by this means I shall be able to make myself known to them."

3. According to *Vital Records of Montague, Massachusetts*, Lovisa Mack was married to Joseph Tuttle on January 31, 1780. Note that Lucy would have been four and a half years old when Lovisa was married. (See Anderson, *Heritage*, p. 75.)

4. Lovina died in 1794 when Lucy was about nineteen years old (see Anderson, *Heritage*, p. 69).

5. Lucy's first visit to Tunbridge, Orange County, Vermont, a journey of about ninety miles, was sometime in 1794 and into 1795.

6. Lucy's brother Stephen was nine years older than she, and certainly took the "parental role" he had once been given by his mother for Lucy.

7. Lucy returned to Tunbridge sometime in 1795 and was married to Joseph Smith on January 24, 1796. Joseph Smith was born July 12, 1771, at Topsfield, Essex County, Massachusetts. Lucy was twenty and Joseph was twenty-four, and their marriage would last until Joseph's death, September 14, 1840, a total of over forty-four and a half years.

CHAPTER 9

A wedding present of one thousand dollars from Stephen Mack and John Mudget to Lucy. Six years on the farm at Tunbridge, Vermont. Two children, Alvin and Hyrum, added to the Smith family. Move to Randolph, Vermont.

January 1796 to spring 1802

Soon after I was married, I went with my husband to see my parents, and as we were about setting out on this visit, my brother Stephen[1] and his partner in business, John Mudget, were making some remarks in regard to my leaving them, and the conversation presently turned upon the subject of giving me a marriage present.

"Well," said Mr. Mudget, "Lucy ought to have something worth naming, and I will give her just as much as you will."

"Done," said my brother. "I will give her five hundred dollars in cash."

"Good," said the other, "and I will give her five hundred dollars more."

So they wrote a check on their bankers for one thousand dollars and presented me with the same. This check I laid aside, as I had other means by me sufficient to purchase my housekeeping furniture.

Having visited my father and mother, we returned again to Tunbridge, where my companion owned a handsome farm upon which we settled ourselves and began to cultivate the soil. We lived on this place about six years, tilling the earth for a livelihood.[2]

Part of Joseph and Lucy Smith's farm in the hills above the town of Tunbridge, Vermont.

In 1802, we rented our farm in Tunbridge and moved to the town of Randolph with our first two children, Alvin and Hyrum,[3] and my husband opened a mercantile establishment.

Hiram son to Joseph & Lucy Smith was born, February ninth 1800 Likewise Sophrona a daughter to the Joseph & Lucy Smith was born May 17th 1803 Certifyed by Joseph Smith Atteft Saml Austin Town Clerk.

Birth entries of Smith children still can be found in the Tunbridge town records.

NOTES

1. Stephen Mack's business enterprises started in Gilsum, New Hampshire, in 1787 when he was twenty-one. He then moved operations to Tunbridge in 1793. He would continue forging a successful career throughout his life and become one of the great developers of Detroit and Pontiac, Michigan, opening stores, running saw and flour mills, farming, and building for many years until his death in 1826. (See Anderson, *Heritage*, pp. 28, 180; Bushman, *Beginnings*, p. 19.)

2. Joseph and Lucy lived on this farm from their marriage in January 1796 until 1802. A note of sadness is found in Joseph Smith Sr.'s patriarchal blessing book of 1834 where he addresses the Smith family and speaks of "three seats" vacated by death among his children: "The Lord in his just providence has taken from me at an untimely birth a son. . . . My next son, Alvin . . . was taken." (See Bushman, *Beginnings*, p. 198.) Joseph and Lucy's firstborn son was taken in death sometime between the middle of 1796 and the spring of 1797.

3. Alvin was born February 11, 1798, and Hyrum was born February 9, 1800, both at Tunbridge, Vermont.

CHAPTER 10

Lucy's sickness and near death at Randolph, Vermont.

Fall 1802

We had lived in Randolph[1] but six months when I took a heavy cold, which caused a severe cough. A hectic fever set in which threatened to prove fatal and the physician believed my case to be confirmed consumption. My mother attended me day and night with much anxiety, sparing herself no pains in administering to my comfort, yet I grew so weak that I could not bear the noise of a footfall except in stocking feet, nor a word to be spoken in the room except in whispers.

One Mr. Murkley, a Methodist exhorter, heard of my afflictions and came to visit me. When he came to the door, he knocked in his usual manner, not knowing that I was so very weak and that the noise would disturb me. This agitated me so much that it was some time before my nerves were settled again. My mother stepped to the door and motioned him to a chair, informing him of my weakness in a whisper.

He seated himself and for a long time seemed pondering in his mind something he wished to say. I thought to myself, "He will ask me if I am prepared to die." I dreaded to have him speak to me, for said I to myself, "I am not prepared to die, for I do not know the ways of Christ," and it seemed to me as though there was a dark and lonely chasm between myself and Christ that I dared not attempt to cross.

I thought as I strained my eyes towards the light (which I knew lay just beyond the gloomy veil before me) that I could discover a faint glimmer.

Mr. Murkley left, and my husband came to my bed and caught my hand and exclaimed as well as he could amidst sobs and tears, "Oh, Lucy! My wife! You must die. The doctors have given you up, and all say you cannot live."

I then looked to the Lord and begged and pled that he would spare my life that I might bring up my children and comfort the heart of my husband. Thus I lay all night, sometimes gazing gradually away to heaven, and then reverting back again to my babies[2] and my companion at my side, and I covenanted with God that if he would let me live, I would endeavor to get that religion that would enable me to serve him right, whether it was in the Bible or wherever it might be found, even if it was to be obtained from heaven by prayer and faith. At last a voice spoke to me and said, "Seek, and ye shall find; knock, and it shall be opened unto you. Let your heart be comforted. Ye believe in God, believe also in me."[3]

In a few moments my mother came in and looked upon me and cried out, "Lucy, you are better." My speech came and I answered, "Yes, Mother, the Lord will let me live. If I am faithful to my promise which I have made to him, he will suffer me to remain to comfort the hearts of my mother, my husband, and my children."

From this time forward I gained strength continually. I said but little upon the subject of religion, although it occupied my mind entirely. I thought I would make all diligence, as soon as I was able, to seek some pious person who knew the ways of God to instruct me in the things of heaven.

I was acquainted with one Deacon Davies, a man of exceeding piety, one who had known my situation and the miraculous manner of my recovery. When I had gained strength enough, I made him a visit, and here I expected the same that I heard from my mother: "The Lord has done a marvelous work; let his name have the praise thereof." But no, from the time I came in sight until I left the house I heard nothing but, "Oh, Mrs. Smith is coming. Run. Build a fire. Make the room warm. Help her in. Fill the teakettle, get the great armchair," etc., etc. Their excessive anxiety for my physical convenience, not tempered with one word pertaining to Christ or godliness, sickened and disgusted me, and I went home disappointed and sorrowful.

About the time the Smiths did business in Randolph,
it was the tenth largest town in Vermont.

In the anxiety of my soul to abide by the covenant which I had entered into with the Almighty, I went from place to place to seek information or find, if possible, some congenial spirit who might enter into my feelings and sympathize with me.

At last I heard that one noted for his piety would preach the ensuing Sabbath in the Presbyterian church. Thither I went in expectation of obtaining that which alone could satisfy my soul—the bread of eternal life. When the minister commenced, I fixed my mind with breathless attention upon the spirit and matter of the discourse, but all was emptiness, vanity, vexation of spirit, and fell upon my heart like the chill, untimely blast upon the starting ear ripening in a summer sun. It did not fill the aching void within nor satisfy the craving hunger of my soul. I was almost in total despair, and with a grieved and troubled spirit I returned home, saying in my heart, there is not on earth the religion which I seek. I must again turn to my Bible, take Jesus and his disciples for an example. I will try to obtain from God that which man cannot give nor take away. I will settle myself down to this. I will hear all that can be said, read all that is written, but particularly the word of God shall be my guide to life and salvation, which I will endeavor to obtain if it is to be had by diligence in prayer.

This course I pursued for many years, till at last I concluded that my mind would be easier if I were baptized. I found a minister who was willing to baptize me and leave me free from membership in any church, a course I continued until my oldest son attained his twenty-second year.[4]

NOTES

1. Randolph was a town located about seven miles west of Tunbridge and had a population at that time of about two thousand inhabitants. Randolph was situated between the Second and Third Branch of the White River, and the gentle-sloping geography allowed for greater growth than in many of the hill-locked villages in Vermont.

2. It is likely the Smiths moved to Randolph in the spring of 1802 and Lucy became ill sometime in the fall of that same year. This means that Lucy's "babies" were four years old (Alvin) and two years old (Hyrum). It is interesting to note that Lucy was in the first three months of her pregnancy with Sophronia, and this could have doubly weakened her during this severe illness.

3. See Matthew 7:7 and John 14:1.

4. Alvin attained age twenty-one on February 11, 1819; therefore he was in his twenty-second year from then until February of 1820. Lucy had been pursuing the fulfillment of her covenant for sixteen years.

CHAPTER 11

Joseph Smith Sr. begins the business of crystallizing ginseng root. He exports a large quantity to China but is taken by fraud and deceit, and the entire venture fails. He loses his business in Randolph and has to sell the Tunbridge farm. Visit of Jason Mack, brother of Lucy, and final correspondence from Jason before his death.

Fall 1802 to late spring 1803

Now I must return to the earlier part of my life and change the subject from spiritual to temporal things. As I said before, my husband followed merchandising for a season in Randolph. Shortly after he commenced business, he ascertained that crystallized ginseng bore an immense value in China, as it was used as a remedy for the plague.[1]

He therefore decided to go into a traffic of this article, crystallizing and exporting the root. When he got a quantity of it on hand, a merchant of Royalton by the name of Stevens came and made him an offer of three thousand dollars for the whole lot, but that was not more than two-thirds of its worth. Mr. Smith refused, saying he would rather ship it himself than accept the offer.

My husband then went immediately to the city of New York[2] and made arrangements to send his ginseng to China on board a vessel that was about to set sail, making arrangements with the captain to sell the ginseng in China and return the avails thereof to my husband. This the captain bound himself to do in a written obligation.

Mr. Stevens, being rather vexed at his failure, repaired immediately to New York, and by taking some pains, he ascertained the vessel on which Mr. Smith was shipping his ginseng, and having some of the same article on hand himself, he made arrangements with the captain to take his also, sending his son to China on the same ship to take charge of the goods.

It appears from circumstances that afterwards transpired that when the son arrived in China, he sold the ginseng which my husband sent and took possession of the avails.

When the vessel returned, Stevens the younger returned with it, and when my husband became apprised of his arrival, he went immediately to him and made inquiry respecting the success of the captain in selling his ginseng. Mr. Stevens told him quite a plausible tale, the particulars of which I have forgotten, but the amount of it was that the sale had been a perfect failure, and the only thing which had been brought for Mr. Smith from China was a small chest of tea, which chest had been delivered into his care for my husband.

In a short time after this, young Stevens hired a house of Major Mack, my brother, employed eight or ten hands, and commenced crystallizing ginseng. When Stevens had fairly set up business, my brother went to see him and found him intoxicated. "Well," said my brother, "you are doing a fine business. You will soon be ready for another trip to China." Then, turning in a gay, social manner, he said, "Oh, Mr. Stevens, how much did Brother Smith's venture bring?"

The man, being under the influence of liquor, was off his guard, so he took my brother by the hand and led him to a trunk and archly observed, "There, sir, is the avails of Mr. Smith's ginseng," exhibiting a large amount of silver and gold.

My brother was astounded but smothered his feelings, talked a while indifferently to him, and then returned home. That night at ten o'clock he ordered his horse and started for Randolph to see my husband. When Mr. Stevens had overcome his intoxication, he began to reflect upon what he had done, and found upon inquiring of the hostler where my brother had gone. Mr. Stevens, conjecturing his business— that he had gone to see my husband respecting the ginseng adventure— went immediately to his establishment, dismissed his hands, called his carriage, and fled, cash and all, for Canada and has not been heard of in the United States since.

My husband pursued him a while, but finding that pursuit was vain, he returned home quite dispirited at the state of his affairs. He then overhauled his books and found that, in addition to the loss that he had met with in the ginseng traffic, he had lost more than two thousand dollars in bad debts and was himself owing eighteen hundred dollars for store goods purchased in the city of Boston. He had expected to discharge the debt at the return of the China expedition; but having invested almost all his means in ginseng, the loss rendered it impossible for him to pay his debt with the property which remained in his hands. The principal dependence left him, in the shape of property, was the farm at Tunbridge, upon which we were then living, having moved back to this place immediately after his venture was sent to China.[3] This farm, which was worth about fifteen hundred dollars, my husband sold for eight hundred dollars in order to make a speedy payment on his debts in Boston. As I had not yet made use of the thousand-dollar present that my brother Stephen and Mr. Mudget had given me, I desired Mr. Smith to add this to the sum which he received for his farm and by this means we would be enabled to liquidate all debts that stood against us; and although we might be poor, we would have the satisfaction of knowing that we had given no man any cause of complaint, and having a conscience void of offense, the society of our children, and the blessing of health, we still might be indeed happy.

He acceded to my proposition and deposited the whole into the hands of Colonel Mack, who took the same to Boston and paid off the demands against us and returned with the receipts which set us free from the embarrassment of debt, but not from the embarrassment of poverty.

While we were living on the Tunbridge farm, my brother Jason made us a visit. He brought with him a young man by the name of William Smith, a friendless orphan whom he had adopted as his own son, and, previous to this time, had kept constantly with him; but he now thought best to leave him with us for the purpose of having him go to school. He remained with us, however, only six months before my brother came again and took him to New Brunswick, which they afterwards made their home, and where my brother had gathered together

some thirty families on a tract of land which he had purchased for the purpose of assisting poor persons to the means of sustaining themselves. He planned their work for them, and when they raised anything which they wished to sell, he took it to market for them. Owning a schooner himself, he took their produce to Liverpool, as it was then the best market.

When Jason set out on the above-mentioned visit to Tunbridge, he purchased a quantity of goods which he intended as presents for his friends, especially his mother and sisters, but on his way thither he

Asael and Mary Smith with their eleven children moved to Tunbridge about November 1791.

found so many objects of charity that he gave away not only the goods, but most of his money. On one occasion he saw a woman who had just lost her husband and who was very destitute; he gave her fifteen dollars in money and a full suit of clothes for herself and each of her children, which were six in number.

This was the last interview I ever had with my brother Jason, but twenty years later he wrote the following letter to my brother Solomon, and that is about all the intelligence I have ever received from him since I saw him:

SOUTH BRANCH OF OROMOCTO, PROVINCE OF NEW BRUNSWICK,

June 30, 1835.

My Dear Brother Solomon:

You will, no doubt, be surprised to hear that I am still alive, although in an absence of twenty years I have never written to you
before. But I trust you will forgive me when I tell you that, for most
of the twenty years, I have been so situated that I have had little or
no communication with the lines, and have been holding meetings,
day and night, from place to place; besides, my mind has been so
taken up with the deplorable situation of the earth, the darkness in
which it lies, that, when my labors did call me near the lines, I did
not realize the opportunity that presented itself of letting you
know where I was. And, again, I have designed visiting you long
since, and annually have promised myself that the succeeding year I
would certainly seek out my relatives, and enjoy the privilege of one
pleasing interview with them before I passed into the valley and
shadow of death. But last, though not least, let me not startle you
when I say, that, according to my early adopted principles of the
power of faith, the Lord has, in his exceeding kindness, bestowed
upon me the gift of healing by the prayer of faith, and the use of
such simple means as seem congenial to the human system; but my
chief reliance is upon him who organized us at the first, and can restore at pleasure that which is disorganized.

The first of my peculiar successes in this way was twelve years
since, and from nearly that date I have had little rest. In addition to
the incessant calls which I, in a short time had, there was the most
overwhelming torrent of opposition poured down upon me that I
ever witnessed. But it pleased God to take the weak to confound the
wisdom of the wise. I have in the last twelve years seen the greatest
manifestations of the power of God in healing the sick, that, with
all my sanguinity, I ever hoped or imagined. And when the learned
infidel has declared with sober face, time and again, that disease had
obtained such an ascendancy that death could be resisted no longer,
that the victim must wither beneath his potent arm, I have seen the
almost lifeless clay slowly but surely resuscitated, and revive, till the

pallid monster fled so far that the patient was left in the full bloom of vigorous health. But it is God that hath done it, and to him let all the praise be given.

I am now compelled to close this epistle, for I must start immediately on a journey of more than one hundred miles, to attend a heavy case of sickness.[4] So God be with you all. Farewell!

Jason Mack

The next intelligence we received concerning Jason, after his letter to Brother Solomon, was that he, his wife, and oldest son were dead, and this concludes my account of my brother Jason.

NOTES

1. Regarding ginseng, a modern reference source reports: "The root of the ginseng has for centuries been reputed to be a panacea for cancer, rheumatism, diabetes, . . . and aging. The claims date back to ancient China, and the root was long of great value there." In 1718 a wild species of ginseng was discovered in Quebec that came to be known as wild American ginseng. In response to Chinese calls for this American species, Daniel Boone and many others in North America made great efforts to search for it. The result was that millions of pounds of the root were exported to China. "The American ginseng . . . grows wild in North American woodlands. It stands up to 60 cm (2 ft) tall, has leaves up to 15 cm (6 in) long, and bears greenish white flowers." (*The New Grolier Multimedia Encyclopedia*, Release 6, 1993, s.v. "ginseng.") To this day, the lucrative ginseng trade is still active in Randolph, Vermont, with an annual market where representatives from the Orient come and purchase the locally harvested wild root.

2. One-way travel time from central Vermont to New York City at the beginning of the nineteenth century was about six days (see Bushman, *Beginnings*, p. 199).

3. This move back to the farm at Tunbridge likely took place in late 1802 or early 1803.

4. The gift of healing seemed to be resident in the Mack line, as we observe it in use with Lucy Mack Smith in her own healing and in the healing of her daughter Sophronia from the "typhus fever." We also later see Joseph Smith the Prophet exercising this gift, especially on July 22, 1839, when hundreds of the Saints were healed from the malarial fevers.

CHAPTER 12

Lucy's dream of the two beautiful trees by a very pure and clear stream in a magnificent meadow. Interpretation is given about Joseph Smith Sr. and his older brother, Jesse Smith.

Spring or summer 1803

While we were yet living in the town of Tunbridge, my mind became deeply impressed with the subject of religion, which probably was occasioned by my singular experience during my sickness at Randolph. I commenced attending Methodist meetings and endeavored to persuade my husband to attend with me. He went a few times to gratify me, but he had so little faith in the doctrine taught by them that my feelings were the only inducement for him to go.

As soon as his father and Brother Jesse[1] heard that we were attending Methodist meetings, they were much displeased. His father came to the door one day and threw Tom Paine's *Age of Reason* into the house and angrily bade him read it until he believed it.[2] They also told him that he ought not to let me go to the meetings and it would be far better for him to stop going. Accordingly, my husband requested me not to go, as he considered it hardly worth our while to attend any longer, and it would prove of but little advantage to us, and it gave our friends such disagreeable feelings.

I was very much hurt by this, but did not reply to him then. I retired to a grove of handsome wild cherry trees not far distant and prayed to the Lord that he would influence the heart of my husband that it might be softened so as to receive the true gospel whenever it was preached, or that he might become more religiously inclined. After praying some time in this manner, I returned to the house much depressed in spirit, which state of feeling continued until I retired to my bed. That night I had the following dream:

I thought that I stood in a large and beautiful meadow, which lay a short distance from the house in which we lived, and that everything around me wore an aspect of peculiar pleasantness. The first thing that attracted my special attention in this magnificent meadow was a very pure and clear stream of water which ran through the midst of it; and as I traced this stream, I discovered two trees standing upon its margin, both of which were on the same side of the stream. These trees were very beautiful. They were well proportioned, and towered with majestic beauty to a great height. Their branches, which added to their symmetry and glory, commenced near the top and spread themselves in luxurious grandeur around. I gazed upon them with wonder and admiration, and after beholding them a short time, I saw one of them was surrounded with a bright belt that shone like burnished gold, but far more brilliantly. Presently, a gentle breeze passed by, and the tree encircled with this golden zone bent gracefully before the wind and waved its beautiful branches in the light air. As the wind increased, this tree assumed the most lively and animated appearance and seemed to express in its motions the utmost joy and happiness. If it had been an intelligent creature, it could not have conveyed by the power of language the idea of joy and gratitude so perfectly as it did; and even the stream that rolled beneath it shared, apparently, every sensation felt by the tree, for, as the branches danced over the stream, it would swell gently, then recede again with a motion as soft as the breathing of an infant, but as lively as the dancing of a sunbeam. The belt also partook of the same influence, and, as it moved in unison with the motion of the stream and of the tree, it increased continually in refulgence and magnitude until it became exceedingly glorious.

I turned my eyes upon its fellow, which stood opposite; but it was not surrounded with the belt of light as the former, and it stood erect and fixed as a pillar of marble. No matter how strong the wind blew over it, not a leaf was stirred, not a bough was bent, but obstinately stiff it stood, scorning alike the zephyr's breath, or the power of the mighty storm.

Joseph Smith Sr. likely attended this Universalist church in North Tunbridge, Vermont.

I wondered at what I saw, and said in my heart, What can be the meaning of all this? And the interpretation given me was that these personated my husband and his oldest brother, Jesse Smith; that the stubborn and unyielding tree was like Jesse; that the other, more pliant and flexible, was like Joseph, my husband; that the breath of heaven, which passed over them, was the pure and undefiled gospel of the Son of God, which gospel Jesse would always resist, but which Joseph, when he was more advanced in life, would hear and receive with his whole heart and rejoice therein; and unto him would be added intelligence, happiness, glory, and everlasting life.

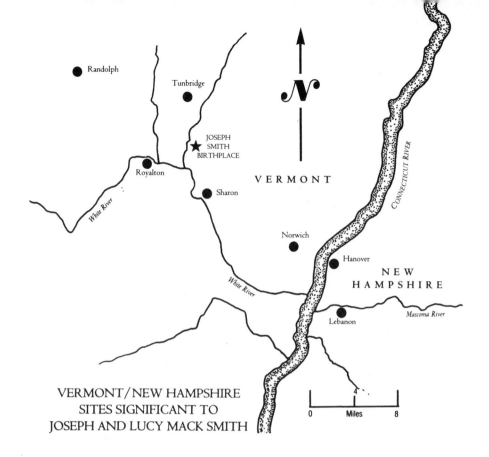

VERMONT/NEW HAMPSHIRE
SITES SIGNIFICANT TO
JOSEPH AND LUCY MACK SMITH

NOTES

1. Jesse Smith was particularly opposed to organized religion. He was the only one of the four living sons of Asael and Mary Smith who did not accept the restored gospel.

2. Part I of Thomas Paine's *Age of Reason*, which consisted of fifty-two pages, was first published in Paris in 1794 and part 2, consisting of ninety-six pages, was first published in 1795. Perhaps Joseph's father, Asael, hoped he would, at least, be attracted to Paine's first page, which in part reads: "It has been my intention, for several years past, to publish my thoughts upon religion. . . . I believe in one God, and no more; and I hope for happiness beyond this life. I believe in the equality of man; and I believe that religious duties consist in doing justice, loving mercy, and endeavoring to make our fellow creatures happy. But, lest it should be supposed that I believe many other things in addition to these, I shall, in the progress of this work, declare the things I do not believe, and my reason for not believing them." (*The Age of Reason. Part the First. Being an Investigation of True and of Fabulous Theology.* 3rd ed. [London: R. Carlile, 1819], p. 1.) Asael Smith was likely encouraging his son Joseph to be cautious in his study of the religions of the day.

CHAPTER 13

The Smiths move from Tunbridge to Royalton, then to Sharon, Windsor County, Vermont, where they rent a farm from Solomon Mack, Lucy's father. Births of Joseph Jr., Samuel Harrison, Ephraim, and William mentioned. First and second in a series of seven visions or dreams given to Joseph Smith Sr. First, the dream of the box, and second, the dream of the tree of life.

Summer 1803 to late summer 1812

The loss of the Tunbridge farm was a considerable trial to us, for it deprived us at once not only of the comforts and conveniences of life, but also a home of any description. After selling the farm at Tunbridge, we took our three oldest children and moved only a short distance to the town of Royalton.[1] Here we resided a few months, then moved again to Sharon, Windsor County, Vermont.[2] Here my husband rented a farm of my father, which he cultivated in the summer season and in the winter taught school. In this way my husband continued laboring for a few years, during which time our circumstances gradually improved until we found ourselves quite comfortable again.

Here it was that my son Joseph was born, December 23, 1805, one who will act a more conscious part in this work than any other individual.

We moved thence to Tunbridge. Here we had another son, whom we named Samuel Harrison, born March 13, 1808. We lived in this place a short time, then moved to Royalton, where Ephraim was born, March 13, 1810, who died in his infancy.[3] We continued here until we had another son, born March 13, 1811, whom we called William.

*Site of the house, with original front porch stone,
where Joseph Smith the Prophet was born.*

About this time my husband's mind became much excited upon the subject of religion; yet he would not subscribe to any particular system of faith, but contended for the ancient order, as established by our Lord and Savior Jesus Christ and his Apostles.

One night my husband retired to his bed in a very thoughtful state of mind, contemplating the situation of the Christian religion, or the confusion and discord that were extant. He soon fell into a sleep, and before waking had the following vision, which I shall relate in his own words just as he told it to me the next morning:[4]

"I seemed to be traveling in an open, barren field, and as I was traveling, I turned my eyes towards the east, the west, the north, and the south, but could see nothing save dead, fallen timber.[5] Not a vestige of life, either animal or vegetable, could be seen; besides, to render the scene still more dreary, the most deathlike silence prevailed. No sound of anything animate could be heard in all the field. I was alone in this gloomy desert, with the exception of an attendant spirit, who kept constantly by my side. Of him I inquired the meaning of what I saw, and why I was thus traveling in such a dismal place. He answered thus: 'This field is the world which now lieth inanimate and dumb in regard to the true religion or plan of salvation, but travel on and by the wayside you will find on a certain log a box, the contents of which, if you eat thereof, will make you wise, and give unto you wisdom and understanding.'

"I carefully observed what was told me by my guide, and proceeding a short distance, I came to the box. I immediately took it up, and placed it under my left arm. Then with eagerness I raised the lid and began to taste of its contents; upon which all manner of beasts, horned cattle, and roaring animals rose up on every side in the most threatening manner possible, tearing the earth, tossing their horns, and bellowing most terrifically all around me, and they finally came so close upon me, that I was compelled to drop the box and fly for my life. Yet, in the midst of all this I was perfectly happy, though I awoke trembling."[6]

From this time forward, my husband seemed more confirmed than ever in the opinion that there was no order or class of religionists that knew any more concerning the kingdom of God than those of the world, or such as made no profession of religion whatever.

In 1811, we moved from Royalton, Vermont, to the town of Lebanon, New Hampshire.[7] Soon after arriving here, my husband received another very singular vision, which I will relate:

"I thought," said he, "I was traveling in an open, desolate field which appeared to be very barren. As I was thus traveling, the thought suddenly came into my mind that I had better stop and reflect upon what I was doing before I went any farther. So I asked myself, 'What motive can I have in traveling here, and what place can this be?'

"My guide, who was by my side as before, said, 'This is the desolate world, but travel on.' The road was so broad and barren that I wondered why I should travel in it, for, said I to myself, 'Broad is the road, and wide is the gate that leads to death, and many there be that walk therein; but narrow is the way, and strait is the gate that leads to everlasting life, and few there be that go in thereat.'[8]

"Traveling a short distance further, I came to a narrow path. This path I entered, and, when I had traveled a little way in it, I beheld a beautiful stream of water which ran from the east to the west. Of this stream I could see neither the source nor yet the mouth, but as far as my eyes could extend I could see a rope, running along the bank of it about as high as a man could reach, and beyond me was a low but very pleasant valley in which stood a tree such as I had never seen before. It was exceedingly handsome, insomuch that I looked upon it with wonder and admiration. Its beautiful branches spread themselves somewhat like an umbrella, and it bore a kind of fruit, in shape much like a chestnut bur, and as white as snow, or, if possible, whiter. I gazed upon the same with considerable interest, and as I was doing so, the burs or shells commenced opening and shedding their particles, or the fruit which they contained, which was of dazzling whiteness. I drew near and began to eat of it, and I found it delicious beyond description.

"As I was eating, I said in my heart, 'I cannot eat this alone, I must bring my wife and children, that they may partake with me.' Accordingly, I went and brought my family, which consisted of a wife and seven children, and we all commenced eating and praising God for this blessing. We were exceedingly happy, insomuch that our joy could not easily be expressed.

"While thus engaged, I beheld a spacious building standing opposite the valley which we were in, and it appeared to reach to the very heavens. It was full of doors and windows, and they were all filled with people, who were very finely dressed. When these people observed us in the low valley, under the tree, they pointed the finger of scorn at us, and treated us with all manner of disrespect and contempt. But their contumely we utterly disregarded.

"I presently turned to my guide and inquired of him the meaning of the fruit that was so delicious. He told me it was the pure love of God, shed abroad in the hearts of all those who love him and keep his commandments. He then commanded me to go and bring the rest of my children. I told him that we were all there. 'No,' he replied, 'look yonder, you have two more, and you must bring them also.' Upon raising my eyes, I saw two small children standing some distance off. I immediately went to them and brought them to the tree, upon which they commenced eating with the rest, and we all rejoiced together.[9] The more we ate, the more we seemed to desire, until we even got down upon our knees and scooped it up, eating it by double handfuls.

"After feasting in this manner a short time, I asked my guide what was the meaning of the spacious building which I saw. He replied, 'It is Babylon, it is Babylon, and it must fall. The people in the doors and windows are the inhabitants thereof, who scorn and despise the Saints of God because of their humility.' I soon awoke, clapping my hands together for joy."[10]

NOTES

1. The birth date of Sophronia, oldest daughter of Joseph and Lucy Smith, was recorded in Tunbridge as May 17, 1803; Mother Smith cites it as May 18, 1803. At the time of this move from Tunbridge eight miles to Royalton, Alvin would have been five years old, Hyrum three, and Sophronia a few weeks to a few months old.

2. The farm the Smiths rented from Solomon Mack is located on the line dividing the townships of Sharon and Royalton near the summit of old Dairy Hill about five to six miles from Royalton. The move to here could have been as early as the summer of 1803 and as late as the early winter of 1804.

3. Ephraim lived but eleven days. Note that three of Joseph and Lucy Smith's sons were born on the same date (March 13); namely, Samuel, Ephraim, and William.

4. This begins a series of at least seven dreams or visions given to Joseph Smith, the father of the Prophet, between the years of 1811 and 1819. Concerning this vision or dream of her husband, Lucy states in the Preliminary Manuscript the following heading: "First Vision of Joseph Smith, Sr. Received the next month after William was born." That would mark the date of this vision in the month of April 1811. The Lord said through the prophet Joel: "And it shall come to pass afterward, that I will pour out my spirit upon all flesh; and your sons and your daughters shall prophesy, your old men shall dream dreams, your young men shall see visions: and also upon the servants and upon the handmaids in those days will I pour out my spirit" (Joel 2:28–29).

5. Hugh Nibley makes an interesting point about this part of Joseph Smith Sr.'s dream: "When the prophet's father dreamed himself lost in 'this field [of] the world,' he 'could see nothing save dead, fallen timber,' a picture which of course faithfully recalls his own frontier background" (*Lehi in the Desert*. . . . [Provo, Utah: Deseret Book Co., and Foundation for Ancient Research and Mormon Studies, 1988], p. 44).

6. In one of the prophet Lehi's visions, he was commanded to read from a book (similar to partaking of the contents of a box), and as he did so "he was filled with

the Spirit of the Lord. . . . And . . . his soul did rejoice, and his whole heart was filled, because of the things which he had seen, yea, which the Lord had shown unto him." (See I Nephi 1:8–15.)

7. Lebanon is located about twenty-five miles southeast of Royalton, Vermont, just across the Connecticut River into New Hampshire. This was the Smiths' longest move in New England and took place likely in the late spring of 1811, sometime after the birth of William, or early summer of that same year. By the time of this move, Joseph and Lucy had six children: Alvin, thirteen; Hyrum, eleven; Sophronia, eight; Joseph, five; Samuel, three; and William, a few weeks to a few months old.

8. See Matthew 7:13–14.

9. It is most likely that this dream was given to Joseph Smith Sr. sometime in the summer of 1812, after the birth of Catharine (July 28, 1812). The two children that were yet to be born in the Smith family were Don Carlos (March 25, 1816) and little Lucy (July 18, 1821). It is also possible that in the vision the two children that were to be gathered in with the family were their firstborn son, who had died, and Ephraim, who lived only eleven days.

10. Over thirty correlations exist between Joseph Smith Sr.'s dream and Lehi's dream or vision of the tree of life found in I Nephi 8.

CHAPTER 14

The Smiths settle in Lebanon, New Hampshire. The older children start school. Typhoid fever epidemic rages, and all the Smith children contract the disease. Sophronia's ninety-day siege, near death, and miraculous recovery.

Fall 1811 to summer 1813

In Lebanon we settled down and began to congratulate ourselves upon our prosperity and also to renew our exertions to obtain a greater abundance of this world's goods. We looked around us and said, What do we now lack? There is nothing of which we have not a sufficiency to make us and our children perfectly comfortable, both for food and raiment, as well as that which is necessary to a respectable appearance in society both at home and abroad.

Taking this view of the subject, we thought it time to begin to provide for the future wants of our family and ourselves when the decline of life would come upon us. This raised our ambition much. I commenced by laying in for the ensuing winter one hundred pounds of candles, that we might better pursue our labors;[1] two hundred yards of cloth for a stock of clothing for my family; and as my children had been deprived of school, we made every arrangement to supply the deficiency. Our second son, Hyrum, we established in the academy in Hanover.[2] The remainder who were old enough attended a school nearby,[3] whilst their father and myself were industriously laboring late and early to do all in our power for their future welfare.[4]

We met with success on every hand, but the scene soon changed. In 1813, the typhus fever came into Lebanon and raged there horribly.[5] Among the rest who were seized with this complaint was my oldest daughter, Sophronia, who was sick four weeks; next, Hyrum came from Hanover sick with the same disease; then, Alvin, my oldest, and so on until there was not one of my family left well, save Mr. Smith and myself. Here I must request my readers to bear with me, for I shall probably detain them some time.[6]

Sophronia was very low and remained so eighty-nine days. On the ninetieth day the attendant physician declared that she was so far gone that it was impossible for her to receive any benefit from the effects of medicine and discontinued his attendance upon her. That night she lay utterly motionless, with her eyes wide open with that peculiar set which most strikingly exhibits the hue of death. I gazed upon my child as a mother looks on the last shade of life in a darling child. In the distraction of the moment, my husband and I clasped our hands together and fell upon our knees by the bedside and poured our grief and supplications into his ears who hath numbered the hair upon our heads.

Did the Lord hear our petition? He did hear us. And I felt assured that he would answer our prayers; but when we rose to our feet, the appearance was far otherwise. My child had apparently ceased to breathe. I seized a blanket, threw it round her, caught her in my arms, and commenced pacing the floor. Those present remonstrated with me, saying, "Mrs. Smith, it's all of no use. You are certainly crazy. Your child is dead." Notwithstanding, I would not, for a moment, relinquish the hope of again seeing her breathe and live.

My reader, are you a parent? Place yourself in the same situation. Are you a mother who has ever been in like circumstances? Feel for your heartstrings. Can you tell me how I felt with my expiring child strained to my bosom, which thrilled with all a mother's love, a mother's tender yearnings for her own offspring? Would you then feel to deny that God had power to save to the uttermost all who call on him? I did not then and I do not now.

At last, she sobbed. I still pressed her to my breast and walked the floor. She sobbed again and then looked up into my face with an

The typhoid fever epidemic of 1812 and 1813 left six thousand dead in the Connecticut River Valley.

appearance of natural life, breathing freely. My soul was satisfied but my strength was gone. I laid her on the bed and sank down beside her, overpowered by a swell of feeling.

From this time forward Sophronia continued mending, until she entirely recovered.

NOTES

1. This large quantity of candles was to provide light in their home through the long, dark New England nights so that they could work late to achieve their goals.

2. Hyrum, at age eleven or twelve, was sent to Moor's Charity School, which was associated with Dartmouth in Hanover (see Porter, "Origins," pp. 25, 26).

3. Alvin, thirteen, and Sophronia, eight, attended a public school in the vicinity, while younger children Joseph, five; Samuel, three; and William, six months, stayed at home.

4. It was here at Lebanon, New Hampshire, that another baby girl was added to the Smith family, Catharine, born July 28, 1812. Catharine would outlive all the Smith children, living to age eighty-seven, and pass away in Fountain Green, Illinois, on February 2, 1900. She is buried in the old Webster Cemetery near Fountain Green.

5. Lucy calls this "typhus fever," but it was "typhoid fever." It swept through the upper Connecticut River Valley beginning in 1812 and left six thousand dead. (See Bushman, *Beginnings*, p. 32.)

6. It was common at the turn of the nineteenth century among the poor for all the children of the household to sleep in one bed, and thereby disease would spread quickly from one child to all the others. Seven children under the age of fifteen had the fever in the Smith home at this time, including Catharine, who was likely but a few months old.

Chapter 15

Seven-year-old Joseph Smith Jr. suffers from a large fever sore, then contracts osteomyelitis in his left leg. Medical efforts to relieve his suffering. Drs. Smith, Perkins, Stone, et al. perform an experimental operation on Joseph's leg in an attempt to save it. Joseph, now on crutches, eventually recovers and goes to Salem, Massachusetts, with his uncle.

Summer 1813 to late fall 1813

I shall here be under the necessity of turning the subject to my third son, Joseph, who had so far recovered that he could sit up. Then, one day, he suddenly screamed out with a severe pain in his shoulder and seemed in such extreme distress that we were fearful that something dreadful was about to ensue, and sent immediately for the doctor. When he arrived and had examined the patient, he said he was of the opinion that it was a sprain, but the child said this could not be the case, as he had not been hurt; but a sharp pain had taken him very suddenly, and he knew no cause for it.

The physician insisted upon the truth of his first opinion and anointed the shoulder with bone liniment, but the pain remained as severe as ever for two weeks. When the doctor came again, he made a closer examination and found that a very large fever sore had gathered between Joseph's breast and shoulder. He immediately lanced it, upon which it discharged a full quart of matter.[1]

As soon as this sore had discharged itself, the pain left it and shot like lightning (as he said) down his side into the marrow of his leg bone on the same side.[2] The boy was almost in total despair and cried out, "Oh, Father, the pain is so severe! How can I bear it?"

His leg immediately began to swell and he continued in the most excruciating pain for two weeks longer. During this time, I carried him in my arms nearly continually, soothing him and doing all that my utmost ingenuity could suggest to ease his sufferings, until nature was exhausted and I was taken severely ill myself.

Then Hyrum, who was always remarkable for his tenderness and sympathy, desired that he might take my place.[3] As he was a good, trusty boy, we let him do so, and, in order to make the task as easy for him as possible, we laid Joseph upon a low bed and Hyrum sat beside him, almost incessantly day and night, grasping the most painful part of the affected leg between his hands and, by pressing it closely, enabled the little sufferer the better to bear the pain which otherwise seemed almost ready to take his life.

At the end of three weeks, he became so low that we sent again for the surgeon. When he came, he made an incision of eight inches on the front side of the leg between the knee and ankle. This somewhat relieved the pain, and the patient was quite comfortable until the wound began to heal, when the pain became as violent as ever.

The surgeon was called again, and he this time enlarged the wound, cutting to the bone. It commenced healing the second time, and as the healing progressed, the swelling continued to rise till we deemed it wisdom to call a council of surgeons; and when they met in consultation, they decided that there was no remedy but amputation.[4]

Soon after coming to this conclusion, they rode up to the door, and I invited them into another room apart from the one where Joseph lay. "Now," said I, "gentlemen [for there were seven of them],[5] what can you do to save my boy's leg?"

They answered, "We can do nothing. We have cut it open to the bone and find the bone so affected that it is incurable, and that amputation is absolutely necessary in order to save his life."

This was like a thunderbolt to me. I appealed to the principal surgeon present, saying, "Dr. Stone, can you not try once more? Can you not, by cutting around the bone, take out the diseased part? There may be a part of the bone that is sound which will heal over, and thus you may save the leg. You will not, you must not, take off his leg, until you try once more. I will not consent to your entering his room until you promise this."

After a short consultation, they agreed to do as I requested; then we went to my suffering son. The doctor said, "My poor boy, we have come again." "Yes," said Joseph. "I see you have; but you have not come to take off my leg, have you, sir?" "No," said the surgeon. "It is your mother's request that we should make one more effort, and that is what we have now come for."

My husband, who was constantly with the child, seemed to contemplate for an instant my countenance; then, turning his eyes upon his boy, at once all his sufferings together with my intense anxiety rushed upon his mind. He burst into a flood of tears and sobbed like a child.

The principal surgeon, after a moment's conversation, ordered cords to be brought to bind Joseph fast to the bedstead, but Joseph objected. When the doctor insisted that he must be confined, Joseph

Dr. Nathan Smith's saddlebag for house calls was likely present for Joseph's operation.

said decidedly, "No, Doctor. I will not be bound. I can bear the process better unconfined."

"Then," said the doctor, "will you take some wine? You must take something, or you can never endure the severe operation to which you must be subjected."

"No," answered the boy. "I will not touch one particle of liquor, nor will I be tied down, but I will tell you what I will do. I will have my father sit on the bed close by me, and then I will do whatever is necessary to be done in order to have the bone taken out. But, Mother, I want you to leave the room. I know that you cannot endure to see me suffer so. Father can bear it. But you have carried me so much and watched over me so long, you are almost worn out." Then, looking up into my face, his eyes swimming with tears, he said beseechingly, "Now, Mother, promise me you will not stay, will you? The Lord will help me. I shall get through with it, so do leave me and go a way off, till they get through with it."

To this I consented. So, after bringing a number of folded sheets to lay under his leg, I left and went several hundred yards from the house in order to be out of hearing.

The surgeons began operating by boring into the bone of his leg, first on one side of the affected part, then on the other side, after which they broke it loose with a pair of forceps or pincers. Thus, they took away nine large pieces of the bone. When they broke off the first piece, he screamed so loud with the pain of his leg that I could not forbear running to him, but as soon as I entered the room, he cried out, "Oh, Mother! Go back! Go back! I do not want you to come in. I will tough it out, if you will go."

When the third fracture was taken away, I burst into the room again, and, oh, my God, what a spectacle for a mother's eye! The wound torn open to view, my boy and the bed on which he lay covered with the blood that was still gushing from the wound. Joseph was pale as a corpse, and the big drops of sweat were rolling down his face, every feature of which depicted agony that cannot be described.

I was forced from the room and detained until they finished the operation. After they had placed him upon a clean bed with fresh clothing and had cleared the room from every appearance of blood and any apparatus used in the extraction, I was permitted to enter.[6]

Jesse Smith and young Joseph came here to Salem, Massachusetts, for the sea breezes.
The Prophet Joseph would return here in 1836.

Joseph now began to recover, and when he was able to travel he went with his uncle Jesse Smith to Salem[7] for the benefit of his health, hoping that the sea breezes might help him. In this, we were not disappointed, for he soon became strong and healthy.

After one whole year of affliction, we were able once more to look upon our children and each other in health, and I assure you, my gentle reader, we realized the blessing, for I believe we felt more to acknowledge the hand of God in preserving our lives through such a desperate siege of disease, pain, and trouble than if we had enjoyed health and prosperity during the interim.

NOTES

1. Joseph Smith Jr. later recalled this time and dictated to Willard Richards in December 1842 the following for his manuscript history: "When I was five years old or thereabouts I was attacked with the typhus fever, and at one time, during my sickness, my father despaired of my life. The doctors broke the fever, after which it settled under my shoulder, and Dr. Parker called it a sprained shoulder and anointed it with bone ointment, and freely applied the hot shovel, when it proved to be a swelling under the arm, which was opened, and discharged freely; after which the disease removed and descended into my left leg and ankle and terminated in a fever sore of the worst kind, and I endured the most acute suffering for a long time under the care of Drs. Smith, Stone, and Perkins of Hanover." (*Papers*, p. 268.)

2. The left side.

3. Hyrum was thirteen years old at this time.

4. This "council of surgeons," likely including some medical students, was headed by Dr. Nathan Smith, founder of Dartmouth Medical School, and Dr. Cyrus Perkins. The disease that Joseph contracted after the fevers was osteomyelitis. Concerning this condition, a modern reference source states that it is "a bacterial, fungal, or rickettsial infection within bone and bone marrow" that is commonly related to infections located elsewhere in the body. In children, osteomyelitis usually starts "near the ends of long bones in the legs, and spreads through the marrow and other bone channels, causing high fever, chills, pain, and an abscess at the infection site." This source goes on to say that without antibiotic treatment, there is risk of bone destruction. (*The New Grolier Multimedia Encyclopedia*, Release 6, 1993, s.v. "osteomyelitis.")

5. Joseph recalled the scene in the following way: "At one time eleven doctors came from Dartmouth Medical College, at Hanover, New Hampshire, for the purpose of amputation, but, young as I was, I utterly refused to give my assent to the operation, but I consented to their trying an experiment by removing a large portion of the bone from my left leg, which they did, and fourteen additional pieces of bone afterwards worked out before my leg healed, during which time I was reduced so very low that my mother could carry me with ease; and after I began to get about I went on crutches till I started for the state of New York" (*Papers*, p. 268). Joseph was on crutches for over three years and had a slight limp the rest of his life.

6. It appears from the record that from the time of Joseph's crying out in pain with the fever sore under his arm until the day of the operation on his leg, the passage of time was between fifty and sixty-four days.

7. This is Salem, Massachusetts, and was approximately 130 miles away.

PART 3

New York/Pennsylvania
Beginnings of the Restoration

CHAPTER 16

The Smiths move to Norwich, Vermont. Three successive years of crop failures. Removal of the Smith family to Palmyra, New York. They obtain one hundred acres of virgin land. Lucy goes to tea with neighbors in Palmyra. Record of Joseph Smith Sr.'s third and sixth visions: the vision of the beautiful garden with twelve wooden images; the vision of going to meeting on the Day of Judgment.

Spring 1814 to spring 1819

When health returned to us, it found us, as may well be supposed, in very low circumstances. Sickness, with all its attendant expenses of nurses, medical attendants, and other necessary articles, reduced us so that we were now compelled to make arrangements for going into some kind of business to provide for present wants, rather than future prospects, as we had previously contemplated.

My husband now determined to change his residence. Accordingly, we moved to Norwich in Vermont[1] and established ourselves on a farm belonging to Squire Moredock. The first year our crops failed, and we bought our bread with the proceeds of the orchard and our own industry. The second year they failed again. In the ensuing spring, Mr. Smith said that we would plant once more on this farm, and if he did not succeed better, we would go to New York, where the farmers raise wheat in abundance.[2]

This next year was like the preceding seasons. An untimely frost blighted the vegetation, and being the third year in succession in which the crops had failed, it well nigh produced a famine.[3] This was enough.

The Smith home and farm, 1814–16.
Here crop failures would drive them to New York.

My husband was now altogether decided upon going to New York. One day he came into the house and sat down, and after meditating some time, he said that could he so arrange his affairs, he would be glad to start soon for New York with one Mr. Howard, who was going to Palmyra. "But," said he, "I cannot leave or you could not get along without me. Besides, I am owing some debts that I must pay."

I told him I thought that he might call upon both his debtors and creditors and by so doing make an arrangement between them that would be satisfactory to all parties. As for the rest, I thought I could prepare myself and my family to follow him by the time he might be ready for us. He accordingly called upon all those with whom he had any dealings and settled up his accounts with them, but there were some who neglected to bring forward their books, consequently they were not balanced, or there were no entries made in them to show the settlement; but in cases of this kind he called witnesses that there might be evidence of the fact.

Having thus arranged his business, Mr. Smith set out for Palmyra, New York, with Mr. Howard. My sons Alvin and Hyrum followed their father with a heavy heart some distance. After the departure of my husband, we toiled faithfully until we considered that we were fully prepared to leave at a moment's warning. We soon received a letter from Mr. Smith requesting us to make ourselves ready to take up a journey for Palmyra immediately. A messenger soon arrived with a conveyance for myself and my family.[4]

As we were starting out on this journey, several of those gentlemen who had withheld their books in the time of settlement now brought them forth and claimed the accounts which had been settled, and which they had, in the presence of witnesses, agreed to erase. We were all ready for the journey, and the teams were waiting on expense. Under these circumstances, I concluded it would be more to our advantage to pay their unjust claims than to hazard a lawsuit. Thus I was compelled to pay 150 dollars out of the means reserved for bearing our expenses in traveling. This I made shift to do and saved sixty or eighty dollars for the journey.[5]

A gentleman by the name of Flagg, a wealthy settler living in the town of Hanover, also a Mr. Howard, who resided in Norwich, were both acquainted with the circumstances mentioned above. They were very indignant at it and requested me to give them a sufficient time to get the witnesses together, and they would endeavor to recover that which had been taken from me by fraud. I told them I could not do so, for my husband had sent teams for me, which were on expense; moreover, there was an uncertainty in getting the money back again, and in case of failure, I should not be able to raise the means necessary to take the family where we contemplated moving.

They then proposed raising some money by subscription, saying, "We know the people feel as we do concerning this matter, and if you

will receive it, we will make you a handsome present." This I utterly refused. The idea of receiving assistance in such a way as this was indeed
very repulsive to my feelings, and I rejected their offer.

We set out with Mr. Howard, a cousin of the gentleman who
traveled to New York with Mr. Smith. I had prepared a great quantity
of woolen clothing for my children; besides I had on hand a great deal
of diaper and pulled cloth in the web. My mother was with me. She had
been assisting in my preparations for traveling. She was now returning
to her home in Royalton, where she resided until she died, which was
two years afterwards, in consequence of an injury which she received by
getting upset in a wagon while traveling with us.[6]

When we arrived there, I had a task to perform which was a severe
trial to my feelings, one to which I shall ever look back with peculiar
sensations that can never be obliterated. I was here to take leave of that
pious and affectionate parent to whom I was indebted for all the religious instructions as well as most of the educational privileges which I
had ever received. The parting hour came. My mother wept over me
long and bitterly. She told me that it was not probable she should ever
behold my face again. "But, my dear child," said she, "I have lived long.
My days are nearly all numbered. I must soon exchange the things of
earth for another state of existence, where I hope to enjoy the society of
the blessed. And now as my last admonition, I beseech you to continue
faithful in the exercise of every religious duty to the end of your days,
that I may have the pleasure of embracing you in another, fairer world
above."

This parting scene was at one Willard Pierce's, a tavern keeper.
From his house my mother went to Daniel Mack's, with whom she
afterwards lived until her decease.

After this I pursued my journey, but it was only a short time until I
discovered that the man who drove the team in which we rode was an
unprincipled, unfeeling wretch by the manner in which he handled my
goods and money, as well as his treatment of my children, especially
Joseph. This child was compelled by Mr. Howard to travel for miles at a
time on foot, though he was still somewhat lame.[7] We bore patiently
with repeated aggravations until we came twenty miles west of Utica,
when one morning we were preparing as usual for starting on the day's
journey. My oldest son came to me and said, "Mother, Mr. Howard has

Lucy, with her children, parted from her mother, Lydia Gates Mack, here in Royalton, Vermont.

thrown the goods out of the wagon and is about getting off with the team." I told him to call the man in. I met him in the barroom, where there was a large company of travelers, both male and female, and I demanded his reason for such a procedure. He answered that the money which I had given him was all exhausted and he could go no farther.

I turned to those present and said, "Gentlemen and ladies, please give me your attention for a moment. Now, as there is a God in heaven, that wagon and horses, as well as the goods that accompany them, are mine. This man is determined to take away from me every means of proceeding on my journey, leaving me with eight little children, utterly destitute. But I forbid you, Mr. Howard, from driving one step with my wagon or horses. And here I declare that the teams, goods, and children, with myself, shall go together to my husband and their father. As for you, sir, I have no use for you, and you can ride or walk the rest of the way as you please; but I shall take charge of my own affairs."[8] I then proceeded on my way, and in a short time I arrived in Palmyra with a small portion of my effects, my babes, and two cents in money, but perfectly happy in the society of my family.[9]

The joy I felt in throwing myself and my children upon the care and affection of a tender husband and father doubly paid me for all I had suffered. The children surrounded their father, clinging to his neck, covering his face with tears and kisses that were heartily reciprocated by him.

We all now sat down and maturely counseled together as to what course it was best to take, and how we should proceed to business in our then destitute circumstances. It was agreed by each one of us that it was most advisable to apply all our energies together and endeavor to obtain a piece of land, as this was then a new country and land was low, being in its rude state. But it was almost a time of famine. Wheat was $2.70 per bushel and other things in proportion. "How shall we," said my husband, "be able to sustain ourselves and have anything left to buy land?" I had done considerable at painting oilcloth coverings for tables, stands, etc. Therefore, I concluded to set up a business, and if prospered, I would try to supply the wants of the family. In this I succeeded so well that it was not long until we not only had an abundance of good and wholesome provision, but I soon began to replenish my household furniture, a fine stock of which I had sacrificed entirely in moving.

My husband and our two oldest sons, Alvin and Hyrum, set themselves about raising the means of paying for one hundred acres of land for which Mr. Smith had contracted with a land agent. In one year's time, we made nearly all of the first payment.[10] The agent advised us to build a log house on the land and commence clearing it. We did so, and it was not long until we had thirty acres ready for cultivation.[11]

Now the second payment was coming due, and we had no means as yet of meeting it. Alvin accordingly proposed that his father should take the business at home in his entire charge, "whilst," he said, "I will go abroad to see if I cannot make the second payment and the remainder of the first." By my son's persevering industry, he was able to return to us after much labor, suffering, and fatigue with the necessary amount of money for all except the last payment. In two years from the time we entered Palmyra, strangers, destitute of friends, home, or employment, we were able to settle ourselves upon our own land in a snug, comfortable though humble habitation, built and neatly finished by our own industry.[12]

If we might judge by any collateral manifestation, we had every reason to believe that we had many good and affectionate friends, for never have I seen more kindness or attention shown to any person or family than we received from those around us. Again we began to rejoice in our prosperity, and our hearts glowed with gratitude to God for the manifestations of his favor that surrounded us.

I shall change my theme for the present, but let not my reader suppose that because I shall pursue another topic for a season that we stopped our labor. We never during our lives suffered one important interest to swallow up every other obligation, but whilst we worked with our hands we endeavored to remember the service of and the welfare of our souls.

Permit me here to relate a little circumstance, by way of illustration, of a friend of mine having invited several of her associates to take tea with her one afternoon.[13] She also sent an urgent request for me to call on her with the rest. The ladies invited were some wealthy merchants' wives and the minister's lady. We spent the time quite pleasantly, each seeming to enjoy those reciprocal feelings which render the society of our friends delightful to us.

When tea was served up, we were proffering some good-natured remarks to each other when one lady observed, "Well, I declare, Mrs. Smith ought not to live in that log house of hers any longer. She deserves a better fate, and I say she must have a new house."

"So she should," said another, "for she is so kind to everyone. She ought to have the best of everything."

"Ladies," said I, "thank you for your compliments, but you are quite mistaken. I will show you that I am the wealthiest woman that sits at this table."

"Well," said they, "now make that appear."

"Now mark," I answered them. "I have never prayed for the riches of this world as perhaps you have, but I have always desired that God would enable me to use enough wisdom and forbearance in my family to set a good example before my children, whose lives I always besought the Lord to spare, as also to secure the confidence and affection of my husband. I have hoped that we, acting together in the education and instruction of our children, might in our old age reap the reward of circumspection and parental tenderness—that is, the pleasure of seeing our children signify their father's name by an upright and honorable course of conduct in life.

"I have been gratified so far in all this, and though I have to this time suffered many disagreeable disappointments in life with regard to property, I now find myself as comfortably situated as any of you are. What we have has not been obtained at the expense or the comfort of any human being. We owe no man; we never distressed any man, which circumstance almost invariably attends the mercantile life, so I have no reason to envy those who are so engaged."

To the minister's lady, I said, "I ask you how many nights of the week you are kept awake with anxiety about your sons who are in habitual attendance on the grog shop and gambling house." They all said, with a look that showed conviction, "Mrs. Smith, you have established the fact."

Reader, I merely relate this that you may draw a moral therefrom that may be useful to you.

In the spring after we moved onto the farm, we commenced making maple sugar, of which we averaged one thousand pounds per year. We then began to make preparations for building a house. The land agent of whom we purchased our farm was dead, and we could not make the last payment. We also planted a large orchard and made every possible preparation for ease when advanced age should deprive us of the ability to make those physical exertions of which we were then capable.

I shall now deviate a little from my subject, in order to relate another very singular dream which my husband had about this time, which is as follows:[14]

"I dreamed," said he, "that I was traveling on foot, and I was very sick, and so lame I could hardly walk. My guide, as usual, attended me. Traveling some time together, I became so lame that I thought I could go no farther. I informed my guide of this and asked him what I should do. He told me to travel on till I came to a certain garden. So I arose and started for this garden. While on my way thither, I asked my guide how I should know the place. He said, 'Proceed until you come to a very large gate; open this and you will see a garden, blooming with the most beautiful flowers that your eyes ever beheld, and there you shall be healed.'

"By limping along with great difficulty, I finally reached the gate; and, on entering it, I saw the before-mentioned garden, which was beautiful beyond description, being filled with the most delicate flowers of every kind and color. In the garden were walks about three and a half feet wide, which were set on both sides with marble stones. One of the walks ran from the gate through the center of the garden; and on each side of this was a very richly carved seat, and on each seat were placed six wooden images, each of which was the size of a very large man. When I came to the first image on the right side, it arose and bowed to me with much deference. I then turned to the one which sat opposite me, on the left side, and it arose and bowed to me in the same manner as the first. I continued turning, first to the right and then to the left, until the whole twelve had made their obeisance, after which I was entirely healed.

"I then asked my guide the meaning of all this, but I awoke before I received an answer."

The scripture which saith, "Your old men shall dream dreams,"[15] was fulfilled in the case of my husband, for, about this time, he had another vision, which I shall here relate; this, with one more, is all of his that I shall obtrude upon the attention of my readers. He received two more visions, which would probably be somewhat interesting, but I cannot remember them distinctly enough to rehearse them in full.[16] The following, which was the sixth, ran thus:

"I thought I was walking alone; I was much fatigued, nevertheless, I continued traveling. It seemed to me that I was going to meeting, that it was the Day of Judgment, and that I was going to be judged.

"When I came in sight of the meetinghouse, I saw multitudes of people coming from every direction, and pressing with great anxiety towards the door of this great building; but I thought I should get there in time, hence there was no need of being in a hurry. But, on arriving at the door, I found it shut. I knocked for admission and was informed by the porter that I had come too late. I felt exceedingly troubled and prayed earnestly for admittance.

"Presently I found that my flesh was perishing. I continued to pray, still my flesh withered upon my bones. I was in a state of almost total despair, when the porter asked me if I had done all that was necessary in order to receive admission. I replied that I had done all that was in my power to do. 'Then,' observed the porter, 'justice must be satisfied; after this, mercy hath her claims.'

"It then occurred to me to call upon God, in the name of his Son Jesus; and I cried out, in the agony of my soul, 'Oh, Lord God, I beseech thee, in the name of Jesus Christ, to forgive my sins.' After which I felt considerably strengthened and I began to mend. The porter or angel then remarked that it was necessary to plead the merits of Jesus, for he was the advocate with the Father, and a Mediator between God and man.

"I was now made quite whole and the door was opened, but on entering, I awoke."

The following spring,[17] we commenced making preparations for building another house, one that would be more comfortable for persons in advanced life.[18]

NOTES

1. This move was just across the Connecticut River into Vermont. It is between eight and nine miles from the cabin site in Lebanon to the home site in Norwich.

2. "The Vermont newspapers advertised new land in the Genesee country [western New York] for $2 to $3 an acre" (Bushman, *Beginnings*, p. 41).

3. The year 1816 was known in New England as "the year without a summer." On June 8 that year, several inches of snow fell and ice formed on the ponds. Due to the crop failures, the next two years saw such a huge migration from Vermont, the state would not recover from the loss for a century. (See Bushman, *Beginnings*, p. 40.) This freakish weather is thought to have been caused by the huge volcanic eruption of Mount Tambora in Indonesia the previous year (see Bushman, *Beginnings*, p. 200).

4. Don Carlos Smith was born to the Smith family March 25, 1816, at Norwich. This move from Norwich, Vermont, to Palmyra, New York, likely in November or December of 1816, was just over three hundred miles and would likely have taken the Smiths between eight and twelve days. Lucy now would move with eight children: Alvin, eighteen; Hyrum, sixteen; Sophronia, thirteen; Joseph, ten; Samuel, eight; William, five; Catharine, four; and Don Carlos, eight or nine months old.

5. A family just ready to move was particularly vulnerable at the moment of taking leave. "Under ordinary circumstances creditors knew that the scarcity of money made collection impractical and waited patiently for credits to balance the account. Departure was, of course, the last opportunity to collect, and furthermore it was a time when the family, having sold all of its possessions to obtain cash for the trip, was most liquid." (Bushman, *Beginnings*, p. 41.)

6. From the writings of Joseph Smith Jr. we learn: "Although the snow was generally deep through the country during this journey, we performed the whole on wheels, except the first two days, when we were accompanied by my mother's mother, Grandmother Lydia Mack, who was injured by the upsetting of the sleigh and, not wishing to accompany her friends west, tarried by the way with her friends in Vermont; and we soon after heard of her death, supposing that she never recovered from the injury received by the overturn of the sleigh" (*Papers*, p. 269). Lydia Gates Mack died in 1818 at the home of her son Daniel in Royalton, Vermont. Her husband, Solomon, spent his last days in Gilsum, New Hampshire, with Solomon Jr., and died in 1820.

7. Joseph Smith Jr. describes the move: "We fell in with a family by the name of Gates, who were traveling west, and Howard drove me from the wagon and made me travel in my weak state through the snow forty miles per day for several days, during which time I suffered the most excruciating weariness and pain; and all this that Mr. Howard might enjoy the society of two of Mr. Gates' daughters which he took on the wagon where I should have rode. And thus he continued to do day after day through the journey. And when my brothers remonstrated with Mr. Howard for his treatment to me, he would knock them down with the butt of his whip." (*Papers*, p. 268.)

8. Joseph Smith Jr. adds this commentary: "On our way from Utica I was left to ride on the last sleigh in the company (the Gates family were in sleighs), but when that came up, I was knocked down by the driver, one of Gates' sons, and left to wallow in my blood until a stranger came along, picked me up, and carried me to the town of Palmyra" (*Papers*, pp. 268–69).

9. Joseph Smith Jr. describes the last part of the journey: "Howard having spent all our funds, my mother was compelled to pay our landlords' bills from Utica to Palmyra in bits of cloth, clothing, etc., the last payment being made with the drops

[earrings] taken from sister Sophronia's ears for that purpose" (*Papers*, p. 269). The distance from "twenty miles west of Utica" to Palmyra is approximately one hundred miles, about a three days' journey.

10. This would be the fall of 1817.

11. "When first purchased by Joseph Smith, Sr., and Alvin, the Smith farm, like much of the land in the area, was covered with a magnificent stand of hardwood forest. Many of the trees were from 350 to 400 years old. Maples, beech, hophornbeam, and wild cherry dominated, interspersed with ash, oak, hickory, and elm. This forest supported as many as 120 trees per acre, nearly all a foot or more in diameter.

"Numerous trees in this ancient forest grew to tremendous size. . . . A few had diameters of 7 feet or more. . . . [Some] likely reached massive proportions of 9 to 10 feet in diameter.

"The upper canopy of this forest . . . reach[ed] heights of more than 100 feet." (Donald L. Enders, "The Sacred Grove," *Ensign*, April 1990, p. 16.)

12. The Smiths could have moved into their twenty-by-thirty-foot "snug log house" by late fall of 1818.

13. The following story was not printed in the 1853 version of Lucy Mack Smith's history nor any succeeding versions. Surely Mother Smith wanted to draw the great contrast here between the kindnesses shown to her and her family before Joseph's first vision and the mobocracy and hatred heaped upon them afterwards.

14. This is Joseph Smith Sr.'s third recorded dream.

15. Joel 2:28.

16. Because Mother Smith did not record or could not remember her husband's fourth and fifth dreams, they are lost to us.

17. These contemplations began in the spring of 1819. Construction on this new and larger house would not begin until 1822.

18. Joseph Smith Sr. was, by the summer of 1819, forty-eight years old, and Lucy was forty-four.

CHAPTER 17

∂❧

Assassination attempt upon fourteen-year-old Joseph. The seventh and final vision of Joseph Smith Sr. Religious excitement in the region of Palmyra. Young Joseph wants to know which church he should join. Account of the First Vision. Account of the first three visits of the angel Moroni.

December 1819 to September 22, 1823

I now come to the history of Joseph, who was born December 23, 1805.[1] I shall say nothing respecting him until he arrived at the age of fourteen.[2] However, in this I am aware that some of my readers will be disappointed, for I suppose, from questions which are frequently asked me, that it is thought by some that I shall be likely to tell many very remarkable incidents which attended his childhood; but, as nothing occurred during his early life except those trivial circumstances which are common to that state of human existence, I pass them in silence.

At the age of fourteen an incident occurred which alarmed us much, as we knew not the cause of it. Joseph being a remarkably quiet, well-disposed child, we did not suspect that anyone had aught against him. He was out on an errand one evening about twilight. When he was returning through the dooryard, a gun was fired across his pathway with evident intention of killing him. He sprang to the door, threw it open, and fell upon the floor with fright.

We went in search of the person who fired the gun, but found no trace of him until the next morning when we found his tracks under a wagon where he lay when he fired. We found the balls that were discharged from his piece the next day in the head and neck of a cow that stood opposite the wagon in a dark corner, but we never found out the man, nor ever suspected the cause of the act.[3]

I shall here insert the seventh vision that my husband had, which was received in the year 1819.[4] It was as follows:

"I dreamed," said he, "that a man, with a peddler's budget[5] on his back came in and thus addressed me: 'Sir, will you trade with me today? I have now called upon you seven times, I have traded with you each time, and have always found you strictly honest in all your dealings. Your measures are always heaped and your weights overbalance; and I have now come to tell you that this is the last time I shall ever call on you, and that there is but one thing which you lack in order to secure your salvation.' As I earnestly desired to know what it was I still lacked, I requested him to write the same upon paper. He said he would do so. I then sprang to get some paper, but in my excitement, I awoke."[6]

Shortly after my husband received the foregoing vision, there was a great revival in religion, which extended to all the denominations of Christians in the surrounding country in which we resided.[7] Many of the world's people, becoming concerned about the salvation of their souls, came forward and presented themselves as seekers after religion. Most of them were desirous of uniting with some church but were not decided as to the particular faith which they would adopt. When the numerous meetings were about breaking up, and the candidates and the various leading church members began to consult upon the subject of adopting the candidates into some church or churches, as the case may be, a dispute arose, and there was a great contention among them.

While these things were going forward, Joseph's mind became considerably troubled with regard to religion; and the following extract from his history will show, more clearly than I can express, the state of his feelings and the result of his reflections on this occasion:[8]

"I was at this time in my fifteenth year. My father's family was proselyted to the Presbyterian faith, and four of them joined that church, namely, my mother, Lucy, my brothers Hyrum and Samuel Harrison; and my sister Sophronia.

"During this time of great excitement my mind was called up to serious reflection and great uneasiness; but though my feelings were deep and often poignant, still I kept myself aloof from all those parties,

Palmyra Four Corners:
(from left) Methodist, Episcopalian, Presbyterian, and Baptist churches.

though I attended their several meetings as often as occasion would permit. In process of time my mind became somewhat partial to the Methodist sect, and I felt some desire to be united with them; but so great were the confusion and strife among the different denominations, that it was impossible for a person young as I was, and so unacquainted with men and things, to come to any certain conclusion who was right and who was wrong.

"My mind at times was greatly excited, the cry and tumult were so great and incessant. The Presbyterians were most decided against the Baptists and Methodists, and used all the powers of both reason and sophistry to prove their errors, or, at least, to make the people think they were in error. On the other hand, the Baptists and Methodists in their turn were equally zealous in endeavoring to establish their own tenets and disprove all others.

"In the midst of this war of words and tumult of opinions, I often said to myself: What is to be done? Who of all these parties are right; or, are they all wrong together? If any one of them be right, which is it, and how shall I know it?

"While I was laboring under the extreme difficulties caused by the contests of these parties of religionists, I was one day reading the Epistle of James, first chapter and fifth verse, which reads, 'If any of you lack wisdom, let him ask of God, that giveth to all men liberally, and upbraideth not; and it shall be given him.'

"Never did any passage of scripture come with more power to the heart of man than this did at this time to mine. It seemed to enter with great force into every feeling of my heart. I reflected on it again and again, knowing that if any person needed wisdom from God, I did; for how to act I did not know, and unless I could get more wisdom than I then had, I would never know; for the teachers of religion of the different sects understood the same passages of scripture so differently as to destroy all confidence in settling the question by an appeal to the Bible.[9]

Joseph Smith put the promise of James to the test and found it to be good.

"At length I came to the conclusion that I must either remain in darkness and confusion, or else I must do as James directs, that is, ask of God. I at length came to the determination to 'ask of God,' concluding that if he gave wisdom to them that lacked wisdom, and would give liberally, and not upbraid, I might venture.

"So, in accordance with this, my determination to ask of God, I retired to the woods to make the attempt. It was on the morning of a beautiful, clear day, early in the spring of eighteen hundred and twenty. It was the first time in my life that I had made such an attempt, for amidst all my anxieties I had never as yet made the attempt to pray vocally.

"After I had retired to the place where I had previously designed to go, having looked around me, and finding myself alone, I kneeled down and began to offer up the desires of my heart to God. I had scarcely done so, when immediately I was seized upon by some power which entirely overcame me, and had such an astonishing influence over me as to bind my tongue so that I could not speak. Thick darkness gathered around me, and it seemed to me for a time as if I were doomed to sudden destruction.[10]

"But, exerting all my powers to call upon God to deliver me out of the power of this enemy which had seized upon me, and at the very moment when I was ready to sink into despair and abandon myself to destruction—not to an imaginary ruin, but to the power of some actual being from the unseen world, who had such marvelous power as I had never before felt in any being—just at this moment of great alarm, I saw a pillar of light exactly over my head, above the brightness of the sun, which descended gradually until it fell upon me.

"It no sooner appeared than I found myself delivered from the enemy which held me bound. When the light rested upon me I saw two Personages, whose brightness and glory defy all description, standing above me in the air. One of them spake unto me, calling me by name and said, pointing to the other—*This is My Beloved Son. Hear Him!*[11]

"My object in going to inquire of the Lord was to know which of all the sects was right, that I might know which to join. No sooner, therefore, did I get possession of myself, so as to be able to speak, than I asked the Personages who stood above me in the light, which of all the sects was right (for at this time it had never entered into my heart that all were wrong)—and which I should join.

"I was answered that I must join none of them, for they were all wrong; and the Personage who addressed me said that all their creeds were an abomination in his sight; that those professors were all corrupt; that: 'they draw near to me with their lips, but their hearts are far from me, they teach for doctrines the commandments of men, having a form of godliness, but they deny the power thereof.'

"He again forbade me to join with any of them; and many other things did he say unto me, which I cannot write at this time. When I came to myself again, I found myself lying on my back, looking up into heaven. When the light had departed, I had no strength; but soon recovering in some degree, I went home. And as I leaned up to the fireplace, mother inquired what the matter was. I replied, 'Never mind, all is well—I am well enough off.' I then said to my mother, 'I have learned for myself that Presbyterianism is not true.' It seems as though the adversary was aware, at a very early period of my life, that I was destined to prove a disturber and an annoyer of his kingdom; else why should the powers of darkness combine against me? Why the opposition and persecution that arose against me, almost in my infancy?

"Some few days after I had this vision, I happened to be in company with one of the Methodist preachers, who was very active in the before mentioned religious excitement; and, conversing with him upon the subject of religion, I took occasion to give him an account of the vision which I had had.[12] I was greatly surprised at his behavior; he treated my communication not only lightly, but with great contempt, saying it was all of the devil, that there was no such thing as visions or revelations in these days; that all such things had ceased with the apostles, and that there would never be any more of them.

"I soon found, however, that my telling the story had excited a great deal of prejudice against me among professors of religion, and was the cause of great persecution, which continued to increase; and though I was an obscure boy, only between fourteen and fifteen years of age, and my circumstances in life such as to make a boy of no consequence in the world, yet men of high standing would take notice sufficient to excite the public mind against me, and create a bitter persecution; and this was common among all the sects—all united to persecute me.

"It caused me serious reflection then, and often has since, how very strange it was that an obscure boy, of a little over fourteen years of age,

*Joseph saw
Heavenly Father
and his Son
Jesus Christ
here in the
Sacred Grove.*

and one, too, who was doomed to the necessity of obtaining a scanty maintenance by his daily labor, should be thought a character of sufficient importance to attract the attention of the great ones of the most popular sects of the day, and in a manner to create in them a spirit of the most bitter persecution and reviling. But strange or not, so it was, and it was often the cause of great sorrow to myself.

"However, it was nevertheless a fact that I had beheld a vision. I have thought since, that I felt much like Paul, when he made his defense before King Agrippa, and related the account of the vision he had when he saw a light, and heard a voice; but still there were but few who believed him; some said he was dishonest, others said he was mad; and he was ridiculed and reviled. But all this did not destroy the reality of his vision. He had seen a vision, he knew he had, and all the persecution under heaven could not make it otherwise; and though they should persecute him unto death, yet he knew, and would know to his latest breath, that he had both seen a light and heard a voice speaking unto him, and all the world could not make him think or believe otherwise.

"So it was with me. I had actually seen a light, and in the midst of that light I saw two Personages, and they did in reality speak to me; and though I was hated and persecuted for saying that I had seen a vision, yet it was true; and while they were persecuting me, reviling me, and speaking all manner of evil against me falsely for so saying, I was led to say in my heart: Why persecute me for telling the truth? I have actually seen a vision; and who am I that I can withstand God, or why does the world think to make me deny what I have actually seen? For I had seen a vision; I knew it, and I knew that God knew it, and I could not deny it, neither dared I do it; at least I knew that by so doing I would offend God, and come under condemnation."

We were still making arrangements to build us a comfortable house, the management and control of which devolved chiefly upon Alvin.[13] And when November 1822 arrived, the frame was raised, and all the materials necessary for its speedy completion were procured. This opened to Alvin's mind the pleasing prospect of seeing his father and mother once more comfortable and happy. He would say, "I am going to have a nice, pleasant room for Father and Mother to sit in and everything arranged for their comfort, and they shall not work anymore as they have done."

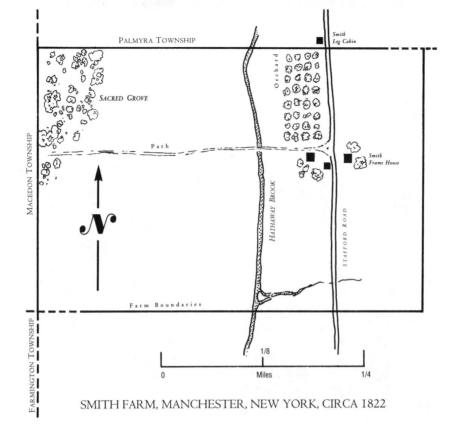

PALMYRA TOWNSHIP

Smith
Log Cabin

SACRED GROVE

Orchard

MACEDON TOWNSHIP

Path

Smith
Frame House

HATHAWAY BROOK

STAFFORD ROAD

N

Farm Boundaries

FARMINGTON TOWNSHIP

1/8

0   Miles   1/4

SMITH FARM, MANCHESTER, NEW YORK, CIRCA 1822

From this time until the twenty-first of September, 1823, Joseph continued, as usual, to labor with his father, and nothing during this interval occurred of very great importance—though he suffered every kind of opposition and persecution from the different orders of religionists.

The third harvest time had now arrived since we opened our new farm, and all our sons were actively employed in assisting their father to cut down the grain and store it away in order for winter.

On the evening of the twenty-first of September, as he recorded:[14]

"After I had retired to my bed for the night, I betook myself to prayer and supplication to Almighty God for forgiveness of all my sins and follies, and also for a manifestation to me, that I might know of my state and standing before him; for I had full confidence in obtaining a divine manifestation, as I previously had one.[15]

"While I was thus in the act of calling upon God, I discovered a light appearing in my room, which continued to increase until the room was lighter than at noonday, when immediately a personage appeared at my bedside, standing in the air, for his feet did not touch the floor.

*Moroni visited Joseph in the cabin on this site
where the family lived from 1818 to 1825.*

"He had on a loose robe of most exquisite whiteness. It was a whiteness beyond anything earthly I had ever seen; nor do I believe that any
earthly thing could be made to appear so exceedingly white and brilliant.
His hands were naked, and his arms also, a little above the wrist; so, also,
were his feet naked, as were his legs, a little above the ankles. His head
and neck were also bare. I could discover that he had no other clothing
on but this robe, as it was open, so that I could see into his bosom.

"Not only was his robe exceedingly white, but his whole person was
glorious beyond description, and his countenance truly like lightning.[16]
The room was exceedingly light, but not so very bright as immediately
around his person. When I first looked upon him, I was afraid; but the
fear soon left me.[17]

"He called me by name, and said unto me that he was a messenger
sent from the presence of God to me, and that his name was Moroni;
that God had a work for me to do; and that my name should be had for

good and evil among all nations, kindreds, and tongues; or that it should be both good and evil spoken of among all people.

"He said there was a book deposited, written upon gold plates, giving an account of the former inhabitants of this continent, and the source from whence they sprang. He also said that the fulness of the everlasting Gospel was contained in it, as delivered by the Savior to the ancient inhabitants; also, that there were two stones in silver bows—and these stones, fastened to a breastplate, constituted what is called the Urim and Thummim—deposited with the plates; and the possession and use of these stones were what constituted "seers" in ancient or former times; and that God had prepared them for the purpose of translating the book.[18]

"After telling me these things, he commenced quoting the prophecies of the Old Testament. He first quoted part of the third chapter of Malachi; and he quoted also the fourth or last chapter of the same prophecy, though with a little variation from the way it reads in our Bibles. Instead of quoting the first verse as it reads in our books, he quoted it thus: 'For behold, the day cometh that shall burn as an oven, and all the proud, yea, and all that do wickedly shall burn as stubble; for they that come shall burn them, saith the Lord of Hosts, that it shall leave them neither root nor branch.'

"And again, he quoted the fifth verse thus: 'Behold, I will reveal unto you the Priesthood, by the hand of Elijah the prophet, before the coming of the great and dreadful day of the Lord.'

"He also quoted the next verse differently: 'And he shall plant in the hearts of the children the promises made to the fathers, and the hearts of the children shall turn to their fathers. If it were not so, the whole earth would be utterly wasted at his coming.'

"In addition to these, he quoted the eleventh chapter of Isaiah, saying that it was about to be fulfilled. He quoted also the third chapter of Acts, twenty-second and twenty-third verses, precisely as they stand in our New Testament. He said that that prophet was Christ; but the day had not yet come when 'they who would not hear his voice should be cut off from among the people,' but soon would come.

"He also quoted the second chapter of Joel, from the twenty-eighth verse to the last. He also said that this was not yet fulfilled, but was soon to be. And he further stated the fulness of the Gentiles was soon to come in. He quoted many other passages of scripture, and offered many explanations which cannot be mentioned here.

"Again, he told me, that when I got those plates of which he had spoken—for the time that they should be obtained was not yet ful-filled—I should not show them to any person;[19] neither the breastplate with the Urim and Thummim; only to those to whom I should be commanded to show them; if I did I should be destroyed. While he was conversing with me about the plates, the vision was opened to my mind that I could see the place where the plates were deposited, and that so clearly and distinctly that I knew the place again when I visited it.

"After this communication, I saw the light in the room begin to gather immediately around the person of him who had been speaking to me, and it continued to do so until the room was again left dark, except just around him; when, instantly I saw, as it were, a conduit open right up into heaven, and he ascended till he entirely disappeared, and the room was left as it had been before this heavenly light had made its appearance.

"I lay musing on the singularity of the scene, and marveling greatly at what had been told to me by this extraordinary messenger; when, in the midst of my meditation, I suddenly discovered that my room was again beginning to get lighted, and in an instant, as it were, the same heavenly messenger was again by my bedside.

"He commenced, and again related the very same things which he had done at his first visit, without the least variation; which having done, he informed me of great judgments which were coming upon the earth, with great desolations by famine, sword, and pestilence; and that these grievous judgments would come on the earth in this generation. Having related these things, he again ascended as he had done before."

When the angel ascended the second time, he left Joseph over-whelmed with astonishment, yet gave him but a short time to contem-plate the things which he had told him before he made his reappear-ance, and rehearsed the same things over, adding a few words of caution and instruction, thus: that he must beware of covetousness, and he must not suppose the record was to be brought forth with the view of getting gain, for this was not the case, but that it was to bring forth light and intelligence, which had for a long time been lost to the world; and that when he went to get the plates, he must be on his guard or his mind would be filled with darkness. The angel then told him to tell his father all which he had both seen and heard.

NOTES

1. Joseph Smith the Prophet was born in the township of Sharon, Windsor County, Vermont, just after the winter solstice (the longest night of the year)—when the light begins to return to the earth.

2. Joseph Smith turned fourteen years old December 23, 1819.

3. This attempted assassination of young Joseph occurred just a few months before the First Vision.

4. This is Joseph Smith Sr.'s seventh vision that Mother Smith gives any record of or reference to.

5. A peddler's budget was a small pack, bag, or pouch.

6. This vision or dream was likely given just six months or less before the first vision of Joseph Smith the Prophet.

7. From the records we learn that the most active congregations in Palmyra were the Methodists, Baptists, Presbyterians, and Episcopalians.

8. Joseph Smith—History 1:7–25; or *History of the Church* 1:3–8.

9. In the 1832 recital of the First Vision, Joseph wrote: "By searching the scriptures I found that mankind did not come unto the Lord but that they had apostatized from the true and living faith, and there was no society or denomination that built upon the gospel of Jesus Christ as recorded in the New Testament; and I felt to mourn for my own sins and for the sins of the world, for I learned in the scriptures that God was the same yesterday, today, and forever, that he was no respecter [of] persons, for he was God" (*Papers*, pp. 5–6).

10. Further insight is received from the 1835 recital of the First Vision: "My tongue seemed to be swollen in my mouth, so that I could not utter; I heard a noise behind me like someone walking towards me. I strove again to pray, but could not; the noise of walking seemed to draw nearer; I sprang upon my feet and looked round, but saw no person or thing that was calculated to produce the noise of walking." (In Milton V. Backman Jr., *Joseph Smith's First Vision*, 2d ed. [Salt Lake City: Bookcraft, 1980], p. 159.)

11. The 1835 account states: "A pillar of fire appeared above my head; which presently rested down upon me, and filled me with unspeakable joy. A personage appeared in the midst of this pillar of flame, which was spread all around and yet nothing

consumed." (In Backman, *First Vision,* p. 159.) Joseph's 1832 account records: "I was filled with the Spirit of God and the Lord opened the heavens upon me, and I saw the Lord and he spake unto me, saying, 'Joseph, my son, thy sins are forgiven thee. Go thy way. Walk in my statutes and keep my commandments. Behold, I am the Lord of glory. I was crucified for the world, that all those who believe on my name may have eternal life.'" (*Papers,* p. 6.) In the Wentworth letter (1842) Joseph said, "I was en-wrapped in a heavenly vision, and saw two glorious personages, who exactly resembled each other in features and likeness, surrounded with a brilliant light which eclipsed the sun at noon day" (*History of the Church* 4:536).

12. Some have speculated that perhaps the Reverend George Lane, a Methodist circuit preacher, had become friends with young Joseph and had tried to help him in his search for the true religion. William Smith, brother of the Prophet, reported: "Rev. Mr. Lane of the Methodists preached a sermon on 'What church shall I join?' And the burden of his discourse was to ask God, using as a text, 'If any man lack wisdom let him ask of God who giveth to all men liberally.' And of course when Joseph went home and was looking over the text he was impressed to do just what the preacher had said, and going out in the woods with child like, simple trusting faith believing that God meant just what He said, kneeled down and prayed." (*Deseret Evening News,* Salt Lake City, January 20, 1894.) Oliver Cowdery added the following: "Mr. Lane's manner of communication was peculiarly calculated to awaken the intellect of the hearer, and arouse the sinner to look about him for safety—much good instruction was always drawn from his discourses on the scriptures, and in common with others, our brother's [Joseph's] mind became awakened" (in *Papers,* p. 46). Some also feel that this Reverend George Lane is the "Methodist preacher" whom Joseph took the opportunity to tell his first vision to on this occasion. (For a thorough treatise on the possible influences of the Reverend Mr. Lane on Joseph Smith, see Porter, "Origins," pp. 49–64.)

13. A daughter, Lucy, was added to the Smith home on July 18, 1821. Her father was fifty years old at her birth and her mother was forty-six.

14. This account, now found in the Pearl of Great Price, was likely inserted in the revised manuscript of Lucy Mack Smith's history that was the basis for the 1853 edition, presumably to give Joseph's fuller, more accurate account of Moroni's first visits rather than Lucy's more general description. In her Preliminary Manuscript she records the events as follows: "One evening we were sitting till quite late conversing upon the subject of the diversity of churches that had risen up in the world and the many thousand opinions in existence as to the truths contained in scripture. Joseph never said many words upon any subject but always seemed to reflect more deeply than common persons of his age upon everything of a religious nature. After we ceased conversation, he went to bed and was pondering in his mind which of the churches was the true one. But he had not lain there long till he saw a bright light enter the room where he lay. He looked up and saw an angel of the Lord standing by him. The angel spoke: 'I perceive that you are inquiring in your mind which is the true church. There is not a true church on earth—no, not one—and has not been since

Peter took the keys of the Melchizedek Priesthood after the order of God into the kingdom of heaven. The churches that are now upon the earth are all man-made churches. There is a record for you, Joseph, but you cannot get it until you learn to keep the commandments of God, for it is not to get gain, but it is to bring forth that light and intelligence which has been long lost in the earth. Now, Joseph, beware or when you go to get the plates, your mind will be filled with darkness and all manner of evil will rush into your mind to prevent you from keeping the commandments of God. You must tell your father of this, for he will believe every word you say. The record is on a side of the hill of Cumorah, three miles from this place. Remove the grass and moss, and you will find the record under it, lying on four pillars of cement."

15. Oliver Cowdery wrote of this moment: "His heart was drawn out in fervent prayer, and his whole soul was so lost to every thing of a temporal nature, that earth, to him, had lost its claims, and all he desired was to be prepared in heart to commune with some kind messenger who could communicate to him the desired information of his acceptance with God.

"At length the family retired, and he, as usual, bent his way, though in silence, where others might have rested their weary frames 'locked fast in sleep's embrace;' but repose had fled, and accustomed slumber had spread her refreshing hand over others beside him—he continued still to pray. . . .

"In this situation hours passed unnumbered—how many or how few I know not, neither is he able to inform me; but supposes it must have been eleven or twelve, and perhaps later, as the noise and bustle of the family, in retiring, had long since ceased." (In *Papers*, pp. 50, 51.)

16. Oliver Cowdery insightfully comments here: "It is no easy task to describe the appearance of a messenger from the skies—indeed, I doubt there being an individual clothed with perishable clay, who is capable to do this work" (in *Papers*, p. 51). Joseph gives the best description of an angel available to man.

17. Oliver Cowdery continues with further insight about the angel's appearing to Joseph: "The first sight was as though the house was filled with consuming and unquenchable fire. This sudden appearance of a light so bright, as must naturally be expected, occasioned a shock or sensation, visible to the extremities of the body. It was, however, followed with a calmness and serenity of mind, and an overwhelming rapture of joy that surpassed understanding, and in a moment a personage stood before him." (In *Papers*, p. 51.)

18. This Urim and Thummim was the same that was given to the brother of Jared upon the mount. See D&C 17:1; also Ether 3:22–24.

19. David Whitmer claimed that he "had conversations with several young men who said that Joseph Smith had certainly gold plates, and that before he attained them he had promised to share with them, but had not done so, and they were very much incensed with him" (quoted in Cook, *Whitmer Interviews*, p. 60).

CHAPTER 18

Joseph tells his father of the visits of Moroni. His father believes every word and tells Joseph to do as he is commanded. Joseph goes to the hill and finds the ancient record hidden in a stone box. Joseph is shown by contrast the powers of darkness and light. Moroni informs Joseph that the time has not yet come for the record to come forth. Evening after evening Joseph teaches his family about the ancient inhabitants of America.

September 22, 1823 to November 1823

The next day Joseph, his father, and his brother Alvin[1] were reaping in the field together. Suddenly, Joseph stopped and seemed to be in a deep study for some time. Alvin hurried him, saying, "Joseph, you must keep to work or we shall not get our task done." Joseph worked again diligently, then stopped in the same way a second time. When his father saw that Joseph was very pale, he urged him to go to the house and tell his mother that he was sick. He went a short distance till he came to a beautiful green under an apple tree. Here he lay down on his face, for he was so weak he could go no farther.

He was here but a short time, when the messenger whom he had seen the night before came to him again and said, "Why did you not tell your father what I told you?" Joseph said he was afraid his father would not believe him. "He will believe every word you say to him," said the angel.[2]

Joseph then promised to do as he was told by the angel and rose up and returned to the field, where he had left my husband and Alvin; but when he got there, his father had just gone to the house, as he was somewhat unwell. Joseph then requested Alvin to go to the house and ask his father to the field, for, said he, "I have something to tell him." When his father came to him, Joseph rehearsed all that had passed between him and the angel the previous night. Having heard this account, his father charged him not to fail in attending strictly to the instruction which he had received from this heavenly messenger.

Soon after Joseph had this conversation with his father, he repaired to the place where the plates were deposited, which place he describes as follows:

"Convenient to the village of Manchester, Ontario county, New York, stands a hill of considerable size, and the most elevated of any in the neighborhood. On the west side of this hill, not far from the top, under a stone of considerable size, lay the plates, deposited in a stone box.[3] This stone was thick and rounding in the middle on the upper side, and thinner towards the edges, so that the middle part of it was visible above the ground, but the edge all around was covered with earth.

"Having removed the earth, I obtained a lever, which I got fixed under the edge of the stone, and with a little exertion raised it up. I looked in, and there indeed did I behold the plates, the Urim and Thummim, and the breastplate, as stated by the messenger."

While Joseph remained here, the angel told him, "Now I will show you the distance between light and darkness, and the operation of a good spirit and an evil one. An evil spirit will try to crowd your mind with every evil and wicked thing to keep every good thought and feeling out of your mind, but you must keep your mind always staid upon God, that no evil may come into your heart."[4]

The angel showed him, by contrast, the difference between good and evil, and likewise the consequences of both obedience and disobedience to the commandments of God, in such a striking manner, that the impression was always vivid in his memory until the very end of his days; and in giving a relation of this circumstance, not long prior to his death, he remarked that ever afterwards he was willing to keep the commandments of God.[5]

*The west side of the Hill Cumorah, not far from the top,
is the area where Moroni met with Joseph.*

Furthermore, the angel told him at the interview mentioned last that the time had not yet come for the plates to be brought forth to the world; that he could not take them from the place wherein they were deposited until he had learned to keep the commandments of God— not only till he was willing, but able to do it. The angel bade Joseph come to this place every year, at the same time of the year, and he would meet him there and give him further instructions.[6]

When Joseph came in that evening, he told the whole family all that he had made known to his father in the field and also of finding the record, as well as what passed between him and the angel while he was at the place where the plates were deposited.

We sat up very late and listened attentively to all that he had to say to us, but his mind had been so exercised that he became very much fatigued. When Alvin saw this he said, "Now, brother, let us go to bed. We will get up early in the morning and go to work so as to finish our day's labor by an hour before sunset, and if Mother will get our suppers early, we will then have a fine, long evening and all sit down and hear you talk."

The next day we worked with great ambition and were ready by sunset to give our whole attention to the discourse of my son, pertaining to the obtaining of the plates, the goodness of God, his knowledge and power, our own liability to error and transgression, and the great salvation that lay before the faithful. "Now," said he, "Father and Mother, the angel of the Lord says that we must be careful not to proclaim these things or to mention them abroad, for we do not any of us know the weakness of the world, which is so sinful, and that when we get the plates they will want to kill us for the sake of the gold, if they know we have them.[7] And as soon as they do find that we pretend to have any such thing, our names will be cast out as evil, and we shall be scoffed at and all names of evil spoken concerning us."

This astonished us very much, and we wondered in our hearts how these things could be. Why would anyone have a disposition to take our lives merely for a thing like this? But he continued, "If we are wise and prudent in that which is revealed to us, God is able to make all things known to us. Do you believe it?" said he to his father.

"Why, yes, certainly," answered Mr. Smith. "He has all power and wisdom, knowledge and understanding and, of course, can teach us all things if we are worthy, and we will try to live in such a way as to deserve the favor of God, that he may be pleased to instruct from day to day."

From this time forth Joseph continued to receive instructions from time to time, and every evening we gathered our children together and gave our time up to the discussion of those things which he instructed to us. I think that we presented the most peculiar aspect of any family that ever lived upon the earth, all seated in a circle, father, mother, sons, and daughters, listening in breathless anxiety to the religious teachings of a boy eighteen years of age who had never read the Bible through by course in his life. For Joseph was less inclined to the study of books than any child we had, but much more given to reflection and deep study.

Fields where Joseph and his family worked were planted in wheat, corn, beans, and flax.

We were convinced that God was about to bring to light something that we might stay our minds upon, something that would give us a more perfect knowledge of the plan of salvation and the redemption of the human family than anything which had been taught us heretofore, and we rejoiced in it with exceeding great joy. The sweetest union and happiness pervaded our house. No jar nor discord disturbed our peace, and tranquility reigned in our midst.

In the course of our evening conversations, Joseph gave us some of the most amusing recitals which could be imagined. He would describe the ancient inhabitants of this continent, their dress, their manner of traveling, the animals which they rode, the cities that they built, and the structure of their buildings with every particular, their mode of warfare, and their religious worship as specifically as though he had spent his life with them. It will be recollected by the reader that all that I mentioned and much more took place within the compass of one short year.

NOTES

1. At this date Alvin was twenty-five years old and engaged to be married; and unbeknownst to any in the family, he would pass away in just fifty-eight days.

2. Joseph recorded: "I started with the intention of going to the house; but, in attempting to cross the fence out of the field where we were, my strength entirely failed me, and I fell helpless on the ground, and for a time was quite unconscious of anything. The first thing that I can recollect was a voice speaking unto me, calling me by name. I looked up, and beheld the same messenger standing over my head, surrounded by light as before. He then again related unto me all that he had related to me the previous night, and commanded me to go to my father and tell him of the vision and commandments which I had received. I obeyed; I returned to my father in the field, and rehearsed the whole matter to him. He replied to me that it was of God, and told me to go and do as commanded by the messenger." (Joseph Smith—History 1:48–50; or *History of the Church* 1:14–15.)

3. Oliver Cowdery visited the Hill Cumorah in 1830 and later gave this detailed description: "The hill of which I have been speaking, at the time mentioned, presented a varied appearance: the north end rose suddenly from the plain, forming a promontory without timber, but covered with grass. As you passed to the south you soon came to scattering timber, the surface having been cleared by art or by wind; and a short distance further left, you are surrounded with the common forest of the country. It is necessary to observe, that even the part cleared was only occupied for pasturage, its steep ascent and narrow summit not admitting the plow of the husbandman, with any degree of ease or profit. It was at the second mentioned place where the record was found to be deposited, on the west side of the hill, not far from the top down its side; and when myself visited the place in the year 1830, there were several trees standing: enough to cause a shade in summer, but not so much as to prevent the surface being covered with grass— which was also the case when the record was first found." (In *Papers*, pp. 81–82.)

4. In the Preliminary Manuscript, Lucy relates that the angel made this comment while Joseph still lay exhausted in the field. However, it seems more consistent with the rest of the message from the angel given at the hill.

5. One example of this in Joseph's life was in 1834 when he wrote: "No month ever found me more busily engaged than November; but as my life consisted of activity and unyielding exertions, I made this my rule: *When the Lord commands, do it*" (*History of the Church* 2:170).

6. Joseph came to the hill on the same date, September 22, in each of the years 1823, 1824, 1825, 1826, and 1827. In one of the many later interviews with David Whitmer, it was reported that "three times has he [David] been at the hill Cumorah and seen the casket that contained the tablets. . . . Eventually the casket had been washed down to the foot of the hill, but it was to be seen when he last visited the historic place." (In Cook, *Whitmer Interviews*, p. 7.)

7. In an 1878 *Deseret Evening News* article reporting on an interview with David Whitmer, he is quoted as saying: "I saw the place where the plates were found, and a great many did so, and it awakened an excitement at the time, because the worst enemies of 'Mormonism' stirred up the confusion by telling about the plates which Joseph found, and the 'gold bible' which he was in possession of, so he was in constant danger of being robbed and killed" (in Cook, *Whitmer Interviews*, pp. 22–23).

CHAPTER 19

⁊❧

Alvin Smith's illness and death. He speaks to each of his brothers and sisters and to his parents, encourages them, and bids them farewell. Cause of his death is determined. His funeral. Alvin's great zeal for the work of the Lord.

November 15, 1823 to end of November 1823

On the fifteenth of November, 1823, about ten o'clock in the morning, Alvin was taken very sick with the bilious colic. He came to the house in great distress and requested his father to go immediately for a physician, which he accordingly did. But the doctor who generally attended upon our family being absent, Mr. Smith was compelled to go further than he expected. However, he found in the next village one Dr. Greenwood, who, when he came, immediately administered a heavy dose of calomel to the patient, although he objected much against it.

This calomel lodged in his stomach, and all the powerful medicine which was afterwards prescribed by skillful physicians could not remove it.

On the third day of his sickness,[1] Dr. McIntyre, the favorite of the family and a man of great skill and experience, was brought and with him four other professors of medicine. But all their exertions were of no avail, just as Alvin had declared would be the case. He said, "The calomel is still lodged in the same place and you cannot move it. Consequently, it must take my life."

He then called Hyrum[2] to him and said, "Hyrum, I must die, and now I want to say a few things to you that you must remember. I have done all that I could do to make our dear parents comfortable. I now

Alvin lovingly completed much of the workmanship in the Smith home
before he passed away.

want you to go on and finish the house and take care of them in their old age[3] and do not let them work hard anymore."

He then called Sophronia[4] to him and said, "Sophronia, you must be a good girl and do all that lies in your power for Father and Mother. Never forsake them. They have worked hard, and they are now getting old. Be kind to them and remember what they have done for us."

In the latter part of the fourth night he called for all the children and again exhorted them separately to the same effect as before. But to Joseph[5] he said, "Joseph, I am going to die now. The distress which I suffer and the sensations that I have tell me my time is very short. I want you to be a good boy and do everything that lies in your power to obtain the record. Be faithful in receiving instruction and in keeping every commandment that is given you. Your brother Alvin must now leave you, but remember the example which he has set for you, and set a good example for the children that are younger than you. Always be kind to Father and Mother."

He then asked me to take his little sister Lucy[6] up and bring her to him, for he wished to see her. This child was the youngest of the family, and he was extremely fond of her and was in the habit of taking her up and caressing her, which naturally attached her to him. She could not then talk plainly, and always called her brother "Amby." I went to her and said, "Lucy, Amby wants to see you." At this she started out of her sleep and screamed out, "Oh, Amby, Amby." We took her to him, and she sprang from my arms and caught him round the neck and cried out, "Oh, my Amby," and kissed him again and again.

To Lucy he said, "You must be the best girl in the world and take care of Mother. You can't have your Amby anymore. Amby is going away; he must leave little Lucy." He then kissed her and said, "Take her away. I think my breath offends her." We took hold of the child, but she clenched hold of him with such a desperate grasp that it was very difficult to disengage her hands.

As I turned with the child, Alvin said, "Father, Mother, brothers, sisters, farewell! I can now breathe out my life as calmly as a clock," and immediately closed his eyes in death.[7]

The child still cried to go back to Alvin. One present said to her, "Alvin is gone. An angel has taken his spirit to heaven." When the babe heard this, she renewed her cries, and as I bent over his corpse with her in my arms, she again threw her arms around him and kissed him repeatedly, screaming as before. And until the body was taken from the house, she continued constantly crying and showing such manifestation of affection mingled with terror at the scene before her as is seldom witnessed in a child.[8]

This harrowed up our feelings almost to distraction, for Alvin was a youth of singular goodness of disposition—kind and amiable manners, so much so that lamentation and mourning filled the whole neighborhood where we lived, and, of course, more than usual grief filled the hearts of those from whose immediate circle he was taken, those who felt and saw the effects of his nobleness and generosity every hour of his existence.[9]

It was the wish of the principal physician that Alvin's body should be cut open to ascertain, if possible, the cause of his disease and death. When this was done, they found the calomel still lodged in the upper bowels, untouched by anything which he had taken to carry it off. It

*Alvin Smith is buried in the Swift Cemetery
located just a few hundred feet north
of downtown Palmyra.*

was as near in its natural state as it could be, surrounded as it was with gangrene.

Dr. McIntyre and Dr. Robinson performed the operation. The last named doctor was seventy years of age. He spoke long and earnestly to the younger physicians upon the danger of administering powerful medicine without the thorough knowledge of the practice of physic. "Here," he said "is one of the loveliest youth that ever trod the streets of Palmyra destroyed, murdered as it were, by him at whose hand relief was expected, cast off from the face of the earth by a careless quack who even dared to trifle with the life of a fellow mortal."

When the time for interment arrived, the inhabitants of the surrounding country gathered together, and during the funeral obsequies they gave the most affectionate manifestations of their sympathy; but there was one that felt our grief more deeply than the rest—a lovely young woman who was engaged to be married to my son. The disconsolate girl was rendered most desolate by his unexpected death, and as long as we knew her, she never recovered her wonted animation and good spirits.

Thus was our happiness blasted in a moment. When we least expected the blow, it came upon us. The poisoned shaft entered our very hearts' core and diffused to deadly effect throughout our veins. We were for a time almost swallowed up in grief, so much so that it seemed impossible for us to interest ourselves at all about the concerns of life. The feeling of every heart was to make speedy preparation to follow him who had been too much the idol of our hearts. And then if it pleased God to take us also, we would receive the call as a favor at his hands from whom it came.

Alvin had ever manifested a greater zeal and anxiety, if it were possible, than any of the rest with regard to the record which had been shown to Joseph, and he always showed the most intense interest concerning the matter. With this before our minds, we could not endure to hear or say one word upon that subject, for the moment that Joseph spoke of the record it would immediately bring Alvin to our minds with all his kindness, his affection, his zeal, and piety. And when we looked to his place and realized that he was gone from it, to return no more in this life, we all wept with one accord over our irretrievable loss, and we could "not be comforted, because he was not."[10]

NOTES

1. November 17, 1823.
2. Hyrum was twenty-three years old.
3. Joseph Smith Sr. was fifty-two years old and Lucy Mack Smith was forty-eight.
4. Sophronia was twenty years old.
5. Joseph was one month less than eighteen years old.
6. Little Lucy was twenty-eight months old at this time.
7. He died sometime in the early morning hours of November 19, 1823.
8. Crossed out in the Preliminary Manuscript is this poignant sentence about

little Lucy's grief: "She would run out of the house and drag in a board and lie beside the corpse, then take a white cloth and wrap herself in it and lie down on the board by his side."

9. On August 22, 1842, Joseph expressed his love for his dear brother taken in his prime: "Alvin, my oldest brother—I remember well the pangs of sorrow that swelled my youthful bosom and almost burst my tender heart when he died. He was the oldest and the noblest of my father's family. He was one of the noblest of the sons of men. Shall his name not be recorded in this book [the Book of the Law of the Lord]? Yes, Alvin, let it be had here and be handed down upon these sacred pages for ever and ever. In him there was no guile. He lived without spot from the time he was a child. . . . He was one of the soberest of men, and when he died the angel of the Lord visited him in his last moments." (*History of the Church* 5:126–27.)

10. See Matthew 2:18; Jeremiah 31:15. The Smiths had now lost three children; that is, Alvin, Ephraim, and their firstborn son. The vision given in the Kirtland Temple, January 21, 1836 (twelve years after Alvin's death), was especially powerful to Joseph: "The heavens were opened upon us, and I beheld the celestial kingdom of God, and the glory thereof. . . . I saw the transcendent beauty of the gate through which the heirs of that kingdom will enter; . . . also the blazing throne of God, whereon was seated the Father and the Son. . . . I saw Father Adam and Abraham; and my father and my mother; my brother Alvin, that has long since slept; and marveled how it was that he had obtained an inheritance in that kingdom, seeing that he had departed this life before the Lord had set his hand to gather Israel the second time, and had not been baptized for the remission of sins. Thus came the voice of the Lord unto me, saying: All who have died without a knowledge of this gospel, who would have received it if they had been permitted to tarry, shall be heirs of the celestial kingdom of God; also all that shall die henceforth without a knowledge of it, who would have received it with all their hearts, shall be heirs of that kingdom; for I, the Lord, will judge all men according to their works, according to the desire of their hearts." (D&C 137:1, 2, 3, 5–9.)

CHAPTER 20

·

A man tries to unify the churches in Palmyra. Joseph gives a prophecy about Deacon Jessup that is fulfilled. Joseph goes to the hill September 22, 1824, and is unable to obtain the plates. A lesson from the angel on keeping all the commandments. Joseph works for Josiah Stowell in Harmony, Pennsylvania. The frame house is completed. Joseph becomes acquainted with Emma Hale.

Winter 1824 to December 1825

Shortly after the death of Alvin, a man began laboring in the neighborhood to effect a union of all the churches, that all denominations might be agreed and thus worship God with one mind and one heart.

This, I thought, looked right. I wished to join them, and I tried to persuade my husband to do so, and it was the inclination of all the family to unite with their numbers, except Joseph. He refused from the first to attend the meetings with us.[1] He would say, "Mother, I do not wish to prevent you from going to meeting or joining any church you like, or any of the family who desire the like; only do not ask me to do so, for I do not wish to go. But I will take my Bible and go out into the woods and learn more in two hours than you could if you were to go to meeting for two years."[2]

To gratify me, my husband attended some two or three meetings, but peremptorily refused going any more, either for my gratification or any other person's. But he did not object to myself and such of the children as chose to go or to become church members, if we wished.

During this excitement, Joseph said, "It will do you no hurt to join them, but you will not stay with them long, for you are mistaken in them. You do not know the wickedness of their hearts. I will," said he, "give you an example, and you may set it down as a prophecy. Now, you look at Deacon Jessup. You hear him talk very piously. Well, you think he is a very good man, but suppose that one of his poor neighbors owes him the value of one cow. This man has eight small children. Suppose the poor man should be taken sick and die, leaving his wife with one cow but destitute of every means of support for herself and family. Now, I tell you that Deacon Jessup, religious as he is, wouldn't hesitate to take the last cow from the widow and orphans rather than lose the debt, although he has an abundance of everything." This seemed impossible, but it was not one year from the time this was spoken until we saw the very thing fulfilled.

After a short time, the first shock occasioned by Alvin's death passed off, and we began to resume our usual avocations.

The angel had informed Joseph that he might make an effort to obtain the plates on the twenty-second of the ensuing September [1824].³ Accordingly, when the time arrived he visited the place where the plates were hid; and supposing at this time that the only thing required, in order to possess them until the time for their translation, was to be able to keep the commandments of God—and he firmly believed he could keep every commandment which had been given him—he fully expected to carry them home with him. Having arrived at the place appointed, he removed the moss and grass from the surface of the rock, and then pried up the flat stone, according to the directions which he had received. He then discovered the plates lying on four pillars in the inside of the box. He put forth his hand and took them up, but when he lifted them from their place, the thought flashed across his mind that there might be something more in the box that would be of a pecuniary benefit to him. In the excitement of the moment, he laid the record down in order to cover up the box, lest someone should come along and take away whatever else might be deposited there. When he turned again to take up the record, it was gone, but where he knew not, nor did he know by what means it had been taken away.

He was much alarmed at this. He knelt down and asked the Lord why it was that the record was taken from him. The angel appeared to him and told him that he had not done as he was commanded, for in a former revelation he had been commanded not to lay the plates down, or put them for a moment out of his hands, until he got into the house and deposited them in a chest or trunk having a good lock and key; and contrary to this, he had laid them down with the view of securing some fancied or imaginary treasure that remained.

In the moment of excitement, Joseph was overcome by the powers of darkness and forgot the injunction that was laid upon him.

After some further conversation, Joseph was permitted to raise the stone again, and there he beheld the plates, the same as before. He reached forth his hand to take them, but was hurled to the ground with great violence. When he recovered, the angel was gone, and he arose and returned to the house, weeping for grief and disappointment.

As he was aware that we would expect him to bring the plates home with him, he was greatly troubled, fearing that we might doubt his having seen them. As soon as he entered the house, my husband asked if he had obtained the plates. The answer was, "No, Father, I could not get them."

His father then said, "Did you see them?"

"Yes," replied Joseph, "I saw them, but could not take them."

"I would have taken them," rejoined his father, with much earnestness, "if I had been in your place."

"Why," returned Joseph, in quite a subdued tone, "you do not know what you say. I could not get them, for the angel of the Lord would not let me."[4]

Joseph then related the circumstance in full, which gave

To the Public.

WHEREAS reports have been industriously put in circulation, that my son *Alvin* had been removed from the place of his interment and dissected, which reports, every person possessed of human sensibility must know, are peculiarly calculated to harrow up the mind of a parent and deeply wound the feelings of relations—therefore, for the purpose of ascertaining the truth of such reports, I, with some of my neighbors, this morning repaired to the grave, and removing the earth, found the body which had not been disturbed.

This method is taken for the purpose of satisfying the minds of those who may have heard the report, and of informing those who have put it in circulation, that it is earnestly requested they would desist therefrom; and that it is believed by some, that they have been stimulated more by a desire to injure thh reputation of certain persons than a philanthropy for the peace and welfare of myself and friends.   JOSEPH SMITH.
Palmyra, Sept. 25th, 1824.   53

Notice which appeared in the Wayne Sentinel, Wednesday, September 29, 1824.[5]

us much uneasiness, as we were afraid that he might utterly fail of obtaining the record through some neglect on his part. We, therefore, dou-
bled our diligence in prayer and supplication to God, in order that he
might be more fully instructed in his duty and be preserved from all the
wiles and machinations of him "who lieth in wait to deceive."[6]

Having the building of the house already paid for, we thought it
would be well to set the mechanics at work and have it completed. We
accordingly did so, and ere long, we had a pleasant, commodious habitation ready to receive us. Mr. Stoddard, the principal workman on the
house, would have been very glad to have purchased it for fifteen hundred dollars, but that was no temptation. Nothing could persuade Mr.
Smith to abandon the scene of his labor and the toiling of this family,
for here they had borne the burden and heat of the day. We contemplated with much happiness the enjoyment of the fruit of our labors.

A short time before the house was completed, a man by the name
of Josiah Stowell[7] came from Chenango County, New York, with the
view of getting Joseph to assist him in digging for a silver mine.[8] He
came for Joseph on account of having heard that he possessed certain
means by which he could discern things invisible to the natural eye.

Mr. Stowell came into the Palmyra district with Joseph Knight Sr.[9]
to buy grain. In that way he became acquainted with the Smith family.

This project of Stowell's was undertaken from this cause—an old
document had fallen into his possession, in some way or other, containing information of silver mines being somewhere in the neighborhood
in which he resided.

Joseph endeavored to divert him from his vain pursuit, but he was
inflexible in his purpose and offered high wages to those who would dig
for him in search of said mine, and still insisted upon having Joseph to
work for him. Accordingly, Joseph and several others returned with him
and commenced digging. After laboring for the old gentleman about a
month without success, Joseph prevailed upon him to cease his operations, and it was from this circumstance of having worked by the
month, at digging for a silver mine, that the very prevalent story arose
of Joseph's having been a money digger.

While Joseph was in the employ of Mr. Stowell, he boarded a short
time with one Isaac Hale, and it was during this interval that Joseph

The spacious Smith frame house had four upstairs bedrooms and four rooms on the main floor.

became acquainted with his daughter, Miss Emma Hale,[10] to whom he immediately commenced paying his addresses, and was subsequently married.

When Mr. Stowell relinquished his project of digging for silver, Joseph returned to his father's house.[11]

Soon after his return we received intelligence of the arrival of a new agent for the Evertson land, of which our farm was a portion. This reminded us of the last payment, which was still due and which must be made before we could obtain a deed to the place.

Having made the acquaintance of a couple of gentlemen from Pennsylvania, Mr. Stowell and Mr. Knight, who were desirous of purchasing a quantity of wheat, which we had down on the place, we agreed with them that if they would furnish us with a sum of money requisite for the liquidation of this debt, the wheat should be carried to them in flour the ensuing season.

Having made this arrangement, Mr. Smith sent Hyrum to the new agent in Canandaigua to inform him that the money should be forthcoming as soon as the twenty-fifth of December 1825. This, the agent said, would answer every purpose, and he agreed to retain the land until that time. Thus assured that all was safe, we gave ourselves no further uneasiness about the matter.

When the time had nearly come for my husband to set out for Pennsylvania to get the money, Joseph called Mr. Smith and myself aside and told us that he had felt so lonely ever since Alvin's death, that he had come to the conclusion of getting married if we had no objections. He thought that no young woman that he ever was acquainted with was better calculated to render the man of her choice happy than Miss Emma Hale, a young lady whom he had been extremely fond of since his first introduction to her. His father was highly pleased with Joseph's choice, and told him that he was not only willing that he should marry her but desired him to bring her home with him, that we might have the pleasure of her society.

Since Mr. Smith was going to Mr. Stowell's and Mr. Knight's to get the money to bring up the arrearages on the farm, Joseph concluded to set off with him as soon as the necessary preparations could be made.

NOTES

1. Probably Joseph did not mingle with other churches at this time, in response to these two statements from the First Vision: "I was expressly commanded 'to go not after them,' at the same time receiving a promise that the fullness of the Gospel should at some future time be made known unto me" (*History of the Church* 4:536). Also, "I asked the Personages who stood above me in the light, which of all the sects was right . . . and which I should join. I was answered that I must join none of them, for they were all wrong. . . . He [the Personage who addressed Joseph] again forbade me to join with any of them." (Joseph Smith—History 1:18–19, 20.)

2. Joseph the Prophet would later state: "Could you gaze into heaven five minutes, you would know more than you would by reading all that ever was written on the subject" (*History of the Church* 6:50).

3. In all former versions of this work, Lucy's story of Joseph's 1824 visit to the Hill Cumorah has been placed before the death of Alvin. This was because Lucy's account of his death was recorded as November 19, 1824, rather than the correct year of 1823. In this version the accounts have been placed in their proper chronological order.

4. Catharine (or Katharine) Smith Salisbury (Joseph's younger sister) spoke of this time: "I well remember the trials my brother had, before he obtained the records. After he had the vision, he went frequently to the hill, and upon returning would tell us, 'I have seen the records, also the brass plates and the sword of Laban with the breast plate and interpreters.' He would ask father why he could not get them. The time had not yet come." (In Backman, *Eyewitness Accounts*, p. 53.)

5. Preston Nibley wrote of this: "There is something pathetic in the publication of this 'notice' by Father Smith. It is evident that various unfounded and harmful rumors were being circulated in the neighborhood regarding the Smith family, probably directed against Joseph, Jr., who had related the story of his visions. Then the rumors grew, and some uninspired yokel put out the story that Father Smith had allowed certain physicians to remove Alvin's body from its grave to be dissected. Father Smith's prompt denial and publication of the notice effectually put an end to these rumors." (In Lucy Mack Smith, *History of Joseph Smith by His Mother*, ed. Preston Nibley [Salt Lake City: Bookcraft, 1954], p. 332.)

6. It appears that the Lord was preparing not only Joseph to receive the record but the whole Smith family as well; for all would face severe trials from the world for their support of Joseph.

7. Josiah Stowell was born at Winchester, New Hampshire (just twenty-three miles south of where Lucy Mack Smith was born), in 1770. Josiah's last name has also been spelled Stoal and Stowel.

8. It is well to note that Joseph was, of course, on the Hill Cumorah, September 22, 1825. Joseph recorded in his history: "In the month of October, 1825, I hired with an old gentleman by name of Josiah Stowel" (*History of the Church* 1:17). At this time, the Smith family house had been under construction for three years, and Joseph first became acquainted with Emma Hale; that is, in late fall 1825.

9. Joseph Knight Sr. was born in 1772 at Oakham, Massachusetts. He married Polly Peck about 1795 and moved in 1810 to a farm at Colesville, Broome County, New York, where he and his family remained for nineteen years. (See *Papers*, p. 496.) Joseph and Polly had seven children, including Newel and Joseph Jr. The Knight family would play a critical role in the Restoration by helping provide the means for Joseph to translate the Book of Mormon and being a constant support to him throughout his life.

10. Emma Hale was born July 10, 1804 (she was seventeen months older than Joseph), in Harmony, Susquehanna County, Pennsylvania. Isaac and Elizabeth Hale lived in a comfortable home (foundation dimensions are thirty by forty-two feet) with their nine children.

11. Clearly Joseph was trying to help raise the money for the last payment on the farm. Joseph came back to the farm sometime in November 1825.

CHAPTER 21

Evil-designing men purchase deed to Smith property and press for immediate eviction of the Smiths. Mr. Durfee helps them, and they become tenants on their own land. Joseph's and Hyrum's marriages. Three-hour reprimand from Moroni to Joseph. The time is near for the plates to be received.

December 1825 to spring 1827

Immediately after my husband's departure,[1] I set myself to work to put my house in order for the reception of my son's bride. I felt that pride and ambition in doing this that is common to mothers upon such occasions. My oldest son, previous to this, had married a wife[2] that was one of the most excellent of women, and I anticipated as much happiness with my second daughter-in-law, as I had received great pleasure from the society of the first. There was nothing in my heart which could give rise to any forebodings as to an unhappy connection.

One very pleasant afternoon, immediately subsequent to this, being by myself and somewhat at leisure, having just finished arranging my house for the reception of my son and his bride, I looked around me upon the various comforts with which I found myself surrounded and which seemed to surpass our most flattering expectations, and I fell into a very agreeable train of reflections. I poured out my soul to God in thanks and praise for the many blessings which he had conferred upon us as a family. The day was exceeding fine and would of itself have produced fine feelings, but everything seemed to contribute to raise in the heart those soothing and grateful emotions that we all have reason to enjoy when the mind is at rest and the circumstances favorable.

*The comfortable front room in the Smith frame house
was just as son Alvin had desired it to be.*

As I stood musing upon the busy, bustling life we had led, and the apparent prospect of a quiet and comfortable old age, my attention was suddenly attracted across the yard to a trio of strangers who were entering. Upon their nearer approach, I recognized Mr. Stoddard, the man who took charge of building the house that we now occupied. When they entered, I seated them and we commenced commonplace conversation, but one of them soon began to ask impertinent questions as to our making the last payment on the place and if we did not want to sell the house; where Mr. Smith and my son had gone; etc., etc.

"Sell the house?" I replied. "No, sir, we have no occasion to sell the house. We have made every necessary arrangement for getting the deed and have an understanding with the agent, so we are quite secure about the matter."

To this they made no answer but went out to meet Hyrum, who was then coming in. They propounded the same questions to him and received the same answers. When they had experimented in this way to their satisfaction, they proceeded to inform my son that he need not put himself to any further trouble with regard to the farm, "for," said they, "we have bought the place and paid for it, and we forbid you touching anything on the farm. Moreover, we warn you to leave forthwith and give possession to the lawful owners, as we have got the deed in our possession."

This conversation passed within my hearing. When they reentered the house, I said, "Hyrum, what does this mean? Is this a reality, or is it a sham to startle and deceive me?" One collected look at the men convinced me of their purpose. I was overcome and fell back into a chair, almost deprived of sensibility.

When I recovered, Hyrum and I talked to them at length to reason them out of what they seemed determined to do, namely, to rush us out of our premises straightway into the common air like the beasts of the field or the fowls of heaven, with naught but the earth for a resting place and the canopy of the skies for a covering. But our only answer was, "Well, we've got the place, and d——m you, help yourselves if you can."

Hyrum went straightway to Dr. Robinson, an old friend of ours who lived in Palmyra and a man of influence and notoriety. He told the doctor the whole story. Then this gentleman sat down and wrote the character of my family, our industry and faithful exertions to obtain a home in the forest where we had settled ourselves, with many commendations calculated to beget confidence in us as to business transactions. This writing he took in his own hands and went through the village, and in an hour there was attached to the paper the names of sixty subscribers. He then sent the same by the hand of Hyrum to the land agent in Canandaigua.

The agent was enraged when he found out the facts of the case. He said that the men told him that Mr. Smith and his son Joseph had run away and that Hyrum was cutting down the sugar orchard, hauling off the rails, burning them, and doing all possible manner of mischief to everything on the farm. Believing this, he had sold them the place, got his money, and given them a deed to the premises.

Hyrum related the circumstances under which his father and brother had left home and also informed him that there was a probability of their being detained on the road on business. Hearing this, the agent directed him to write to his father by the first mail and have letters deposited in every public house on the road which Mr. Smith traveled. It might be that some of these letters would meet his eye and cause him to return more speedily than he otherwise would.

The agent then dispatched a messenger to bring the men who had taken the deed of our farm, in order to make some compromise with them and, if possible, get them to relinquish their claim on the place. But they refused to come. The agent then sent another message to them, that if they did not make their appearance forthwith, he would fetch them with a warrant. To this they gave heed, and they came without delay.

The agent used all the persuasion possible to convince them of the unjust, impolitic, and disgraceful measures which they had taken and urged them to retract from what they had done and let the land go back into Mr. Smith's hands. But they were for a long time inexorable, answering every argument with taunting sneers like the following, "We've got the land, sir, and we have got the deed, so just let Smith help himself. Oh, no matter about Smith. He has gold plates, gold money; he's rich. He don't want anything." At length, however, they agreed that if Hyrum could raise one thousand dollars by Saturday at ten o'clock in the evening, they would give up the deed.

It was now Thursday near noon, and Hyrum was at Canandaigua, which was nine miles distant from home, and hither he must ride before he could make the first move towards raising the required amount. He came home with a heavy heart, supposing it impossible to effect anything towards redeeming the land, but when he arrived there he found his father, who had found one of the letters within fifty miles of home.

The next day Mr. Smith requested me to go to an old gentleman who was a Quaker, a man with whom we had been intimate since our first commencement on the farm now in question, and who always admired the neatness and arrangement of the same. He had manifested a great friendship for us from our first acquaintance with him. We hoped that he would be able to furnish the requisite sum to purchase the place, that we might reap the benefit, at least, of the crops which were then sown on the farm. But in this we were disappointed, not in his will or disposition, but in his ability. This man had just paid out to the land agent all the money he could spare, within five dollars of his last farthing, in order to redeem a piece of land belonging to a friend in his immediate neighborhood. Had I arrived at his house thirty minutes earlier, I would have found him with fifteen hundred dollars in his pocket.

When I told him what had occurred, he was much distressed for us and regretted having no means of relieving our necessity. He said, however, "If I have no money, I will try to do something for you. So, Mrs. Smith, say to your husband that I will see him as soon as I can and let him know what the prospects are."

It was near nightfall, the country new, and my road lay through a dense forest. I had ten miles to ride alone; however, I hastened to inform my husband of the disappointment.

The old gentleman, as soon as I left, started in search of someone who could afford us assistance, and hearing of a Mr. Durfee, who lived four miles distant, he came the same night, and directed us to go and see what he could devise for our benefit.

Mr. Smith went immediately and found Mr. Durfee still in his bed, as it was not light. He sent Mr. Smith still three miles further to his son, who was a high sheriff, and bid him say to the young man that his father wished to see him as soon as possible. Mr. Durfee, the younger, came without delay. After breakfasting, the three preceded together to the farm. It was now Saturday at ten o'clock a.m. They tarried a short time, and then rode on to meet the agent and our competitors.

What I felt and suffered in that short day no one can imagine who has not experienced the same. I did not feel our early losses so much, for I realized that we were young and might by exertion better our situation. I, furthermore, had not felt the inconvenience of poverty so much as I had now done and consequently did not appreciate justly the value of property.[3] I looked upon the proceeds of our industry, which smiled on every side of me, with a yearning attachment that I had never felt before.

Mr. Smith and the Messrs. Durfee arrived at Canandaigua at half past nine o'clock in the evening. The agent immediately sent for Mr. Stoddard and his friends, who, when they came, averred that the clock was too slow, that it was really past ten. However, being overcome in this, they received the money and gave up the deed to Mr. Durfee, the high sheriff, who now came into possession of the farm.

With this gentleman, we were now renters.[4] Mr. Durfee gave us the privilege of the place for one year with this provision—that Samuel, our fourth son, was to labor for him six months.[5] These things were all settled upon with the conclusion that if after we had kept the place in this way one year, we chose to remain, we still could have the privilege.

Now Joseph, who had returned from his journey with his father, began to turn his mind again to what had occupied his attention previous to our disaster. He set out for Pennsylvania a second time and had such fine success that in January he returned in fine health and spirits.[6]

Soon after this, Mr. Smith had occasion to send Joseph to Manchester on business. He set out in good time, and we expected him to be home as soon as six o'clock in the evening, but he did not arrive. We had always had a peculiar anxiety about this child, for it seemed as though something was always occurring to place his life in jeopardy, and if he was absent one-half an hour longer than expected, we were apprehensive of some evil befalling him.

It is true he was now a man, grown and capable of using sufficient judgment to keep out of common difficulties.[7] But we were now aware that God intended him for a good and an important work; consequently we expected that the powers of darkness would strive against him more than any other, on this account, to overthrow him.

But to return to the circumstances which I commenced relating. He did not return home until the night was considerably advanced. When he entered the house, he threw himself into a chair, seemingly much exhausted. He was pale as ashes. His father exclaimed, "Joseph, why have you stayed so late? Has anything happened to you? We have been in distress about you these three hours."

As Joseph made no answer, he continued his interrogations, until finally I said, "Now, Father, let him rest a moment—don't trouble him now—you see he is home safe, and he is very tired, so pray wait a little."

The fact was, I had learned to be a little cautious about matters with regard to Joseph, for I was accustomed to see him look as he did on that occasion, and I could not easily mistake the cause thereof.

After Joseph recovered himself a little, he said, "Father, I have had the severest chastisement that I ever had in my life."

My husband, supposing that it was from some of the neighbors, was quite angry and observed, "Chastisement indeed! Well, upon my word, I would like to know who has been taking you to task and what their pretext was. I would like to know what business anybody has to find fault with you."

Joseph smiled to see his father so hasty and indignant. "Father," said he, "it was the angel of the Lord. He says I have been negligent, that the time has now come when the record should be brought forth, and that I must be up and doing, that I must set myself about the things which God has commanded me to do.[8] But, Father, give yourself no uneasiness as to this reprimand, for I know what course I am to pursue, and all will be well."

It was also made known to him, at this interview, that he should make another effort to obtain the plates, on the twenty-second of the following September, but this he did not mention to us at that time.[9]

NOTES

1. December 1825.

2. Hyrum was married to Jerusha Barden on November 2, 1826. It appears that the chronology of events here is not correct inasmuch as Mother Smith's description of the problems with the farm which follows took place in December 1825.

3. Crossed out in the Preliminary Manuscript is this comment of Lucy's: "But at this time I now felt that all must go at one fell swoop if this last resort failed, and we be left in the decline of life destitute, a burden upon our children's hands."

4. In the Preliminary Manuscript, Lucy crossed out the following ending to this sentence: "upon premises which one week before we considered ourselves as much the entire possessors as did Adam and Eve the Garden of Eden before Satan entered it."

5. It appears that they would have the right to stay on the farm from December 1825 to December 1826. Samuel was seventeen years old, then turned eighteen, during the six-month indenture.

6. This likely marks the marriage of Joseph and Emma. Joseph had worked either for Josiah Stowell or for the Joseph Knight family through most of the year 1826 and often went to visit Emma in Harmony. He returned to Manchester to meet the requirements for his annual visit to the Hill Cumorah on September 22, 1826. It appears that after his visit he returned immediately to the Knights' and may have even missed Hyrum's November 2 wedding. (See Bushman, *Beginnings*, p. 76.)

Joseph Knight helped in the courtship of Joseph and Emma. He recorded: "I paid him the money and I furnished him with a horse and cutter [sled] to go and see his girl" (quoted in William G. Hartley, "The Knight Family: Ever Faithful to the Prophet," *Ensign*, January 1989, p. 44). In January 1827, Emma came on a visit to the Stowells' home some twenty-five miles from Harmony. As she later recounted to her eldest son: "I had no intention of marrying when I left home; but during my visit at Mr. Stowell's, your father visited me there. My folks were bitterly opposed to him; and being importuned by your father, aided by Mr. Stowell, who urged me to marry him, and preferring to marry him to any other man I knew, I consented." (Quoted in Bushman, *Beginnings*, p. 77.) Joseph and Emma were married on January 18, 1827, in South Bainbridge (now Afton), Chenango County, New York. Joseph was twenty-one and Emma was twenty-two.

7. Joseph was twenty-one years old at this time.

8. This marked the ninth visit of Moroni to Joseph (of which we have record) and probably occurred in the late winter or early spring of 1827.

9. Joseph was told he could obtain the plates on September 22, 1827.

CHAPTER 22

Joseph Knight and Josiah Stowell arrive at the Smith home on September 20, 1827. Joseph and Emma go to the Hill Cumorah. Joseph receives the plates from the angel Moroni. Description of the Urim and Thummim. Money diggers gather and by evil means conjure to find the gold plates. Joseph hides the plates in an old birch log. Joseph brings the plates home and is accosted by three men. Admonition of Moroni to Joseph.

September 1827

On the twentieth of September[1] Mr. Knight came with his friend Mr. Stowell to see how we were managing matters with Mr. Stoddard and company. They remained with us until the twenty-second. On the night of the twenty-first, I sat up very late, as my business pressed upon my hands, and I did not retire until past twelve. About twelve o'clock, Joseph came to me and asked me if I had a chest with a lock and key. I knew in a moment what he wanted it for and was alarmed,[2] fearing that this might be a matter of great importance to him at that time. But Joseph replied, "Never mind, I can do very well just now without it. Be calm. All is right." But I found it very difficult to do so, for I had not forgotten the first failure.

Shortly after this, Joseph's wife passed through the room with her bonnet and riding dress; and in a few minutes they left together, taking Mr. Knight's horse and wagon.[3] I spent the night in prayer and supplication to God, for the anxiety of my mind would not permit me to sleep. At a reasonable time for rising, I went to preparing breakfast, my

*Pantry in the Smiths' Manchester frame house,
with period utensils, crockery, and implements.*

heart fluttering at every footfall, for I now expected Joseph and Emma every moment and was in dread of a second disappointment in his obtaining the plates.

When the male part of the family sat down to breakfast, Mr. Smith inquired for Joseph (as no one knew where he had gone but myself). I told him that I thought I would not call Joseph, for I would like to have him take breakfast with his wife that morning.

"No, no," said my husband. "I must have Joseph come and eat with me."

"Well, now, Mr. Smith," said I, "do let him eat with his wife *this morning.* He almost always takes breakfast with you. Just indulge him a little this time."

His father finally consented to eat without him, and I thought that there would be no danger of any further inquiry as to the cause of Joseph's absence, but in a few minutes Mr. Knight came in quite disturbed.

"Why, Mr. Smith," said he, "my horse is gone. I can't find him on the premises and I want to start home in half an hour."

"Never mind the horse," said I. "Mr. Knight does not know all the nooks and corners in the pasture. I will call William;[4] he will soon bring the horse."

This satisfied him for a little while, but he soon made another discovery. His wagon also was gone, and now he concluded that some rogue had stolen them both.

"Well, now," said I, "do be quiet. I would be ashamed to have you go about gearing your own horse and waiting upon yourself. Just go out and talk with Mr. Smith till William comes. If you really must go home, you shall be attended upon like a gentleman." He went, and while he was absent, Joseph returned.[5]

I trembled so much with fear lest all might be lost again by some small failure in keeping the commandments, that I was under the necessity of leaving the room to conceal my feelings. Joseph saw this and followed me. "Mother," said he. "Do not be uneasy. All is right. See here," said he, "I have got the key."

I knew not what he meant, but took the article in my hands and, examining it with no covering but a silk handkerchief, found that it consisted of two smooth three-cornered diamonds set in glass, and the glasses were set in silver bows connected with each other in much the same way that old-fashioned spectacles are made. He took them again and left me, but did not tell me anything of the record.[6]

Soon after he came again and asked my advice what was best to do about getting a chest made. I told him to go to a cabinetmaker who had been making some furniture for my oldest daughter,[7] and tell the man we would pay him for making a chest as we did for the other things he had made for us, namely one-half in cash and one-half in produce.

Joseph said that he would, but that he did not know where the money would come from, for there was not a shilling in the house.[8]

In one of the bedrooms in this home, the Prophet informed Joseph Knight of his obtaining the plates.

The next day Mr. Warner came to him from Macedon and requested Joseph to go with him to a widow's house in Macedon. The widow, by the name of Wells, wanted a wall of a well taken up, and she would pay Joseph money for the labor. As this afforded us an opportunity to pay the cabinetmaker for the chest, Joseph accompanied Mr. Warner to Macedon according to Mrs. Wells's request. Since this woman had never seen one of the family before, but had sent purposely for Joseph, we considered it a provision of Providence to enable us to pay the money we were owing the cabinetmaker.

Joseph had been absent but a little while when one of the neighbors began to ask Mr. Smith many questions about the plates. Here let me mention that no one knew anything of them from us except one of my husband's confidential friends to whom he had spoken of them some two or three years before.[9] It now seemed that Satan had stirred up the hearts of those who had in any way gotten a hint of the matter, to search into it and make every possible move towards preventing the work.[10]

Mr. Smith was soon informed that ten or twelve men were clubbed together, with one Willard Chase, a Methodist class leader, at their head, and what was more ridiculous, they had sent some sixty miles for a conjuror to come to divine by magic art the place where the record was deposited.

We supposed that Joseph had taken the plates and secreted them somewhere, and we were somewhat uneasy lest they might be discovered by our enemies. Accordingly, the morning after we heard of their plans, Mr. Smith went over a hill which lay east of us to see what he could discover among the neighbors. At the first house he came to, he found the conjuror and Willard Chase, together with the company. This was the house of one Mr. Lawrence.[11] Making an errand, he went in and sat down near the door, leaving it ajar, for the men were so near that he could overhear their conversation. They stood in the yard near the door and were devising many plans and schemes to find "Joe Smith's gold bible," as they termed it. The conjuror was really animated, although he had traveled sixty miles during the latter part of the day and the night before.

Presently, the woman of the house became uneasy at the exposures they were making. She stepped through a back door into the yard and called to her husband in a suppressed voice (but so loud that Mr. Smith heard every word distinctly). "Sam, Sam," said she. "You are cutting your own throat." At this, the conjuror bawled out at the top of his voice, "I am not afraid of anybody. We will have the plates in spite of Joe Smith or all the devils in hell."

When the woman came in again, Mr. Smith laid aside a paper which he had been holding in his hand with the pretense of reading, and coolly remarked that he believed he could not then finish the article which he was reading. He then left the house, and returned home.

Mr. Smith, on returning home, asked Emma if she knew anything of the record—whether Joseph had taken them out of their place of deposit or where they were. She said she did not know. My husband then related what he had both seen and heard.

Upon this, Emma said that she did not know what to do, but she thought if Joseph was to have the record, he *would* get it, and that they would not be able to prevent him.

"Yes," said Mr. Smith, "he will, if he is watchful and obedient; but remember that for a small thing Esau lost his birthright and blessing. It may be so with Joseph."

"Well," said Emma, "if I had a horse I would go and see him."

Mr. Smith said she should have one in fifteen minutes, for although his team was gone, there had been a stray horse on the premises for two days. So he sent William immediately for the horse.

In a few minutes William brought the horse with a large hickory withe around his neck (as it was according to law to put a withe round the neck of a stray horse before turning him into an enclosure), and Emma was soon on her way to her husband.

Joseph kept the Urim and Thummim constantly about his person, by the use of which he could in a moment tell whether the plates were in any danger. Having just looked into them before Emma got there, he perceived her coming, came up out of the well, and met her. When she informed him of what had occurred, he told her that the record was perfectly safe, for the present; nevertheless, he concluded to return with his wife, as something might take place that would render it necessary for him to be at home where he could take care of it.[12]

He went immediately to Mrs. Wells and told her that he must return home to attend to some important business. She was not willing for him to leave, but upon his promising to come back when he was at liberty again, she consented. She sent a boy to bring him a horse, which he mounted in his linen frock, with his wife by his side on her horse, decorated as before with a green hickory withe on his neck. And thus they rode through the village of Palmyra.

When he came, he met his father about a mile from the house pacing back and forth in great anxiety of mind. "Father," said Joseph, "there is no danger. All is perfectly safe. There is no cause of alarm."

When he had refreshed himself a little, he sent Carlos, my youngest son, to his brother Hyrum's to ask him to come up immediately, as he wished to see him.[13] When Hyrum came, Joseph requested him to get a chest that had a good lock and key and, "Have it here," said Joseph, "so that it may be ready by the time I get home."

The plates were secreted about three miles from home in the following manner: Finding an old birch log much decayed, excepting the bark, which was in a measure sound, he took his pocketknife and cut

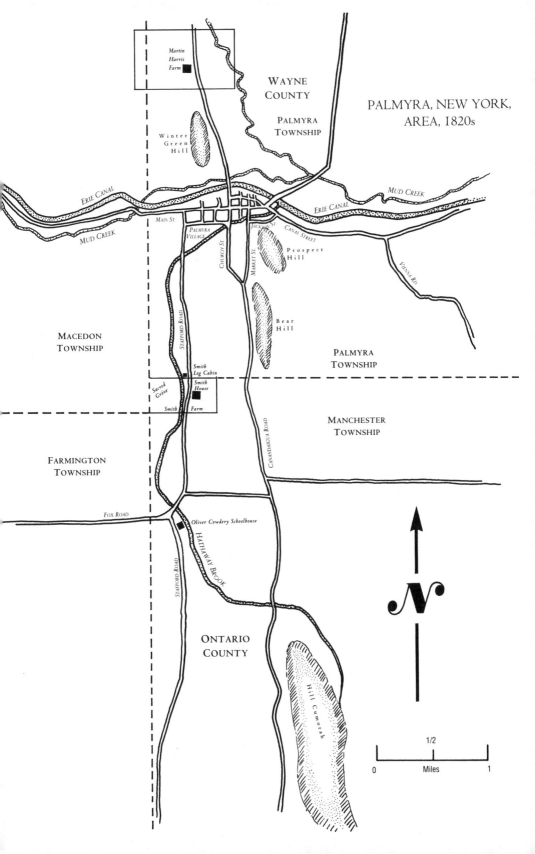

the bark with some care, then turned it back and made a hole of sufficient size to receive the plates, and laying them in the cavity thus formed, he replaced the bark; after which he laid across the log in several places some old stuff that happened to lie near, in order to conceal, as much as possible, the place in which they were deposited.

Joseph took the plates from their place and, wrapping them in his linen frock, put them under his arm and started for the house. After walking a short distance in the road, he thought it would be safer to go across through the woods. Traveling some distance after he left the road, he came to a large windfall, and as he was jumping over a log, a man sprang up from behind and gave him a heavy blow with a gun. Joseph turned around and knocked him to the ground, and then ran at the top of his speed. About half a mile further, he was attacked again in precisely the same way. He soon brought this one down also and ran on again, but before he got home, he was accosted the third time with a severe stroke with a gun. When he struck the last one, he dislocated his thumb, which, however, he did not notice till he came in sight of the house. He threw himself down in the corner of the fence to recover his breath. As soon as he was able, he rose and finished his race for the house, where he arrived altogether speechless from fright and exhaustion.[14]

After a moment's rest, he said, "Mother, send Carlos for Father and Mr. Knight and his friend Stowell, and tell them to go and see if they can find some men who have been pursuing me. Then let Carlos go tell Hyrum to bring his chest."

When Carlos went into Hyrum's house, he found him at tea with two of his wife's sisters. Carlos touched his brother's shoulder just as he was raising his cup to his mouth. Without waiting to hear a word of the child's errand, Hyrum dropped his cup, sprang from the table, fetched up the chest, turned it upside down, and, leaving the contents on the floor, left the house in an instant with the chest on his shoulder.

The young ladies were much surprised at his singular behavior and protested to his wife (who was bedfast, her oldest daughter, Lovina, being but four days)[15] that her husband was positively crazy. She laughed heartily, "Oh, not in the least. He has just thought of something that he has neglected, and it's just like him to fly off on a tangent when he thinks of anything that way."

When the chest came, Joseph locked up the record and threw himself on the bed. After resting himself a little so that he could converse, he went out and related his adventure to his father, Mr. Knight, Mr. Stowell, and others, who had come back from their scouting expedition without seeing anyone. He showed them his thumb, saying, "I must stop talking, Father, and get you to put my thumb in place, for it is very painful."

When this was done, he related to our guests the whole history of the record, which interested them very much. They listened and believed all that was told them.

When Joseph first took the plates into his hands, the angel of the Lord stood by and said:

"Now you have got the record into your own hands, and you are but a man, therefore you will have to be watchful and faithful to your trust, or you will be overpowered by wicked men, for they will lay every plan and scheme that is possible to get them away from you. And if you do not take heed continually, they will succeed. While they were in my hands I could keep them, and no man had power to take them away, but now I give them up to you. Beware, and look well to your ways, and you shall have power to retain them until the time for them to be translated."

That of which I spoke, which Joseph termed a key, was indeed nothing more nor less than a Urim and Thummim by which the angel manifested those things to him that were shown him in vision; by which also he could at any time ascertain the approach of danger, either to himself or the record, and for this cause he kept these things constantly about his person.

NOTES

1. It appears that Josiah Stowell and Joseph Knight were aware of the date when Joseph would be able to receive the plates. Joseph Knight Jr. recorded that in November 1826 Joseph Smith "made known to us that he had seen a vision, that a personage had appeared to him, and told him where there was a gold book of ancient

date buried, and that if he would follow the direction of the Angel, he could get it. We were told this in secret." (Quoted in William G. Hartley, "The Knight Family: Ever Faithful to the Prophet," *Ensign*, January 1989, p. 44.)

2. In the Preliminary Manuscript the following phrase of Lucy's is crossed out: "frightened for the issue, as I had broken every lock in the house in moving."

3. It must be noted here that Joseph Smith Jr. and Joseph Knight Sr. had known each other and worked closely together for nearly two years by this time.

4. William was sixteen years old.

5. Heber C. Kimball, who at this time lived just eighteen miles from the Smiths and was as yet unaware of the Restoration, later recorded: "I had retired to bed, when John P. Greene, who was living within a hundred steps of my house, came and waked me up, calling upon me to come out and behold the scenery in the heavens. I woke up and called my wife [Vilate] and Sister Fanny Young [sister to Brigham], who was living with us, and we went out-of-doors.

"It was one of the most beautiful starlight nights, so clear that we could see to pick up a pin. We looked to the eastern horizon, and beheld a white smoke arise toward the heavens; as it ascended it formed itself into a belt, and made a noise like the sound of a mighty wind, and continued southwest, forming a regular bow dipping in the western horizon. After the bow had formed, it began to widen out and grow clear and transparent, of a bluish cast; it grew wide enough to contain twelve men abreast.

"In this bow an army moved, commencing from the east and marching to the west; they continued marching until they reached the western horizon. They moved in platoons, and walked so close that the rear ranks trod in the steps of their file leaders, until the whole bow was literally crowded with soldiers. We could distinctly see the muskets, bayonets and knapsacks of the men, who wore caps and feathers like those used by the American soldiers in the last war with Britain; and also saw their officers with their swords and equipage, and the clashing and jingling of their implements of war, and could discover the forms and features of the men. The most profound order existed throughout the entire army; when the foremost man stepped, every man stepped at the same time; I could hear the steps. When the front rank reached the western horizon a battle ensued, as we could distinctly hear the report of arms and the rush.

"No man could judge of my feelings when I beheld that army of men, as plainly as ever I saw armies of men in the flesh; it seemed as though every hair of my head was alive. This scenery we gazed upon for hours, until it began to disappear.

"After I became acquainted with Mormonism, I learned that this took place the same evening that Joseph Smith received the records of the Book of Mormon from the angel Moroni." (Quoted in Orson F. Whitney, *Life of Heber C. Kimball*, Collector's Edition [Salt Lake City: Bookcraft, 1992], pp. 15–17.)

6. Joseph Knight recorded: "[In] the forepart of September [1827], I went to Rochester on business and returned by Palmyra to be there by the 22nd of September. I was there several days. . . . That night we went to bed and in the morning I got up and my horse and carriage were gone. . . . After a while he [Joseph Smith] came home [with] the horse. All came into the house to breakfast but nothing [was]

said about where they had been. After breakfast Joseph called me into the other room. . . . He set his foot on the bed, leaned his head on his hand and said, . . . 'It is ten times better than I expected.' Then he went on to tell length and width and thickness of the plates; and said he, 'They appear to be gold.' But he seemed to think more of the glasses or the Urim and Thummim than he did of the plates, for, said he, 'I can see anything; they are marvellous. Now they are written in characters and I want them translated.'" (In Backman, *Eyewitness Accounts*, p. 72.)

7. The oldest daughter was Sophronia, who was twenty-four years old at this time and would marry Calvin Stoddard in a little over two months—on December 2, 1827.

8. This shows the destitute circumstances of the Smiths and emphasizes Joseph's words about himself, "one, too, who was doomed to the necessity of obtaining a scanty maintenance by his daily labor" (Joseph Smith—History 1:23).

9. This confidential friend was Martin Harris, a respected and well-to-do farmer of Palmyra. Martin Harris was born on May 18, 1783, in Easttown, Saratoga County, New York.

10. Because of Joseph's involvement with the Josiah Stowell affair near Harmony (in digging for buried treasure or a silver mine), it appears that those who worked with Joseph may have felt that any of the group who found buried treasure (including Joseph) would share it equally with the others. Martin Harris stated: "The money-diggers claimed that they had as much right to the plates as Joseph had, as they were in company together. They claimed that Joseph had been traitor, and had appropriated to himself that which belonged to them. For this reason Joseph was afraid of them, and continued concealing the plates." (Quoted in Porter, "Origins," pp. 81–82.)

11. This was one Samuel Lawrence, "a neighbor who had pretensions to seership and knew about the plates and the annual visits." Apparently Lawrence was one of the local "money-diggers." (Bushman, *Beginnings*, pp. 81, 216.)

12. The 1853 edition of Lucy Mack Smith's history gives a slightly different account of the order of events, reading: "Just before Emma rode up to Mrs. Wells, Joseph, from an impression that he had had, came up out of the well in which he was laboring, and met her not far from the house. Emma immediately informed him of what had transpired, whereupon he looked in the Urim and Thummim, and saw that the Record was as yet safe." (*Biographical Sketches*, pp. 103–4.)

13. Don Carlos was at this time eleven years old.

14. Martin Harris estimated the weight of the plates at between forty and fifty pounds. William Smith, who was once allowed to heft the plates while they were covered by a pillowcase, estimated the weight at sixty pounds (see Backman, *Eyewitness Accounts*, p. 70). It is interesting to note the weight of the plates and observe the physical strength of Joseph running three miles with them under his arm.

15. Lucy stated here that Lovina was but four days old. In fact, since her date of birth was September 16, 1827, she must have been older at the time of this event. It was clearly at least one or two days after Joseph had obtained the plates on September 22, 1827.

CHAPTER 23

Detailed description of the breastplate. Mob action. Hiding the plates under the hearthstone in the house and then in the cooper's shop. Martin Harris involves himself in the work. Dealing with Lucy Harris. Lucy Harris's remarkable dream. Joseph and Emma move to Harmony, Pennsylvania. Martin and Lucy Harris visit soon thereafter. Lucy Harris actively tries to destroy Joseph's reputation.

End of September 1827 to March 1828

After bringing home the plates, Joseph now commenced work with his father on the farm in order to be as near as possible the treasure that was committed to his care.[1]

Soon after this, he came in from work one afternoon, and after remaining a short time, he put on his greatcoat and left the house. I was engaged at the time in an upper room in preparing some oilcloths for painting. When he returned, he requested me to come downstairs. I told him that I could not leave my work just then, yet upon his urgent request, I finally concluded to go down and see what he wanted, upon which he handed me the breastplate spoken of in his history.

It was wrapped in a thin muslin handkerchief, so thin that I could see the glistening metal and ascertain its proportions without any difficulty.

It was concave on one side and convex on the other, and extended from the neck downwards as far as the center of the stomach of a man of extraordinary size. It had four straps of the same material for the purpose of fastening it to the breast, two of which ran back to go over the shoulders, and the other two were designed to fasten to the hips. They were just the width of two of my fingers (for I measured them), and they had holes in the end of them to be convenient in fastening.

The whole plate was worth at least five hundred dollars. After I had examined it, Joseph placed it in the chest with the Urim and Thummim.

Shortly after this circumstance, Joseph came to the house in great haste and inquired if there had been a company of men there. I told him no one had come to the house since he left. He then said that a mob would be there that night, if not before, to search for the record, and that it must be removed immediately.

Soon after, one Mr. Braman came from the neighboring village of Livonia, a German man in whom we reposed much confidence and who was well worthy of the same. Joseph told him his apprehensions of a mob being there that night and that they must prepare themselves to drive them away; but the first thing to be attended to was to secrete the record and breastplate.

It was resolved that a portion of the hearth should be taken up and the plates and breastplate should be buried under the same, and then the hearth relaid to prevent suspicion.

This was carefully and speedily done, but the hearth was scarcely relaid when a large company of armed men came rushing up to the house. Joseph threw the door open and, taking a hint from the stratagem of his Grandfather Mack, hallooed as if he had a legion at hand, giving the word of command with great importance. At the same time, the males that belonged to the house, from the father down to little Carlos,[2] ran out with such vehemence upon the mob that it struck them with terror and dismay, and they fled before our little Spartan band away into the woods, where they dispersed themselves to their several homes.

We had but a few days rest, however, before Joseph received another intimation of the approach of a mob and the necessity of removing the record and breastplate again from their hiding place. Consequently, Joseph took them out of the box in which they had been placed, wrapped them in clothes, carried them across the road to a cooper's shop, and laid them in a quantity of flax which was stowed in the shop loft. He then nailed up the box as before and tore up the floor and put the box under it.

*The ancient record and breastplate were hidden
under one of the hearthstones in the Smith home.*

As soon as it was dark, the mob came and ransacked the place, but did not come into the house. After making a satisfactory search, they went away.

The next morning we found the floor of the cooper's shop taken up and the wooden box which was put under it split to pieces.

In a few days we learned the cause of this last move and why their curiosity had led them in the direction of the cooper's shop. A young woman, who was a sister to Willard Chase, had found a green glass through which she could see many wonderful things, and among the rest of her discoveries, she said she had found out the exact place where

"Joe Smith kept his gold bible." And so in pursuance to her directions, they gathered their forces and laid siege to the cooper shop, but went away disappointed.

This did not shake their confidence in Miss Chase, for they still went from place to place by her suggestion, determined to get possession of the object of their research.[3]

Not long after the circumstance of the mob's going into the cooper's shop, Joseph began to take some measures to accomplish the translation of the record into English. The first step that he was instructed to take in regard to this work was to make a facsimile of the characters composing the alphabet, which were called reformed Egyptian, and send them to all the most learned men of this generation and ask them for the translation of the same.[4]

Joseph was very solicitous about the work, but as yet no means had come into his hands of accomplishing it.

The reader will notice that on a preceding page of this book, I spoke of a confidential friend to whom Mr. Smith mentioned the existence of the record two or three years before it came forth. This was no other than Martin Harris, one of the witnesses to the Book of Mormon after it was translated.

To him Joseph desired me to go one afternoon, as he wished to see him. But this was an errand that I somewhat disliked, for his wife was a peculiar sort of a woman, one that was habitually of a very jealous temperament, and being hard of hearing, she was always suspicious that it was some secret which was designedly kept from her. So I told Joseph that I would rather not go, unless I could approach her upon the subject before I spoke to him about it. Joseph consented to this, and I went according to his request.

When I arrived there, I carefully detailed the particulars of Joseph's finding the record, as far as wisdom dictated and necessity demanded, in order to satisfy Mrs. Harris's mind, but she did not wait for me to get through with my story till she commenced urging me to receive a considerable amount of money, which she had at her own command, a kind of private purse which her husband permitted her to keep to satisfy her peculiar disposition. She also had a sister living in the house who was extremely anxious to help to the amount of seventy-five dollars to get the record translated.

I told her I came on no such business, that I did not want her money, and that Joseph would attend to his own affairs; but I would like to speak with Mr. Harris for a moment and then I would return home, as my family would soon be expecting me back. Notwithstanding all this, she said that she was determined to assist in the business, for she knew that he would want money and she could spare two hundred as well as not.

After detaining me a few minutes, finally she went with me to her husband and told him I wanted to speak to him. He said he wasn't going to stop his work, for, he said, "I am now just laying the last brick of this hearth."

"You see," said he, "this is the last work that I have to do for one year on the house or about the house or on the farm, and when this is done, I am going to hire a hand to work a year for me, as I shall travel twelve months before I settle myself at home again."

He soon left, and after being gone a short time, he came and told me that he was now a free man, his hands were altogether untied to go and come and do as he pleased.

I told him, in short, the errand on which I had come. He said that he would see Joseph in a few days. At this his wife exclaimed, "Yes, and I am coming to see him, too, and I will be there Tuesday afternoon and will stop overnight."

Accordingly, when Tuesday afternoon arrived, Mrs. Harris made her appearance. As soon as she came in and was well seated, she began to importune my son as to the truth of what he said concerning the record, declaring that if he really had any gold plates, she *would* see them and she was resolved to help him in publishing them.

He told her that she was mistaken—that she could not see them, as he was not permitted to exhibit them to anyone except those whom the Lord should appoint to testify of them. "And as to assistance," said Joseph, "I always prefer dealing with men, rather than their wives."

This highly displeased Mrs. Harris, for she was a woman who considered herself altogether superior to her husband. "Well, now, Joseph," said she, "are you not telling me a lie? Can you look full in my eye and say before God that you have, in reality, found that record as you pretend?"

He said indifferently, "Why, yes, Mrs. Harris. I would as soon look into your face and say so as not, if you would be at all gratified by it."

"Now, Joseph," said she, "I will tell what I will do. If I can get a witness that you do speak the truth, I will believe it, and I shall want to do something about the translation—and I mean to help you anyway."

This closed the evening's conversation. She went to bed, and in the morning told us a very remarkable dream. She said that a personage had appeared to her the night before and said to her that inasmuch as she had disputed the servant of the Lord, said that his word was not to be believed, and asked him many improper questions, she had done that which was not right in the sight of God. Then he said, "Behold, here are the plates, look upon them and believe."

She then described the record minutely and again said that she had made up her mind as to what she would do; namely, that she had in her possession twenty-eight dollars that her mother had given her just before she died, when she was on her deathbed. Joseph should take that, and if he *would* he might give his note, but he would certainly accept of it on some terms.

This last proposition he acceded to in order to get rid of her importunities.

Shortly after this, Alva Hale, Joseph's brother-in-law, came to our house from Pennsylvania for the purpose of moving my son and his wife to Joseph's father-in-law's house, as word had been sent to them that it was their wish to go there as soon as Joseph could settle up his business in New York. During the short interval of Alva's stay with us, Alva and Joseph were one day in Palmyra at a public house doing some business with the landlord, when Mr. Harris entered the room. Many strangers were present. When he came in, he walked up to my son, gave him his hand, and said, "How do you do, Mr. Smith?" Then, taking a bag of silver from his pocket, he said, "Here, Mr. Smith, is fifty dollars. I give it to you to do the Lord's work with. No," said he, "I give it to the Lord for his own work."

"No," said Joseph. "We will give you a note, and Mr. Hale, I presume, will sign it with me."

"Yes," replied Alva. "I will."

But Mr. Harris persisted that he would give the money to the Lord and called upon all present to witness to the fact that he gave it freely and did not demand any compensation or return for the same, that it was for the purpose of helping Mr. Smith do the Lord's work.

It was soon arranged so that Joseph was ready to set out for Pennsylvania with the breastplate and record. These were securely nailed up in a box and the box put into a strong cask made for the purpose. The cask was then filled with beans and headed up again.

When it became generally known that Joseph was about moving to Pennsylvania, a mob of fifty men collected and went to Dr. McIntyre and requested him to take the command of the company, stating that their object was to "follow Joe Smith and take his gold bible away from him." Dr. McIntyre's ideas and feelings did not altogether harmonize with theirs, and he told them they must be a pack of devilish fools and bid them go home and mind their own business; that if Smith had anything of that sort to attend to, he was capable of doing it, and they would do better to busy themselves about that which concerned them more.

A quarrel then arose as to who should be captain and ran so high that it broke up the expedition.[5]

Joseph started in December for Pennsylvania.[6] It was agreed upon that Martin Harris should follow him as soon as Joseph should have sufficient time to transcribe some of the Egyptian characters. Then Mr. Harris was to take the characters to the East and through the country in every direction, and on his way he was to call on all who were professed linguists to give them an opportunity of showing their talents in giving a translation of the characters.[7]

When Mrs. Harris heard this, she declared her intention of accompanying her husband; but he concluded that it would be better to go without her, and without giving her any intimation of his intention, he left quite suddenly with Hyrum.

Copy of original reformed Egyptian characters taken from the plates and sent to "the learned."

Mrs. Harris soon missed her husband and came to me to find out if I knew where he was. I told her what he had said to me about leaving, suppressing, however, his remarks pertaining to herself.

She was highly enraged and accused me of framing the whole affair. I told her I had nothing to do with the plan, nor the execution of it, but that the business of the house, which was the natural cares of a woman, was all that I attempted to dictate or interfere with, unless by my husband's or son's requests.

Mrs. Harris then said that she had property, and she knew how to take care of it, and she would show me that.

"Now, stop," I replied. "Do you not know that we never asked you for money or property? Had we been disposed to take advantage of your liberality, might we not have gotten possession of at least two hundred and seventy dollars of your money?" She answered in the affirmative, but went home in anger, determined to have satisfaction in some way for the slight which she had received.

When a short space of time had elapsed, Mr. Harris returned, and his wife's anger kindled afresh at her husband's presence, so much so that she prepared a bed and room for him alone, which she refused to enter.

A young man by the name of Dikes had been paying his addresses to Miss Lucy Harris, Martin's oldest daughter.[8] Of this young gentleman the father of the girl was very fond, and the young lady was not at all averse to him. Of course, Mrs. Harris was decidedly upon the negative, but just at this juncture, a scheme entered her brain that changed her deportment to Mr. Dikes very materially. She told Mr. Dikes that if he would contrive to get the Egyptian characters out of Martin's possession, hire a room in Palmyra, transcribe them accurately, and bring her the transcript, she would give him her daughter, Lucy, to wife.

Mr. Dikes readily agreed to this, and suffice it to say, he succeeded to the woman's satisfaction and received the promised reward.

When Mr. Harris began to make preparations to start for Pennsylvania a second time, with the view of writing for Joseph, his wife told him that she fully decreed in her heart to go also.[9] Mr. Harris, having no particular objections, informed her that she might go with him and stay a week or two on a visit, and then he would take her home and go again to do the work of writing the book. She acceded to this very cheerfully, but her husband did not suspect what he was about to encounter. The

*The structure in the center is where Joseph and Emma
were living in Harmony, Pennsylvania.*[10]

first time he exhibited the Egyptian characters, she took out of her
pocket an exact copy of them and informed those present that "Joe
Smith" was not the only one that was in possession of this great curiosity, that she herself had the same characters and they were quite as genuine as those displayed to them by Mr. Harris. This course she continued to pursue wherever she went, until she reached my son's house.

As soon as she arrived there, she said she had come to see the
plates and would never leave until she had accomplished it. Without
delay she began ransacking every nook and corner of the house—

chest, cupboard, trunk, etc.; consequently, Joseph was compelled to take both the breastplate and the record out of the house and secrete them elsewhere. Not finding them in the house, she concluded that Joseph had buried them, and the next day she went out and hunted the ground over, adjacent to the house. She kept up the search till two o'clock in the afternoon, when she came in very ill-natured and, after warming herself a little, enquired of Emma if they had snakes there in the wintertime. "I was walking around in the woods," said she, "to look at the situation of your place, and as I turned round to come home, a tremendous, great black snake stuck up its head before me and commenced hissing at me."

The woman was so disappointed and perplexed in everything she undertook that she left the house and took lodgings at the house of a near neighbor. Here she stated to the hostels that she was in search of the plates, that when she came to a place where she thought they must be buried, upon stooping down to scrape away the snow and leaves in order to examine the spot, she encountered a horrible black snake which frightened her so badly that she ran to the house as fast as possible.

While this woman remained in the neighborhood, she did all that her ingenuity could contrive to injure Joseph in the estimation of his neighbors. She told them that he was a grand imposter, that he had deceived her husband with his specious pretensions and was exerting all his deceptive powers in order to induce Mr. Harris to give his property into Joseph's hands, that he might, by robbing her husband, make himself rich.[11] When she returned home, which was about two weeks from the time she arrived in Harmony, she endeavored to dissuade Mr. Harris from having anything further to do with the writing or translating of the record. But Mr. Harris paid but little attention to her, and as he had agreed to go back and write for a season at least, he did so.

After Mr. Harris left again for Pennsylvania, his wife went from place to place and from house to house, telling her grievances to everyone she met, but particularly bewailing that the deception which Joe Smith was practicing upon the people was about to strip her of all that she possessed. "But," said the woman, "I know how to take care of my property, and I'll let them see that pretty shortly." So she carried away her furniture, linen and bedding, and other movable articles, till she well-nigh divested the premises of everything which could conduce to comfort or convenience. These things she deposited with her friends in whom she reposed sufficient confidence to assure her of the safety of her property.

NOTES

1. Joseph received the plates on Saturday, September 22, 1827, in the early hours before sunrise. He would have begun work on the farm the last week of September and early October 1827.

2. Carlos was eleven and a half years old at the time.

3. Dr. John Stafford spoke of this woman's activities: "The neighbors used to claim Sally Chase could look at a stone she had, and see money. Willard Chase used to dig when she found where the money was. Don't know as anybody ever found any money." (Quoted in Porter, "Origins," p. 81.)

4. Martin Harris was the man who took the facsimile of the characters from the plates to the East in February 1828. His own account states: "I went to the city of New York and presented the characters which had been translated, with the translation thereof, to Professor Charles Anthon, a gentleman celebrated for his literary attainments. Professor Anthon stated that the translation was correct, more so than any he had before seen translated from the Egyptian.

"I then showed him those which were not yet translated, and he said that they were Egyptian, Chaldaic, Assyric, and Arabic, and he said that they were true characters. He gave me a certificate certifying to the people of Palmyra that they were true characters and that the translation of such of them as had been translated was also correct. I took the certificate and put it into my pocket, and was just leaving the house, when Mr. Anthon called me back and asked me how the young man found out that there were gold plates in the place where he found them. I answered that an angel of God had revealed it unto him. He then said to me, 'Let me see that certificate.' I accordingly took it out of my pocket and gave it to him, when he took it and tore it to pieces, saying that there was no such thing now as ministering of angels, and that if I would bring the plates to him, he would translate them. I informed him that part of the plates were sealed, and that I was forbidden to bring them. He replied, 'I cannot read a sealed book.' I left him and went to Dr. Mitchel [Samuel L. Mitchill], who sanctioned what Professor Anthon had said respecting both the characters and the translation." (In *Papers*, pp. 285–86.)

5. Martin Harris reported: "The excitement in the village upon the subject had become such that some had threatened to mob Joseph, and also to tar and feather him. They said he should never leave until he had shown the plates. It was unsafe for him to remain. . . . He wrote to his brother-in-law Alva, requesting him to come for him. I advised Joseph that he must pay all his debts before starting. I paid them for him, and furnished him money for the journey. I advised him to take time enough to get ready so that he might start a day or two in advance: for he would be mobbed if it was known when he started. We put the box of plates in a barrel about one-third full of beans and headed it up. I informed Mr. Hale of the matter, and advised them to cut each a good cudgel [a short, heavy stick to be used as a weapon or club] and put into the wagon with them, which they did. It was understood that they were to start on Monday; but they started on Saturday night and got through safe. This was the last of October, 1827. It might have been the first of November." (Quoted in Porter, "Origins," p. 83.)

6. On this journey of 135 miles, Emma was in the first three months of pregnancy with her and Joseph's first child.

7. In Joseph's 1832 account of this he states: "I obtained the plates and in December following [1827] we moved to Susquehanna by the assistance of a man by the name of Martin Harris, who became convinced of the visions and gave me fifty dollars to bare my expenses. And because of his faith and this righteous deed, the Lord appeared unto him in a vision and showed unto him his marvelous work which he was about to do. And he immediately came to Susquehanna and said the Lord had shown him that he must go to New York City with some of the characters, so we proceeded to copy some of them, and he took his journey to the eastern cities." (*Papers,* p. 9.)

8. Martin and Lucy Harris (his first cousin) had three children: Duty L., George W., and Lucy (see Cook, *Revelations,* p. 9).

9. This is apparently after Martin Harris's February 1828 trip to New York City and likely took place in March 1828.

10. The buildings on the left and right of the small cabin were added after Joseph and Emma had moved from Harmony. The photograph is by George Edward Anderson, 1907, courtesy of Nelson B. Wadsworth.

11. Surely this spreading of lies, exaggerations, and deceits helped lead to the mob action that eventually drove Joseph out of Harmony to finish the translation in Fayette, Seneca County, New York.

CHAPTER 24

Martin Harris pleads with Joseph to take the sacred manuscript to show to his family. The Lord finally consents to let Martin take the 116 pages, with a solemn covenant to show them only to five of his family members. Emma gives birth to a son who soon after dies. Emma's precarious health condition. Joseph leaves for Palmyra to find Martin. A stranger assures Joseph's safe passage home. The "Book of Lehi" manuscript is lost.

April 12, 1828 to mid-July 1828

Martin Harris, having written some one hundred and sixteen pages for Joseph, asked permission of my son to carry the manuscript home with him in order to let his wife read it, as he hoped it might have a salutary effect upon her feelings.[1] He also wanted to show his family what he had been employed in during his absence from them. Joseph was very partial to Mr. Harris, on account of the friendship which he had manifested in an hour when there seemed to be no earthly friend to succor or to sympathize. Still, Joseph, for a long time, resisted every entreaty of this kind.

At last, however, since Joseph felt a great desire to gratify the man's feelings as far as it was justifiable to do so, he inquired of the Lord to know if he might do as Martin Harris had requested, but was refused. With this, Mr. Harris was not altogether satisfied, and, at his urgent request, Joseph inquired again, but received a second refusal. Still, Martin Harris persisted as before, and Joseph applied again, but the last answer was not like the two former ones.[2] In this, the Lord permitted Martin Harris to take the manuscript home with him, on the condition that my son was responsible for its safety. This my son was willing to do, as he could not conceive it possible for so kind a friend to betray the trust reposed in him. But there is no doubt of this indulgence being given to Joseph in order to show him by another lesson of bitter experience how vain are all human calculations, and also that he might learn not to put his trust in man, nor make flesh his arm.

Mr. Harris now took the most solemn oath that he would not show the manuscript to any save five individuals who belonged to his household.[3] His anxious desires were now gratified, for he hoped that this might be the means of carrying the truth home to their hearts. The idea of effecting a union of sentiment in his family animated him very much.

He was now fully prepared to set out for home, which he did, carrying with him one hundred and sixteen pages of the record in manuscript.[4]

Immediately after Mr. Harris's departure, Emma became the mother of a son, but she had but small comfort from the society of the dear little stranger, for he was very soon snatched from her arms and borne aloft to the world of spirits before he had time to learn good or evil.[5] For some time, the mother seemed to tremble upon the verge of the silent home of her infant. So uncertain seemed her fate for a season that, in the space of two weeks, Joseph never slept one hour in undisturbed quiet. At the expiration of this time she began to recover, but as Joseph's anxiety about her began to subside, another cause of trouble forced itself upon his mind. Mr. Harris had been absent nearly three weeks, and Joseph had received no intelligence whatever from him, which was altogether aside of the arrangement when they separated. He determined that as soon as his wife gained a little more strength, he would make a trip to New York and see after the manuscript. He did not mention the subject to Emma for fear of agitating her mind in her delicate health.

In a few days, however, she soon manifested that she was not without her thoughts upon the subject.[6] She called Joseph to her and asked him what he thought about the manuscript. "I feel so uneasy," said she, "that I cannot rest and shall not be at ease until I know something about what Mr. Harris is doing with it. Do you not think it would be advisable for you to go and inquire into the reason of his not writing or sending any word back to you since he left us?"

*Crude stone in Harmony
marks the grave of little Alvin Smith,
first son of Joseph and Emma.*

Joseph begged her to be quiet and not worry herself, as he could not leave her just then, as he should not dare to be absent from her one hour while her situation was so precarious. "I will," said Emma, "send for my mother and she shall stay with me while you are gone."[7]

After much persuasion, he concluded to leave his wife in the care of her mother for a few days, and set out on the before-mentioned journey.[8] Only one other passenger was in the stage besides himself, and since this individual did not seem inclined to urge conversation, Joseph was left to the solitude of his own imagination. But the sensations which he experienced when he found himself well seated in the stagecoach cannot be imagined by anyone who reads this, for they have not been in like circumstances, and, of course, they cannot be correctly described.

There were various causes acting upon his mind which were calculated to have a very peculiar effect upon him. In the first place was the consideration of the calling which he had received at the hand of God, many years previous, to do a thing unlooked for by the generation in which he lived. He cast his eyes abroad upon the age now present upon the earth, and reflected that he stood alone, an unlearned youth, opposed to all the casuistry and learning and ingenuity of the combined world. He considered that he had been called to extend his search up to the throne of God and bring down the precious things of heaven above into the midst of the sons of men, despite all their preconceived opinions and prejudices. These were so great that in order to gratify a pride of popularity and sustain a fashionable religion, they would and did strive, and even before this had used all their ingenuity, to take away his life to prevent the truth from coming forth—that their own opinions would not receive injury.

But this he did not regard, while he was sure of the strong support of the arm of the Almighty Ruler of men.

There remained another item of consideration of tenfold weight and of more vital importance than any of these. He had not now that feeling of justification which assured him of the especial favor of God, for he feared awfully that he had ventured too far in vouching for the safety of the manuscript after it was out of his possession. Should the manuscript be endangered, the consequence which must ensue was inevitable, which was that he would not be permitted to retain the plates until he should be able to translate them—and perhaps that he might never have the privilege of touching a finger to the work, which until now he had been the blessed instrument in the hands of God to bring to the knowledge of mankind.

Nor was this the worst apprehension that disturbed his mind. The hot displeasure of the Almighty would be kindled against him for turning aside from the injunctions which were laid upon him, and for calling upon his Heavenly Father to grant him an indulgence that was not according to the instructions of the angel of the Lord. For it now appeared to him, upon reflection, that he had acted hastily and in an inconsiderate manner, and that he had regarded man more than his Maker. Whilst these thoughts, accompanied by ten thousand others, pulsed in rapid succession through his brain, there was but small opportunity of rest and little relish for refreshment. Consequently, Joseph neither ate nor slept while on the route.

This was observed by his fellow traveler, insomuch that when Joseph remarked, as he descended from the stage, that he had still twenty miles to travel on foot, the stranger objected, saying, "I have watched you since you first entered the stage, and I know that you have not slept nor eaten since you commenced your journey.[9] You shall not go on foot twenty miles alone this night, for if you must go, I will be your company. And now tell me what can be the trouble which makes you thus desperate and also weighs down your spirits to such an extent that you refuse every proffered comfort and convenience."

Joseph told the gentleman that he had left his wife in so low a state of health that he had reason to fear that he would not find her alive when he returned; also he had buried his first and only child but a few days previous to leaving home. The explanation was given in truth and sincerity, although there was heavy trouble lying at his heart that he did not dare to mention.

"I feel," said the kind stranger, "to sympathize with you, and I will go with you, for I fear that your constitution, which is evidently not strong, will be insufficient to support you. You will be in danger of falling asleep in the forest, and some accident befall you."

Joseph thanked him for his kindness, and they proceeded together. When they arrived at our house, it was nearly daylight.[10] The last four miles of the distance, the stranger was under the necessity of leading Joseph by his arm, for nature was too much exhausted to support him any longer, and he would fall asleep as he stood upon his feet every few minutes.

When they came in, the stranger said, "I have brought your son through the forest because he insisted on coming, but he is sick and wants rest and refreshment. He ought to have some pepper tea immediately to warm his stomach. After you have prepared that, I will thank you for a little breakfast, as I am in haste to be on my journey again."

When we had complied with the first direction, Joseph requested us to send with all possible speed for Martin Harris. We did so, and after the stranger left (whose name we never knew), we prepared breakfast for the family, as soon as we conveniently could—for Martin Harris always came in such haste, when sent for, that we supposed he would be there and ready to take breakfast with us before we were ready.

It was now nearly six o'clock, and he lived three miles distant. At eight o'clock, we set the victuals on the table, looking for him every moment. We waited till nine, and he came not; till ten, and he was not there; till eleven, still he did not make his appearance. At half past twelve we saw him walking with a slow and measured tread toward the house, his eyes fixed thoughtfully upon the ground. When he came to the gate, he did not open it but got upon the fence and sat some time with his hat drawn over his eyes. At last he entered the house. After we sat down and were ready to commence eating, Martin took up his knife and fork as if to use them but dropped them from his hands. Hyrum

In this room Martin Harris revealed to the Smiths
that the 116 pages of manuscript were gone.

said, "Martin, why do you not eat? Are you sick?" Martin pressed his hands upon his temples and cried out in a tone of anguish, "Oh! I have lost my soul. I have lost my soul."

Joseph, who had smothered his fears till now, sprang from the table, exclaiming, "Oh! Martin, have you lost that manuscript? Have you broken your oath and brought down condemnation upon my head as well as your own?"

"Yes," replied Martin, "it is gone and I know not where."

"Oh, my God, my God," said Joseph, clinching his hands together. "All is lost, is lost! What shall I do? I have sinned. It is I who tempted the wrath of God by asking him for that which I had no right to ask, as

I was differently instructed by the angel." And he wept and groaned, walking the floor continually.

At last he told Martin to go back to his house and search again. "No," said Mr. Harris, "it is all in vain, for I have looked in every place in the house. I have even ripped open beds and pillows, and I know it is not there."

"Then must I," said Joseph, "return to my wife with such a tale as this? I dare not do it lest I should kill her at once. And how shall I appear before the Lord? Of what rebuke am I not worthy from the angel of the Most High?"

I besought him not to mourn so, for it might be that the Lord would forgive him, after a short season of humiliation and repentance on his part. But what could I say to comfort him when he saw all the family in the same state of mind that he was? Our sobs and groans and the most bitter lamentations filled the house. Joseph, in particular, was more distressed than the rest, for he knew definitely and by sorrowful experience the consequence of what would seem to others to be a very trifling neglect of duty. He continued walking backwards and forwards, weeping and grieving like a tender infant until about sunset, when we persuaded him to take a little nourishment.

The next morning he went home. We parted with heavy hearts, for it seemed as though all our fond anticipations, that which we had fed upon and which had been the source of so much secret gratification to us, had in a moment fled, and fled forever.

NOTES

1. In the Preliminary Manuscript, Lucy records at this point that Martin first asked to see the plates before he asked to take the manuscript home to show his wife. This appears to be an error in chronology.

2. In the Preliminary Manuscript, Lucy only mentions that Joseph prayed once about allowing Martin to take the 116 manuscript pages. One can only imagine the pressure Joseph was feeling at this time to gratify Martin Harris. Martin was twenty-

two years older than Joseph. He had liquidated Joseph and Emma's debts. He had financed the move from Manchester to Harmony. He was spending all of his time as a scribe on the work. He was risking his good reputation to continue to associate with Joseph. He was losing his wife's confidence and affections and potentially losing his own place in his home. All these considerations must have weighed heavily on Joseph's mind and heart.

3. These five individuals were: Martin's wife, Lucy Harris; his parents, Nathan and Rhoda Harris; his younger brother, Preserved Harris; and his wife's younger sister, Polly Harris Cobb (see *Papers,* p. 286).

4. He departed for Palmyra on Saturday, June 14, 1828, after having worked as scribe since about April 12 of that same year (a total of sixty-three days). In his possession were 116 pages of foolscap paper consisting of what is called the "Book of Lehi." Foolscap paper was so named from the watermark of a fool's cap used on such paper (traditional jester cap having several drooping peaks from which bells are hung), and each sheet measured $13\frac{1}{2}$ by 17 inches.

5. This son, named Alvin Smith, was born and passed away on Sunday, June 15, 1828.

6. This date can be approximated as being at the middle to end of the first week of July, 1828.

7. Emma's mother, Elizabeth Lewis Hale, lived just a few hundred feet away. Born November 19, 1766, she was sixty-one at this time.

8. Joseph likely left Harmony about Friday, July 4, or Saturday, July 5, 1828.

9. The stagecoach ride of 135 miles would have been no less than two full days and could have been three.

10. At this time of year, "nearly daylight" would have been between about 4:30 and 4:45 in the morning.

CHAPTER 25

Events in the life of Martin Harris leading to the loss of the 116 manuscript pages. He first shows the manuscript to those he is allowed to, but then forgets his sacred covenant and begins showing it to others. The manuscript is stolen. His crops are blighted and destroyed by a thick fog.

June 17, 1828 to mid-July 1828

I will now give a sketch of the proceedings of Martin Harris, during the time he was absent from Joseph.[1] These brought about the circumstances that seared our bright hopes in the tender bud, ere we were granted the privilege of beholding even the opening leaf.

When he arrived at home,[2] he was not slow to exhibit the manuscript to his wife and family. Thus far he was under no condemnation. His wife seemed highly pleased with what she heard, and entered into the spirit of it so much, that she gave her husband the privilege of locking the manuscript up in a set of drawers which she had never before permitted him to look into. After he had shown the transcript to those who were privileged to see it, according to his oath, he laid it aside and went with Mrs. Harris to visit a relative of hers who lived three miles distant.[3]

After remaining with them a short time, he returned home, but his wife declined accompanying him back. Shortly after he got there, a very particular friend made him a visit to whom he related all he knew concerning the record. The man's curiosity was much excited, and he earnestly desired to see the transcript. Martin was anxious to gratify his

*House (circa 1850) built on the foundation
where Martin Harris's home once stood.*

friend, although it was contrary to his obligation. But when he went to the drawer to get the manuscript, the key was gone. He sought for it some time, but could not find it. Resolved, however, to carry his design into execution, he picked the lock, and in so doing, he injured his lady's bureau considerably. He then took out the manuscript, and after showing it to his friend, he removed it to his own set of drawers. Here he had it at his command, and passing by his oath, he showed it to any good friend that happened to call on him.

When Mrs. Harris returned and beheld the marred and injured state of her bureau, her irascible temper knew no bounds, and an intolerable storm ensued throughout the house which descended with greatest force upon the head of her devoted husband.

Having once made a sacrifice of his conscience, Mr. Harris no longer regarded its scruples, so he continued to exhibit the writings, until a short time before Joseph arrived, to anyone whom he regarded as prudent enough to keep the secret, except our family, but *we* were not allowed to set our eyes upon them.

A heavy fog blighted Martin Harris's crops in these fields the day he realized he had lost the sacred manuscript.

For a short time previous to Joseph's arrival, Mr. Harris had been otherwise engaged and thought but little about the manuscript. When Joseph sent for him, he went immediately to his drawer, but the manuscript was gone! He asked his wife where it was. She solemnly averred that she did not know anything about it whatever.[4] Not regarding what she said, he went through the house and made a faithful search. But it was more vain than Esau's seeking his blessing.

The manuscript has never been found; and there is no doubt but Mrs. Harris took it from the drawer, with the view of retaining it until another translation should be given, then to alter the original translation for the purpose of showing a discrepancy between them, and thus make the whole appear to be a deception.[5]

Martin Harris had not only lost his spiritual blessing, but a great temporal blessing also. The same day on which the foregoing circumstance took place, a heavy fog swept over Mr. Harris's fields and blighted all his wheat, so that he lost about two-thirds of his crop, while the fields on the opposite side of the road remained untouched.[6]

I well remember that day of darkness, both within and without. To us, at least, the heavens seemed clothed with blackness, and the earth shrouded with gloom. I have often said within myself that if a continual punishment, as severe as that which we experienced on that occasion, were to be inflicted upon the most wicked characters who ever stood upon the footstool of the Almighty—if even their punishment were no greater than that, I should feel to pity their condition.

NOTES

1. He was absent from Joseph from June 14, 1828, until approximately the beginning of the second week of July 1828.

2. We can approximate the date of Martin's arrival home as either late on June 16 or sometime on June 17, 1828.

3. The 1853 edition (*Biographical Sketches*, p. 122) says the relative lived ten or fifteen miles distant.

4. In the Preliminary Manuscript, Mother Smith says, "When Joseph arrived, peace was not yet restored, and because of this she was accused of having taken the transcript by stealth and secreted [it]." Since it is not entirely clear who made this accusation, it has not been included in the main text of this edition.

5. In the first edition of the Book of Mormon (1830), Joseph Smith included a preface that stated: "To the Reader—As many false reports have been circulated respecting the following work, and also many unlawful measures taken by evil designing persons to destroy me, and also the work, I would inform you that I translated, by the gift and power of God, and caused to be written, one hundred and sixteen pages, the which I took from the Book of Lehi, which was an account abridged from the plates of Lehi, by the hand of Mormon; which said account, some person or persons have stolen and kept from me, notwithstanding my utmost exertions to recover it again— and being commanded of the Lord that I should not translate the same over again, for Satan had put it into their hearts to tempt the Lord their God, by altering the words, that they did read contrary from that which I translated and caused to be written; and if I should bring forth the same words again, or, in other words, if I should translate the same over again, they would publish that which they had stolen, and Satan would stir up the hearts of this generation, that they might not receive this work: but behold, the Lord said unto me, I will not suffer that Satan shall accomplish his evil design in this thing: therefore thou shalt translate from the plates of Nephi, until ye come to that which ye have translated, which ye have retained; and behold ye shall publish it as the record of Nephi; and thus I will confound those who have altered my words. I will not suffer that they shall destroy my work; yea, I will shew unto them that my wisdom is greater than the cunning of the Devil. Wherefore, to be obedient unto the commandments of God, I have, through his grace and mercy, accomplished that which he hath commanded me respecting this thing."

6. This date can be approximated as being between July 6 and 10, 1828.

CHAPTER 26

Joseph Smith Sr. and Lucy go to see Joseph Jr. and Emma in Harmony, Pennsylvania. Joseph relates details of what happened after the manuscript was stolen. Joseph goes through time of repentance and finally obtains forgiveness. Parts of Doctrine and Covenants 3 and 10 are quoted. Joseph Sr. and Lucy meet Emma's parents, Isaac and Elizabeth Hale.

July 1828 to fall 1828

We never heard from our unfortunate son until two months after, when, being uneasy as to the consequences of his distress of mind, Mr. Smith and myself went down to Harmony to make him a visit.[1] When we came within three-quarters of a mile of the house, Joseph started off to meet us, telling his wife that Father and Mother were coming, although he could not see us. He met us with a countenance blazing with delight, and it was very evident that his joy did not arise wholly from seeing us. When I entered, the first thing which attracted my attention was a red morocco trunk lying on Emma's bureau, which Joseph shortly informed me contained the Urim and Thummim and the plates. He said very little concerning the subject of his earlier trouble until evening. He then related what had taken place since he was in New York with minute precision as follows:

"Immediately after I left you, I returned home. After I arrived here, I commenced humbling myself in mighty prayer before the Lord, and as I poured out my soul in supplication to him, that if possible I might obtain mercy at his hands and be forgiven of all that I had done which

Joseph and Emma's Harmony home was on this site.
Here fifteen revelations were received.

was contrary to his will, an angel stood before me and answered me, saying, that I had sinned in delivering the manuscript into the hands of a wicked man, and as I had ventured to become responsible for this man's faithfulness, I would of necessity suffer the consequences of his indiscretion, and I must now give back the Urim and Thummim[2] into his (the angel's) hands.

"This I did as I was directed, and as I handed them to him he remarked, 'If you are very humble and penitent, it may be you will receive them again; if so, it will be on the twenty-second of next September.' "[3]

Joseph then related a revelation which he received soon after the angel visited him, a part of which is as follows:

> Behold, you have been entrusted with these things, but how strict were your commandments; and remember also the promises which were made to you, if you did not transgress them.

And behold, how oft you have transgressed the commandments and the laws of God, and have gone on in the persuasions of men.

For, behold, you should not have feared man more than God. Although men set at naught the counsels of God, and despise his words—

Yet you should have been faithful; and he would have extended his arm and supported you against all the fiery darts of the adversary; and he would have been with you in every time of trouble.

Behold, thou art Joseph, and thou wast chosen to do the work of the Lord, but because of transgression, if thou art not aware thou wilt fall.

But remember, God is merciful; therefore, repent of that which thou hast done which is contrary to the commandment which I gave you, and thou art still chosen, and art again called to the work;

Except thou do this, thou shalt be delivered up and become as other men, and have no more gift.

And when thou deliveredst up that which God had given thee sight and power to translate, thou deliveredst up that which was sacred into the hands of a wicked man,

Who has set at naught the counsels of God, and has broken the most sacred promises which were made before God, and has depended upon his own judgment, and boasted in his own wisdom.

And this is the reason that thou hast lost thy privileges for a season—

For thou hast suffered the counsel of thy director to be trampled upon from the beginning.

Nevertheless, my work shall go forth, for inasmuch as the knowledge of a Savior has come unto the world, through the testimony of the Jews, even so shall the knowledge of a Savior come unto my people—[4]

And to the Nephites, and the Jacobites, and the Josephites, and the Zoramites, through the testimony of their fathers—

And this testimony shall come to the knowledge of the Lamanites and the Lemuelites, and the Ishmaelites, who dwindled in unbelief because of the iniquity of their fathers, whom the Lord has suffered to destroy their brethren the Nephites, because of their iniquities and their abominations.

And for this very purpose are these plates preserved, which contain these records—that the promises of the Lord might be fulfilled, which he made to his people;

And that the Lamanites might come to the knowledge of their fathers, and that they might know the promises of the Lord, and that they may believe the gospel and rely upon the merits of Jesus Christ, and be glorified through faith in his name, and that through their repentance they might be saved. Amen.

I will now return to Joseph's recital.

"After the angel left me," said he, "I continued my supplications to God, without cessation, and on the twenty-second of September, I had the joy and satisfaction of again receiving the Urim and Thummim, with which I have again commenced translating, and Emma writes for me, but the angel said that the Lord would send me a scribe, and I trust that it will be so. The angel was rejoiced when he gave me back the Urim and Thummim, and he told me that the Lord was pleased with my faithfulness and humility, and loved me for my penitence and diligence in prayer, in the which I had performed my duty so well as to receive the Urim and Thummim and was able to enter upon the work of translation again."

A few months after Joseph received them, he inquired of the Lord, and obtained the following revelation:[5]

> Now, behold, I say unto you, that because you delivered up those writings which you had power given unto you to translate by the means of the Urim and Thummim, into the hands of a wicked man, you have lost them.
>
> And you also lost your gift at the same time, and your mind became darkened.[6]
>
> Nevertheless, it is now restored unto you again; therefore see that you are faithful and continue on unto the finishing of the remainder of the work of translation as you have begun.
>
> Do not run faster or labor more than you have strength and means provided to enable you to translate; but be diligent unto the end.

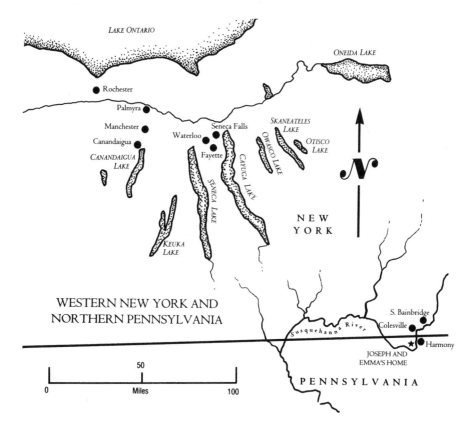

LAKE ONTARIO

ONEIDA LAKE

Rochester

Palmyra

Manchester

Waterloo

Seneca Falls

SKANEATELES LAKE

OWASCO LAKE

OTISCO LAKE

Canandaigua

Fayette

CANANDAIGUA LAKE

CAYUGA LAKE

SENECA LAKE

NEW YORK

KEUKA LAKE

WESTERN NEW YORK AND NORTHERN PENNSYLVANIA

S. Bainbridge

Colesville

Susquehanna River

Harmony

JOSEPH AND EMMA'S HOME

50

0   Miles   100

PENNSYLVANIA

Pray always, that you may come off conqueror; yea, that you may conquer Satan, and that you may escape the hands of the servants of Satan that do uphold his work.

Behold, they have sought to destroy you; yea, even the man in whom you have trusted has sought to destroy you.

And for this cause I said that he is a wicked man, for he has sought to take away the things wherewith you have been entrusted; and he has also sought to destroy your gift.

And because you have delivered the writings into his hands, behold, wicked men have taken them from you.

Therefore, you have delivered them up, yea, that which was sacred, unto wickedness.

And, behold, Satan hath put it into their hearts to alter the words which you have caused to be written, or which you have translated, which have gone out of your hands.

And behold, I say unto you, that because they have altered the words, they read contrary from that which you translated and caused to be written;

And, on this wise, the devil has sought to lay a cunning plan, that he may destroy this work;

For he hath put into their hearts to do this, that by lying they may say they have caught you in the words which you have pretended to translate.

While on this visit, we became acquainted with Emma's father, whose name was Isaac Hale; also his family, which consisted of his wife, Elizabeth; his sons, Jesse, David, Alva, Isaac Ward, and Reuben; and his daughters, Phebe and Elizabeth.[7]

They were a lovely, intelligent, and highly respectable family. They were pleasantly situated, living in fine circumstances in the town of Harmony, on the Susquehannah River, lying a short distance from the foot of a splendid range of mountains. They lived in a large, neatly finished frame home, with every convenient appendage necessary on an extensive and well-cultivated farm.[8] It was a most delightful situation and did honor to the good taste of the intelligent proprietor.

We spent our time very agreeably and returned home relieved of a burden which had seemed too heavy to be borne. The joy we had over the present prosperity of our son with regard to his spiritual concerns far outweighed anything of the kind which we had before experienced. We now had learned to appreciate the sweet from having drunk deeply of the bitter for a season.

NOTES

1. This was likely in October 1828.

2. In the Preliminary Manuscript, Lucy states that Joseph must give back the plates, not the Urim and Thummim.

3. Meaning September 22, 1828.

4. In the 1853 and later editions of Lucy Mack Smith's history, the verses from Doctrine and Covenants 3 end at this point. In the Preliminary Manuscript, Lucy quotes section 3 to its conclusion.

5. Based on Lucy's account, this revelation was not given any earlier than September 22, 1828.

6. Note here the Lord distinguishes between the "gift" Joseph had been given and the Urim and Thummim.

7. The Hale family consisted of nine children (Lucy assumes the reader is aware of Emma, but she omits one other daughter). The children are Jesse (born February 24, 1792); David (March 6, 1794); Alva (November 29, 1795); Phebe (May 1, 1798); Elizabeth (February 14, 1800); Isaac Ward (March 11, 1802); Emma (July 10, 1804); Tryal (November 21, 1806); and Reuben (September 18, 1810). (See Porter, "Origins," p. 116.)

8. It appears that Isaac Hale (and others) had purchased some 623 acres in Harmony Township between 1809 and 1833 (see Porter, "Origins," pp. 115–16).

CHAPTER 27

Sickness in the Smith household. Oliver Cowdery is hired to teach school in Manchester. Oliver becomes acquainted with the history of Joseph Smith Jr. and desires to become a scribe for him. Smiths are forced to move to their old cabin. Oliver and Samuel Smith go to Harmony, Pennsylvania, to see Joseph. Oliver acts as scribe for Joseph in the translation of the Book of Mormon. Joseph and Oliver receive the Aaronic Priesthood and the ordinance of baptism.

January 1829 to May 15, 1829

As had always been the case, our season of rejoicing was soon mingled with anxiety and distress. When we arrived at home, we found Sophronia and Samuel lying at the point of death. Hyrum had shut up his own house and quitted business in order to take care of the children during our absence. Sophronia lay very sick for two months, in which time she was dreadfully salivated by the doctor who attended her.[1]

Soon after we returned, there came a man into our neighborhood by the name of Lyman Cowdery. He went to Hyrum (as he was one of the principal trustees) and applied for the school. A meeting of the trustees was called, and it was settled that Mr. Cowdery should be employed. But the next day, this Mr. Cowdery brought his brother Oliver[2] to the trustees and requested them to receive him in his place, as business had arisen that would oblige him to disappoint them. But he would warrant the prosperity of the school in Oliver's hands, if the trustees would accept of his services. All parties were satisfied, and Oliver requested my husband to take him as a boarder, at least for a little while until he should become acquainted with his patrons in the school.

*School (circa 1848)
built on the foundation of
Oliver Cowdery school.
Original is in background.*

He had not been in the place long until he began to hear about the plates from all quarters and immediately commenced importuning Mr. Smith upon the subject. He did not succeed in eliciting any information from him for a long time. At length, however, he gained my husband's confidence so far as to get a sketch of the facts which related to the plates.

One day, Oliver came home from school in quite a lively manner. As soon as he had an opportunity of conversing with Mr. Smith, he told him that he (Oliver) had been in a deep study all day, and it had been put into his heart that he would have the privilege of writing for Joseph.[3] And when the term of school which he was then teaching was closed, he would go and pay Joseph a visit.

The next day was so very stormy as to render it almost impossible to travel the road between the schoolhouse and our place. The rain fell in torrents all the evening, so I supposed that Oliver would certainly stop with some neighbor who lived nearer the schoolhouse than we did. But he was not to be deterred from coming by any common difficulty, for his mind was now fully set upon a subject which he could not converse upon anywhere else.

When he came in, he said, "I have now resolved what I will do—for the thing which I told you about yesterday seems working in my very bones, insomuch that I cannot for a moment get rid of it. My plan is this: My term of school will be out in March, and I want Hyrum, as he is one of the trustees, to manage to have my school money ready for me as soon as the school closes, that I may be able to set off for Pennsylvania immediately upon making the necessary preparations. Samuel, I understand, is going to stay with Joseph through the spring. I will endeavor to be ready to go by the time he recovers his health again. I have made it a subject of prayer, and I firmly believe that if it is the will of the Lord that I should go, and that there is a work for me to do in this thing, I am determined to attend to it."

We told him that we thought it was his privilege to know whether this was the case and advised him to seek for a testimony for himself. He did so and received the witness spoken of in the book of Doctrine and Covenants, section 8.[4]

From this time Oliver was so entirely absorbed in the subject of the record, that it seemed impossible for him to think or converse about anything else.

As the time for which we had agreed for our place was now drawing to a close, we began to make preparations to remove our family and effects to the log house which was now occupied by Hyrum.[5] When we gave to the new landlord full and entire possession of the last vestige of real estate which we could call our own, we began to feel more seriously than ever before the effects of our lot. Before this, we had the use of our property, although it was not nominally ours. Now the time had come for us to feel the stroke most sensibly.

I thought that it would be impossible in the crowded situation in which we would now have to live for us to make Mr. Cowdery comfortable and mentioned to him the necessity of seeking another boarding place.[6] I also thought this would be a good occasion to bring to his mind the cause of all our present privations, as well the misfortune that he himself was liable to if he turned his back upon the world and set out in the service of God.

The Smiths would now move from their comfortable frame home back to their small cabin.

"Now, Oliver," said I, "just look upon this thing. See what a comfortable home we have had here and what pains each child that we have has taken to provide for us everything necessary to make our old age comfortable, and long life desirable. Here I have to look upon the handiwork of that dear son whom death has removed from our sight. Everything which meets my eyes reminds me of my beloved Alvin.[7] Even upon his deathbed, in his last moments, his dying injunction to his brothers was that they should not, by any means, neglect to finish his work of preparing a place of earthly rest for us— that if possible, through the exertions of our children, our last days might be our best days. There is scarcely anything that I see that has not passed through the hands of that faithful boy and, afterwards, been carefully arranged precisely according to his plan by his brothers who survived him. This shows me in every particular their faithful and affectionate remembrance both of their parents and the brother whom they loved.

"All these tender recollections render our present trial doubly severe, for these relics must now pass into the hands of wicked men who fear not God, neither do they regard man. And upon what righteous principle has all this been brought about? They have never raised a hand to earn any part of that of which they are now to reap the benefit. In consequence of these things, Oliver, we cannot make you comfortable any longer and you will be under the necessity of taking boarding somewhere else, for we shall have to crowd ourselves together in a log house where we shall have none of the convenience that we have here."

"Mother," exclaimed the young man with much feeling, "only let me stay with you, and I can live in any log hut where you and Father live, but I cannot go away from you, so say no more about convenience."

"Well," I continued, "now look around me upon all these things that have been gathered together for my happiness, which has cost the toil of years. You mark. I now give this up for the sake of Christ and salvation, and I pray God to help me do so without a murmur or a tear. In the strength of God I give these up from this time, and I will not cast one longing look upon anything which I leave behind me."

In April, all Mr. Cowdery's affairs being arranged according to his mind, he and Samuel set out for Pennsylvania.[8] The weather, for some time previous, had been very wet and disagreeable—raining, freezing, and thawing alternately, which had made the roads almost impassable, particularly during the middle of the day. But Mr. Cowdery was determined not to be detained by wind or weather and persevered until they arrived at Joseph's house, although Oliver froze one of his toes and he and Samuel suffered much on the road from fatigue.

When they arrived there, Joseph was not at home.[9] He had been so hurried with business and writing, etc., that he could not proceed with the work as fast as it was necessary for him to do. There was also another disadvantage under which he had to labor. Emma had so much of her time taken up with the care of her house that she could write but little for him. Accordingly, two or three days before the arrival of Oliver and Samuel,[10] Joseph called upon his Heavenly Father to send him a scribe as the angel had promised, and he was informed that the same should be forthcoming in a few days.

When Oliver was introduced to Joseph, he said, "Mr. Smith, I have come for the purpose of writing for you." This was not at all unexpected to Joseph, for although he had never seen Mr. Cowdery before, he knew that the Lord was able to perform, and that he had been faithful to fulfill, all his promises.

They then sat down and conversed together until late, and Joseph told Oliver his entire history as far as it was necessary for his information in those things which concerned him. The next morning they commenced the work of translation and were soon deeply engaged. Now the work of writing and translation progressed rapidly.

Joseph and Oliver were baptized in these waters of the Susquehanna River on May 15, 1829.

One morning, however, they sat down to their usual work, when the first thing that presented itself to Joseph was a commandment from God that he and Oliver should repair to the water and each of them be baptized.[11] They immediately went down to the Susquehanna River and obeyed the mandate given them through the Urim and Thummim. As they were on their return to the house, they overheard Samuel, in a secluded spot, engaged in secret prayer. They had now received the authority to baptize, and Joseph said that he considered it a sufficient testimony of Samuel's honesty of heart and zeal for religion that they had found him privately bowing before the Lord in prayer, and that he thought it was an evidence of readiness for baptism. Oliver was of the

same opinion, and they spoke to Samuel, who went with them straightway to the water and was baptized.[12] After this, they again went on with
the translation as before.[13]

NOTES

1. A common medical practice at this time was to give the patient regular doses
of mercury to cause them to salivate a great deal. It was thought that this would bring
about the healing of various maladies. Numerous patients died from the mercury poisoning.

2. Oliver Cowdery was born October 3, 1806, at Wells, Rutland County,
Vermont, the son of William and Rebecca Fuller Cowdery. He married Elizabeth
Ann Whitmer (daughter of Peter and Mary Whitmer) on December 18, 1832.
Together they had six children (Maria Louise, Elizabeth Ann, Josephine Rebecca,
Oliver Peter, Adeline Fuller, and Julia Olive). (See Cook, *Revelations*, p. 14.) Only one
of their children lived to adulthood, Maria Louise, who married but had no children.

3. Joseph the Prophet enlightens the reader from his 1832 account: "The Lord
appeared unto a young man by the name of Oliver Cowdery and showed unto him the
plates in a vision and also the truth of the work and what the Lord was about to do
through me, his unworthy servant; therefore, he was desirous to come and write for
me" (*Papers*, p. 10).

4. Mother Smith's edition of the Doctrine and Covenants was printed in
Nauvoo in 1844 and the section she is referring to is now section 6 in the 1981 edition. She is likely referring specifically to D&C 6:22–24.

5. This appears to be late winter or early spring, 1829.

6. The small twenty-by-thirty-foot cabin at the north end of the one hundred
acres would now be home to eleven people: Hyrum and Jerusha Smith (with eighteen-
month-old Lovina, and Jerusha pregnant); Joseph Sr. and Lucy Mack Smith; Samuel
(age twenty-one); William (eighteen); Catharine (sixteen); Don Carlos (twelve); little
Lucy (seven); and Oliver Cowdery.

7. Alvin had now been gone for nearly five and a half years.

8. Samuel Harrison Smith, age twenty-one, and Oliver Cowdery, age twenty-
two, likely set out on their 135-mile journey on Wednesday, April 1, or Thursday,
April 2, 1829.

9. Oliver recorded: "Near the time of the setting of the sun, Sabbath evening,
April 5, 1829, my natural eyes for the first time beheld this brother. . . . On Monday
the 6th, I assisted him in arranging some business of a temporal nature, and on
Tuesday the 7th commenced to write the Book of Mormon." (In *Papers*, p. 29.)

10. Joseph's fervent prayer was on April 2 or 3, 1829.

11. This was on Friday, May 15, 1829. On this date, Joseph and Oliver were visited by John the Baptist, received the Aaronic Priesthood, and were baptized (see Joseph Smith—History 1:68–72). Joseph recorded: "Immediately on our coming up out of the water after we had been baptized, we experienced great and glorious blessings from our Heavenly Father. No sooner had I baptized Oliver Cowdery, than the Holy Ghost fell upon him, and he stood up and prophesied many things which should shortly come to pass. And again, so soon as I had been baptized by him, I also had the spirit of prophecy, when, standing up, I prophesied concerning the rise of this Church, and many other things connected with the Church, and this generation of the children of men. We were filled with the Holy Ghost, and rejoiced in the God of our salvation." (Joseph Smith—History 1:73.) Oliver Cowdery also recorded: "I shall not attempt to paint to you the feelings of this heart, nor the majestic beauty and glory which surrounded us on this occasion; but you will believe me when I say, that earth, nor men, with the eloquence of time, cannot begin to clothe language in as interesting and sublime a manner as this holy personage [John the Baptist]. No; nor has this earth power to give the joy, to bestow the peace, or comprehend the wisdom which was contained in each sentence as they were delivered by the power of the Holy Spirit!" (Joseph Smith—History 1:71n.)

12. In *History of the Church* these circumstances are recorded a little differently from Mother Smith's account: "We informed him [Samuel] of what the Lord was about to do for the children of men, and began to reason with him out of the Bible. We also showed him that part of the work which we had translated, and labored to persuade him concerning the Gospel of Jesus Christ, which was now about to be revealed in its fulness. He was not, however, very easily persuaded of these things, but after much inquiry and explanation he retired to the woods, in order that by secret and fervent prayer he might obtain of a merciful God, wisdom to enable him to judge for himself. The result was that he obtained revelation for himself sufficient to convince him of the truth of our assertions to him; and on the twenty-fifth day of that same month in which we had been baptized and ordained, Oliver Cowdery baptized him; and he returned to his father's house, greatly glorifying and praising God, being filled with the Holy Spirit." (*History of the Church* 1:44.)

13. Joseph recorded: "Our minds being now enlightened, we began to have the scriptures laid open to our understandings, and the true meaning and intention of their more mysterious passages revealed unto us in a manner which we never could attain to previously, nor ever before had thought of. In the meantime we were forced to keep secret the circumstances of having received the Priesthood and our having been baptized, owing to a spirit of persecution which had already manifested itself in the neighborhood." (Joseph Smith—History 1:74.)

CHAPTER 28

Lucy Harris raises a vexatious lawsuit against Joseph Smith Jr. Mrs. Harris gathers witnesses. Mother Smith prays fervently for her son's protection and receives a direct answer. Conflicting witnesses are confounded. Martin Harris boldly testifies as to Joseph Smith's integrity and the work of the Lord.

Summer 1829

Samuel remained with his brother until July or August, and then came back to the state of New York, bringing us news of Joseph's success and prosperity.[1] This roused in Martin Harris a great desire to go down to Pennsylvania to see how they were prospering for himself, as he was more than commonly interested in the matter. His wife soon came to the knowledge of his intention and fixed in her mind a determination to prevent him from going. She also resolved to bring Joseph into a difficulty which would be the means of hindering him, perhaps entirely, from accomplishing the work which he was about.[2]

To this end she undertook to prove that Joseph never had the record which he professed to have, and that he pretended to have in his possession certain gold plates for the express purpose of obtaining money. Accordingly, she mounted her horse, flew from house to house through the neighborhood, like a dark spirit, making diligent inquiry where she had the least hope of gleaning anything that would subserve her purpose—which was to prove that Joseph did not have the record which he pretended to have, that he pretended to be in possession of certain gold plates for the express purpose of obtaining money from those who might be so credulous as to believe him.[3] After she had as-certained the strength of her adherents, she entered a complaint before a magistrate at Lyons. She then sent word to Lyman Cowdery,[4] request-ing him to come to Lyons, prepared with a good horse to travel posthaste to Pennsylvania (should the case go against Joseph Smith), that he might go with the officers to assist them in securing him and confining him in prison.

Lyman Cowdery was very obedient to her suggestion, and all things seemed to be going on prosperously with Mrs. Harris. She made affi-davit to many things herself, and directed the officers whom to sub-poena. Among the rest, her husband was a principal witness in the case.

When the day of trial came, the neighbors who felt friendly to us informed us that the witnesses were gone to Lyons and were determined to obtain a verdict against Joseph if it could be done by swearing. This very naturally gave me great anxiety for my son. Hyrum came in and I asked him what could be done.

"Why, Mother," said he, "we can do nothing, but look to the Lord, for in him is all help and strength, and he can deliver from every trouble."

I had never neglected this all-important duty, but seeing this confi-dence in my son strengthened me in this hour of trial. This was the first time that a suit was ever brought before any court which affected any of my family, and not being accustomed to such things (as I would become afterwards), I trembled for the issue.[5] But I retired to a secluded place and bowed myself before God and poured out my whole soul in impas-sioned entreaties for the safety of my son. I continued my supplication for some time. At length a spirit fell upon me so powerfully that every feeling of foreboding or distress was entirely removed from my mind, and a voice spoke to me, saying, "Not one hair of his head shall be harmed." I was satisfied, and arose and went into the house. I never felt as happy in my life as I did then. I sat down and began to read, but my feelings were too intense to permit me to do so. My daughter-in-law Jerusha came into the room soon after, and when she turned her eyes upon me, she stopped short, saying, "Why, Mother, what is the matter? I never saw you look so strange in my life."

I told her I never had been so happy before. I said, "My heart is so light and my mind so completely at rest, that it does not seem to me as though I should ever have any more trouble while I lived. I have got a witness from the Lord that Joseph's enemies will have no power over him. I have received a promise that he shall be protected." Overpowered by the strength of my feelings I burst into tears and sobbed aloud.

I will now relate the proceedings of the court. After the setting of the same, the witnesses were sworn. The first witness testified that Joseph Smith had told him that the box which he had contained nothing but sand, and he only said it was gold plates to deceive the people.

The second witness swore that Joseph Smith had told him on a certain occasion that it was nothing but a box of lead, and he was determined to use it as he saw fit.

The third witness declared, under oath, that he inquired of Joseph Smith what he had in that box and Joseph told him that there was nothing in the box, saying, "I have made fools of the whole of you, and all I want is to get Martin Harris's money away from him." This witness also stated that Joseph had already got two or three hundred dollars from Martin by his persuasion.

Next came Mrs. Harris's affidavit, in which she stated that Joseph Smith had but one principal object in view, and that was to defraud her husband in such a way as to induce him to give up all his property into Smith's hands. She said that she did not believe that Joseph Smith had ever been in possession of the gold plates which he talked so much about, and that his pretensions were altogether unreal.

The magistrate then forbade the introduction of any more witnesses until he heard Mr. Harris's testimony. Mr. Harris, being duly sworn, testified with boldness, decision, and energy to a few simple facts. When he rose he raised his hand to heaven and said, "I can swear that Joseph Smith never got one dollar from me since God made me. I did once voluntarily, of my own free will and accord, put fifty dollars into his hands before many witnesses, for the purpose of doing the work of the Lord. This I can pointedly prove, and I can tell you, furthermore, that Joseph has certainly never shown any disposition to get any man's money without giving him a reasonable compensation for the same in return. And as to the plates which he professes to have, gentlemen, if you do not believe it but continue to resist the truth, it will one day be the means of damning your souls."[6]

The judge then told them they need not call any more of their witnesses, but ordered them to bring him what had been written of the testimony already given. This he tore in pieces before their eyes and told them to go home about their business and trouble him no more with such ridiculous folly. They returned home, abashed and confounded, hanging down their heads with shame and confusion.

Notes

1. This date appears to be incorrect, as Joseph moved to Fayette, New York, with David Whitmer, on or about June 1, 1829.

2. It is indicated by Mother Smith later in this chapter that Lucy Harris was willing to have Joseph brought from Pennsylvania by the law if need be, so this suit could have been filed sometime in May, or as late as early June, 1829 (see Bushman, *Beginnings*, p. 224).

3. Shortly before this time, Joseph had received a revelation concerning those who wanted to see the gold plates: "Behold, if they will not believe my words, they would not believe you, my servant Joseph, if it were possible that you should show them all these things which I have committed unto you. Oh, this unbelieving and stiffnecked generation—mine anger is kindled against them. Behold, verily I say unto you, I have reserved those things which I have entrusted unto you, my servant Joseph, for a wise purpose in me, and it shall be made known unto future generations; but this generation shall have my word through you." (D&C 5: 7–10.)

4. Lyman Cowdery, it will be remembered, was Oliver Cowdery's brother.

5. Brigham Young gave us some idea of the future Joseph would face with lawsuits: "Joseph, our Prophet, was hunted and driven, arrested and persecuted, and although no law was ever made in these United States that would bear against him, for he never broke a law, yet to my certain knowledge he was defendant in forty-six lawsuits" (in *JD* 14:199, June 3, 1871).

6. Preston Nibley comments here: "The courage of Martin Harris in thus defending the Prophet is commendable" (footnote in Lucy Mack Smith, *History of Joseph Smith by His Mother*, ed. Preston Nibley [Salt Lake City: Bookcraft, 1954], p. 146).

CHAPTER 29

Joseph is commanded to write David Whitmer and ask him to move them to Fayette, New York. David Whitmer wants a witness of the work. Three strangers arrive and in an extraordinary fashion finish all remaining farmwork. David makes the trip to Harmony and gets Joseph and Oliver. The translation process continues in the home of Peter Whitmer Sr.

End of May to mid-June 1829

In the meantime, Joseph was one hundred and fifty miles distant in Pennsylvania and knew not of the matter, except through an intimation that was given through the Urim and Thummim. One morning as he applied it to his eyes to look upon the record, instead of the words of the book being given to him, he was commanded to write a letter to one David Whitmer, who lived in Waterloo.[1] This man Joseph had never seen, but he was instructed to say to him that he must come with his team immediately, in order to convey Joseph and Oliver back to his house, that they might remain with him there until the translation should be completed, as an evil-designing people were seeking to take away Joseph's life in order to prevent the work of God from going forth among the world.[2] The letter was written and delivered, and Mr. Whitmer showed it to his father, mother, sisters, and brothers, asking their advice as to what it would be best for him to do.

His father said, "Why, David, you know you have sowed as much wheat as you can harrow in tomorrow and the next day, and then you have a quantity of plaster of paris to spread that is much needed on your land. You cannot go unless you get an evidence from God that it is very necessary."[3]

This suggestion pleased David, and he asked the Lord for a testimony that it was his will that he should go. He was told by the voice of the Spirit to harrow in his wheat, and then go straightway to Pennsylvania. The next morning David went to the field and found that he had two heavy days' work before him. He then asked the Lord to enable him to do this work sooner than the same work had ever been done on the farm before—and he would receive it as an evidence that it was God's will that he should do all in his power to assist Joseph Smith in the work in which he was engaged. He then fastened his horses to the harrow, and instead of dividing the field into what is, by farmers, usually termed bands, he drove round the whole of it, continuing thus till noon, when, on stopping for dinner, he looked around, and discovered to his surprise that he had harrowed in full half the wheat. After dinner he again went on as before, and by evening he finished the whole two days' work.

When he informed his father of the fact, his father could not believe it till he examined for himself and ascertained that it was actually true. "Well," said his father, "there must be some overruling power in this thing, and I think you had better go as soon as you get your plaster of paris sown and bring up the man with his scribe."

To this also David agreed. The next morning, as soon as breakfast was over, he took the half-bushel measure under his arm and went out to the place where he supposed the plaster to be, as he knew exactly where he had left it twenty-four hours earlier. But when he came to look for it, behold, it had entirely disappeared! Every vestige of it was gone from the spot where he left it. He ran to his sister's house a few yards distant and inquired if she knew what had become of it.

"Why?" she said, in surprise. "Was it not all spread yesterday?"

"Not to my knowledge," answered David.

"I am astonished at that," replied his sister, "for the children came to me in the forenoon and begged of me to go out and see the men sow plaster in the field, saying that they never saw anybody sow plaster so fast in their lives. I accordingly went and saw three men at work in the field, as the children said, but, supposing that you had hired some help

Reconstruction of the Peter Whitmer Sr. farmhouse,
where the Book of Mormon was translated.

on account of your hurry, I went immediately into the house and gave the subject no further attention."

David made considerable inquiry in regard to the matter, both among his relatives and neighbors, but was not able to learn who had done it. However, the family were convinced that there was an exertion of supernatural power connected with this strange occurrence.

David immediately set out for Pennsylvania and arrived there in two days, without injuring his horses in the least, though the distance was one hundred and thirty-five miles. When he arrived, he was under the necessity of introducing himself to Joseph, as this was the first time that they had ever met.[4]

I will observe that the only acquaintance that existed between the Smith and Whitmer families was that formed by Mr. Smith and myself, when, on our way from Manchester to Pennsylvania to visit Joseph, we stopped with David overnight and gave him a brief history of the record.

When Joseph commenced making preparations for his journey, he inquired of the Lord to know how the plates should be conveyed to their point of destination. His answer was that he should give himself no trouble about that but commit them into the hands of an angel for safety, and after arriving at Mr. Whitmer's house, if he would repair immediately to the garden, the angel would deliver them up again into his hands.

Leaving Emma behind to take charge of affairs, Joseph, Oliver, and David Whitmer started for Waterloo, where they arrived after a short, pleasant journey in health and fine spirits for commencing anew on their labors. On arriving at Waterloo, Joseph received the record according to promise. The next day, he and Oliver resumed the work of translation, which they continued without further interruption until the whole work was accomplished.

NOTES

1. Waterloo is approximately five miles from Fayette, where David Whitmer's parents, Peter and Mary Musselman Whitmer, were living. It is worth noting that Mother Smith often refers to Waterloo and means Fayette or even Seneca Falls. All these villages and towns are within a few miles of each other. Peter Whitmer Sr. was born April 14, 1773, and with his wife, Mary, had eight children: Christian (January 18, 1798); Jacob (January 27, 1800); John (August 27, 1802); David (January 7, 1805); Catherine (April 22, 1807); Peter Jr. (September 27, 1809); Nancy (December 24, 1812—died April 19, 1813); and Elizabeth Ann (January 22, 1815). (See Porter, "Origins," pp. 224–25.)

2. From the beginning even Isaac Hale, Emma's father, was disillusioned about Joseph Smith and published statements against him. Concerning the plates, Isaac reported: "I was informed they had brought a wonderful book of plates down with

them. I was shown a box in which it was said they were contained, which had, to all appearances, been used as a glass box of the common size window-glass. I was allowed to feel the weight of the box, and they gave me to understand, that the book of plates was then in the box—into which, however, I was not allowed to look. . . . After this I became dissatisfied, and informed him that if there was anything in my house of that description, which I could not be allowed to see, he must take it away; if he did not, I was determined to see it. After that the Plates were said to be hid in the woods." (Quoted in Porter, "Origins," pp. 132–33.)

3. A second letter was also sent by Oliver Cowdery telling David that he had "revealed knowledge" concerning the plates and that he was convinced that they contained a record of the people who once inhabited this continent (see Porter, "Origins," p. 235).

4. David Whitmer reported the miraculous nature of his first experience meeting with Joseph and Oliver: "I was a little over two and a half days going, and traveled over 40 miles the first day, and met them on the third day. . . . Oliver told me, they knew just when I started, where I put up at night and even the name on the sign board of the hotel where I stayed each night, for he had asked Joseph to look in the Seer stone, that he did so and told him all these particulars of my journey. Oliver asked me when I first met them, when I left home, where I stayed on the road, and the names of the persons at Hotels. I could not tell the names; but as we returned I pointed out the several houses where I had stopped, when he took out his book and found them to correspond even to the names on the sign boards, all of which he had written before we met. As had been told to him by the Prophet, and which agreed in every particular." (In Cook, *Whitmer Interviews*, p. 123.)

CHAPTER 30

Translation of the Book of Mormon is completed. Oliver Cowdery, David Whitmer, and Martin Harris receive divine witness of the work. Testimony of the Three Witnesses. Testimony of the Eight Witnesses. Contract negotiations completed for publication of the Book of Mormon with E. B. Grandin of Palmyra. Mob gathers to stop Joseph and is confounded. Copyright secured. Careful instructions are given concerning protection of the sacred manuscript.

June 1829 to end of August 1829

As soon as the Book of Mormon was translated, Joseph dispatched a messenger to Mr. Smith, bearing intelligence of the completion of the work and a request that Mr. Smith and myself should come immediately to Waterloo.[1]

That same evening we communicated this intelligence to Martin Harris, for we loved the man although his weakness had cost us much unnecessary trouble. He seemed to have a heart that designed no evil, and we felt a commiseration for the disappointment which his misguided zeal had brought upon him in an evil hour. When he heard that the translation was finally completed, he seemed as greatly rejoiced as if he knew that it affected his salvation, and determined to go straightway to Waterloo as soon as he could get away. The next morning, we accordingly set off together, and before sunset we met Joseph and Oliver at Waterloo.

The evening was spent in reading the manuscript, and it would be superfluous for me to say to anyone who has read these pages that we were greatly rejoiced. It then appeared to us, who did not realize the

Joseph and his scribes worked on the translation in an upper room of the Whitmer home.[2]

magnitude of the work, as though the greatest difficulty was then surmounted. But with Joseph it was not so, for he knew that a dispensation of the gospel had been committed to him, of which the starting bud had scarcely yet made its appearance.

The next morning after breakfast, we repaired to the sitting room, and after attending the morning service, namely reading, singing, and praying, Joseph arose from his knees and approached Martin with a solemnity which thrills through my veins to this day, whenever it comes to my recollection. "Martin Harris," he said, "*you* have got to humble yourself before your God this day and obtain, if possible, a forgiveness of your sins. If you will do this, it is God's will that you and Oliver Cowdery and David Whitmer should look upon the plates."

Soon after this, these four left and went into a grove a short distance from the house, where they continued in earnest supplication to God, until he permitted an angel from his presence to bear to them a message, declaring to them that all which Joseph had testified of concerning the plates was true, and showing them the same.

When they returned to the house, it was between three and four o'clock. Mrs. Whitmer, Mr. Smith, and myself were sitting in a bedroom, myself on a bedside. When Joseph came in, he threw himself down beside me and exclaimed, "Father! Mother! You do not know how happy I am. The Lord has caused the plates to be shown to three more besides me. They have also seen an angel and will have to testify to the truth of what I have said, for they know for themselves that I do not go about to deceive the people. I do feel as though I was relieved of a dreadful burden which was almost too much for me to endure. But they will now have to bear a part, and it does rejoice my soul that I am not any longer to be entirely alone in the world."[3]

Martin Harris then came in. He seemed almost overcome with an excess of joy. He then testified to what he had seen and heard, as did also the others, Oliver and David, who added that no tongue could express the joy of their hearts and the greatness of the things which they had both seen and heard. Their testimony was the same in substance as that in the Book of Mormon:

*The Three Witnesses retired to a nearby grove
and there beheld Moroni and the ancient plates.*

THE TESTIMONY OF THREE WITNESSES

Be it known unto all nations, kindreds, tongues, and people, unto whom this work shall come: That we, through the grace of God the Father, and our Lord Jesus Christ, have seen the plates which contain this record, which is a record of the people of Nephi, and also of the Lamanites, their brethren, and also of the people of Jared, who came from the tower of which hath been spoken. And we also know that they have been translated by the gift and power of God, for his voice hath declared it unto us; wherefore we know of a surety that the work is true. And we also testify that we have seen the engravings which are upon the plates; and they have been shown unto us by the power of God, and not of man. And we declare with words of soberness, that an angel of God came down from heaven, and he brought and laid before our eyes, that we beheld and saw the plates, and the engravings thereon; and we know that it is by the grace of God the Father, and our Lord Jesus Christ, that we beheld and bear record that these things are true. And it is marvelous in our eyes. Nevertheless, the voice of the Lord commanded us that we should bear record of it; wherefore, to be obedient unto the commandments of God, we bear testimony of these things.[4] And we know that if we are faithful in Christ, we shall rid our garments of the blood of all men, and be found spotless before the judgment-seat of Christ, and shall dwell with him eternally in the heavens. And the honor be to the Father, and to the Son, and to the Holy Ghost, which is one God. Amen.

OLIVER COWDERY
DAVID WHITMER
MARTIN HARRIS

Martin Harris seemed particularly willing to give out his feelings in words. He said, "I have now seen an angel from heaven who has of a surety testified of the truth of all that I have heard concerning the record. I have also looked upon the plates and handled them with my hands and can testify of the same to the whole world. I have received for myself a witness that words cannot express, and no tongue can describe, and I bless God in the sincerity of my soul that he has condescended to make me, even me, a witness of the greatness of his work and designs in behalf of the children of men." Oliver and David also joined with him in solemn praises to God for his goodness and mercy.

We returned home the next day, a cheerful, happy little company. In a few days, we were followed by Joseph, Oliver, and the Whitmers, who came to make us a visit and make some arrangements about getting the book printed. Soon after they came, all the male part of the company,

The Eight Witnesses viewed the ancient plates near the area
where Joseph saw the Father and the Son.

with my husband, Samuel, and Hyrum, retired to a grove where the family were in the habit of offering up their secret devotions to God. They went to this place, because it had been revealed to Joseph that the plates would be carried thither by one of the ancient Nephites. Here it was that those eight witnesses, whose names are recorded in the Book of Mormon, looked upon them and handled them, of which they bear record in the following words:

The Testimony of Eight Witnesses

Be it known unto all nations, kindreds, tongues, and people, unto whom this work shall come: That Joseph Smith, Jun., the translator of this work, has shown unto us the plates of which hath been spoken, which have the appearance of gold; and as many of the leaves as the said Smith has translated we did handle with our hands;

and we also saw the engravings thereon, all of which has the appearance of ancient work, and of curious workmanship. And this we bear record with words of soberness, that the said Smith has shown unto us, for we have seen and hefted, and know of a surety that the said Smith has got the plates of which we have spoken. And we give our names unto the world, to witness unto the world that which we have seen. And we lie not, God bearing witness of it."

CHRISTIAN WHITMER
JACOB WHITMER
PETER WHITMER, JUN.
JOHN WHITMER
HIRAM PAGE
JOSEPH SMITH, SEN.
HYRUM SMITH
SAMUEL H. SMITH

After the witnesses returned to the house, the angel again made his appearance to Joseph and received the plates from his hands. That evening we held a meeting in which all the witnesses bore testimony to the facts, as stated above; and all of our family, even to Don Carlos, who was but fourteen years of age,[5] testified of the truth of the latter-day dispensation—that it was ushered in.

In a few days the whole company from Waterloo went to Palmyra for the purpose of contracting with Mr. E. B. Grandin for the printing of the book.[6] They succeeded in making a contract, but did not draw the writings at that time. The next day, the company from Waterloo returned home, excepting Joseph and Peter Whitmer, Joseph remaining to draw writings in regard to the printing of the manuscript, which was to be done on the day following.

When Joseph was about starting for Palmyra, where the writings were to be executed, Dr. McIntyre came in and informed us that forty men were collected in the capacity of a mob, with the view of waylaying Joseph on his way thither; that they requested him (Dr. McIntyre), as they had done once before, to take command of the company; and that upon his refusing to do so, one Mr. Huzzy, a hatter of Palmyra, proffered his services and was chosen as their leader.

On hearing this I besought Joseph not to go; but he smiled at my fears, saying, "Never mind, Mother; just put your trust in God, and nothing will hurt me today." In a short time he set out for Palmyra. On his way thither lay a heavy strip of timber, about half a mile in width, and beyond it, on the right side of the road, lay a field belonging to David Jacaway. When he came to this field, he found the mob seated on the string fence running along the road. Coming to Mr. Huzzy first, he took off his hat and good-naturedly saying, "Good morning, Mr. Huzzy," passed on to the next, whom he saluted in like manner, and the next, and so on till he came to the last.

This struck them with confusion, and while they were pondering in amazement, he passed on, leaving them perched upon the fence like so many roosting chickens, and arrived at Palmyra without being molested. Here he met Mr. Grandin, and writings were drawn up between them to this effect: that half of the price for printing was to be paid by Martin Harris, and the residue by my two sons Joseph and Hyrum. These writings were afterwards signed by all the parties concerned.[7]

When Joseph returned from Palmyra, he said, "Well, Mother, the Lord has been on my side today; the devil has not overpowered me in any of my proceedings. Did I not tell you that I should be delivered from the hands of my enemies? They thought they were going to perform great feats; they have done wonders to prevent me from getting the book printed; they mustered themselves together, and got upon the fence, made me a low bow, and went home, and I'll warrant you they wish they had stayed there in the first place. Mother, there is a God in heaven, and I know it."

Soon after this, Joseph secured the copyright; and before he returned to Pennsylvania, where he had left his wife, he received a commandment, which was in substance as follows:

Joseph was told to see that Oliver transcribed the whole work a second time and that he never take both transcripts to the office, but leave one and carry the other, so that in case one was destroyed, the other would be left. Furthermore, Peter Whitmer was commanded to remain at our house to assist in guarding the writings, and also to accompany Oliver to the office and back, when no other person could be spared from the place, to go and come with him. It was necessary that Oliver should be accompanied by someone to protect him against those who would try to waylay him in order to get the manuscript, and also to protect the house against infestation by those intrusive persons who were willing to sacrifice their character for the sake of putting a stop to the printing, because they were exceedingly mad against the truth and went about to establish their own kind of righteousness.

This astonished us very much, but we did not gainsay the counsel of the Most High; wherefore we did all things according to the pattern that was given; and accordingly, they guarded Oliver on his way to work in the morning, went after him at night, and kept a guard over the house all night long, although we saw no enemy, and knew not that anyone designed evil against us.

After giving these instructions, Joseph returned to Pennsylvania.

NOTES

1. Although it appears that the translation was not yet completed, Joseph deposited the title page of the Book of Mormon in the office of R. R. Lansing, clerk of the Northern District of New York, on Thursday, June 11, 1829, to obtain the copyright (see Bushman, *Beginnings,* p. 107).

2. David Whitmer reported, "In regard to the translation, it was a laborious work for the weather was very warm, and the days were long and they worked from morning till night. But they [Joseph and Oliver] were both young and strong and were soon able to complete the work." (In Cook, *Whitmer Interviews,* p. 115.)

3. Oliver Cowdery witnessed: "I beheld with my eyes, and handled with my hands, the gold plates. . . . I also saw with my eyes and handled with my hands the 'holy interpreters.' That book is *true.* . . . It contains principles of salvation; and if you, my hearers, will walk by its light and obey its precepts, you will be saved with an everlasting salvation in the kingdom of God on high." (Quoted in *Millennial Star* 27 [January 28, 1865]: 58.) Elizabeth Whitmer Cowdery, wife of Oliver, testified of her husband: "From the hour when the glorious vision of the Holy Messenger revealed to mortal eyes the hidden prophecies which God had promised his faithful followers should come forth in due time, until the moment when he passed away from earth, he always without one doubt or shadow of turning affirmed the divinity and truth of the Book of Mormon" (quoted in Richard Lloyd Anderson, *Investigating the Book of Mormon Witnesses* [Salt Lake City: Deseret Book Co., 1981], p. 63).

Martin Harris testified: "I know what I know. I have seen what I have seen, and I have heard what I have heard. I have seen the gold plates. . . . An angel appeared to me and others." He further testified: "I might as well doubt my own existence as to doubt the divine authenticity of the Book of Mormon or the divine calling of Joseph Smith." (Quoted in Anderson, *Investigating*, p. 117.)

David Whitmer boldly averred: "I have been visited by thousands of people, believers and unbelievers, men and ladies of all degrees, sometimes as many as 15 in one day, and have never failed in my testimony. And they will know some day that my testimony is true. I had a mob of from four to five hundred surrounding me at one time, demanding that I should deny my published statement in the Book of Mormon; but the testimony I bore the mob made them tremble before me. I heard the voice of the Angel just as stated in said Book, and the engravings on the plates were shown to us, and we were commanded to bear record of them; and if they are not true, then there is no truth, and if there is no truth there is no God; if there is no God then there is no existence. But there is a God, and I know it." (In Cook, *Whitmer Interviews*, pp. 95–96.)

4. One correspondent reported David Whitmer's description of God's voice as "a voice that seemed to fill all space, musical as the sighing of a wind through the forest." Of Whitmer's experience of hearing Moroni's voice, the same correspondent wrote: "The voice, majestic, ringing out from earth to the mighty dome of space, still lingers in his ears like a chime of silver bells." (In Cook, *Whitmer Interviews*, pp. 75, 78–79.)

5. Don Carlos was in his "fourteenth year."

6. After an initial refusal by E. B. Grandin, Joseph and his companions had tried to get printers in nearby Rochester, New York, to do the work; but the contract eventually came to Grandin after he relented. Egbert Bratt Grandin was born in 1806 and died in 1845. He was the editor of the local newspaper, the *Wayne Sentinel.* He was twenty-three years old when he printed the Book of Mormon.

7. The publishing contract was for five thousand copies to be printed at a cost of three thousand dollars. Martin Harris was to guarantee the payment within eighteen months by a security agreement and mortgage on his farm. The agreement was signed August 26, 1829. To complete the obligation, Martin Harris's farm was sold at public auction on April 7, 1831.

CHAPTER 31

Group of religionists meet and plan to thwart the work of publishing the Book of Mormon. Mother Smith spends the night with the manuscript in a trunk under her bed. She contemplates many scenes she has passed through. Three men visit the Smiths with intentions of distracting Lucy, seizing the manuscript, and immediately burning it. Their scheme fails.

Early fall 1829

Oliver Cowdery commenced the work immediately after Joseph left, and the printing went on very well for a season, but the clouds of persecution again began to gather. The rabble, and a party of restless religionists, began to counsel together as to the most efficient means of putting a stop to our proceedings.

About the first council of this kind was held in a room adjoining that in which Oliver and young Mr. Robinson, son of our friend, Dr. Robinson, were printing. They suspected that something was agitated among these men that was not right, and Oliver proposed to Mr. Robinson that he should put his ear to a hole in the partition wall, and by this means he overheard the following remarks and resolutions: One said, "Now, gentlemen, this golden bible which the Smiths have got is destined to break down everything before it, if a stop is not put to it. This very thing is going to be a serious injury to all religious denominations, and in a little while, many of our excellent minister goodmen, who have no means of obtaining a respectable livelihood except by their ministerial labor, will be deprived of their salaries, which is their living. Shall we endure this, gentlemen?"

Cries of "No! No!"

"Well, how shall we put a stop to the printing of this thing?"

It was then moved, seconded, and carried without a dissenting voice to appoint three of their company to come to our house on the following Tuesday or Wednesday, when the men were not about the house, and request me to read the manuscript to them; and that after I had done reading it, two of the company should attract my attention toward something else than the manuscript, and while they were doing this, the third should seize the writing from the drawer and throw the same into the fire and burn it up.

"Again," said the speaker, "suppose that we fail in this—or any other plan—and the book is published in defiance of all that we can do. What is then to be done? Shall we buy their books and suffer our families to read them?" They all responded, "No!" They then entered into a solemn covenant, binding themselves by tremendous oaths, that they would never own a single volume, nor would they permit one member of their families to do so, and thus they would nip the dreadful calamity while it was in the bud.

Oliver came home that evening and related the whole affair with solemnity, for he was greatly troubled by it. "Mother, what shall I do with the manuscript? Where shall I put it to keep it away from them?"

"Oliver," said I, "do not think the matter so serious after all, for there is a watch kept constantly about the house, and I need not take out the manuscript to read it to them unless I choose, and for its present safety I can have it deposited in a chest, under the head of my bed, in such a way that it never will be disturbed." I then placed it in a chest, raised up the head of my bedstead, and shoved the chest under it, letting the bedstead fall, so that the chest was securely closed, although it had neither lock nor key.

At night we all went to rest at the usual hour except Peter Whitmer, who spent the night on guard. As for myself, soon after I lay down upon my bed, I fell into a train of reflections which occupied my mind until the day appeared. I called up to my recollection the past history of my life, and scene after scene seemed to rise in succession before me. The principles of early piety which were taught me when my mother called me, with my brothers and sisters, around her knee and instructed us to feel our constant dependence upon God, our accountability to

*Lucy Smith spent a night sleeping with the sacred manuscript
in a chest beneath her headboard.*[1]

him, our liability to transgression, the necessity of prayer, and of a
death and judgment to come.

Then again, I seemed to hear the voice of my brother Jason declaring to the people that the true religion and faith of the Church of Jesus
Christ, which He established on the earth, was not among the Christian
denominations of the day, and beseeching them, by the love of God, to
seek to obtain that faith which was once delivered to the Saints.

Again, I seemed to stand at the bedside of my sister Lovisa, and saw her exemplify the power of God in answer to the prayer of faith by an almost entire resuscitation, while her livid lips moved but to express one sentiment—which was the power of God over disease and death.

The next moment I was conveyed to the closing scene of my sister Lovina's life, and heard her last admonition to her mates and myself re-iterated in my ear. Then my soul thrilled to the plaintive notes of the favorite hymn which she repeated in the last moments of her existence on earth. Oh, how often I had listened to the beautiful music of the voices of these two sisters and drunk in their tones as if I might ne'er hear them again.

After that, I seemed to live again the season of gloominess, of prayers and tears, that preceded my sister's death, when my heart was burdened with anxiety, distress, and fear lest I, by any means, should fail in that preparation which is needful in order to meet my sisters in that world for which they had taken their departure.

It was then I began to feel the want of a living instructor in matters of salvation. How intensely I felt this deficiency when, a few years after-wards, I found myself upon the very verge of the eternal world; and al-though I had an intense desire for salvation, yet I was totally devoid of any satisfactory knowledge or understanding of the laws or require-ments of that Being before whom I expected shortly to appear. But I labored faithfully in prayer to God, struggling to be freed from the power of death.

When I recovered, I sought unceasingly for someone who could im-part to my mind some definite idea of the requirements of heaven with regard to mankind. But like Esau seeking his blessing, I found them not, though I sought the same with tears. For days and months and years I continued asking God continually to reveal to me the hidden treasures of his will. Although I was always strengthened, I did not receive answer to my prayers for many years.

I had always believed confidently that God would raise up some-one who would effect a reconciliation among those who desired to do his will at the expense of all other things. But what was my joy and astonishment to hear my own son, though a boy of fourteen years of age, declare that he had been visited by an angel from heaven![2]

My mind rested upon the hours which I had spent listening to the instructions which Joseph had received, and which he faithfully committed to us. We received these with infinite delight, but none were more engaged than the one from whom we were doomed to part, for Alvin was never so happy as when he was contemplating the final success of his brother in obtaining the record.

And now I fancied I could hear him with his parting breath conjuring his brother to continue faithful that he might obtain the prize that the Lord had promised him. But when I cast my mind upon the disappointment and trouble which we had suffered while the work was in progress, my heart beat quickly and my pulse rose high, and in my best efforts to the contrary, my mind was agitated. I felt every nervous sensation which I experienced at the time the circumstances took place.

At last, as if led by an invisible spirit, I came to the time when the messenger from Waterloo informed me that the translation was actually completed. My soul swelled with a joy that could scarcely be heightened, except by the reflection that the record which had cost so much labor, suffering, and anxiety was now, in reality, lying beneath my own head—that this identical work had not only been the object which we as a family had pursued so eagerly, but that prophets of ancient days, angels, and even the great God had had his eye upon it. "And," said I to myself, "shall I fear what man can do? Will not the angels watch over the precious relic of the worthy dead and the hope of the living? And am I indeed the mother of a prophet of the God of heaven, the honored instrument in performing so great a work?" I felt that I was in the purview of angels, and my heart bounded at the thought of the great condescension of the Almighty.

Thus I spent the night surrounded by enemies and yet in an ecstasy of happiness. Truly I can say that my soul did magnify and my spirit rejoiced in God, my Savior.

On the fourth day after they had met, the three men delegated by the council came to perform the work assigned them. They began, "Mrs. Smith, we hear you have a gold bible, and we came to see if you would be so kind as to show it to us?"

"No, gentlemen," said I, "we have no gold bible, but we have a translation of some gold plates, which have been brought forth to bring to the world the plainness of the gospel and to give to the children of men a history of the people that used to inhabit this continent." I then proceeded to give them the substance of what is contained in the Book of Mormon, particularly the principles of religion which it contains. I endeavored to show them the similarity between these principles and the simplicity of the gospel taught by Jesus Christ in the New Testament. "But," added I, "the different denominations are very much opposed to us. The Universalists come here wonderfully afraid that their religion will suffer loss. The Presbyterians are frightened lest their salary will come down. The Methodists come and they rage, for they worship a God without body or parts, and the doctrine we advocate comes in contact with their views."

"Well," said the foremost gentleman with whom I was acquainted, "can we see the manuscript?"

"No, sir, you *cannot* see it. We have done exhibiting the manuscript altogether. I have told you what is in it, and that must suffice."

He did not reply to this, but said, "Mrs. Smith, you, Hyrum, Sophronia, and Samuel have belonged to our church for some time, and we respect you very highly. You say a great deal about the book which your son has found and believe much of what he tells you, but we cannot bear the thoughts of losing you, and they do wish—I wish—that if you do believe those things, you never would proclaim anything about them. I do wish you would not."[3]

"Deacon Beckwith," said I, "even if you should stick my body full of faggots and burn me at the stake, I would declare, as long as God should give me breath, that Joseph has that record, and that I know it to be true."

He then turned to his companions and said, "You see, it is no use to say anything more to her, for we cannot change her mind." Then, addressing me, he said, "Mrs. Smith, I see that it is not possible to persuade you out of your belief, and I do not know that it is worthwhile to say any more about the matter."

"No, sir," said I, "it is of no use. You cannot affect anything by all that you can say."

He then bid me farewell and went out to see Hyrum, when the following conversation took place between them:

Deacon Beckwith: "Mr. Smith, do you not think that you may be deceived about that record which your brother pretends to have found?"

Hyrum: "No, sir, I do not."

Deacon Beckwith: "Well, now, Mr. Smith, if you find that you are deceived, and that he has not got the record, will you confess the fact to me?"

Hyrum: "Will you, Deacon Beckwith, take one of the books, when they are printed, and read it, asking God to give you an evidence that you may know whether it is true?"

Deacon Beckwith: "I think it beneath me to take so much trouble; however, if you will promise that you will confess to me that Joseph never had the plates, I will ask for a witness whether the book is true."

Hyrum: "I will tell you what I will do, Mr. Beckwith, if you do get a testimony from God that the book is not true, I will confess to you that it is not true."

Upon this they parted, and the deacon next went to Samuel, who quoted to him Isaiah 56:9–11:

"All ye beasts of the field, come to devour, yea, all ye beasts in the forest. His watchmen are blind: they are all ignorant, they are all dumb dogs, they cannot bark; sleeping, lying down, loving to slumber. Yea, they are greedy dogs which can never have enough, and they are shepherds that cannot understand: they all look to their own way, every one for his gain, from his quarter."

Here Samuel ended the quotation, and the three gentlemen left without ceremony.

NOTES

1. The bedroom depicted is on the upper floor of the Smith frame house in Manchester. It appears, however, that the Smiths had already moved back to their little cabin at the north end of the one hundred acres when these events occurred. This cabin no longer exists.

2. In the Preliminary Manuscript Lucy does not mention the visit of God the Father and Jesus Christ to her son Joseph. Joseph did state, however, in his 1835 recital of the First Vision: "I saw many angels in this vision" (in Milton V. Backman Jr., *Joseph Smith's First Vision*, 2d ed. [Salt Lake City: Bookcraft, 1980], p. 159).

3. In the March 10, 1830, session records of the Western Presbyterian Church in Palmyra, it is stated that "the committee appointed to visit Hyrum Smith, Lucy Smith, and Samuel Harrison Smith reported that they had visited them and received no satisfaction. They acknowledged that they had entirely neglected the ordinances of the church for the last eighteen months and that they did not wish to unite with us anymore. Whereupon resolved that they be cited to appear before the session on the 24th day of March inst. at 2:00 p.m. at the meetinghouse to answer to the following charge, to wit: neglect of public worship and the sacrament of the Lord's Supper for the last eighteen months." The committee appointed one P. West to summon Lucy, Hyrum, and Samuel to appear before the session on March 24, 1830, but to no avail. They were thereafter "censured for their contumacy" and "suspended from the sacrament of the Lord's Supper." (Session records, Presbyterian church, microfilm, LDS Church Archives. See also Backman, *First Vision*, pp. 182–83.)

CHAPTER 32

Work of printing the Book of Mormon continues. Hyrum Smith is led by the Spirit to go to the press on the Sabbath. He and Oliver Cowdery discover Abner Cole pilfering the Book of Mormon, publishing it in a series in his small newspaper. They ask him to cease and desist. Joseph is brought in from Pennsylvania, warns Cole he will use the law, and convinces Cole to stop his illegal activities. Citizens of Palmyra combine and agree to never purchase the "gold bible." The Book of Mormon is published.

Fall 1829 to March 26, 1830

The work of printing still continued with little or no interruption. The bargain which they had made with E. B. Grandin entitled them to use the press every day except Sunday. Then one Sunday afternoon, Hyrum became very uneasy. He told Oliver that his peculiar feelings led him to believe that something was going wrong at the printing office. Oliver asked if he thought there would be any harm in going to the office because it was Sunday. They debated some time about this, until at last Hyrum said, "I shall not stop to consider the matter any longer, for I am going. You may suit yourself about the matter, but I will not suffer such uneasiness any longer without knowing the cause."

In a few minutes they were on their way to the printing establishment. When they arrived there, they found an individual by the name of Cole very busy at work printing a paper which seemed to be a weekly periodical. Hyrum said, "Why, Mr. Cole, you seem to be busy at work. How is it that you work on Sunday?"

*Twenty-six-year-old John Gilbert worked here
and set the type for the Book of Mormon.*[1]

Mr. Cole answered, "I cannot have the press during the week, and I am obliged to print nights and Sundays."

Hyrum took up one of the papers and discovered that the man was printing the Book of Mormon by piecemeal. In the prospectus, Mr. Cole agreed to publish one form of "Joe Smith's gold bible" each week, and thereby furnish his subscribers with the principal portion of the book for a comparatively small sum. His paper was entitled *Dogberry Paper on Winter Hill,* and here he had thrown together the most disgusting and insignificant stuff that could be conceived of in juxtaposition with the portion of the Book of Mormon which he had pilfered. He was thus classing the beautiful, unaffected simplicity of this inspired writing with the lowest and most contemptible doggerel that ever was imposed upon any community. Hyrum was shocked at this perversion of common sense and moral feeling, as well as indignant at the unfair and dishonest course Mr. Cole had taken to get possession of the work.

"Mr. Cole," said he, "what right have you to print the Book of Mormon in this way? Do you not know that we have secured a copyright?"

"It is none of your business, sir," said Mr. Cole. "I have hired the press and I will print what I please, so help yourself."

"Mr. Cole," replied Hyrum, "I forbid you printing any more of that sacred book in your paper. You must stop it."

"Smith," exclaimed Cole, "I don't care a d———n for you. That d———d gold bible is going into my paper, in spite of all you can do."

Hyrum and Oliver both contended with him a long time to dissuade him from his purpose, but finding they could do nothing with him, they returned home, and Mr. Cole issued his paper as he had done several other times. We discovered that he had already issued some six or eight numbers, and had managed to keep them out of our sight.[2]

Hyrum and Oliver returned immediately home, and after connecting with Mr. Smith, it was considered necessary to send for Joseph. Accordingly my husband set out as soon as possible for Pennsylvania and returned with Joseph the ensuing Sunday.[3] The day on which they were expected home was one of the most blustery, cold, and disagreeable that I ever experienced. But they breasted the storm all day long,

*The Grandin Company building in downtown Palmyra
had a press, a bindery,[4] and a bookstore.*

and when they arrived there, they were nearly stiffened with the cold. However, Joseph made himself comfortable, and, as soon as he could, he went the same night to the printing office.

As it was Sunday, the day in which Mr. Cole published his *Dogberry Paper*, Joseph saluted him very good-naturedly with, "How do you do, Mr. Cole? You seem hard at work."

"How do you do, Mr. Smith?" said Cole dryly.

Joseph then examined his paper and said, "Mr. Cole, that book and the right of publishing it belongs to me, and I forbid you meddling with it in the least degree."

Mr. Cole threw off his coat and, rolling up his sleeves, came towards my son in a great rage, smacking his fists together with vengeance and roaring out, "Do you want to fight, sir? Do you want to fight? I will publish just what I've a mind to, and now if you want to fight, just come on."

Joseph could not help smiling at his grotesque appearance, for his behavior was too ridiculous to excite indignation. "Well, now, Mr. Cole," said he, "you had better keep on your coat, for it's cold, and I am not going to fight you nor do anything of the sort. Nevertheless, you have got to stop printing my book, sir, I assure you, for I know my

The 1830 edition of the Book of Mormon
had no verses or columns and contained 590 pages.[5]

THE BOOK OF MORMON:

AN account written by the hand of Mormon, upon plates, taken from the plates of Nephi.
Wherefore it is an abridgment of the Record of the People of Nephi, and also of the Lamanites; written to the Lamanites, which are a remnant of the House of Israel; and also to Jew and Gentile; written by way of commandment, and also by the spirit of Prophecy and of Revelation. Written, and sealed up, and hid up unto the LORD, that they might not be destroyed; to come forth by the gift and power of GOD unto the interpretation thereof; sealed by the hand of Moroni, and hid up unto the LORD, to come forth in due time by the way of Gentile; the interpretation thereof by the gift of GOD; an abridgment taken from the Book of Ether.

Also, which is a Record of the People of Jared, which were scattered at the time the LORD confounded the language of the people when they were building a tower to get to Heaven: Which is to shew unto the remnant of the House of Israel how great things the LORD hath done for their fathers; and that they may know the covenants of the LORD, that they are not cast off forever; and also to the convincing of the Jew and Gentile that JESUS is the CHRIST, the ETERNAL GOD, manifesting Himself unto all nations. And now if there be fault, it be the mistake of men; wherefore condemn not the things of GOD, that ye may be found spotless at the judgement seat of CHRIST. BY JOSEPH SMITH, JUNIOR, Author and Proprietor.

The above work, containing about 600 pages, large Duodecimo, is now for sale, wholesale and retail, at the Palmyra Bookstore, by
HOWARD & GRANDIN.
Palmyra, March 26, 1830.   339

Notice appearing Friday, March 26, 1830, in the
Wayne Sentinel in Palmyra, New York.

rights and shall maintain them."

"Sir," bawled out Cole, "if you think you are the best man, just take off your coat and try it."

"Mr. Cole," said Joseph, in a low, significant tone, "there is law, and you will find that out, if you did not know it before; but I shall not fight you, for that will do no good. There is another way of disposing of the affair that will answer my purpose better than fighting."

At this, the ex-justice began to cool off a little, and finally concluded to submit to an arbitration, which decided that he should stop his proceedings forthwith, so that he made us no further trouble.

Joseph, after disposing of this affair, returned to Pennsylvania, but it was not long till another difficulty arose. The inhabitants of the surrounding country, perceiving that the work still went on, were becoming uneasy again and called a large meeting. They gathered their forces together, far and near, and organizing themselves into a committee of the whole, they passed a resolution that they would not purchase the book or suffer their families to do so, as they had done in a former meeting. Not content with this, they sent a deputation to E. B. Grandin who informed him of the resolution passed by the meeting, and also told him the evil consequences which would result to him therefrom.

The men who were appointed to this errand fulfilled their mission to the letter and urged upon Mr. Grandin the necessity of his putting a stop to the printing, as the Smiths had lost all their property and consequently would be unable to pay him for his work, except by the sale of books. And this they would never be able to do, for the people would not purchase them. This information caused Mr. Grandin to stop printing, and we were again compelled to send for Joseph. These trips back and forth from New York to Pennsylvania cost everything that we could raise, but they seemed unavoidable.[6]

When Joseph came, he went immediately with Martin Harris to Grandin and succeeded in removing his fears, so that he went on with the work until the books were printed, which was in the spring of 1830.

NOTES

1. When the manuscript came to the printer it needed to be paragraphed, capitalized, and punctuated, and needed to have spelling corrected. John H. Gilbert won the trust of Hyrum and Oliver, and was allowed to take a few sheets of the printer's copy of the manuscript home and work on them at night. Gilbert reported: "But one copy of the manuscript was furnished the printer. I never heard of but one. As quick as Mr. Grandin got his type and got things all ready to commence work, Hyrum Smith brought to the office 24 pages of manuscript on foolscap paper, closely written

and legible, but not a punctuation mark from beginning to end. . . . Oliver Cowdery was not engaged as compositor on the work or was not the printer. He was a frequent visitor . . . to the office during the printing of the Mormon Bible. The manuscript was supposed to be in the handwriting of Cowdery. Every Chapter, if I remember correctly, was one solid paragraph, without a punctuation mark, from beginning to end. . . . I punctuated it to make it read as I supposed the Author intended, and but very little punctuation was altered in proofreading. . . . [Some nights I took the manuscript] home with me and read it, and punctuated it with a lead pencil. . . . Cowdery held and looked over the manuscript when most of the proofs were read. Martin Harris once or twice, and Hyrum Smith once, Grandin supposing these men could read their own writing as well, if not better, than anyone else; and if there are any discrepancies between the Palmyra edition and the manuscript these men should be held responsible." (Quoted in Porter, "Origins," p. 89. See also Backman, *Eyewitness Accounts*, pp. 180–81.)

2. Abner Cole began publishing this Palmyra weekly, entitled *The Reflector*, on September 2, 1829. In the January 2, 1830, issue he published material corresponding to the present 1 Nephi 1 through 1 Nephi 2:3. After Joseph threatened legal action, Cole finally backed off and ceased publishing parts of the Book of Mormon. The issues of *The Reflector* dated January 13 and January 22 were the last numbers to carry the pilfered parts of the Book of Mormon. (See Bushman, *Beginnings*, pp. 108–9.) Lucy Mack Smith "remembered the paper was called *Dogberry Paper on Winter Hill.* There never was any paper published under this name, but the editor and proprietor of the *Reflector* called himself O. Dogberry and occasionally inserted a note that the paper was published at the 'Bower on Wintergreen Hill.' And so, putting these facts partially together in her memory many years later, Mother Smith remembered it incorrectly as *Dogberry Paper on Winter Hill.*" (Russell R. Rich, "The Dogberry Papers and the Book of Mormon," *BYU Studies* 10 [Spring 1970]: 318–19.)

3. This shows that the round trip of 270 miles from Palmyra to Harmony took about six or seven days. The date that Joseph arrived to deal with Cole can be reasonably estimated as either Sunday, January 3, or Sunday, January 10, 1830. It could have also been as late as Sunday, January 17, 1830, but this is unlikely, since Joseph would yet return to Harmony, then back to Palmyra, all in the month of January.

4. The binding was done in partnership with Luther Howard on the second floor (see Porter, "Origins," p. 90).

5. The press used by Grandin printed sheets of paper with eight Book of Mormon pages on each side. After one side was printed, the sheet was hung on a line to dry before the other side was printed. One of these sheets, containing sixteen pages, after being folded, stitched, and cut into a booklet, was called a signature. To print five thousand copies of the first edition of the Book of Mormon, the printer would have needed at least 185,000 sheets of paper, not counting any mistakes or extras.

6. This action took place sometime in January 1830.

CHAPTER 33

Legal organization of the Church at the home of Peter Whitmer Sr. in Fayette, New York. Joseph's parents are baptized. Samuel Harrison Smith called on a mission to surrounding area. An account of his challenges. He meets with John P. Greene.

April 1830 to July 1830

During the fall and winter we held no meetings, because of the plotting schemes of the people against us, but in the spring, about the first of April of the same year in which the Book of Mormon was published, Joseph came from Pennsylvania and preached to us several times. My husband and Martin Harris were baptized. Joseph stood on the shore when his father came out of the water, and as he took him by the hand he cried out, "Praise to my God! I have lived to see my own father baptized into the true Church of Jesus Christ," and covered his face in his father's bosom and wept aloud for joy as did Joseph of old when he beheld his father coming up into the land of Egypt.[1] This took place on the sixth of April, 1830, the day on which the Church was organized.[2]

Shortly after this, my sons were all ordained to the ministry, even Don Carlos, who was but fourteen years of age. Samuel was directed to take a number of the Books of Mormon and go on a mission to Livonia,[3] to preach and make sale of the books, if possible. Whilst he was making preparations to go on this mission, Miss Almira Mack arrived in Manchester from Pontiac. This young woman was a daughter

The Church was organized in the home of Peter Whitmer Sr. on Tuesday, April 6, 1830.[4]

of my brother Stephen Mack, whose history I have already given. She received the gospel as soon as she heard it, and was baptized immediately, and has ever since remained a faithful member of the Church.

On the thirtieth of June,[5] Samuel started on the mission to which he had been set apart by Joseph, and in traveling twenty-five miles, which was his first day's journey, he stopped at a number of places in order to sell his books, but was turned out of doors as soon as he declared his principles. When evening came on, he was faint and almost discouraged,[6] but coming to an inn, which was surrounded with every appearance of plenty, he called to see if the landlord would buy one of his books. On going in, Samuel inquired of him, if he did not wish to purchase a history of the origin of the Indians.

"I do not know," replied the host; "how did you get hold of it?"

"It was translated," rejoined Samuel, "by my brother, from some gold plates that he found buried in the earth."

"You liar!" cried the landlord. "Get out of my house—you shan't stay one minute with your books."

Samuel was sick at heart, for this was the fifth time he had been turned out of doors that day. He left the house and traveled a short distance and washed his feet in a small brook, as a testimony against the man. He then proceeded five miles further on his journey, and seeing an apple tree a short distance from the road, he concluded to pass the night under it; and here he lay all night upon the cold, damp ground. In the morning, he arose from his comfortless bed, and observing a small cottage at no great distance, he drew near, hoping to get a little refreshment. The only inmate was a widow, who seemed very poor. He asked her for food, relating the story of his former treatment. She prepared him victuals, and, after eating, he explained to her the history of the Book of Mormon. She listened attentively and believed all that he told her, but, in consequence of her poverty, she was unable to purchase one of the books. He presented her with one and proceeded to Bloomington, which was eight miles further.

Here he stopped at the house of John P. Greene,[7] who was a Methodist preacher and was at that time about starting on a preaching mission. He, like the others, did not wish to make a purchase of what he considered at that time to be a nonsensical fable; however, he said

Samuel Harrison Smith first preached the gospel
in this countryside of western New York.

that he would take a subscription paper, and if he found anyone on his route who was disposed to purchase, he would take his name, and in two weeks Samuel might call again and he would let him know what the prospect was of selling.[8] After making this arrangement, Samuel left one of his books with him, and returned home. At the time appointed, Samuel started again for the Reverend John P. Greene's, in order to learn the success which this gentleman had met with in finding sale for the Book of Mormon. This time, Mr. Smith and myself accompanied him, and it was our intention to have passed near the tavern where Samuel was so abusively treated a fortnight previous, but just before we came to the house, a sign of smallpox intercepted us. We turned aside, and meeting a citizen of the place, we inquired of him, to what extent this disease prevailed. He answered that the tavern keeper and two of his family had died with it not long since, but he did not know that anyone else had caught the disease, and that it was brought into the neighborhood by a traveler who stopped at the tavern overnight.

This is a specimen of the peculiar disposition of some individuals, who would sacrifice their soul's salvation rather than give a Saint of

God a meal of victuals.[9] According to the word of God, it will be more tolerable for Sodom and Gomorrah, in the Day of Judgment, than for such persons.

We arrived at Esquire Beaman's, in Livonia, that night. The next morning Samuel took the road to Mr. Greene's, and, finding that he had made no sale of the books, we returned home the following day.

Notes

1. It appears from Joseph Knight's record that Joseph Smith Sr. and Martin Harris were baptized on the Smith farm at Manchester (therefore not on the actual day of the legal formation of the Church). Knight recorded: "We went home to [Joseph's] father's and Martin with us. Martin stayed at his father's and slept in a bed on the floor with me. . . . I stayed a few days waiting for some Books [of Mormon] to be bound. Joseph said there must be a church built up. I had been there several days. Old Mr. Smith and Martin Harris came forward to be baptized. . . . They found a place in a lot a small stream ran through, and they were baptized in the evening because of persecution. They went forward and was baptized, being the first I saw baptized in the new and everlasting covenant. . . . There was one thing I will mention that evening that old Brother Smith and Martin Harris was baptized. Joseph was filled with the Spirit to a great degree . . . he burst out with . . . joy and seemed as though the world could not hold him. He went out into the lot and appeared to want to get out of sight of everybody and would sob and cry and seemed to be so full that he could not live. Oliver and I went after him and came to him and after a while he came in. But he was the most wrought upon that I ever saw any man. . . . His joy seemed to be full." (Dean Jessee, "Joseph Knight's Recollection of Early Mormon History," *BYU Studies* 17 [Autumn 1976]: 37.) George A. Smith seems to have agreed that Joseph Sr. was not baptized on the day of the organization of the Church, for he crossed out the reference to this date in his marked copy of the 1853 *Biographical Sketches* (see George A. Smith, Edited 1853, p. 151). It is worthy of note that George A. Smith made no textual changes (save it be genealogical data in chapter 9 of the 1853 edition) until this chapter (current chapter 33) (see George A. Smith, Edited 1853, pp. 1–151). It is possible that the baptism took place on the *evening* of April 6. Apparently Lucy herself was baptized on the same occasion that her husband was. (See *History of the Church* 1:79; Bushman, *Beginnings,* pp. 144, 237.)

2. There are several extant lists attempting to document those comprising the original six founding members of the Church, not all of them corresponding to each

other. From the records of Joseph Smith, Brigham Young, Joseph Knight Jr., and David Whitmer, Richard Lloyd Anderson has identified at least seven lists. William E. McLellin also gives a list. Traditionally, the six were: Oliver Cowdery, Joseph Smith Jr., Hyrum Smith, Peter Whitmer Jr., Samuel H. Smith, and David Whitmer. McLellin is the only one to include Lucy Mack Smith among the original six. (See *Papers*, p. 241.) In the 1839 draft of Joseph's history, he recorded concerning this day: "We had received commandment to organize the Church, and accordingly we met together . . . and proceeded as follows at the house of the above-mentioned Mr. Whitmer—Having opened the meeting by solemn prayer to our Heavenly Father, . . . I proceeded to lay my hands upon Oliver Cowdery—and ordained him an Elder of The Church of Jesus Christ of Latter-day Saints, after which he ordained me. . . . We then took bread, blessed it, and brake it with them; also wine, blessed it, and drank it with them. We then laid our hands on each individual member of the Church present, to confirm them members of the Church of Jesus Christ, and that they might receive the Holy Ghost, when immediately the Holy Ghost was poured out upon us all [what follows was all crossed out in the original] in a miraculous manner. . . . Many spoke with new tongues, and some several of our number were so completely overpowered for a time, that we were obliged to lay them upon beds . . . , and when bodily sensibility was restored to them they shouted hosannas to God and the Lamb, and declared that the heavens had been opened unto them, . . . that they had seen Jesus Christ sitting at the right hand of the Majesty on high, and many other great and glorious things." (*Papers*, pp. 241, 242–43.)

3. Livonia, New York, is a little over fifty miles west of Fayette.

4. The Peter and Mary Whitmer cabin was reconstructed and completed for the celebration of the sesquicentennial of the Church on April 6, 1980.

5. Though he had already been involved in missionary activities, Samuel started on this mission twelve weeks after the Church was organized in Fayette and is generally given credit for being the first missionary of the Church. However, Solomon Chamberlain, a resident of Lyons, New York, had heard of the Book of Mormon in 1829 and, being led by the Spirit, came to the Smith home. He entered the house and asked, "Is any one here that believes in visions or revelations?" Hyrum replied, "Yes, we are a visionary house." Solomon explained to them that an angel had revealed to him "that all churches and denominations on the earth had become corrupt . . . but that [God] would shortly raise up a Church, that would never be confounded nor brought down and be like unto the Apostolic Church." He then asked if they could make known to him any of their discoveries. He recorded: "Now the Lord revealed to me by the gift and power of the Holy Ghost that this was the work I had been looking for." Hyrum took Solomon to the Grandin press and pulled the first sixty-four pages of the Book of Mormon that had been printed and gave them to him. He immediately took leave to Canada and preached the gospel by the way to "both high and low, rich and poor." Solomon continued: "And thus you see this was the first that ever printed Mormonism was preached to this generation." Solomon Chamberlain was baptized by the Prophet Joseph and remained faithful all his days.

He died in Washington County, Utah, on March 26, 1862. (See Porter, "Origins," pp. 360–64.)

6. In her Early Notebook, dictated to Martha Jane Coray, Mother Smith states that "he had not eat[en] anything since he left home" (Early Notebook, p. 27).

7. John P. Greene was born in 1793 in Herkimer County, New York. He married Rhoda Young (Brigham's sister) and was living in Mendon at the time of Samuel's visit.

8. In her Early Notebook Lucy states one reason why John Greene did this: "He was willing to do any one a kindness" (Early Notebook, p. 31).

9. In her Early Notebook, Mother Smith comments: "He purchased his death for a few shillings, but sacrificed his soul's salvation" (Early Notebook, p. 33).

CHAPTER 34

Joseph Smith Sr. and Don Carlos set out on a mission to bring the gospel to the extended Smith family. They are well treated by all the family, save Jesse. Extract from brother John Smith's journal. Meeting with Parley P. Pratt. Trouble in Colesville, New York. Joseph is arrested and tried before false witnesses. John Reed is led by the Spirit to defend Joseph.

Summer 1830 to fall 1830

In the summer after the Church was organized,[1] my husband set out, with Don Carlos, to visit his father, Asael Smith.[2] After a tedious journey, they arrived at the house of John Smith, my husband's brother.[3] His wife, Clarissa, had never before seen my husband, but as soon as he entered, she exclaimed, "There, Mr. Smith, is your brother Joseph."

John, turning suddenly, cried out, "Joseph, is this you?"

"It is I," said Joseph. "Is my father still alive? I have come to see him once more before he dies."[4]

For a particular account of this visit, I shall give my readers an extract from brother John Smith's journal.[5] He writes as follows:

"The next morning after brother Joseph arrived, we set out together for Stockholm to see our father, who was living at that place with our brother Silas.[6] We arrived about dark at the house of my brother Jesse, who was absent with his wife. The children informed us that their parents were with our father, who was supposed to be dying. We hastened without delay to the house of brother Silas, and upon arriving there, were told that Father was just recovering from a severe fit, and, as it was not considered advisable to let him or Mother know that Joseph was there, we went to spend the night with brother Jesse.

"As soon as we were settled, brothers Jesse and Joseph entered into conversation respecting their families. Joseph briefly related the history of his family, the death of Alvin, etc. He then began to speak of the discovery and translation of the Book of Mormon. At this Jesse grew very angry, and exclaimed, 'If you say another word about that Book of Mormon, you shall not stay a minute longer in my house, and if I can't get you out any other way, I will hew you down with my broadaxe.'

"We had always been accustomed to being treated with much harshness by our brother, but he had never carried it to so great an extent before. However, we spent the night with him, and the next morning visited our aged parents.[7] They were overjoyed to see Joseph, for he had been absent from them so long that they had been fearful of never beholding his face again in the flesh.

"After the usual salutations, enquiries, and explanations, the subject of the Book of Mormon was introduced. Father received with gladness that which Joseph communicated; and remarked, that he had always expected that something would appear to make known the true gospel.[8]

"In a few moments brother Jesse came in, and on hearing that the subject of our conversation was the Book of Mormon, his wrath rose as high as it did the night before. 'My father's mind,' said Jesse, 'is weak; and I will not have it corrupted with such blasphemous stuff, so just shut up your head.'[9]

"Brother Joseph reasoned mildly with him, but to no purpose. Brother Silas then said, 'Jesse, our brother has come to make us a visit, and I am glad to see him and am willing he should talk as he pleases in my house.' Jesse replied in so insulting a manner and continued to talk so abusively, that Silas was under the necessity of requesting him to leave the house.

"After this, brother Joseph proceeded in conversation, and Father seemed to be pleased with every word which he said. But I must confess that I was too pious, at that time, to believe one word of it.

"I returned home the next day, leaving Joseph with my father. Soon after which Jesse came to my house and informed me that all my brothers were coming to make me a visit, 'and as true as you live,' said he, 'they all believe that cursed Mormon book, every word of it, and they are setting a trap for you to make you believe it.'

"I thanked him for taking so much trouble upon himself to inform me that my brothers were coming to see me, but told him that I considered myself amply able to judge for myself in matters of religion. 'I know,' he replied, 'that you are a pretty good judge of such things, but I tell you that they are as wary as the devil. And I want you to go with me and see our sister Susan and sister-in-law Fanny, and we will bar their minds against Joseph's influence.'

"We accordingly visited them, and conversed upon the subject as we thought proper, and requested them to be at my house the next day.

"My brothers arrived according to previous arrangement, and Jesse, who came also, was very careful to hear every word which passed among us, and would not allow one word to be said about the Book of Mormon in his presence. They agreed that night to visit our sisters the following day, and as we were about leaving, brother Asael took me aside and said, 'Now, John, I want you to have some conversation with Joseph, but if you do, you must cheat it out of Jesse. And if you wish, I can work the card for you.'

"I told him that I would be glad to have a talk with Joseph alone, if I could get an opportunity.

"'Well,' replied Asael, 'I will take a certain number in my carriage, and Silas will take the rest, and you may bring out a horse for Joseph to ride, but when we are out of sight, take the horse back to the stable again, and keep Joseph overnight.'

"I did as Asael advised, and that evening Joseph explained to me the principles of 'Mormonism,' the truth of which I have never since denied.

"The next morning, we (Joseph and myself) went to our sisters, where we met our brothers. Jesse censured me very sharply for keeping Joseph overnight.

"In the evening, when we were about to separate, I agreed to take Joseph in my wagon twenty miles on his journey the next day. Jesse rode home with me that evening, leaving Joseph with our sisters. As Joseph did not expect to see Jesse again, when we were about starting, Joseph gave Jesse his hand in a pleasant, affectionate manner, and said, 'Farewell, brother Jesse.'

"'Farewell, Jo, forever,' replied Jesse, in a surly tone.

"'I am afraid,' returned Joseph, in a kind, but solemn manner, 'it will be forever, unless you repent.'

"This was too much for even Jesse's obdurate heart. He melted into tears; however, he made no reply, nor ever mentioned the circumstance afterwards.[10]

"I took my brother twenty miles on his journey the next day, as I had agreed. Before he left me, he requested me to promise him that I would read a Book of Mormon, which he had given me, and even should I not believe it, that I would not condemn it; 'for,' said he, 'if you do not condemn it, you shall have a testimony of its truth.' I fulfilled my promise, and thus proved his testimony to be true."

Just before my husband's return, as Joseph was about commencing a discourse on Sunday morning, Parley P. Pratt came in, very much fatigued. He had heard of us at considerable distance and had traveled very fast in order to get there by meeting time, as he wished to hear what we had to say, that he might be prepared to show us our error. But when Joseph had finished his discourse, Mr. Pratt arose and expressed his hearty concurrence in every sentiment advanced. The following day he was baptized and ordained.[11] In a few days he set off for Canaan, New York, where his brother Orson resided, whom he baptized on the nineteenth of September, 1830.

About this time Joseph's trouble commenced at Colesville with the mob, who served a writ upon him and dragged him from the desk as he was about taking his text to preach.[12] But as a relation of this affair is given in his history, I shall mention only one circumstance pertaining to it, for which I am dependent upon Esquire Reed, Joseph's counsel in the case, and I shall relate it as near in his own words as my memory will admit:

"I was so busy at that time, when Mr. Smith sent for me, that it was almost impossible for me to attend the case, and never having seen Mr. Smith, I determined to decline going. But soon after coming to this conclusion, I thought I heard someone say to me, 'You *must* go, and deliver the Lord's Anointed!' Supposing it was the man who came after me, I replied, 'The Lord's Anointed? What do you mean by the Lord's Anointed?' He was surprised at being accosted in this manner, and replied, 'What do you mean, sir? I said nothing about the Lord's Anointed.' I was convinced that he told the truth, for these few words filled my mind with peculiar feelings, such as I had never before experienced; and I immediately hastened to the place of trial. Whilst I was engaged in the case, these emotions increased, and when I came to speak upon it, I was inspired with an eloquence which was altogether new to me, and which was overpowering and irresistible. I succeeded, as I expected, in obtaining the prisoner's discharge.[13] This the more enraged the adverse party, and I soon discovered that Mr. Smith was liable to abuse from them, should he not make his escape. The most of them being fond of liquor, I invited them into another room to drink, and thus succeeded in attracting their attention until Mr. Smith was beyond their reach. I knew not where he went, but I was satisfied that he was out of their hands."[14]

Since this circumstance occurred, until this day, Mr. Reed has been a faithful friend to Joseph, although he has never attached himself to the Church.

After escaping the hands of the mob, Joseph traveled till daybreak the next morning, before he ventured to ask for victuals, although he had taken nothing, save a small crust of bread, for two days.[15] About daybreak he arrived at the house of one of his wife's sisters, where he found Emma, who had suffered great anxiety about him since his first arrest. They returned home together, and immediately afterwards Joseph received a commandment by revelation to move his family to Waterloo.

Joseph had at this time just completed a house, which he had built on a small farm that he had purchased of his father-in-law; however, he locked up his house[16] with his furniture in it, and repaired with Emma immediately to Manchester. About the time of his arrival at our house, Hyrum had settled up his business, for the purpose of being at liberty to do whatever the Lord required of him, and he requested Joseph to ask the Lord for a revelation concerning the matter. The answer given was that he should take a bed, his family, and what clothing he needed for them, and go straightway to Colesville, for his enemies were combining in secret chambers to take away his life. At the same time, Mr. Smith received a commandment to go forthwith to Waterloo and prepare a place for his family, as our enemies also sought his destruction in the neighborhood in which we then resided, but in Waterloo he should find favor in the eyes of the people. The next day, by ten o'clock, Hyrum was on his journey. Joseph and Emma left for Macedon, and William went away from home in another direction, on business. Samuel was absent on a third mission to Livonia, for which he had set out on the first of October, soon after the arrival of my husband and Don Carlos from their visit to father Smith. Catharine and Don Carlos were also away from home. Calvin Stoddard and his wife, Sophronia, had moved several miles distant some time previous. This left no one but Mr. Smith, myself, and our little girl, Lucy, at home.

NOTES

1. This was the summer of 1830.

2. Asael and Mary Duty Smith had eleven children, seven sons and four daughters, Jesse (1768–1853), Priscilla (1769–1867), Joseph (1771–1840), Asael (1773–1848), Mary (1775–1844), Samuel (1777–1830), Silas (1779–1839), John (1781–1854), Susan (1783–1849), Stephen (1785–1802), and Sarah (1789–1824).

3. Most of the Smiths were at this time living in the area of Stockholm, St. Lawrence County, New York, about two hundred miles from Fayette. Joseph Smith's father, Asael Smith, accepted the message of the restored gospel but died shortly after the visit (October 31, 1830). Of the thirteen members of Joseph's family, seven accepted it, three died before they had the opportunity, and three rejected it (see Bushman, *Beginnings*, p. 198). Jesse Smith was always violently opposed to organized religion and made no pretense about that in his family.

4. At this point the Early Notebook states: "[Joseph] then preached a beautiful sermon" (Early Notebook, p. 15). Asael was eighty-six years old. He read the Book of Mormon all the way through without the aid of glasses (which he took as a miracle) and died in a few short months.

5. John Smith, it will be remembered, was Joseph Smith Sr.'s younger brother. John was the first of the extended Smith family to join the Church (1832), and remained ever true to the gospel.

6. Silas Smith was a younger brother of Joseph Smith Sr., accepted the gospel, and was faithful until his death in 1839.

7. Joseph Smith Sr.'s eighty-seven-year-old mother, Mary Duty Smith, readily accepted the gospel, moved with the Saints to Kirtland, Ohio, and died there when she was ninety-two.

8. Asael Smith told his grandson, George A. Smith, "that he always knew that God was going to raise up some branch of his family to be a great benefit to mankind" (George A. Smith, "Memoirs," p. 2, Brigham Young University Special Collections, Provo, Utah). George A. Smith also stated, "My grandfather, Asahel Smith, heard of the coming forth of the Book of Mormon, and he said it was true, for he knew that something would turn up in his family that would revolutionize the world" (in *JD* 5:102).

9. The Early Notebook states, "so just shut up your heart" (Early Notebook, p. 18).

10. Mother Smith's Early Notebook states: "This lowered even the almost invulnerable Jesse Smith and he wept like a child all the while we were riding four miles" (Early Notebook, p. 23).

11. Parley P. Pratt recounted his story: "I accordingly visited the village of Palmyra, and inquired for the residence of Mr. Joseph Smith. I found it some two or three miles from the village. As I approached the house at the close of the day I overtook a man who was driving some cows, and inquired of him for Mr. Joseph Smith, the translator of the *"Book of Mormon."* He informed me that he now resided in Pennsylvania; some one hundred miles distant. I inquired for his father, or for any of the family. He told me that his father had gone a journey; but that his residence was a small house just before me; and, said he, I am his brother. It was Mr. Hyrum Smith. I informed him of the interest I felt in the Book, and of my desire to learn more about it. He welcomed me to his house, and we spent the night together; for neither of us felt disposed to sleep. We conversed most of the night, during which I unfolded to him much of my experience in my search after truth, and my success so far; together with that which I felt was lacking, viz: a commissioned priesthood, or apostleship to minister in the ordinances of God.

"He also unfolded to me the particulars of the discovery of the Book; its translation; the rise of the Church of Latter-day Saints, and the commission of his brother Joseph, and others, by revelation and the ministering of angels, by which the apostleship and authority had been again restored to the earth. After duly weighing the whole matter in my mind I saw clearly that these things were true; and that myself and the whole world were without baptism, and without the ministry and ordinances of God; and that the whole world had been in this condition since the days that inspiration and revelation ceased—in short, that this was a *new dispensation* or *commission,* in fulfilment of prophecy, and for the restoration of Israel, and to prepare the way before the second coming of the Lord."

As Parley left the next morning, Hyrum gave him a copy of the Book of Mormon. Later that day, Parley read of the Savior's visit to the American continent, and realized that the book had preserved the gospel message in its purity. He recalled: "This discovery greatly enlarged my heart, and filled my soul with joy and gladness. I esteemed the Book, or the information contained in it, more than all the riches of the world. Yes; I verily believe that I would not at that time have exchanged the knowledge I then possessed, for a legal title to all the beautiful farms, houses, villages and property which passed in review before me, on my journey through one of the most flourishing settlements of western New York." (Pratt, *Autobiography*, pp. 20, 22.)

12. These actions of the mob and the trials took place starting the last two days of June and the first days of July, 1830 (see Bushman, *Beginnings*, pp. 160–62, 240).

13. Joseph recorded: "Mr. Davidson and Mr. Reed followed in my behalf. They held forth in its true colors the nature of the prosecution, the malignancy of intention, and apparent disposition to persecute their client rather than to afford him justice. They took up the different arguments which had been brought by the lawyers for the prosecution and, having showed their utter futility and misapplication, then proceeded to scrutinize the evidence which had been adduced, and each in his turn thanked God that he had been engaged in so good a cause as that of defending a man whose character stood so well the test of such scrutinizing enquiry. In fact, these men (although not regular lawyers) were upon this occasion able to put to silence their opponents—and convince the court that I was innocent. They spoke like men inspired of God, whilst the lawyers who were arrayed against me trembled under the sound of their voice, and quailed before them like criminals before a bar of justice." (*Papers*, p. 257.)

14. Joseph had been taken to South Bainbridge, Chenango County, New York, tried, acquitted, and then immediately taken to Broome County on another warrant. An abusive constable had taken him into custody to hold him until the following trial. Joseph recorded: "He [the constable] then took me to a tavern, and gathered in a number of men who used every means to abuse, ridicule, and insult me. They spit upon me, pointed their fingers at me, saying to me, 'Prophesy, prophesy,' and in many other ways did they insult me. I applied for something to eat. The constable ordered me some crusts of bread and some water, which was the only fare I that night received." (*Papers*, p. 255.)

15. The Colesville mob had designed to tar and feather Joseph the first time he was arrested and were in cahoots with the constable. Joseph recorded: "The constable informed me soon after he had arrested me that the plan of those who had got out this warrant was to get me into the hands of the mob who were now lying in ambush for me, but that he was determined to save me from them, as he had found me to be a different kind of person from what had been represented to him. We had a wagon to travel in and soon found that he had told me the truth in this matter, for not far from Mr. Knight's house the wagon was surrounded by the mob, who seemed only to await some signal from the constable, but to their great disappointment, he gave the horse the whip and drove me out of their reach. However, whilst we were driving pretty quickly along, one of our wheels came off, which left us very nearly once more in their power, as they were in close pursuit; however, we managed to get the wheel on again, and once more left them behind." (*Papers*, p. 252.)

16. Joseph and Emma had been living in this place since December 1827. Joseph officially secured title for the property on August 25, 1830, for two hundred dollars. He later sold the property to Joseph McKune, a neighbor, on June 8, 1833, for three hundred dollars. Joseph and Emma did not live in the home after early 1831. (See Porter, "Origins," pp. 133–34.)

CHAPTER 35

A Quaker calls upon Joseph Smith Sr. to pay a debt for fourteen dollars. Joseph cannot pay but is given the option to burn the Book of Mormon and be forgiven the debt. Joseph refuses and goes to jail. A large mob gathers to pilfer the Smith home when only Lucy and little Lucy are present. Mother Smith prays that her family will be safe. Son William Smith arrives and immediately breaks up the mob. Samuel goes to help his father in jail. Joseph Sr. works for thirty days in the jail yard to pay his debt, preaches the gospel, and baptizes two people.

Fall 1830

On the same day that Hyrum left for Colesville, which was Wednesday, the neighbors began to call, one after another, and inquire very particularly for Hyrum.

This gave me great anxiety, for I knew that they had no business with him. The same night my husband was taken rather ill, and, continuing unwell the next day, he was unable to take breakfast with me. About ten o'clock I commenced preparing him some milk porridge, but before it was ready for him, a Quaker gentleman called to see him, and the following is the substance of their conversation:

Quaker: "Friend Smith, I have a note against thee for fourteen dollars, which I have lately bought, and I have come to see if thou hast the money for me."

Mr. Smith: "Why, sir, did you purchase that note? You certainly were in no want of the money?"

Quaker: "That is business of my own; I want the money, and must have it."

Mr. Smith: "I can pay you six dollars now—the rest you will have to wait for, as I cannot get it for you."

Quaker: "No, I will not wait one hour; and if thou dost not pay me immediately, thou shalt go forthwith to the jail, unless"—running to the fireplace and making violent gestures with his hands towards the fire "thou wilt burn up those Books of Mormon; but if thou wilt burn them up, then I will forgive thee the whole debt."

Mr. Smith (decidedly): "That I shall not do."

Quaker: "Then, thou shalt go to jail."

"Sir," I interrupted (taking my gold beads from my neck and holding them towards him), "these beads are the full value of the remainder of the debt. I beseech you to take them and be satisfied to give up the note."

Quaker: "No, I will not. Thou must pay the money, or thy husband shall go straightway to jail."

"Now, here, sir," I replied, "just look at yourself as you are. Because God has raised up my son to bring forth a book, which was written for the salvation of the souls of men, for the salvation of your soul as well as mine, you have come here to distress my family and me by taking my husband to jail; and you think, by this, that you will compel us to deny the work of God and destroy a book which was translated by the gift and power of God. But, sir, we shall not burn the Book of Mormon, nor deny the inspiration of the Almighty."

The Quaker then stepped to the door and called a constable, who was waiting there for the signal. The constable came forward and, laying his hand on Mr. Smith's shoulder, said, "You are my prisoner."

I entreated the officer to allow me time to get someone to become my husband's security, but he refused. I then requested that he might be permitted to eat the porridge which I had been preparing, as he had taken no nourishment since the night before. This was also denied, and the Quaker ordered my husband to get immediately into a wagon which stood waiting to convey him to prison.

After they had taken him to the wagon, the Quaker stood over him as guard and the officer came back and ate up the food which I had prepared for my husband, who sat in the burning sun, faint and sick.

Wives, who love your husbands and would sacrifice your lives for theirs, how do you think I felt at that moment? I will leave you to imagine. Suffice it for the present to say that after devouring the last mouthful of provisions which we had in the house, they drove away with my husband, and I was left alone again with Lucy, my youngest child.[1]

The next morning I went on foot several miles to see a friend by the name of Abner Lackey, who, I hoped, would assist me. I was not disappointed. He went without delay to the magistrate's office and had my papers prepared, so that I could get my husband out of the prison cell, although he would still be confined in the jail yard.

Shortly after I returned home, a pesty young gentleman came in and asked if Mr. Hyrum Smith was at home. I told him, as I had others, that he was in Colesville. The young man said that Hyrum was owing a small debt to Dr. McIntyre (who was then absent), and the doctor wished him to call at my house to see if it would be convenient for him to settle the debt. I told the young man that all my son's business was left in order, and that the agreement with Dr. McIntyre was that the debt was to be paid in corn and beans, which I would send to him the next day.

I then hired a man to take the produce the following day to the doctor's house, which was accordingly done, and, when the man returned, he informed me that the clerk agreed to erase the account. It was now too late in the day to set out for Canandaigua, where my husband was confined in prison, and I concluded to defer going till the next morning, in hopes that some of my sons would return during the interval.

The night came on, but neither of my sons made their appearance. When the night closed in, the darkness was hideous; scarcely any object was discernible. I sat down and began to contemplate the situation of myself and family. My husband, an affectionate companion and as tender a father as ever blessed the confidence of a family, was an imprisoned debtor, torn from his family and immured in a dungeon, where he had already lain two dismal nights, and now another must be added to the number before I could reach him to render him any assistance. And where were his children? Alvin was murdered by a quack physician; but still he lay at peace. Hyrum was flying from his home and why I knew not; the secret combinations of his enemies were not yet fully developed. Joseph had but recently escaped from his persecutors, who sought to accomplish his destruction. Samuel was gone, without purse or scrip, to preach the gospel, for which he was as much despised and hated as were the ancient disciples. William was also gone, and I had not, unlike Naomi, even my daughters-in-law to comfort my heart in this the hour of my affliction.

While I was thus meditating, a heavy rap at the door brought me suddenly to my feet. I bade the stranger enter. He asked me, in a hurried manner, where Hyrum was. I answered the question as usual. Just then a second person came in, and the first observed to a second, "Mrs. Smith says her son is not at home." The person addressed looked suspiciously around and remarked, "He is at home, for your neighbors have seen him here today."

"Then, sir," I replied, "they have seen what I have not."

"We have a search warrant," rejoined he, "and if you do not give him up, we shall be under the necessity of taking whatever we find that belongs to him." Finding some corn stored in the chamber above the room where Hyrum had lived, they declared their intention of taking it, but I forbade their meddling with it.

At this instant a third stranger entered, and then a fourth. The last observed, "I do not know, but you will think strange of so many of us coming in, but my candle was out, and I came in to relight it by your fire."

I told him I did not know what to think. I had but little reason to consider myself safe either day or night, and that I would like to know what their business was, and for what cause they were seizing upon our property. The foremost replied that it was wanted to settle a debt which Hyrum was owing to Dr. McIntyre. I told him that it was paid. He disputed my word, and ordered his men to take the corn.

As they were going upstairs, I looked out of the window, and one glance almost turned my head giddy. As far as I could see by the light of two candles and a pair of carriage lamps, the heads of men appeared in every direction, some on foot, some on horseback, and the rest in wagons. I saw that there was no way but for me to sit quietly down, and see my house pillaged by a banditti of blacklegs, religious bigots, and cutthroats, who were united in one purpose, namely, that of destroying us from the face of the earth.

However, there was one resource, and to that I applied. I went aside, and kneeled before the Lord and begged that he would not let my children fall into their hands, and that they might be satisfied with plunder without taking life.

Just at this instant, William bounded into the house. "Mother," he cried, "in the name of God, what is this host of men doing here? Are they robbing or stealing? What are they about?"

I told him, in short, that they had taken his father to prison, and had now come after Hyrum, but, not finding him, they were plundering the house. Hereupon, William seized a large handspike, sprang up the stairs, and, in one instant, cleared the scoundrels out of the chamber. They scampered downstairs; he flew after them, and, bounding into the very midst of the crowd, he brandished his handspike in every direction, exclaiming, "Away from here, you cut-throats, instantly, or I will be the death of every one of you."

The lights were immediately extinguished, yet he continued to harangue them boisterously, until he discovered that his audience had left him. They seemed to believe what he said, and fled in every direction, leaving us again to ourselves.

Between twelve and one o'clock, Calvin Stoddard and his wife, Sophronia, arrived at our house. Calvin said he had been troubled about us all afternoon, and, finally, about the setting of the sun, he told Sophronia that he would even then start for her father's, if she felt inclined to go with him.

Within an hour after their arrival, Samuel came. He was much fatigued, for he had traveled twenty-one miles after sunset. I told him our situation, and that I wished him to go early the next morning to Canandaigua and procure his father's release from the dungeon. "Well, Mother," said he, "I am sick; fix me a bed, that I may lie down and rest myself, or I shall not be able to go, for I have taken a heavy cold, and my bones ache dreadfully."

However, by a little nursing and some rest, he was able to set off by sunrise, and arrived at Canandaigua at ten o'clock. After informing the jailor of his business, he requested that his father might be immediately liberated from the cell. The jailor refused, because it was Sunday, but permitted Samuel to go into the cell, where he found my husband confined in the same dungeon with a man committed for murder. Upon Samuel inquiring what his treatment had been, Mr. Smith replied as follows:

"Immediately after I left your mother, the men by whom I was taken commenced using every possible argument to induce me to re-nounce the Book of Mormon, saying, 'how much better it would be for you to deny that silly thing, than to be disgraced and imprisoned, when you might not only escape this, but also have the note back, as well as the money which you have paid on it.' To this I made no reply. They still went on in the same manner till we arrived at the jail, when they hurried me into this dismal dungeon. I shuddered when I first heard these heavy doors creaking upon their hinges; but then I thought to my-self, I was not the first man who had been imprisoned for the truth's sake; and when I should meet Paul in the paradise of God, I could tell him that I, too, had been in bonds for the gospel which he had preached. And this has been my only consolation.

"From the time I entered until now, and this is the fourth day, I have had nothing to eat, save a pint basin full of very weak broth; and there [pointing to the opposite side of the cell] lies the basin yet."

Samuel was very much wounded by this, and, having obtained per-mission of the jailor, he immediately went out and brought his father some comfortable food. After which he remained with him until the next morning, when the business was attended to, and Mr. Smith went out into the jail yard to a cooper's shop, where he obtained employment at coopering, and followed the same until he was released, which was thirty days.[2] He preached during his confinement there every Sunday, and when he was released, he baptized two persons whom he had thus converted.

Notes

1. Little Lucy was nine years old at this time. It appears that Joseph Smith Sr. was incarcerated in the Canandaigua jail between October 7, 1830, and November 5, 1830, or perhaps from September 30 (one week earlier) until October 29, 1830 (see Porter, "Origins," p. 268; see also Bushman, *Beginnings*, p. 242).

2. Apparently Joseph Smith Sr. earned enough money not only to pay off the fourteen-dollar debt but also to bring home some extra clothing for the family (see Bushman, *Beginnings*, p. 173).

CHAPTER 36

Samuel's account of his third mission to Livonia, New York. John and Rhoda Greene, Phineas Young, Brigham Young, and others join the Church through Samuel's efforts. The Smiths move from the farm at Manchester to Waterloo, New York, and are treated with great kindness and enjoy a season of peace.

Fall 1830

Samuel returned from Canandaigua the same day that my husband was liberated from the cell.[1] After relating to us the success he had met with at Canandaigua, he gave us an account of his third mission to Livonia:

"When I arrived at Mr. Greene's," said he, "Mrs. Greene informed me that her husband was absent from home, that there was no prospect of selling my books, and even the one which I had left with them, she expected I would have to take away, as Mr. Greene had no disposition to purchase it, although she had read it herself, and was much pleased with it. I then talked with her a short time and, binding my knapsack upon my shoulders, rose to depart; but, as I bade her farewell, it was impressed upon my mind to leave the book with her. I made her a present of it, and told her that the Spirit forbade me taking it away. She burst into tears, and requested me to pray with her.[2] I did so, and afterwards explained to her the most profitable manner of reading the book which I had left with her; which was, to ask God, when she read it, for a testimony of the truth of what she had read, and she would receive the Spirit of God, which would enable her to discern the things of God. I then left her, and returned home."

I shall now turn aside from my narrative, and give a history of the above book. When Mr. Greene returned home, his wife requested him to read it, informing him very particularly with regard to what Samuel had said to her, relative to obtaining a testimony of the truth of it.[3] This, he, for a while, refused to do, but finally yielded to her persuasions and took the book and commenced perusing the same, calling upon God for the testimony of his Spirit. The result of which was that he and Mrs. Greene were in a short time baptized. They gave the book to Phineas Young, Mrs. Greene's brother, who read it, and commenced preaching it forthwith. It was next handed to Brigham Young, and from him to Mrs. Murray, his sister, who is also the mother of Heber C. Kimball's wife. They all received the work without hesitancy, and rejoiced in the truth thereof. Joseph Young was at this time in Canada, preaching the Methodist doctrine; but, as soon as Brigham became convinced of the truth of the gospel, as contained in the Book of Mormon, he went straightway to his brother Joseph and persuaded him to cease preaching Methodism and embrace the truth, as set forth in the Book of Mormon, which he carried with him.

Thus was this book the means of convincing this whole family and bringing them into the Church, where they have continued faithful members from the commencement of their career until now. And, through their faithfulness and zeal, some of them have become as great and honorable men as ever stood upon the earth.[4]

I shall now resume my subject. The first business which Samuel set himself about after he returned home was preparing to move the family to Waterloo, according to the revelation given to Joseph.[5] And after much fatigue and perplexities of various kinds, he succeeded in getting us there. We moved into a house belonging to an individual by the name of Kellog. Shortly after arriving there, we were made to realize that the hearts of the people were in the hands of the Lord; for we had scarcely unpacked our goods, when one of our new neighbors, a Mr. Osgood, came in and invited us to drive our stock and teams to his barnyard, and feed them from his barn, free of cost, until we could make further arrangements. Many of our neighbors came in and welcomed us to Waterloo, among whom was Mr. Hooper, a tavern keeper, whose wife came with him, and brought us a present of some delicate eatables. Such manifestations of kindness as these were shown us from day to

day, during our continuance in the place. And they were duly appreci-
ated, for we had experienced the opposite so severely, that the least show
of good feeling gave rise to the liveliest sensations of gratitude.

Having settled ourselves in this place, we established the practice of
spending the evenings in singing and praying. The neighbors soon became aware of this, and it caused our house to become a place of
evening resort for some dozen or twenty persons. One evening, soon
after we commenced singing, a couple of little boys came in, and one of
them, stepping softly up to Samuel, whispered, "Mr. Smith, won't you
pray pretty soon? Our mother said we must be home by eight o'clock,
and we would like to hear you pray before we go."

Samuel told them that prayer should be attended to immediately.
Accordingly, when we had finished the hymn, which we were then
singing, we closed the evening services with prayer, in order that the
little boys might be gratified. After this, they were never absent during
our evening devotions while we remained in the neighborhood.

NOTES

1. This was probably during the first part of October 1830.

2. Lucy records in her Early Notebook, as dictated to Martha Jane Coray, that
Rhoda Young Greene "afterwards told me that she never saw a man that had such an
appearance or ever heard such a prayer in her life. 'My God,' said she, 'it seemed as
though the very heavens were rent and the Spirit of God was poured down upon us.'"
(Early Notebook, pp. 35–36.)

3. In the Early Notebook, Mother Smith gives more detail of the conversation
Rhoda Greene had with her husband, John: "'Now, Mr. Greene,' said she, 'you certainly ought to do so and I will tell you how Mr. Smith says you must read.' She then
repeated Samuel's testimony to her and added, 'I do know that he would not tell an
untruth for any inducement. I know he must be a good man if there ever was one.'"
(Early Notebook, p. 37.)

4. In the Early Notebook, Lucy states: "Thus was Samuel's sufferings in this instance the means of converting some of the most substantial and the greatest men
who have ever subscribed their names to the truth; men who have never faltered nor
slacked their zeal through every scene of trouble and privation for the truth's sake"

(Early Notebook, pp. 38–39). Through the instrumentality of Samuel Harrison Smith, nearly all of the extended Young family came into the Church. Apparently Phineas had received a copy (separate from the John Greene copy) of the Book of Mormon from Samuel and, being religiously inclined, decided to study the matter. "I thought it my duty to read it," Phineas recorded, "as I had promised, and search out the errors, and as a teacher in Israel, expose such errors and save the people from the delusion. . . . I commenced and read every word in the book in the same week. The week following I did the same, but to my surprise, I could not find the errors that I anticipated, but felt a conviction that the book was true. . . . My father [John Young] then took the book home with him, and read it through. I asked him his opinion of it. He said it was the greatest work and the clearest of error he had ever seen, the Bible not excepted. I then lent the book to my sister, Fanny Murray. She read it and declared it a revelation. Many others did the same." Phineas continued to preach the gospel as he understood it, trying to tie Methodism (which he had previously followed) to Mormonism. He could see that would not work. "About this time my brother Brigham came to see me," Phineas continued in his account, "and very soon told me that he was convinced that there was something to Mormonism. I told him I had long been satisfied of that." Within a short time the following were baptized: Father Young and his wife, Hannah; Brigham and Miriam Young; Phineas H. and Clarissa Young; Joseph Young; Lorenzo D. and Persis Young; John P. and Rhoda Young Greene; and Fanny Young Murray. The rest of the family would soon follow, including Susannah; Louisa; Nancy Young Kent and her husband, Daniel; and John Jr. (See Leonard J. Arrington and JoAnn Jolley, "The Faithful Young Family: The Parents, Brothers, and Sisters of Brigham," *Ensign*, August 1980, pp. 55–56.)

5. The move to Waterloo took place sometime in October or November 1830. Waterloo was located about twenty-five miles east and south of the Smith farm in Manchester. The house where they lived was actually within the boundaries of Seneca Falls, the neighboring community (see Bushman, *Beginnings*, p. 173).

CHAPTER 37

Parley P. Pratt, Ziba Peterson, Peter Whitmer Jr., and Oliver Cowdery are called on a mission to the Lamanites. Lucy's description of the indomitable Emma. The four missionaries stop in Ohio to preach the gospel, and hundreds respond to the message of the Restoration, including Sidney Rigdon and Edward Partridge. Sidney and Edward come to Waterloo to meet the Prophet. The Lord commands the Church to gather in Ohio. Joseph and Emma move to Kirtland, Ohio.

October 1830 to February 1831

I mentioned in a foregoing chapter that when Joseph and Emma left Manchester they went to Macedon.[1] Here he commenced his ministerial labors and continued, for some time, to preach successively in this place, Colesville, Waterloo, Palmyra, and Manchester, till finally he sent to Pennsylvania for his goods and settled himself in Waterloo.[2] Soon after which, a revelation was given commanding Parley P. Pratt, Ziba Peterson, Peter Whitmer, and Oliver Cowdery to take a mission to Missouri, preaching by the way.[3] As soon as this revelation was received, Emma Smith and several other sisters began to make arrangements to furnish those who were set apart for this mission with the necessary clothing, which was no easy task, as the most of it had to be manufactured out of the raw material.

Emma's health at this time was quite delicate,[4] yet she did not favor herself on this account, but whatever her hands found to do she did with her might, until so far beyond her strength that she brought upon herself a heavy fit of sickness, which lasted four weeks. And, although her strength was exhausted, still her spirits were the same, which, in fact, was always the case with her, even under the most trying circumstances. I have never seen a woman in my life who would endure every species of fatigue and hardship from month to month and from year to year with that unflinching courage, zeal, and patience which she has ever done; for I know that which she has had to endure—she has been tossed upon the ocean of uncertainty—she has breasted the storms of persecution, and buffeted the rage of men and devils, which would have borne down almost any other woman.[5] It may be that many may yet have to encounter the same—I pray God that this may not be the case; but, should it be, may they have grace given them according to their day, even as has been the case with her.

As soon as those men designated in the revelation were prepared to leave home, they started on their mission, preaching and baptizing on their way wherever an opportunity afforded. On their route they passed through Kirtland, where they preached a short time and raised up a branch of twenty or thirty members.[6] Before leaving this place, they addressed a letter to Joseph, desiring him to send an elder to preside over the branch which they had raised up. Accordingly, Joseph dispatched John Whitmer to take the presidency of the Church at Kirtland; and when he arrived there, those appointed to go to Missouri proceeded on their mission, preaching and baptizing as before.[7]

In December of the same year, Joseph appointed a meeting at our house. While he was preaching, Sidney Rigdon[8] and Edward Partridge came in and seated themselves in the congregation. When Joseph had finished his discourse, he gave all who had any remarks to make the privilege of speaking. Upon this, Mr. Partridge arose, and stated that he had been to Manchester with the view of obtaining further information respecting the doctrine which we preached; but, not finding us, he had made some inquiry of our neighbors concerning our characters, which they stated had been unimpeachable, until Joseph deceived them relative to the Book of Mormon. He also said that he had walked over our farm, and observed the good order and industry which it exhibited; and, having seen what we had sacrificed for the sake of our faith, and having heard that our veracity was not questioned upon any other point

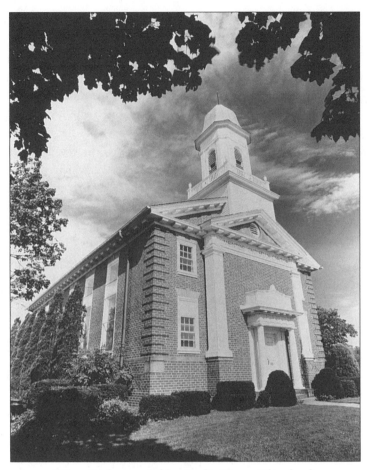

Sidney Rigdon preached here in this Mentor, Ohio, church.
He accepted the restored gospel.

than that of our religion, he believed our testimony and was ready to be baptized, "if," said he, "Brother Joseph will baptize me."

"You are now," replied Joseph, "much fatigued, Brother Partridge, and you had better rest today and be baptized tomorrow."

"Just as Brother Joseph thinks best," replied Mr. Partridge, "I am ready at any time."

He was accordingly baptized the next day.[9] Before he left, my husband returned home from prison, bringing along with him considerable clothing, which he had earned at coopering in the jail yard.[10]

The latter part of the same month, Joseph received a letter from John Whitmer, desiring his immediate assistance at Kirtland in regulating the affairs of the Church there. Joseph inquired of the Lord and received a commandment to go straightway to Kirtland with his family and effects;[11] also to send a message to Hyrum to have him take the branch of the Church over which he presided and start immediately for the same place.[12] And my husband was commanded, in the same revelation, to meet Hyrum at the most convenient point and accompany him to Kirtland. Samuel was sent on a mission into the same region of country, while I and my two sons William and Carlos were to be left till the ensuing spring, when we were to take the remainder of the branch at Waterloo and move also to Kirtland.

It was but a short time till Joseph and Emma were on their way, accompanied by Sidney Rigdon, Edward Partridge, Ezra Thayre, and Newel Knight.[13] When they were about starting, they preached at our

Joseph Knight Sr.'s farm in Colesville, New York,
was the site of the first branch of the Church.

Joseph and Emma arrived here in front of the Gilbert and Whitney store on February 1, 1831.

house on the Seneca River; and on their way they preached at the house of Calvin Stoddard,[14] and likewise at the house of Preserved Harris.[15] At each of these places, they baptized several individuals into the Church.

On Joseph's arrival at Kirtland,[16] he found a church consisting of nearly one hundred members, who were, in general, good brethren, though a few of them had imbibed some very erroneous ideas, being greatly deceived by a singular power which manifested itself among them in strange contortions of the visage, and sudden, unnatural exertions of the body. This they supposed to be a display of the power of God. Shortly after Joseph arrived, he called the Church together in order to show them the difference between the Spirit of God and the spirit of the devil. He said, if a man arose in meeting to speak, and was seized with a kind of paroxysm that drew his face and limbs in a violent and unnatural manner which made him appear to be in pain; and if he gave utterance to strange sounds which were incomprehensible to his audience, they might rely upon it, that he had the spirit of the devil. But, on the contrary, when a man speaks by the Spirit of God, he speaks from the abundance of his heart—his mind is filled with intelligence, and even should he be excited, it does not cause him to do anything ridiculous or unseemly. He then called upon one of the brethren to speak, who arose and made the attempt, but was immediately seized with a kind of spasm which drew his face, arms, and fingers in a most astonishing manner.

Hyrum, by Joseph's request, laid his hands on the man, whereupon he sank back in a state of complete exhaustion. Joseph then called upon another man to speak who stood leaning in an open window. This man also attempted to speak, but was thrown forward into the house, prostrate, unable to utter a syllable. He was administered to, and the same effect followed as in the first instance.

These, together with a few other examples of the same kind, convinced the brethren of the mistake under which they had been laboring; and they all rejoiced in the goodness of God in once more condescending to lead the children of men by revelation and the gift of the Holy Ghost.[17]

NOTES

1. Macedon is about six miles west of the Manchester Smith farm.

2. This was in late fall 1830.

3. This revelation (section 32 of the Doctrine and Covenants) was given in October 1830. After calling Parley Pratt and Ziba Peterson to join Oliver Cowdery and Peter Whitmer Jr., the Lord said: "And I myself will go with them and be in their midst; and I am their advocate with the Father, and nothing shall prevail against them" (D&C 32:3).

4. In the fall of 1830 Emma was pregnant with twins.

5. In the seventeen years of Joseph and Emma's marriage, they moved sixteen times, and perhaps only three or four times lived in a home of their own (Harmony, Kirtland, Far West [for a brief time], and Nauvoo).

6. Parley Pratt recorded: "At length Mr. Rigdon and many others became convinced that they had not authority to minister in the ordinances of God; and that they had not been legally baptized and ordained. They, therefore, came forward and were baptized by us, and received the gift of the Holy Ghost by the laying on of hands, and prayer in the name of Jesus Christ.

"The news of our coming was soon noised abroad, and the news of the discovery of the Book of Mormon and the marvelous events connected with it. The interest and excitement now became general in Kirtland, and in all the region round about. The people thronged us night and day, insomuch that we had no time for rest and retirement. Meetings were convened in different neighborhoods, and multitudes came together soliciting our attendance; while thousands flocked about us daily; some to be taught, some for curiosity, some to obey the gospel, and some to dispute or resist it.

"In two or three weeks from our arrival in the neighborhood with the news, we had baptized one hundred and twenty-seven souls, and this number soon increased to one thousand. The disciples were filled with joy and gladness; while rage and lying was abundantly manifested by gainsayers; faith was strong, joy was great, and persecution heavy." (Pratt, *Autobiography*, pp. 35–36.)

7. Parley recorded that as the missionaries came to the state of Missouri, "we travelled on foot for three hundred miles through vast prairies and through trackless wilds of snow—no beaten road; houses few and far between; and the bleak northwest wind always blowing in our faces with a keenness which would almost take the skin off the face. We travelled for whole days, from morning till night, without a house or fire, wading in snow to the knees at every step, and the cold so intense that the snow did not melt on the south side of the houses, even in the mid-day sun, for nearly six weeks. We carried on our backs our changes of clothing, several books, and corn bread and raw pork. We often ate our frozen bread and pork by the way, when the bread would be so frozen that we could not bite or penetrate any part of it but the outside crust.

"After much fatigue and some suffering we all arrived in Independence, in the county of Jackson, on the extreme western frontiers of Missouri, and of the United States.

"This was about fifteen hundred miles from where we started, and we had performed most of the journey on foot, through a wilderness country, in the worst season of the year, occupying about four months, during which we had preached the gospel to tens of thousands of Gentiles and two nations of Indians; baptizing, confirming and organizing many hundreds of people into churches of Latter-day Saints." (Pratt, *Autobiography,* p. 40.)

8. Sidney Rigdon and Edward Partridge arrived on December 10, 1830. Sidney Rigdon, born at St. Clair Township, Allegheny County, Pennsylvania, February 19, 1793, was the son of William and Nancy Gallaher Rigdon. Sidney was baptized November 14, 1830, and played a key role in the Restoration. He served as Joseph's scribe during the inspired translation of the Bible, accompanied Joseph to Missouri, dedicated the land of Zion, saw the vision of the three degrees of glory with Joseph, was mobbed in Hiram, Ohio, with Joseph, participated in the dedication of the Kirtland Temple, was with Joseph in Liberty Jail, was a member of the First Presidency, and ran (on the ticket with Joseph) as a vice-presidential candidate of the United States. Joseph spoke of Sidney's great sacrifice in leaving behind his employment of preacher and joining with the true fold of Christ: "The honors and applause of the world were showered down upon him, his wants were abundantly supplied, and were anticipated. He was respected by the entire community, and his name was a tower of strength. His [counsel] was sought for, respected and esteemed. But if he should unite with the Church of Christ, his prospects of wealth and affluence would vanish; his family dependent upon him for support, must necessarily share his humiliation and poverty. He was aware that his character and his reputation must suffer in the estimation of the community." (*Times and Seasons* 4 [September 1, 1843]: 304.) Sidney became disaffected from the Church and from Joseph, moving away from the body of the Saints. Upon his attempt to wrest the leadership of the Church after the martyrdom of Joseph, he was excommunicated September 8, 1844, and never returned to the Church. He died July 14, 1876 (age 83), in Friendship, New York. (See Cook, *Revelations,* pp. 52–53.)

9. Edward Partridge was baptized by Joseph Smith on December 11, 1830, in the Seneca River. He was referred to by the Prophet Joseph as "a pattern of piety, and one of the Lord's great men." Edward, born in Pittsfield, Berkshire County, Massachusetts, August 27, 1793, was the son of William and Jemima Bidwell Partridge. As a youth, "the Spirit of the Lord strove with him a number of times, insomuch that his heart was made tender, and he went and wept; and sometimes he went silently and poured the effusions of his soul to God in prayer. . . . At the age of twenty he had become disgusted with the religious world. He saw no beauty, comeliness, or loveliness in the character of God as represented by the teaching of the various religious sects. He however heard a Universalist Restorationer preach upon the love of God: this sermon gave him exalted opinions of God, and he concluded that

Universal Restoration was right according to the Bible. He continued in this belief till 1828, when he and his wife were baptized into the 'Campbellite' church by Sidney Rigdon, in Mentor, [Ohio]. . . . He continued a member of this church, though doubting at times its being the true one, until Elders Parley P. Pratt, Oliver Cowdery, Peter Whitmer, Jun., and Ziba Peterson came with the Book of Mormon." (*History of the Church* 1:128–29.) Edward wanted to meet the Prophet Joseph before he made a decision to be baptized. He first heard him preach the night they arrived in Waterloo (December 10, 1830).

10. This date is difficult to coordinate with other records, but it appears from Lucy's account that Joseph Smith Sr. had been incarcerated in Canandaigua Jail from the middle of November until this mid-December 1830 period. As noted previously, however, other sources estimate that Joseph Sr. was incarcerated basically throughout the month of October, being released probably no later than November 5, 1830 (see p. 243, note 1).

11. See Doctrine and Covenants 37. In part this revelation said: "Behold, I say unto you that it is not expedient in me that ye should translate [the Bible] any more until ye shall go to the Ohio, and this because of the enemy and for your sakes. . . . And again, a commandment I give unto the church, that it is expedient in me that they should assemble together at the Ohio." (D&C 37: 1, 3.)

12. Hyrum presided over the Colesville Branch of the Church, which, at that time, had about seventy members.

13. It is well to note that Emma made this dead-of-winter journey while seven months pregnant with twins.

14. This was Lucy Mack Smith's son-in-law, husband to Sophronia.

15. Preserved Harris was a younger brother of Martin Harris.

16. Joseph and Emma arrived in Kirtland, pulled by horses in a sleigh, on or about Tuesday, February 1, 1831.

17. Joseph recorded: "With a little caution and some wisdom, I soon assisted the brethren and sisters to overcome [the strange notions and false spirits that had crept in among them]. . . . and the false spirits were easily discerned and rejected by the light of revelation." (*History of the Church* 1:146, 147.)

PART 4

The Gathering
in Ohio

Chapter 38

Lucy Mack Smith leads a group of families from Fayette (Waterloo), New York, to Kirtland, Ohio, the gathering place for the Saints. They sing hymns and preach sermons along the Erie Canal. They arrive at Buffalo and the harbor is closed because of ice. The Saints murmur because of their ill comfort, hunger, and thirst, but Lucy continues to encourage and strengthen them. She calls upon them to exercise their faith and the way will be opened for them. The twenty-foot-thick ice bursts apart like the roar of thunder and they make their passage out of the harbor, then upon Lake Erie to Fairport, Ohio. Joyous meeting with the Prophet Joseph. Safe arrival in Kirtland.

Late April 1831 to mid-May 1831

Soon after my husband and Joseph left for Kirtland, William, being one of the teachers, assisted the Church by calling on every family (as is our custom). He prayed with them and did not leave the house until every member of the family over eight years old had prayed vocally.[1]

When the brethren considered the spring sufficiently open for traveling on the water, a time was set when the Church members were to meet at my house and set off for Kirtland in the same boat. When we were thus collected, we numbered eighty, including the children.

We went on board a boat which was owned by a Methodist preacher. His wife generally went on the boat with him and did his work, but when she found that he was going to take a company of Mormons, she refused to go and sent a hired girl in her stead. When we were ready to start, the people from all the surrounding country came in droves to bid us farewell, which they did, universally invoking the blessing of heaven upon our heads. Just before we shoved off from shore, an old brother by the name of Humphrey[2] came from Potsdam.[3] He had been brought into the Church by Don Carlos's preaching at the time that he visited his grandfather in company with my husband. At this time, Brother Humphrey was the oldest elder in the Church and Don Carlos the youngest.

On account of Brother Humphrey's age, I wished him to take charge of the company, but he refused to do so, saying that everything should be done just as Mother Smith said, and that I, with my sons William and Carlos, should have the entire dictation. "Yes," the whole company responded together, "we will do just as Mother Smith says." Just then Esquire Chamberlain came on board and inquired if I had what money I needed to make my family comfortable. I told him that I had an abundance of everything for myself and my children, but it was

Lucy Mack Smith and her group of eighty Saints went by boat along the Erie Canal to Buffalo.[4]

possible that he might find some who had been unable to provide sufficient means to take them through. "Well," he said, "here is a little cash," and handed me seventeen dollars. "You may spend it as you like." I again told him I did not need it. "You can deal it out to such as do," he said. I took the money and soon had reason to rejoice that I did.

After bedding him with our own acquaintances and giving our affectionate farewells, the boat was shoved off from shore and we were soon under fine headway.[5] I then began to think how I was to set about the task which was laid upon me. I called the brethren and sisters together and reminded them, "Now, brothers and sisters, we have set out just as father Lehi did to travel, by the commandment of the Lord, to a land that he will show us if we are faithful. I want you all to be solemn and lift your hearts to God in prayer continually, that we may be prospered. And for the present, let the sisters take seats on one side of the boat and the brethren on the other, and we will sing a hymn." They did as I desired, and when we struck into the second hymn, the captain cried out to his mate, "Do, for God's sake, come here and take the helm and let me go, for I must hear that singing." When we finished the hymn, he expressed his surprise and pleasure in the warmest terms and mentioned that his wife had left the boat because he had taken a Mormon company on board, which he regretted, for he thought she would have enjoyed our society very much.

At evening Brother Humphrey and Brother Page[6] asked me if I thought it was best to have prayers twice a day. This pleased me, for it was what I intended before. We seated ourselves and sang a hymn, and the solemn music rose in such sweet melancholy on the clear air and died away so beautifully upon the water, that it melted every heart that heard it. And when we bowed down before the Lord in prayer, our souls burned within us with love, and we felt most sensibly that God indeed bestowed his Spirit upon men, even in these last days as in former days.

When the evening service was ended, I went round among the brethren to ascertain how many of them had prepared themselves with food for the journey, and to my surprise I discerned that there was no less than twenty who had no more than two meals' victuals on hand. This was unaccountable to me at first, but I afterwards learned that they had converted their substance into clothing. These all, as well as thirty children, I supported entirely by feeding them from meal to meal clear to the end of the journey. They would have been obliged to have turned back or else suffer for the want of proper sustenance, for those who had provided for themselves had done no more, although some of them might have supplied others and themselves. But they did not seem to consider that the revelation that they should help each other was binding upon them.

I soon discovered among the mothers in our company a carelessness with regard to their children, even when their lives were in danger, which gave me great anxiety. For instance, if children were on deck when the boat passed under a bridge, they could be thrown overboard or bruised in such a manner as was terrible to think of. I called the sisters together and tried to make them realize their children's danger and their own responsibility. "Sisters," said I, "God has given you children to be a blessing to you, and it is your duty to take care of them, to keep them out of every possible danger, and especially in such a place as this, to have them always by your side. I warn you now to attend better to your duty in this respect, or your children will by some unforeseen accident be taken from you."

After this we received news by another boat of the death of a small child that had occurred the day before on the same river. It was killed by being on deck when the boat was passing under a bridge. I thought that this accident and what I had said, taken together, would rouse the sisters to greater attention, but in this I was mistaken, for they took no thought of either, and their excuse for their neglecting their children was that they could not make them mind. I told them that I could make them mind me easily enough, and since they wouldn't control them, I should.

I then got the children together around me and said, "Now, mark what I say to you. When I come up the stairs and raise my hand, you must every one of you run to me as fast as you can and you must not stop a minute. Will you do so?" They all answered heartily, "Yes, ma'am, we will." And to their credit I would say that they kept their faith better than some very great folks do in these days—for they never failed to do just as I told, not only in that but everything else, while I was with them.

When we got halfway to Buffalo, the canal broke and we were stopped from traveling.[7] This circumstance gave rise to many evil forebodings and much murmuring and discontentment. "Well, here we are," said they, "the canal is broke and we can go no further, and what's next? We have left our good homes, and now we have no means of getting a living, and here we must starve."[8]

"No," said I, "you will not starve, brethren, nor any such thing. Only do stop murmuring and be patient, for I have no doubt that the hand of the Lord is over us for good. Perhaps it is best for us to be here a short time. After all, it is quite likely that the steamboats cannot leave Buffalo Harbor because it is blockaded with ice, and the town is crowded with families who are waiting for it to break away so that the boats can start. Are we not more comfortable here in a habitation which is paid for, and we have not the expense of renting a house?"

"Well," said the sisters, "I suppose you know best, but it does seem that we would have done better to have remained at home, for there we might sit in our rocking chairs and take as much comfort as we were a mind to, and here we are tired out and have no place to rest ourselves." I could not help reflecting upon the contrast between their care, fatigue, and cause for complaint and my own.

While I was talking, a citizen of the place where we had landed came into the boat and inquired what profession we were. I told him that we were Mormons, or Latter-day Saints. "Ah!" said he, "that is a denomination which I never heard of before. Do they ever preach?"

"They do," I replied.

"Have you any preachers on board," he said, "that would preach for us while you are stopping here?"

I told him that there were some elders in our company and I would speak to them about the matter. I went immediately to Brothers Humphrey and Page to ask them if they would preach that day. They were glad of an opportunity of addressing the people, and gave an appointment for meeting at one o'clock that afternoon. At the appointed hour, a congregation of one hundred persons collected on a beautiful green bordering the canal. We had a very pleasant meeting, and our fainthearted brethren and sisters were much strengthened. The people were anxious to have the elders preach again, but the canal was repaired by eleven o'clock the next morning, and we proceeded on our journey and arrived at Buffalo on Friday, about an hour and a half before sunset. It was the fifth day after we had set out from Waterloo.[9]

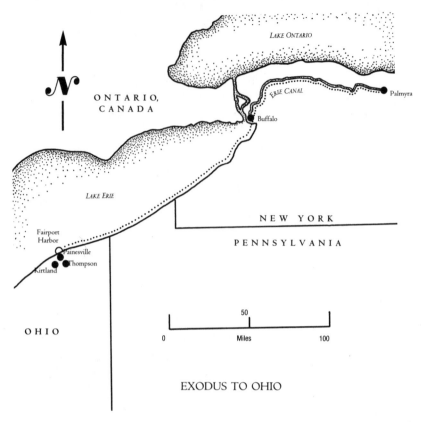

EXODUS TO OHIO

Here we met the brethren from Colesville, who had been detained a week in this place to wait for navigation to open. Since Mr. Smith and Hyrum were directed to be in Kirtland by the first of April, they had gone the remainder of the journey by land. I inquired of the Colesville brethren if they had told the people that they were Mormons. They seemed surprised at the question and replied, "No, by no means—and don't you do it for the world, for if you do, you will not get a boat nor a house, and here you must stay or go back."

I told them I would let the people know exactly who I was and what I professed. "If you," said I, "are ashamed of Christ, you will not be prospered as much as I shall, and we will get to Kirtland before you."

While we were yet talking with the Colesville brethren, another boat came up which had on board about thirty Mormon brethren, and Brother Thomas Marsh[10] was one of the company. He came to me and, perceiving the drift of our conversation, said, "Now, Mother Smith, if you do sing and have prayers and acknowledge that you are Mormons here in this place, as you have done all along, you will be mobbed before morning."

"Well, mob it is, then," said I, "for we shall sing and attend to prayers before sunset, mob or no mob."

"Then," said Marsh, considerably irritated, "I shall go into my own boat."

I then called William and told him to tell Elder Humphrey and Elder Page that I would like to see them. When they came, we counseled together, and concluding that it was best to make what diligence we could to get onto our journey's end, I requested them to go round among the boats and inquire for Captain Blake, and if they found him to bargain with him to take us to Fairport, for he was the captain of a boat that formerly belonged to General Mack, my brother of Detroit. They soon found the person in question, and he agreed to take us all on board the next morning. He said, however, that he would not be able to furnish us with fresh water, and also he was uncertain about starting, as the ice might not be out in a fortnight from that time. The morning after, we commenced moving our goods on board Captain Blake's boat and were finished two hours before sunset. The captain of the boat that brought us to Buffalo went with us and said he would stay with us as long as we were there for the sake of religious instruction.

When we were fairly settled, it commenced raining. This rendered our situation very uncomfortable, for we were under the necessity of taking a deck passage, and some of the sisters complained bitterly because we had not hired a house till the boat was ready to start. In fact, their case was rather a trying one, for some of them had sick children.

I told them that I did not believe it would be an easy matter to get a house, for the other brethren had informed me that it was almost impossible, but they could not content themselves. In consequence, I asked Brother Hiram Page to try to get a room for them, but after a tiresome search, he returned and informed them that there was no vacant house to be found in the whole place. At this the women grumbled again and declared that they would have a house, let the consequences be what they might. "Well, well," I said, "I will go myself and see what I can do for you, and a room you shall have if there is a possibility of getting one, on any terms whatsoever."

The rain was still falling in torrents, but William went with me and held an umbrella over my head. I went to the nearest tavern and asked the landlord if he could let me have a room for some women to bring their beds into and sleep, that their children were unwell, and they were so much exposed that I was fearful for their health. "Yes," said he. "I can easily make room for them." At this, a woman who was ironing in the room turned upon him very sharply and said, "I have put up here myself and I am not going to be encumbered with anybody's things in my way. I warrant the children have got the whooping cough or measles or some other catchin' disease, and if they come, I'll go somewhere else to board."

"Why madam," said the landlord, "that is not necessary. You can still have one large room."

"Well, I don't care," said she. "I want them both, and if I can't have them, I won't stay."

"Never mind," said I, "it's no matter. I will go somewhere else. I presume I can get some other room just as well."

"No, you can't though," answered the lady, "for we hunted all over the town and couldn't find one single room until we came here." This instance of human nature carries its own moral, therefore it needs no remarks.

I left immediately and soon came to a long row of rooms, and as one of them seemed to be almost at liberty, I ventured to call and inquire if I could not rent it a few days. I found the proprietor to be a fine, cheerful old lady, probably near seventy years of age. When I asked her if she had a room which she could spare me at any price, stating the circumstances as I had done to the landlord before, she said, "Well, I don't know. Where are you going?"

"To Kirtland," I said.

"What be you?" said she. "Be you Baptists?"

"No," said I. "We are Mormons."

"Mormons!" said she in a quick but low and good-natured tone. "Why, I never heard of them before. What be they?"

I told her that we did not acknowledge the name, but the world called us so, and I said so that she might know who we were, but our proper name was Latter-day Saints.

"Latter-day Saints," said she. "I never heard of them before."

"I am," said I, "the mother of the prophet who brought forth the work and translated the Book of Mormon."

"What!" said she with increased surprise. "A prophet in these days! Why, I never heard the like in my life. Will you come, if I let you have a room?" I told her that I wanted the room for the sisters who were with me, but that I would come with them and stay that day with her.

"You will come in and sit with me and tell me all about it. I don't know why 'twas, but just as soon as I saw you, I felt as though I wanted you to stay with me and I could not bear to have you go away."

I returned to the boat, told the sisters what the prospects were, and they made haste to the room, having their beds taken also. The old lady was very prompt in removing the furniture from the room, and as soon as this was done, she came to me and said, "Now come and sit down with me and tell me all about what you was talking about."

I went in and sat down, and we commenced conversation. I explained to her how the Lord was performing a work which was designed for the salvation of the people, and in order that they might be saved, it is necessary for them to repent of all their sins and be baptized for the remission of their sins, and have hands laid on them that they may receive the Holy Ghost.

"Receive the Holy Ghost," said she. "What do you mean by that?" I gave her an explanation in full of this and many other matters, and she was so inquisitive and anxious to hear, that she kept me up until two o'clock in the morning. The next day my sisters and I were up betimes, and the old lady was not at all behind us. She offered every assistance possible about our cooking and arrangements, and when breakfast was over and I was about starting back to the boat, she urged me to stay, saying, "I felt as soon as I saw you that there was something more than common, and I would have not let my room go to any person in the world but you."

When we removed to the boat again, Captain Blake requested the passengers to remain on board, as he wished from that time to be ready to start at a moment's warning; at the same time he sent out a man to measure the depth of the ice, who, when he returned, reported that it was piled up to the height of twenty feet, and that it was his opinion that we would remain in the harbor at least two weeks longer.

At this, Porter Rockwell started on shore to see his uncle. His mother endeavored to prevent him, but he paid no attention to her, and she then appealed to me, saying, "Mother Smith, do get Porter back, for he won't mind anybody but you." I told him that, if he went, we should leave him on the shore, but he could do as he liked. He left the boat, and several others were about following him; but when I spoke to them, they replied, "We will do just as you say, Mother Smith," and returned immediately.

Just then, William whispered in my ear, "Mother, do see the confusion yonder; won't you go and put a stop to it!"

I went to that part of the boat where the principal portion of our company were. There I found several of the brethren and sisters engaged in a warm debate, others murmuring and grumbling, and a number of young ladies were flirting, giggling, and laughing with gentlemen passengers who were entire strangers to them, whilst hundreds of people on shore and on other boats were witnessing this scene of clamor and vanity among our brethren with great interest. I stepped into their midst, "Brethren and sisters," said I, "we call ourselves Saints and profess to have come out from the world for the purpose of serving God at the expense of all earthly things; and will you, at the very onset, subject the cause of Christ to ridicule by your own unwise and improper conduct? You profess to put your trust in God, then how can you feel to murmur and complain as you do? You are even more unreasonable than the children of Israel were; for here are my sisters pining for their rocking chairs, and brethren from whom I expected firmness and energy declare that they positively believe they shall starve to death before they get to the end of their journey. And why is it so? Have any of you lacked? Have I not set food before you every day, and made you who had not provided for yourselves as welcome as my own children? And even if this were not the case, where is your faith? Where is your confidence in God? Do you not know that all things are in his hands, that he made all things and overrules them? If every Saint here would just lift their desires to him in prayer, that the way might be opened before us, how easy it would be for God to cause the ice to break away, and in a moment's time we could be off on our journey. But how can you expect the Lord to prosper you when you are continually murmuring against him?"

Just then a man cried out from the shore, "Is the Book of Mormon true?"

"That book," said I, "was brought forth by the power of God and translated by the same power, and if I could make my voice sound as loud as the trumpet of Michael, the archangel, I would declare the truth from land to land and from sea to sea, and echo it from isle to isle, until everyone of the whole family of man was left without excuse—for all should hear the truth of the gospel of the Son of God. I would sound in every ear that he has again revealed himself to man in these last days, and set his hand to gather his people together upon a goodly land. If they will fear him and walk uprightly before him, it shall be unto them for an inheritance; but if they rebel against his law, his hand will be against them to scatter them abroad and cut them off from the face of the earth.

"God is now going to do a work upon the earth for the salvation of all who will believe it unto the uttermost, even all who call on him, and man cannot hinder it. It will prove unto everyone who stands here this day a savior of life unto life or of death unto death—a savior of life unto life if ye will receive it, but of death unto death if ye reject the counsel of God unto your own condemnation. For every man shall have the desires of his heart. If he desires the truth, the way is open, and he may hear and live. Whereas if he treat the truth with contempt, and trample upon the simplicity of the word of God, he will shut the gate of heaven against himself."

Then, turning to our own company, I said, "Now, brethren and sisters, if you will all of you raise your desires to heaven that the ice may be broken before us, and we be set at liberty to go on our way, as sure as the Lord lives, it shall be done." At that moment a noise was heard like bursting thunder. The captain cried out, "Every man to his post," and the ice parted, leaving barely a pathway for the boat that was so narrow that, as the boat passed through, the buckets were torn with a crash from the waterwheel. This, with the noise of the ice, the confusion of the spectators, the word of command from the captain, and the hoarse answering of the sailors, was truly dreadful. We had barely passed through the avenue, when the ice closed together again, and the Colesville brethren were left in Buffalo, unable to follow us.

As we were leaving the harbor, I heard one man on shore say, "There goes the Mormon company! That boat is sunk in the water nine inches deeper than it was before, and mark it, she will sink—there is nothing surer." Our boat and one other had just time enough to get

Here at Buffalo Harbor the Saints witnessed the
opening of the ice to allow their passage west.

through, and the ice closed again and remained three weeks longer. The Colesville brethren were left in Buffalo, unable to follow us. The bystanders were so sure we would sink that they went straight to the office and had it published that we were sunk, so that when we arrived at Fairport, we read in the papers the news of our own death.

After our miraculous escape from the wharf and passage into the lake, I spoke to Brother Humphrey and requested him to call the brethren and sisters together, that we had seen a great manifestation of the power of God in our behalf, and it was near time for prayers. I thought it would be well to sing a little, and then have a kind of prayer meeting, so that all could pray that felt disposed so to do. We sang and prayed, but we had not got halfway through, when I received a message from the captain requesting me to have the Saints stop praying, for, he said, "We shall all go to hell together. We cannot keep one single hand to his post, even if we should go to the devil, for they are so taken up with the praying of your children." (He said "my children" because they all called me "Mother.")

We soon, however, had a formidable difficulty to encounter. We began to feel the effects of the motion of the boat, which brought many of our number down upon their backs with seasickness. There was a cry for water, but the captain had told the cook not to furnish the passengers with water, except where arrangements had been made. Yet, the Saints, especially those who were sick, were in great anxiety. I went to the cook and handed him twenty-five cents, and asked him if he could not let me have some hot water occasionally for the sick folks. He complied very readily with my request, and I was furnished with the means to make them comfortable for a season.

We had not been on board long until the captain found me to be the sister of General Mack. He seemed highly pleased to find in me a relative of his old friend. From that time until I left his boat, I never lacked for anything, and I never was treated with greater respect than on this boat.

A short time before we arrived at Fairport, Brother Humphrey and myself went on shore, and I bought a quantity of bread and some molasses for the little children, for there were thirty on board that I supplied myself. After we went back, Brother Humphrey called me to one side and said, "Mother Smith, you must stop this slavish work or you will kill yourself, and from now on let those women wait upon their own children and do the work for themselves and their husbands. As for myself, I shall not stay on board much longer." I told him I thought there was no danger of my injuring myself but, thanking him for his kindness, went on as before. They told me afterwards that he left us at the next landing, but I did not observe it at the time.

When we were approaching the landing at Fairport, the passengers, sailors, and even the cooks came round and took me by the hand and wept as they bade me farewell. After landing, with our things put on shore, the company were more disheartened than ever.[11] Several of the men came round me, asking what was to be done. "Here we are," they said. "We and our goods are without any shelter, and we have no hopes of houses here and no means of conveying ourselves to Kirtland. Even if we could get there, it is not at all probable that we should have a shelter. Now, won't you set our wives to work and have them sew up some blankets into tents, and we will camp out here by our goods and watch them."

*The Fairport, Ohio, lighthouse on Lake Erie marked the end of
the water journey for the Saints headed for Kirtland.*

I looked round at the sisters and found them sitting about, some crying, others pointing, others attending to their business, but the last was the fewest number. I told them I should not set their wives to work; they might do as they liked. "But yonder," said I, raising my eyes, "sits a man, and I shall inquire of him for information and see what can be done by the way of settling ourselves."

I came to the man and asked him how far it was to Kirtland. He started up and exclaimed, "Is this Mother Smith?"

"Yes, sir," I said. "We would like to know whether there is any chance of procuring teams to take our goods to Kirtland."

"And is it possible that this is Mother Smith?" said he. "I have sat here three days and nights looking for you. Do not give yourself any uneasiness. Brother Joseph is expected here every hour, and in less than twenty-four hours there will be twenty teams on hand to take the goods from here to houses that are waiting to receive them."

When he mentioned Joseph's name I started, for I just began to realize that I was so soon to see my husband and three oldest sons. As I turned from the stranger, the first thing that met my eyes was Samuel coming towards me. We met in tears of joy, but before I could speak to him, Joseph came up and caught hold of my other hand. "Mother," said Samuel. "I was warned of God in a dream to come immediately to this place to meet the company from Waterloo, and I was afraid that some dreadful thing had befallen you. Indeed, I feared that you were dead and that I should only meet your corpse."

Joseph also seemed overjoyed to find me in so good health and said, "I was myself in great fear for your life, for Brother Humphrey came to Kirtland three days since and told me he thought there was great danger of your wearing yourself out before you got here. He said you had been a perfect servant to the company all the way along, but Mother, I shall now take you away from them and you shall have no more to do with it."

As soon as this was spoken, the women gathered round me. "Oh, Mother Smith, what shall we do? You must not leave us. Can't we go with you?" Joseph told them that they could go as far as Painesville and said, "Your husbands and the other brethren will remain until the teams come for the goods, but tomorrow I shall take her away from the whole of you, for she has done enough."

The other women and I got into the wagons, and we were taken to Brother Partridge's. When we arrived there we found an excellent dinner prepared for us. After this, Brother Kingsbury came and took me in his carriage so that I could have a good night's rest, the which I had not taken since I left Waterloo. From here, I set out with my sons for Kirtland in Brother Kingsbury's handsome and comfortable carriage, which Joseph had provided for the purpose before my arrival. Joseph and the brethren had also engaged houses in Kirtland and Painesville for the rest of the company, so that in a little while they were well situated and ready to commence business for the future support of their families.

The first house that I entered was Brother Morley's.[12] Here I met with my beloved husband, and great was my joy. Many of my readers know my present situation. These can imagine, perhaps, with what feelings I rehearse these recitals.[13] But no, how can you? No woman lives upon the earth that could tell an experience like mine, and when I retrace my life in scenes like this, I seem again to press the warm hand that I then held within my own, and rest my weary head upon that affectionate breast that supports it now no more. But oh, my God, give

Isaac and Lucy Morley's farm was a gathering place
for many of the Saints, including the Smiths.

me strength and be thou my God and help in every time of need, and support me yet a little longer, until my work is done, and then may the angels waft me to my home in heaven. But enough, I must not indulge my heart, for my tale of woe is to be told hereafter.

The evening after we arrived at Kirtland, we visited Emma. She was very much pleased to see us. She said she had heard of our situation and was afraid that we would be drowned on the lake. This evening she had a pair of twins brought in that was given to her a few days before. These children were taken to supply the place of a pair of twins which she had lost.[14]

NOTES

1. William may have been working in an effort to unite the Saints to follow the commandment to move from New York to Ohio. From John Whitmer's record it appears that some of the Saints were upset about the move to Ohio. "After the Lord had manifest the above words [D&C 38], through Joseph the Seer, there were some divisions among the congregation, some would not receive the above as the word of the Lord: but that Joseph had invented it himself to deceive the people that in the end he might get gain. Now this was because, their hearts were not right in the sight of the Lord, for they wanted to serve God and man; but our Savior had declared that it was impossible to do so." (Quoted in Porter, "Origins," pp. 311–12.)

2. This was Solomon Humphrey, born September 23, 1775. He was just two months younger than Lucy Smith. He served a mission to the "eastern lands" and baptized George A. Smith, cousin to Joseph the Prophet and future Apostle. Solomon was a member of Zion's Camp in 1834 and died later that same year in Clay County, Missouri. (See Cook, *Revelations*, p. 78.)

3. Potsdam is located just six or seven miles from Stockholm, New York, where the extended Smith family were living.

4. The Fayette (Waterloo) company was divided into two groups, one under Mother Smith and the other under Thomas B. Marsh. The groups would have likely traveled east on the Cayuga and Seneca Canal (which ran in front of the Smith home in Waterloo), then followed the Seneca River as it proceeded generally east through the village of Seneca Falls, northeast to the north end of Cayuga Lake, then generally north through the Montezuma swamps, and into the Erie Canal. (See Porter, "Origins," p. 316.)

5. It appears that this group of eighty Saints left on Monday, May 2, 1831. An editorial in the *Wayne Sentinel* dated May 27, 1831, gave a report of the exodus of another group of the Saints from the Palmyra area. "Several families, numbering about fifty souls, took up their line of march from this town [Palmyra] this week for the 'promised land,' among whom was Martin Harris, one of the original believers in the 'Book of Mormon.' Mr. Harris was among the early settlers of this town, and has ever borne the character of an honorable and upright man, and an obliging and benevolent neighbor. He had a respectable fortune—and he has left a large circle of acquaintances and friends to pity his delusion." (Quoted in Porter, "Origins," p. 321.) It is worthy to note that there were three main groups making the exodus to Ohio, namely: the Waterloo/Fayette Saints (about eighty in number under the guidance of Mother Smith and Thomas B. Marsh); the Palmyra Saints (about fifty in number under the leadership of Martin Harris); and the Colesville Branch (approximately seventy Saints under the direction of Newel Knight).

6. This is most likely referring to Hiram Page, one of the Eight Witnesses to the Book of Mormon. Hiram, born in 1800 in Vermont, married Catherine Whitmer

(sister to David Whitmer) November 10, 1825. They had nine children (five sons and four daughters). (See Cook, *Revelations,* p. 40.)

7. The trip from Waterloo to Buffalo on the canal system was a little over one hundred miles and took this group of Saints about five days to complete, including the waiting time for the "break" in the canal.

8. In leaving their homes for a new promised land, the Saints, like the children of Israel and Lehi and his family before them, were following the exodus pattern. At this point where the canal is broken, it is worth inserting a correlating verse from Lehi's journey: "And it came to pass that the daughters of Ishmael did mourn exceedingly, because of the loss of their father, and because of their afflictions in the wilderness; and they did murmur against my father, because he had brought them out of the land of Jerusalem, saying: Our father is dead; yea, and we have wandered much in the wilderness, and we have suffered much affliction, hunger, thirst, and fatigue; and after all these sufferings we must perish in the wilderness with hunger." (1 Nephi 16:35.)

9. If this day of the week is correct, then this group arrived at Buffalo on Friday, May 6, 1831. The Colesville Saints had arrived here May 1, 1831. Mother Smith states that they had been detained a week in this place. (See Porter, "Origins," pp. 317–18.)

10. Thomas Baldwin Marsh, son of James and Molly Law Marsh, was born in Acton, Middlesex County, Massachusetts, on November 1, 1799 or 1800. He was baptized by David Whitmer on September 3, 1830, and was named by the Lord as a "physician unto the church" (D&C 31:10). Thomas would be called as one of the original Twelve Apostles. He was excommunicated on March 17, 1839, for apostasy, and rebaptized eighteen years later. He died in full fellowship of the Church in January 1866. (See Cook, *Revelations,* pp. 42–43.)

11. William Smith stated: "After a long and tedious passage, facing many storms, cold winds and rains, we at length arrived at Fairport, about eleven miles distant from the settlement of the brethren [Kirtland]. I started on foot with Bro. J. [Jenkins] Salisbury [William's brother-in-law], to find them. We soon discovered their place of residence, and with great joy in our hearts we again conversed with them face to face; while they on their part very gladly received us and bade us welcome." (Quoted in Porter, "Origins," p. 320.)

12. The Morley farm was a gathering place for the Smiths and many of the Saints coming from New York. After Joseph and Emma's arrival in Kirtland, they first stayed in the home of Newel and Elizabeth Whitney for a few weeks. After this they were invited to live on the Isaac and Lucy Morley farm. Here they made their residence until September 12, 1831, whereupon they moved to Hiram, Portage County, Ohio, to live with the John and Elsa Johnson family.

13. By the time of the recounting of her life story in 1844–45, Lucy had lost her husband and five of her adult sons. Remembering this past moment of family reunion in Kirtland was very painful for her.

14. On Saturday, April 30, 1831, Emma had given birth to twins, a boy and a girl, who were named Thaddeus and Louisa. They lived but three hours and died. On

that same day, Julia Clapp Murdock, wife of John Murdock, gave birth to twins, a boy and a girl, and she passed away six hours later. Brother Murdock had three other small children, Orrice, John Riggs, and Phebe, and felt that giving the twins to Joseph and Emma (at nine days of age) would allow them to be raised in a place where they could be "taught in the faith and principles of salvation," and would perhaps assuage the pain of both families. The adopted twins were named Joseph Murdock Smith and Julia Smith. (See Cook, *Revelations,* p. 80. See also Karl Ricks Anderson, *Joseph Smith's Kirtland: Eyewitness Accounts* [Salt Lake City: Deseret Book Co., 1989], p. 32; John Murdock Journal, Typescript, Brigham Young University Archives, p. 9.)

CHAPTER 39

The Smiths settle on a farm in Kirtland. Joseph, Samuel, and Hyrum leave on missions for Missouri. Lucy Mack Smith inserts a number of revelations given at this time concerning the building up of Zion, the keeping of the commandments, and the preaching of the gospel among the congregations of the wicked, including, in part or whole, sections 52, 58, 59, 60, and 61 of the Doctrine and Covenants.

Mid-May 1831 to August 12, 1831

Mr. Morley gave us the use of a room which we occupied but two weeks, when we moved onto a farm which was purchased by Joseph for the Church. On this farm my family were all established with this arrangement, that we were to cultivate the farm, and from the fruits of our labors we were to support our several families and sustain strangers who were traveling, either members of the Church or others in search of the truth or on a visit to the place.

Immediately after we moved onto the farm, Joseph received a request from the brethren who were in Missouri to send some elders to assist them. Joseph inquired of the Lord and received the following revelation[1]:

> Behold, thus saith the Lord unto the elders whom he hath called and chosen in these last days, by the voice of his Spirit—
> Saying: I, the Lord, will make known unto you what I will that ye shall do from this time until the next conference,[2] which shall be held in Missouri, upon the land, which I will consecrate unto my

people, which are a remnant of Jacob, and those who are heirs according to the covenant.

Wherefore, verily I say unto you, let my servants Joseph Smith, Jun., and Sidney Rigdon take their journey as soon as preparations can be made to leave their homes, and journey to the land of Missouri.

And inasmuch as they are faithful unto me, it shall be made known unto them what they shall do;

And it shall also, inasmuch as they are faithful, be made known unto them the land of your inheritance. . . .

And also [let] my servant John Murdock, and my servant Hyrum Smith, take their journey unto the same place by the way of Detroit.

And let them journey from thence preaching the word by the way, saying none other things than that which the prophets and apostles have written, and that which is taught them by the Comforter through the prayer of faith.

Let them go two by two, and thus let them preach by the way in every congregation, baptizing by water, and the laying on of the hands by the water's side. . . .

Let my servants Reynolds Cahoon and Samuel H. Smith also take their journey. . . .

And thus, even as I have said, if ye are faithful ye shall assemble yourselves together to rejoice upon the land of Missouri, which is the land of your inheritance, which is now the land of your enemies.

But, behold, I, the Lord, will hasten the city in its time, and will crown the faithful with joy and with rejoicing.

Behold, I am Jesus Christ, the Son of God, and I will lift them up at the last day. Even so. Amen.[3]

It will be observed in this revelation that Samuel H. Smith and Reynolds Cahoon were appointed to go in company together.

On their way to Missouri, they called at a town, and going into a large store, they inquired of the clerk, who was William E. McLellin,[4] if they had any preaching evenings in the place. "Yes," answered Mr. McLellin, "we do, when any preacher comes along. What denomination do you belong to?"

"We are Latter-day Saints," said Samuel.

"Can you preach?" said Mr. McLellin. "I would like to hear you, for that is a denomination that I have never heard of, and if you will preach, I will get a house and light it up and call the people together in good season."

Samuel replied that he would be glad of the opportunity. Mr. McLellin went out, and in a short time he had a large congregation seated in a convenient room, well lit up at his expense. After the meeting was dismissed, Mr. McLellin urged them to stay in the place and preach again, but they refused, as their directions were to go forward without any further delay than to warn the people as they passed.

Soon after they left, which was the next morning, Mr. McLellin grew uneasy, and he afterwards told me the following story:

"When night came I was unable to sleep, for I thought that I ought to have gone with them, as I had an excellent horse, and I could have assisted them much on their journey. This worked upon my mind, so that I determined to set out after them the next morning, cost what it might. I accordingly told my employer what I had concluded to do, and obtaining his consent, I set out in pursuit of my new acquaintances. I did not overtake them, but I pursued my route in the same direction, until I came to Jackson County, Missouri, where I was baptized."

On their route, Samuel and Brother Cahoon suffered great privations, such as want of rest and food. On this journey, they passed through Quincy. There were only thirty-two houses then in the place, and they preached the first sermon that ever was delivered in that town.[5]

At the time that they started for Missouri, near fifty others also set out for the same place, all taking different routes. When they arrived in Jackson, the elders had mostly got there before them.[6]

Soon after their arrival Joseph received a revelation, of which the following is an extract:[7]

> Hearken, O ye elders of my church, and give ear to my word, and learn of me what I will concerning you, and also concerning this land unto which I have sent you.
>
> For verily I say unto you, blessed is he that keepeth my commandments, whether in life or in death; and he that is faithful in

tribulation, the reward of the same is greater in the kingdom of heaven.

Ye cannot behold with your natural eyes, for the present time, the design of your God concerning those things which shall come hereafter, and the glory which shall follow after much tribulation.[8]

For after much tribulation come the blessings. Wherefore the day cometh that ye shall be crowned with much glory; the hour is not yet, but is nigh at hand.

Remember this, which I tell you before, that you may lay it to heart, and receive that which is to follow.

Behold, verily I say unto you, for this cause I have sent you—that you might be obedient, and that your hearts might be prepared to bear testimony of the things which are to come;

And also that you might be honored in laying the foundation, and in bearing record of the land upon which the Zion of God shall stand. . . .

Wherefore, be subject to the powers that be, until he reigns whose right it is to reign, and subdues all enemies under his feet. . . .

And now, verily, I say concerning the residue of the elders of my church, the time has not yet come, for many years, for them to receive their inheritance in this land, except they desire it through the prayer of faith, only as it shall be appointed unto them of the Lord. . . .

For, verily, the sound must go forth from this place into all the world, and unto the uttermost parts of the earth—the gospel must be preached unto every creature, with signs following them that believe.

And behold the Son of Man cometh. Amen.

After the elders had collected in Jackson, they dedicated the spot for the temple,[9] and four days later Joseph received the following revelation:[10]

Behold, blessed, saith the Lord, are they who have come up unto this land with an eye single to my glory, according to my commandments.

Here in Independence, Jackson County,
over twelve hundred Saints would gather to try to establish Zion.

For those that live shall inherit the earth, and those that die shall rest from all their labors, and their works shall follow them; and they shall receive a crown in the mansions of my Father, which I have prepared for them.

Yea, blessed are they whose feet stand upon the land of Zion, who have obeyed my gospel; for they shall receive for their reward the good things of the earth, and it shall bring forth in its strength.[11]

And they shall also be crowned with blessings from above, yea, and with commandments not a few, and with revelations in their time—they that are faithful and diligent before me.

Wherefore, I give unto them a commandment, saying thus: Thou shalt love the Lord thy God with all thy heart, with all thy might, mind, and strength; and in the name of Jesus Christ thou shalt serve him.

Following the Missouri conference the elders who had been appointed to return to the East desired to know how they should proceed, and by what route and manner they should travel.[12] In response, on Monday, August 8, 1831, Joseph received the following revelation:[13]

Behold, thus saith the Lord unto the elders of his church, who are to return speedily to the land from whence they came: Behold, it pleaseth me, that you have come up hither;

But with some I am not well pleased, for they will not open their mouths, but they hide the talent which I have given unto them, because of the fear of man. Wo unto such, for mine anger is kindled against them.

And it shall come to pass, if they are not more faithful unto me, it shall be taken away, even that which they have.

For I, the Lord, rule in the heavens above, and among the armies of the earth; and in the day when I shall make up my jewels, all men shall know what it is that bespeaketh the power of God.

But, verily, I will speak unto you concerning your journey unto the land from whence you came. Let there be a craft made, or bought, as seemeth you good, it mattereth not unto me, and take your journey speedily for the place which is called St. Louis.

And from thence let my servants, Sidney Rigdon, Joseph Smith, Jun., and Oliver Cowdery, take their journey for Cincinnati;

And in this place let them lift up their voice and declare my word with loud voices, without wrath or doubting, lifting up holy hands upon them. For I am able to make you holy, and your sins are forgiven you.

And let the residue take their journey from St. Louis, two by two, and preach the word, not in haste, among the congregations of the wicked, until they return to the churches from whence they came.

And all this for the good of the churches; for this intent have I sent them.

And let my servant Edward Partridge impart of the money which I have given him, a portion unto mine elders who are commanded to return;

And he that is able, let him return it by the way of the agent; and he that is not, of him it is not required.

And now I speak of the residue who are to come unto this land.

Behold, they have been sent to preach my gospel among the congregations of the wicked; wherefore, I give unto them a commandment, thus: Thou shalt not idle away thy time, neither shalt thou bury thy talent that it may not be known.

And after thou hast come up unto the land of Zion, and hast proclaimed my word, thou shalt speedily return, proclaiming my word among the congregations of the wicked, not in haste, neither in wrath nor with strife.

And shake off the dust of thy feet against those who receive thee not, not in their presence, lest thou provoke them, but in secret; and wash thy feet, as a testimony against them in the day of judgment.

Behold, this is sufficient for you, and the will of him who hath sent you.

And by the mouth of my servant Joseph Smith, Jun., it shall be made known concerning Sidney Rigdon and Oliver Cowdery. The residue hereafter. Even so. Amen.

On August 9, 1831, in company with ten elders, Joseph left Independence landing (on the Missouri River) for Kirtland. Nothing

While along the banks of the Missouri, William W. Phelps saw the destroyer riding upon the waters.

very important occurred till the third day, when many of the dangers so
common upon the western waters manifested themselves; and after they
had encamped upon the bank of the river, Brother William W. Phelps,
in open vision by daylight, saw the destroyer in his most horrible power
ride upon the face of the waters; others heard the noise, but saw not the
vision. The next morning after prayer, Joseph received a revelation,[14] an
extract of which follows:

> Behold, verily thus saith the Lord unto you, O ye elders of my
> church, who are assembled upon this spot, whose sins are now for-
> given you, for I, the Lord, forgive sins, and am merciful unto those
> who confess their sins with humble hearts;
>
> But verily I say unto you, that it is not needful for this whole
> company of mine elders to be moving swiftly upon the waters,
> whilst the inhabitants on either side are perishing in unbelief.
>
> Nevertheless, I suffered it that ye might bear record; behold,
> there are many dangers upon the waters, and more especially here-
> after. . . .
>
> And now, concerning the residue, let them journey and declare
> the word among the congregations of the wicked, inasmuch as it is
> given. . . .
>
> And let them journey together, or two by two, as seemeth them
> good, only let my servant Reynolds Cahoon, and my servant
> Samuel H. Smith, with whom I am well pleased, be not separated
> until they return to their homes, and this for a wise purpose in me.

Here let me say that Samuel was never censured by revelation to my
knowledge, for he always performed his missions faithfully and his
work was well approved.[15]

NOTES

1. This revelation was given June 7, 1831, and is now known as section 52 of
the Doctrine and Covenants. Mother Smith gave instructions in the Preliminary

Manuscript to include extracts from several revelations at this point in her history. Two paragraphs have been added in this chapter to give a bridge of continuity between them. They have been correspondingly footnoted as they appear.

2. This first conference in Missouri was held on Thursday, August 4, 1831, in the home of "Brother Joshua Lewis, in Kaw township, in the presence of the Colesville branch of the Church" (*History of the Church* 1:199). Joshua Lewis, born in 1795, was one of the early settlers of Jackson County and converted to the Church through the efforts of the Lamanite missionaries (Ziba Peterson, Peter Whitmer Jr., Oliver Cowdery, Parley P. Pratt, and Frederick G. Williams) in late fall 1830 (see *Papers*, pp. 497–98).

3. Those who had been called on missions to Missouri, as recorded in section 52 of the Doctrine and Covenants, were: Lyman Wight, John Corrill, John Murdock, Hyrum Smith, Thomas B. Marsh, Ezra Thayre, Isaac Morley, Ezra Booth, Edward Partridge, Martin Harris, David Whitmer, Harvey Whitlock, Parley P. Pratt, Orson Pratt, Solomon Hancock, Simeon Carter, Edson Fuller, Jacob Scott, Levi Hancock, Zebedee Coltrin, Reynolds Cahoon, Samuel H. Smith, Wheeler Baldwin, William Carter, Newel Knight, and Selah J. Griffin. Joseph Wakefield and Solomon Humphrey were called to the "eastern lands."

4. William E. McLellin, son of Charles McLellin, was born January 18, 1806, in Smith County, Tennessee. He was one of the original Twelve Apostles, ordained February 15, 1835. He later publicly opposed Church leadership, was excommunicated in 1838, and never returned to the Church. He spent the last thirteen years of his life trying to convince David Whitmer to start a new church. He died at Independence, Jackson County, Missouri, April 24, 1883. (See Cook, *Revelations*, pp. 106–7.)

5. Quincy, Illinois, would, nearly eight years later, be a place of refuge for thousands of the Saints who had been driven from Missouri.

6. Joseph recorded: "The meeting of our brethren, who had long waited our arrival, was a glorious one and moistened with many tears. It seemed good and pleasant for brethren to meet together in unity. But our reflections were great: coming as we had from a highly cultivated state of society in the east, and standing now upon the confines or western limits of the United States, and looking into the vast wilderness of those that sat in darkness, how natural it was to observe the degradation, leanness of intellect, ferocity and jealousy of a people that were nearly a century behind the times; and to feel for those who roamed about without the benefit of civilization, refinement or religion!—yea, and exclaim in the language of the prophets:—when will the wilderness blossom as the rose; when will Zion be built up in her glory, and where will thy Temple stand unto which all nations shall come in the last days?" (*Papers*, p. 357.)

7. Mother Smith instructed in her Preliminary Manuscript that "suitable extracts" be taken from this revelation and be inserted into the history. For a full reading of this revelation, see Doctrine and Covenants 58:1–65.

8. This was a foreshadowing of all that would transpire in Missouri.

9. The spot for the temple was dedicated on Wednesday, August 3, 1831. The 87th Psalm was read and Joseph recorded: "The scene was solemn and impressive." (*History of the Church* 1:199.) This was the humble beginning of laying the foundation for the great Zion, the New Jerusalem that prophets through the ages had seen in vision and hoped and longed for. Here, on that obscure summer day, on a small plot of land in a frontier wilderness, and unknown to the world, the small beginning was laid for the city of God which will someday become the envy of all nations.

10. This revelation was given on the Sabbath day, August 7, 1831. Mother Smith instructed in her Preliminary Manuscript that "suitable extracts" be taken from this revelation and be inserted into the history. For a full reading of this revelation, see Doctrine and Covenants 59:1–24.

11. These first verses are especially poignant and personal. Polly Knight, stalwart and faithful wife of Joseph Knight Sr., and a member of the Colesville, New York, Branch of the Church, had desired with all of her soul to see Zion, but her health had been failing quite rapidly. The twelve-hundred-mile journey was arduous. Newel Knight recorded: "She would not consent to stop traveling; her only, or her greatest desire was to set her feet upon the land of Zion, and to have her body interred in that land. I went on shore and bought lumber to make a coffin in case she should die before we arrived at our place of destination—so fast did she fail. But the Lord gave her the desire of her heart, and she lived to stand upon that land." (*History of the Church* 1:199.) She died on Saturday, August 6, 1831, and was buried the next day. Following the funeral on that day, this revelation was given.

12. The bridging paragraph here is taken from the headnote to section 60 in the 1981 edition of the Doctrine and Covenants.

13. Mother Smith instructed that the whole revelation, section 60 of the Doctrine and Covenants, be inserted in the history. None of the preceding editions have included this.

14. This paragraph has been inserted from *History of the Church* 1:202–3 to create a bridge for continuity between the revelations Lucy directed be included in her history. This revelation, section 61 of the Doctrine and Covenants, was given on Friday, August 12, 1831.

15. It must be noted that Samuel Harrison Smith passed away on July 30, 1844, just thirty-three days after his brothers Hyrum and Joseph were killed. Lucy recites with pride, poignance, and in the past tense as she comments about her martyred sons.

CHAPTER 40

Lucy recounts her mission with niece Almira Mack, son Hyrum, and others to Detroit and Pontiac, Michigan. Teaching the Book of Mormon aboard ship. Meeting with various relatives (all from the Stephen Mack family). Confrontation with the Reverend Mr. Ruggles of Pontiac. Lucy gives a prophecy to the reverend concerning the missionary work and his congregation. It is all fulfilled. Samuel serves a mission with William McLellin, then an eleven-month mission with newly baptized Orson Hyde.

June 14, 1831 to December 22, 1832

I will now return to the time when the elders set out for Missouri. The reader will recollect that Hyrum Smith, my eldest son, was directed to go by the way of Detroit. I thought it would be a good opportunity to visit the family of my brother Stephen Mack, who had been dead some four or five years, this being 1831, and my brother died in 1826. Hyrum was very anxious to have me accompany him, and as my niece Almira Mack[1] was about returning home, this was another inducement for me to undertake the journey. I accordingly set off in the month of June with Hyrum, Almira, Brother Murdock, Lyman Wight,[2] and Brother Corrill.[3]

When we went on board the boat, we held a consultation to determine whether it was best to say much concerning the gospel. At first, it was concluded that we should be entirely still as to religion, but finally Hyrum said that Mother might say what she was disposed to, and if a difficulty arose, the elders should assist her out of it. We had not been long on board when, as I was sitting one day at the door of the cabin very much engaged reading the Book of Mormon, a lady accosted me thus, "What book have you, madam? You seem very much engaged."

"The Book of Mormon," I replied.

"The Book of Mormon," said she. "What work is that?" I then gave her a brief history of the discovery and translation of the work. This delighted her, and when I mentioned that it was a record of the origin of the Indians of America, she exclaimed, "Is it possible? Why, my husband is a missionary out now among the Indians, and I am going too. How I do wish that I could get a book to carry to him!"

Just then another lady, who was a doctor's wife, came up very near us with the appearance of wishing to hear our conversation. She paced to and fro before us for some time, carrying herself daintily, I assure you. She was sumptuously dressed, and in seeming absence of mind, she allowed her rich scarf to fall down from one shoulder and thus displayed a neck and bosom so splendidly decorated with jewels as almost to dazzle the eyes. After a while she turned sharply upon me, saying, "Now, I don't want to hear any more about that stuff or anything more about Joe Smith either. They say he is a Mormon prophet, but it is nothing but deception and lies. There was one Mr. Murdock who believed in Joe Smith's doctrine; and the Mormons all think that they can cure the sick and can raise the dead. So when Mr. Murdock's wife was sick, he refused to send for a doctor, although the poor woman wanted him to do so, and so by his neglect, his wife died."

I told her I thought she must be a little mistaken in regard to that matter, for my son had taken the twins which she left, and I had an idea that I knew something near the truth of the affair.

"I know all about it," said the lady.

"Well, now, perhaps not," said I. "Just stop a moment and I will explain a little."

"No, that I won't," she said.

"Then I will introduce you to Mr. Murdock himself and let him tell the story," I said, turning to Elder Murdock, who stood near. Just before this, however, the chambermaid, who was very friendly, went downstairs and complained to the lady's husband of his wife's unbecoming behavior. And before she had heard a dozen words from our brother, her husband came bustling upstairs and said, "Here, they tell me you are abusing this old lady," and, taking her hand, drew it within his arm and marched her off at an unusually quick pace. But by this time, a large number of the passengers had gathered round, and the subject being introduced, the elders continued it, and they preached most of the time, except while they were sleeping, until we arrived in Detroit.[4] The impression upon the minds of the passengers was very favorable, and we could have disposed of a quantity of books but we had none with us.

When we landed in Detroit, it was dark,[5] and my niece thought it would be advisable for us to put up at a tavern, as her sister, Mrs. Cooper, the only one of my brother's family who lived in Detroit, was in very ill health with a nervous affection, which she had been under the influence of for several years. The next morning Almira Mack and myself went to her sister's house. Mrs. Cooper was in her room when we arrived, lying on the bed. Almira went to her, but I remained in the sitting room, as her housekeeper thought that our both going in at once would agitate Mrs. Cooper so much that it might be an injury to her. When the usual salutations had passed between the sisters, Almira told Mrs. Cooper that I had come to Detroit and was waiting to see her. She requested the privilege of inviting me into her room.

"Stop, sister," said the elder of the two. "I am so nervous I cannot see her, but I am glad she is here, and I will be happy to have her come in as soon as my nerves are settled again."

"Well, Mrs. Cooper," said Almira, "there is another thing I want to mention to you. Aunt Lucy has some three or four elders with her, who are yet at the tavern, and she wishes to have them invited here also."

"Oh dear, no. I am so nervous that I never could endure it in the world. It would kill me. Do not think of it."

Almira saw that it was in vain to urge the matter, and when Mrs. Cooper's husband thought that she was composed enough to meet me, she directed Almira to call me to her room, but Almira's heart was full to overflowing. She knew that Lovisa—that is, Mrs. Cooper—had received as much of my attention when she was a child as either of my own had received, and that my feelings for all my brother's children were unusually tender. On this account, she felt disagreeable to be the bearer of her sister's refusal to meet her cousin and my son. But after giving vent to her feelings in a flood of tears, she came to me and gave me to understand the situation.

I went into Lovisa's room, and she seemed very much pleased to see me. After some light remarks on both sides, I said, "Lovisa, I have four of my brethren with me. One of them is your cousin Hyrum, and I want to have them invited here if I stay."

"Oh! no, no, no!" she exclaimed. "I never can consent to it! Why, I am so nervous that I am not in a proper situation to see anyone. Company does so agitate me."

"Now, Lovisa," I said. "Do you know what it is that ails you? I can tell you exactly. There is a good spirit and an evil one operating upon you, and the bad spirit has almost got possession of you, and when the good spirit is the least agitated, the evil one strives for the entire mastery and sets the good spirit to faltering, just ready to leave you, because it has so slight a foothold. You have been sick a long time, and you may yet live many years. These men who are with me are clothed with the authority of the priesthood, and through their administration, you might receive a blessing; and even should you not be healed, do you not wish to know something about your Savior before you are called to meet him? Furthermore, if you refuse to receive my brethren into your house, I shall leave it and go myself to the tavern."

She finally concluded to have a sumptuous dinner prepared and have the brethren all invited to dine with her.[6] The necessary directions being given, I told her that I would like to have her calm her mind as much as possible, and when the elders came have them lay hands on her and pray for her. To this she consented, and it was done after dinner. She went to her room again, being a little fatigued. I asked her if she wished them to pray for her again. She answered very readily that she did, for she had been better since they had administered to her. They complied with her request and, bidding her farewell, left the house.

After they were gone, and she found that they were not to be coming again, she seemed very much distressed that she had not urged them to stay and preach. The next morning I set out in the stage for Pontiac,[7] whither the brethren had gone the day before, and where my brother Stephen's wife and her son-in-law and daughter, Mr. and Mrs. Whitermore, lived. As soon as I had settled myself at Mr. Whitermore's, I broached the subject which lay nearest my heart and began to explain to them why the elders visited them and the nature of their mission. Mr. Whitermore paid great attention to what I advanced, as did also my brother's widow, Sister Mack, until near tea time. Then Sister Mack arose and said, "Sister Lucy, you must excuse me, for I find my nerves are so discomposed that I cannot bear conversation any longer. As the subject is an entirely new one, it confuses my mind."

"Stop a moment," I said, and she sat down. I then repeated to her the same, in substance, which I had told her daughter two days before, "but," I added, "if a company of fashionable people were to come in now and begin to talk about parties, balls, and the latest style of making drapes, do you think that would agitate you?"

She smiled, saying, "I do not know as it would, Sister Lucy. You know, those are very common things." I told her that I would excuse her freely now to walk where she liked, but requested her to think of what I had said to her. I then concluded to say no more upon the subject of religion, unless she desired me to do so. Finding that she and I were to occupy the same bed, I even determined to desist from my usual habit of praying at my bedside but retired to another place and besought God to soften her heart to the influence of the truth. A short time after we lay down to rest, my sister said, "Everything is still now and I would be glad to hear you talk, if you are not too much fatigued."

"I should have no objections if you do not think that the subject of religion would make you nervous," said I.

"Oh, not in the least," she replied. "There is no other noise now to confuse my mind." Accordingly we commenced a conversation which lasted till daylight in which she heard and believed the gospel and never after lost her faith.[8]

In a few days Mr. Whitermore accompanied me to the house of another niece, named Ruth Stanly, sister to Mrs. Whitermore. Soon after we arrived, Mr. Whitermore introduced me to the Reverend Mr. Ruggles, the pastor of the Presbyterian church to which he belonged. "And you," said Mr. Ruggles, upon shaking hands with me, "are the mother of that poor, silly, foolish boy, Joe Smith, who pretended to translate the Book of Mormon."

I looked him steadily in the face and replied, "I am, sir, the mother of Joseph Smith, but why may I ask do you call him a foolish, silly boy?"

"Because," said his reverence, "that he should imagine he was going to break down all the churches with that simple Mormon book."

"Did you ever read that book?" I inquired.

"No," said he, "it is too far beneath me to be worthy of my notice."

"Then I think, sir," I said, "you do not abide by that scripture which saith 'search these things'; and now, sir, let me tell you boldly that the Book of Mormon contains the everlasting gospel, and it was written for the salvation of your soul by the gift and power of the Holy Ghost."

"Pooh," said the minister, "nonsense, but I have no fears of any members of my church being led away by such dogmatism, for they have too much intelligence."

"Now, Mr. Ruggles," said I, and I spoke earnestly, for the Spirit of God was upon me, "mark my words: as sure as God lives, before three years we will have more than one-third of your church, and sir, whether you believe it or not, we will take the very deacon too."

This produced a hearty laugh from the company at the expense of the reverend minister.

Not to be tedious, I will say that I remained in this section of the country about three weeks after our brethren left me, making my whole stay four weeks, during which time I labored incessantly for the truth's sake and gained the hearts of many believers, among whom was David Dort and his wife. These were anxious to have me use my influence to have an elder sent into that region of the country, and they pledged that the man who came should not lack for anything. Just as I embarked for home, Mr. Cooper, my nephew of Detroit, said if we would dress our elders in broadcloth instead of homespun, it would add greatly to their influence. I promised him that the next one who came to preach to them should be more genteel.

I arrived home in a few days in perfect health and safety, finding my family well, and at the first opportunity mentioned the state of things where I had been to Joseph. He seemed pleased that I had succeeded in preparing the way for a minister of the gospel, and sent Brother Jared Carter to labor in that country, but not until we had him fitted out, as I promised Mr. Cooper, with a suit of superfine broadcloth. He went into the midst of Mr. Ruggles's church and converted seventy of his best members, and as I said he took the very deacon too. For although I did not know anything about the situation of his church, he had a very intelligent deacon by the name of Samuel Bent, who is now a high councilor in Nauvoo, and he told me the last time I saw him, which was not a week since, that he had never forgotten my prophecy upon his head.[9]

In less than a month after my arrival, Samuel returned home from Missouri and remained until the next October, when a revelation was given commanding him and William McLellin to go to the town of Hiram, which was about thirty miles distant, and warn the people in the name of the Lord. He began to make preparations to set out on this mission, but before he was ready to start, he heard a voice in the night which called to him, saying, "Samuel, arise immediately and go forth on the mission which thou wast commanded to take to Hiram." He arose and took what clothing he had in readiness and set out without eating.

He traveled fifteen miles that day, warning the people by the way, and the next day he arrived at Hiram, where he met William McLellin according to previous appointment, for they had not gone the same route. They held a meeting at noon as they could make arrangements to do so, and being tolerably well received, they continued to preach in Hiram and the surrounding country. They had not been in this place long until they were sent for by a woman who had been sick many months and had prayed much that the Lord would send some of the Mormons into that country, that she might have hands laid on her for the recovery of her health. Samuel went immediately to her and administered to her by the laying on of hands in the name of the Lord, and she was healed and was also baptized.

After finishing this mission, he returned home on December twenty-seventh. However, Samuel was not long permitted to remain at home in quiet; on the first of January he was sent with newly baptized Orson Hyde[10] on a mission into the eastern country. They set out on this mission without delay, calling at public houses as much as possible and warning the people to flee from the wrath to come, until they got to Boston. They preached from city to city, continuing their labors until they were called home by a revelation in which the Lord declared that they should receive the ordinance of the washing of feet, for their skirts were clean of the blood of this generation.[11]

NOTES

1. Almira Mack was the youngest daughter of Stephen and Temperance Bond Mack. Born at Tunbridge, Orange County, Vermont, in 1805 (the same year as her cousin, Joseph the Prophet), Almira was baptized by David Whitmer in 1830. She married William Scobey in 1831, and he died one year later. She married Benjamin Covey in 1836. She followed the Saints through Ohio, Missouri, and Illinois, and crossed the plains to Utah in 1848, dying in Salt Lake City in 1886. (See *Papers*, p. 498.)

2. Lyman Wight, son of Levi and Sarah Cardin Wight, was born at Fairfield, Herkimer County, New York, on May 9, 1796. He married Harriet Benton on January 5, 1823, and together they had six children. He joined the Campbellite movement (with Sidney Rigdon) in May 1829, and was among the "common stock" (a "united order" type group of families in the area of Kirtland, Ohio) with Isaac Morley and Titus Billings. He was baptized November 14, 1830. Lyman spent the years 1830 to 1848 associated with the Church. He was a member of Zion's Camp, was with Joseph in Liberty Jail, was ordained an Apostle on April 8, 1841, and campaigned for Joseph for president of the United States in 1844. He was assigned to try to find a place for the Saints to gather and left for Texas on May 21, 1845. When the Saints followed the Twelve to the Rocky Mountains, he pleaded with them to come to Texas. He never joined with the main body of the Saints and was cut off from the Church December 3, 1848. He died March 31, 1858, at Dexter, Medina County, Texas. (See Cook, *Revelations*, pp. 82–83.)

3. The revelation commanding the elders to go to the land of Missouri was given June 7, 1831. Lucy left on Tuesday, June 14, 1831. John Corrill, born September 17, 1794, at Worcester County, Massachusetts, was baptized January 10, 1831. He suffered with the Saints in Missouri, was imprisoned, then driven from Jackson County. He stood by the Brethren through storms and strife and then published a work against the Church in 1839. He was excommunicated March 17, 1839, and died at Quincy, Illinois, in 1843. (See Cook, *Revelations*, pp. 68–69.)

4. It was twelve miles from Kirtland to Fairport Harbor, and then another 150 miles across Lake Erie to Detroit.

5. John Murdock's journal gives verification of the departure and late arrival: "Agreeable to this revelation [D&C 52] we, Hyrum Smith and Lyman Wight, John Corrill and myself, took our journey from Kirtland June 14th and went on board the steamer Wm. [William] Penn at Fairport and arrived at Detroit Wednesday, 15th, 11 o'clock at night" (John Murdock Journal, Typescript, Brigham Young University Archives, p. 9).

6. In the Preliminary Manuscript, Lucy added and then crossed out at this point: "Meanwhile, they applied for the Methodist church to preach in, but was refused. A minister came the next morning and said that if he had known it to be the request of General Mack's sister, they should have preached in his church. I told him there might yet be an opportunity for him to show his goodwill to us."

7. Pontiac, Michigan, was twenty-five miles from the dock where their ship landed.

8. Temperance Mack joined the Church and gathered with the Saints. She wrote a letter in December 1843 from Nauvoo to her Michigan daughters saying: "Aunt Lucy sends her love, tells me that she wishes you to remember that the work is as true as it was when she saw you" (quoted in Richard Lloyd Anderson, "His Mother's Manuscript: An Intimate View of Joseph Smith," Brigham Young University Forum, January 27, 1976, Typescript, p. 10).

9. The Pontiac Congregational Church records verify this event: "February 9 [1833] observed as a day of fasting and prayer on the occasion of the excommunication of Deacon Bent for embracing the Mormon delusion" (quoted in Anderson, "His Mother's Manuscript," p. 10). Samuel Bent, son of Joel Bent, was born July 19, 1778, at Barre, Worcester County, Massachusetts. Samuel was baptized by Jared Carter in January 1833, was a member of Zion's Camp, served in various leadership positions, received temple ordinances at Nauvoo, left with the Saints for the West, and passed away at Garden Grove, Iowa, August 16, 1846. (See Cook, *Revelations,* p. 254.)

10. Orson Hyde, born January 8, 1805, in Oxford, New Haven County, Connecticut, the son of Nathan and Sally Thorpe Hyde, was a member of Sidney Rigdon's Campbellite movement. Sidney Rigdon baptized Orson a member of the Church on October 2, 1831. He served this mission with Samuel H. Smith, leaving January 25, 1832, and returning eleven months later (having together baptized sixty souls). He and his wife, Marinda, had ten children. He was a member of Zion's Camp, was one of the original Twelve Apostles, and helped open England to the gospel. On April 15, 1840, he left Nauvoo with a mission to dedicate the Holy Land for the return of the Jews, arriving in Jerusalem on October 21, 1841, and dedicating the land on October 24, 1841. He left to go west with the Saints, served another mission to England, presided over the Church at Winter Quarters (1847–1850), and served in the Twelve the rest of his life. He died in Spring City, Utah, November 28, 1878. (See Cook, *Revelations,* pp. 109–10.)

11. Orson Hyde's journal indicates that he served on this mission to the "Eastern Countries" from February 1, 1832, to December 22, 1832, "being absent from Kirtland about 11 months." It also records that the trip home from Boston to Kirtland took thirteen days.

CHAPTER 41

Joseph, Emma, and family move thirty miles south to John Johnson farm in Hiram, Ohio. Joseph and Sidney Rigdon are mobbed, beaten, tarred, and feathered. Little Joseph M. Smith dies five days later. Joseph the Prophet goes to Missouri. An account of a stagecoach accident, poisoning, and safe return to Kirtland. Report of terrible mob action in Missouri. Joseph gathers an army to redeem Zion.

September 12, 1831 to May 5, 1834

I shall now return to the month of September, 1831. Joseph, at this time, was engaged in translating the Bible, and Sidney Rigdon was writing for him. About the first of this month, Joseph came to the conclusion to remove himself and clerk, as well as their families,[1] to Hiram,[2] in order to expedite the work. They moved to the house of Father John Johnson[3] and lived with him in peace until the following March, when a circumstance occurred which I shall relate in his own words:

"On the twenty-fourth of March [1832], the twins before mentioned, which had been sick of the measles for some time, caused us to be broken of our rest in taking care of them, especially my wife. In the evening I told her she had better retire to rest with one of the children, and I would watch with the sicker child.[4] In the night she told me I had better lie down on the trundle bed, and I did so, and was soon after awakened by her screaming murder! when I found myself going out of the door in the hands of about a dozen men; some of whose hands were in my hair, and some had hold of my shirt, drawers, and limbs.

Sixteen revelations were received here in the Johnson farmhouse
within a one-year period.

The foot of the trundle bed was towards the door, leaving only room enough for the door to swing.

"My wife heard a gentle tapping on the windows, which she then took no particular notice of (but which was unquestionably designed for ascertaining whether we were all asleep), and, soon after, the mob burst open the door and surrounded the bed in an instant, and, as I said, the first I knew I was going out of the door in the hands of an infuriated mob. I made a desperate struggle, as I was forced out, to extricate myself, but only cleared one leg with which I made a pass at one man and he fell on the door steps.[5] I was immediately confined again, and they swore by G——, they would kill me if I did not be still, which quieted me. As they passed around the house with me, the fellow that I kicked came to me and thrust his hand into my face all covered with blood (for I hit him on the nose), and with an exultant horse laugh, muttered, 'Gee, gee, G—— d—— ye, I'll fix ye.'

*About a dozen of the fifty in the mob entered this room
and violently tore Joseph from his bed.*[6]

"They then seized me by the throat and held on till I lost my breath. After I came to, as they passed along with me, about thirty rods from the house,[7] I saw Elder Rigdon stretched out on the ground, whither they had dragged him by the heels. I supposed he was dead.

"I began to plead with them, saying, 'you will have mercy and spare my life, I hope.' To which they replied, 'G—— d—— ye, call on yer God for help, we'll show ye no mercy'; and the people began to show themselves in every direction; one coming from the orchard had a plank and I expected they would kill me and carry me off on a plank.[8] They then turned to the right and went on about thirty rods farther—about sixty rods from the house[9] and about thirty from where I saw Elder Rigdon—into the meadow, where they stopped, and one said, 'Simonds, Simonds,' (meaning, I supposed, Simonds Rider), 'pull up his drawers, pull up his drawers, he will take cold.'

"Another replied, 'Ain't ye going to kill 'im? Ain't ye going to kill 'im?' when a group of mobbers collected a little way off and said, 'Simonds, Simonds, come here'; and Simonds charged those who had hold of me to keep me from touching the ground (as they had done all the time), lest I should get a spring upon them. They went and held a council, and as I could occasionally overhear a word, I supposed it was to know whether it was best to kill me.

"They returned, after a while, when I learned that they had concluded not to kill me, but pound and scratch me well, tear off my shirt and drawers, and leave me naked. One cried, 'Simonds, Simonds, where is the tar bucket?'

"'I don't know,' answered one, 'where 'tis, Eli's left it.' They ran back and fetched the bucket of tar, when one exclaimed, with an oath, 'Let us tar up his mouth'; and they tried to force the tar paddle into my mouth; I twisted my head around so that they could not, and they cried out, 'G—— d—— ye, hold up yer head and let us giv ye some tar.' They then tried to force a vial into my mouth and broke it in my teeth.[10] All my clothes were torn off me, except my shirt collar; and one man fell on me and scratched my body with his nails like a mad cat, and then muttered out, 'G—— d—— ye, that's the way the Holy Ghost falls on folks.'

"They then left me, and I attempted to rise, but fell again; I pulled the tar away from my lips, etc., so that I could breathe more freely, and after a while I began to recover and raised myself up, when I saw two lights. I made my way towards one of them and found it was Father Johnson's. When I had come to the door I was naked, and the tar made me look as though I was covered with blood; and when my wife saw me, she thought I was all mashed to pieces and fainted. During the affray abroad, the sisters of the neighborhood had collected at my room. I called for a blanket, they threw me one and shut the door; I wrapped it around me, and went in.

"In the meantime, Brother John Poorman heard an outcry across the cornfield, and running that way met Father Johnson, who had been fastened in his house at the commencement of the assault, by having his

Near this spot, about a thousand feet from the Johnson home,
Joseph was tarred and feathered.

door barred by the mob, but on calling to his wife to bring his gun, saying he would blow a hole through the door, the mob fled, and Father
Johnson, seizing a club, ran after the party that had Elder Rigdon, and
knocked one man, and raised his club to level another, exclaiming:
"What are you doing here?"[11] when they left Elder Rigdon and turned
upon Father Johnson, who, turning to run towards his own house, met
Brother Poorman coming out of the cornfield; each supposing the
other to be a mobber, an encounter ensued, and Poorman gave Johnson
a severe blow on the left shoulder with a stick or stone, which brought
him to the ground. Poorman ran immediately towards Father Johnson's,
and arriving while I was waiting for the blanket, exclaimed: 'I'm afraid
I've killed him.' 'Killed who?' asked one; when Poorman hastily related
the circumstances of the encounter near the cornfield, and went into
the shed and hid himself. Father Johnson soon recovered so as to come
to the house, when the whole mystery was quickly solved concerning
the difficulty between him and Poorman, who, on learning the facts,
joyfully came from his hiding place.[12]

"My friends spent the night in scraping and removing the tar, and
washing and cleansing my body, so that by morning I was ready to be
clothed again. This being Sabbath morning, the people assembled for
meeting at the usual hour of worship, and among them came also the

mobbers, viz., Simonds Rider, a Campbellite preacher and leader of the mob; one McClentic, who had his hands in my hair; one Streeter, son of a Campbellite minister; and Felatiah Allen, Esq., who gave the mob a barrel of whisky to raise their spirits; and many others. With my flesh all scarified and defaced, I preached to the congregation as usual, and in the afternoon of the same day baptized three individuals.

"The next morning I went to see Elder Rigdon and found him crazy, and his head highly inflamed, for they had dragged him by his heels, and those, too, so high from the ground that he could not raise his head from the rough, frozen surface, which lacerated it exceedingly; and when he saw me he called to his wife to bring him his razor. She asked him what he wanted of it; and he replied, to kill me. Sister Rigdon left the room, and he asked me to bring his razor. I asked him what he wanted of it, and he replied he wanted to kill his wife; and he continued delirious some days. The feathers which were used with the tar on this occasion, the mob took out of Elder Rigdon's house. After they had seized him, and dragged him out, one of the banditti returned to get some pillows; when the women shut him in and kept him a prisoner some time.

"During the mobbing, one of the twins contracted a severe cold, and continued to grow worse till Friday and died.[13] The mobbers were composed of various religious parties, but mostly Campbellites, Methodists and Baptists, who continued to molest and menace Father Johnson's house for a long time."

Sidney Rigdon went immediately to Kirtland, but Joseph remained at Father Johnson's to finish his preparations for a journey which he contemplated making to Missouri. Immediately after Sidney's arrival at Kirtland, we met for the purpose of holding a prayer meeting, and, as Sidney had not been with us for some time, the brethren were very anxious to hear a sermon from him. After we waited some time for him, he came in appearing much agitated. He did not go to the stand, but began to pace back and forth through an aisle that was left between the seats. My husband said, "Brother Sidney, we would like to hear a discourse from you today."

Brother Rigdon replied, in a tone of excitement, "The keys of the kingdom are rent from the Church, and there shall not be a prayer put up in this house this day."

Great light and knowledge was poured out upon the Prophet in this room of the Johnson home.

"Oh! no," said my husband, "I hope not."

"They are," said Sidney. "I tell you the keys are rent from this people and no man or woman shall put up a prayer here this day."

This produced a great excitement in the minds of many of the sisters and some brethren. The brethren stared and turned pale, and the sisters cried, and for a few minutes we were at a stand as to what course to take. Sister Howe, in particular, was much terrified.[14] "Oh dear me!" said she, "what shall we do? what shall we do? The keys of the kingdom are taken from us, and what shall we do?"

"I tell you again," said Sidney, with much feeling, "the keys of the kingdom are taken from you, and you never will have them again until you build me a new house."

Hyrum was vexed at this frivolous maneuvering, and, taking his hat, he went out of the house, saying, "I'll put a stop to this fuss, pretty quick; I'm going for Joseph."

"Oh, don't," said Sister Howe, "for pity's sake, don't go for him. Brother Sidney says the keys of the kingdom are taken from us, and where is the use of bringing Joseph here?"

Hyrum paid no attention to her but went for a horse and set out that evening, which was Saturday, to Father Johnson's for Joseph.[15] He arrived there in the afterpart of the night. Joseph was in bed. "Come," said Hyrum. "Joseph, get up. You must go back with me to Kirtland and attend to things there. We are in great trouble. Sidney is telling the people that we have lost the keys of the kingdom, and they are having a terrible time."

Joseph did not know what he meant, but when Hyrum told him what a freak had got into Sidney's head, Joseph said that he would start as soon as he could get his breakfast. Father Johnson offered him a horse, for he was a kind old man and would do anything in his power for Joseph or any of our family.

They were soon on their journey and arrived in Kirtland just after the afternoon meeting began.[16] Joseph got up and told the brethren to be eased of all their fears, for they were under a great mistake, and that they were under no transgression. He said, "I myself hold the keys of this last dispensation, and I forever will hold them in time and in eternity. So set your hearts at rest, for all is well."

After Joseph preached a comforting discourse, he appointed a council to sit the next day, by which Brother Sidney was tried for having lied in the name of the Lord. Joseph told him that he must suffer for what he had done, and Joseph said, "You shall be delivered over to the buffetings of Satan, and the devil will handle you as one man handleth another, and the less priesthood you have the better it will be for you. Therefore, I advise you to give up your license."

Sidney did as he was counseled, yet he had to suffer for his folly, for he afterwards stated that he had the most astonishing encounters with the devil on the following night that ever a man had. He said that he was dragged out of bed three times successively on the same night.[17] Whether this be true or not, one thing is certain, his contrition of soul was apparently as great as a man could well live through.

After he had sufficiently humbled himself, he received another license; but the old one was retained and is now in the hands of Bishop Whitney.

On the second of April, 1832, Joseph set off for Missouri, accompanied by Newel K. Whitney,[18] Peter Whitmer, and Jesse Gause.[19] They were taken by brother Pitkin to the town of Warren, where they were joined by Brother Rigdon, and they all pursued their journey together.

While Joseph was gone, Emma, by her husband's request, was moved to Kirtland. Bishop Whitney wanted her to live at his house and tarry with his wife, until he and Joseph should return home. But when Emma came to Sister Whitney's house and made known Bishop Whitney's request, an elderly maiden aunt named Sarah Smith, who lived there, was highly offended and declared that if Emma stayed, she would go away. Upon this, Sister Whitney invited Emma to leave. This, however, I was never aware of until lately, and although she lived with us and very near us, she said nothing of the mortifying circumstance lest it should injure feelings. She was then young, and being naturally ambitious, her whole heart was occupied in the work of the Lord, and she felt no interest except for the Church and the cause of truth. Whatever her hands found to do, she did with her might, and she did not ask the selfish question, "Shall I be benefitted any more than anyone else?"

If elders were sent away to preach, she was the first to volunteer her services to assist in clothing them for their journey. Whatever her own privations, she scorned to complain. While Joseph was gone, she lived with Brother Reynolds Cahoon and Brother Williams, occasionally spending a short time with us. She labored faithfully for the interest of those with whom she stayed, cheering them by her lively and spirited conversation.

On the twenty-fourth of April, Joseph arrived at Independence.[20] He made haste to attend to the business that lay before him, and wrote this about his return journey:

"On the 6th of May I gave the parting hand to the brethren in Independence, and in company with Brothers Rigdon and Whitney, commenced a return to Kirtland, by stage to St. Louis, from thence to Vincennes, Indiana; and from thence to New Albany, near the falls of the Ohio River. Before we arrived at the latter place, the horses became frightened, and while going at full speed, Bishop Whitney attempted to jump out of the coach, but having his coat fast, caught his foot in the wheel and had his leg and foot broken in several places; at the same time I jumped out unhurt, and we put up at Mr. Porter's public house[21] in Greenville for four weeks, while Elder Rigdon went directly forward to Kirtland.

"During all this time, Brother Whitney lost not a meal of victuals or a night's sleep, and Doctor Porter, our landlord's brother, who attended him, said it was 'a d—— pity we had not got some Mormon there, they can set broken bones or do anything else.'

"I tarried with Brother Whitney and administered to him till he was able to be moved. While at this place I frequently walked out in the woods, where I saw several fresh graves; and one day when I rose from the dinner table, I walked directly to the door and commenced vomiting most profusely. I raised large quantities of blood and poisonous matter, and so great were the muscular contortions of my system, that my jaw was dislocated in a few moments. This I succeeded in replacing with my own hands, and made my way to Brother Whitney (who was on the bed) as speedily as possible. He laid his hands on me and administered in the name of the Lord, and I was healed in an instant, although the effect of the poison had been so powerful as to cause much of the hair to become loosened from my head. Thanks be to my Heavenly Father for his interference in my behalf at this critical moment, in the name of Jesus Christ; Amen.

"Brother Whitney had not had his foot moved from the bed for near four weeks, when I went into his room, after a walk in the grove, and told him if he would agree to start for home in the morning, we would take a wagon to the river, about four miles, and there would be a ferry boat in waiting which would take us quickly across, where we would find a hack which would take us directly to the landing, where we should find a boat in waiting, and we will be going up the river before ten o'clock and have a prosperous journey home. He took courage and told me he would go.

"We started next morning and found everything as I had told him, for we were passing rapidly up the river before ten o'clock and, landing at Wellsville, took stagecoach to Chardon, from thence in a wagon to Kirtland, where we arrived sometime in June."

After Joseph returned, a comfortable home was provided for Emma and her adopted daughter, in a house that belonged to Brothers Whitney and Gilbert, being previously occupied for a store. Soon after Emma moved into this house, Joseph went on a mission to the East, leaving her in the care of Hyrum, who watched over her with the most faithful care and attention. Shortly after Joseph left, Joseph Smith the third was born.[22]

After Joseph returned from his mission to the East, he established a school for the elders, and called them all home from the different parts of the country where they had been laboring. This was called the School of the Prophets (which is spoken of in the Book of Covenants[23]) and was held in an upper room of the house that Joseph occupied.

When my sons returned from their missions and had rested themselves, Joseph took all the male portion of the family into the room where the School of the Prophets was kept and, girding himself, administered to them the ordinance of washing of feet according to the directions of the Savior, who said, "If I then, your Lord and Master, have washed your feet; ye also ought to wash one another's feet."[24] When the ceremony was over, the Spirit of the Lord fell upon them and they spoke in other tongues and prophesied as on the day of Pentecost. The brethren gathered together to witness the manifestation of the power of God.

At that time, I was on the farm a short distance from the place where the meeting was held, but those of my children who could not

*The School of the Prophets first met in this room of
the Gilbert and Whitney store in Kirtland.*[25]

bear that Mother should miss anything dispatched a messenger in great
haste for me. I was putting some loaves of bread into the oven, but the
brother who ran for me would not wait till I had set my bread to bak-
ing. I went and shared with the rest one of the most glorious outpourings of the Spirit of God that had ever been witnessed in the Church at
that time. This produced great joy and satisfaction among the brethren
and sisters, and we felt as though we had about gained the victory over
the adversary. Truly, it was as the poet says:

> We could not believe
> That we ever should grieve,
> Or ever should sorrow again.

But alas! How our joy was measurably turned to grief, for it was not two months before a messenger arrived from Missouri just as my sons were all at work preparing a piece of ground for sowing wheat the ensuing fall. Joseph was standing on the porch near the door washing his face and hands when the dispatch arrived who stated that the brethren were driven, and Brothers Partridge and Allen had been tarred and feathered[26] and put into prison; that some were killed, and Brother Dibble, among others, had been shot.[27]

When Joseph heard this, he was overwhelmed with grief. He burst into tears and sobbed aloud, "Oh, my brethren, my brethren. Oh, that I had been with you to have shared with you your trouble. My God, my God, what shall we do in such a case of trial?"

Joseph was likely standing on this porch as he heard the news of the mobbings in Missouri.[28]

After his first burst of grief was over, Joseph called a council, and it was resolved that the brethren should be called from the surrounding country to Kirtland, and when sufficient time was had to prepare those in Kirtland, and whoever should be called from abroad, that they would set off for Missouri for the purpose of forming a treaty with the mob and also to take clothing and money to relieve them in their distress.[29]

Just before this, Jesse Smith, my husband's nephew, and Amos Fuller arrived in Kirtland from Potsdam, and Jesse determined to go with the camp to Missouri. He was the son of Jesse Smith, my husband's oldest brother, of whose peculiar disposition I have spoken before. Knowing that his father would censure us, I endeavored to dissuade him from going; but to no purpose, for he was determined upon being one of the company.[30]

As soon as they could make the necessary collections and preparations, they started for Missouri with nearly two hundred in their number, thoroughly equipped.[31]

NOTES

1. Joseph's family at this time included Emma and their two adopted twins, Joseph M. and Julia.

2. They moved on Monday, September 12, 1831, to the Johnson farm, located about thirty-one miles south of Kirtland.

3. John Johnson, born April 11, 1778, in Chesterfield, Cheshire County, New Hampshire, was the son of Israel and Abigail Higgins Johnson. He married Elsa Jacobs on June 22, 1800, and they had nine children: Elsa, Fanny, John Jr., Luke S., Olmsted, Lyman E., Emily, Marinda Nancy, and Mary. He was appointed to the first high council at Kirtland, yet later withdrew from the Church. He died out of the Church on July 30, 1843, in Kirtland. The Johnsons had come into the Church because of a miracle they witnessed, as recorded in a non-Mormon source: "Mr. and Mrs. Johnson . . . visited Smith at his home in Kirtland, in 1831. Mrs. Johnson had been afflicted for some time with a lame arm, and was not at the time of the visit able to lift her hand to her head. The party visited Smith partly out of curiosity, and partly to see for themselves what there might be in the new doctrine. During the interview the conversation turned on the subject of supernatural gifts, such as were conferred in

the days of the apostles. Some one said, 'Here is Mrs. Johnson with a lame arm; has God given any power to man now on the earth to cure her?' A few moments later, when the conversation had turned in another direction, Smith rose, and walking across the room, taking Mrs. Johnson by the hand, said in the most solemn and impressive manner: 'Woman, in the name of the Lord Jesus Christ I command thee to be whole,' and immediately left the room. The company were awe-stricken at the infinite presumption of the man, and the calm assurance with which he spoke. The sudden mental and moral shock—I know not how better to explain the well-attested fact—electrified the rheumatic arm—Mrs. Johnson at once lifted it up with ease, and on her return home the next day she was able to do her washing without difficulty or pain." (*Hayden's History of the Disciples,* as quoted in *History of the Church* 1:216.)

4. The sicker child was little Joseph.

5. B. H. Roberts noted that "the man whom the Prophet struck was named Waste. He was regarded, says Luke Johnson, as the strongest man in the Western Reserve [northern Ohio], and had boasted that he could take the Prophet out of the house alone. 'At the time they [the mob] were taking him [the Prophet] out of the house, Waste had hold of one foot. Joseph drew up his leg and gave him a kick, which sent him sprawling into the street. He afterwards said that the Prophet was the most powerful man he ever had hold of in his life.'" (*History of the Church* 1:262.)

6. The mobbing took place late Saturday night, March 24, and into the early hours of the morning on Sunday, March 25, 1832.

7. Nearly five hundred feet from the house.

8. Luke Johnson gave further description of the mobbing: "While Joseph was yet at my father's, a mob of forty or fifty came to his house, a few entered his room in the middle of the night, and Carnot Mason dragged Joseph out of bed by the hair of his head; he was then seized by as many as could get hold of him, and taken about forty rods from the house, stretched on a board, and tantalized in the most insulting and brutal manner; they tore off the few night clothes that he had on, for the purpose of emasculating him, and had Dr. Dennison there to perform the operation; but when the Dr. saw the Prophet stripped and stretched on the plank, his heart failed him, and he refused to operate" (in *Papers,* p. 377).

9. They were now nearly a thousand feet from the house. Sixty rods is 990 feet.

10. When the glass vial was broken in Joseph's mouth, one of his front teeth was also broken, either a large piece of it or the whole. From Benjamin Johnson we learn the following: "The Prophet's lost tooth, to which I alluded was, as generally understood, broken out by the mob at Hiram while trying to pry open his mouth to strangle him with acid, which from that time, until the tooth was replaced by a dentist neighbor, a year or so previous to his death, there [was] a whistle-like sound to accompany all his public speaking" (Benjamin Johnson, Letter to George S. Gibbs, 1903, Church Archives, cited in E. Dale LeBaron, "Benjamin Franklin Johnson: Colonizer, Public Servant, and Church Leader" [master's thesis, Brigham Young University, 1967], pp. 343–44). Luke Johnson reported concerning the vial: "And in attempting to force open his jaws, they broke one of his front teeth, to pour a vial of some obnoxious drug

into his mouth. The mob became divided, and did not succeed; but poured tar over him and then stuck feathers in it and left him, and went to an old brick yard to wash themselves and bury their filthy clothes. At this place a vial was dropped, the contents of which ran out and killed the grass." (In *Papers,* p. 377.)

11. John Johnson was nearly fifty-four years old when he chased after the mob with the club.

12. The blow broke Father Johnson's collar bone, according to a statement by Luke Johnson, his son. "He was taken back to the house, and hands laid upon him by David Whitmer, and immediately healed." (In *Papers,* p. 377.)

13. This was little Joseph Murdock Smith, who died from exposure on Friday, March 30, 1832, age eleven months. The *History of the Church* reports his death as March 29, 1832; however, that date was a Thursday. Many consider this little babe the first martyr of this dispensation.

14. This was likely Harriet Howe, a member of the Church from Painesville, Ohio. She was the sister of Eber D. Howe, publisher of the Painesville *Telegraph* (a local paper with an anti-Mormon slant). (See *Papers,* p. 492.)

15. This was likely Saturday, March 31, 1832.

16. According to this account this would have been Sunday, April 1, 1832.

17. George A. Smith and Elias Smith edited this story out of the version of Lucy Mack's history that was published in 1902. Apparently they doubted its truthfulness, as Lucy herself seems to have. Sidney's head injuries may have still been affecting his perceptions.

18. Joseph Smith had become close friends with Newel Kimball Whitney immediately upon arrival in Kirtland on February 1, 1831. Joseph had gotten off the sleigh and come right into the Gilbert and Whitney store and extended his hand to the man across the counter, saying, "Newel K. Whitney, thou art the man!" Brother Whitney was bewildered and responded with, "I could not call you by name as you have me." Then came the reply, "I am Joseph the Prophet. You have prayed me here, now what do you want of me?" (See Elizabeth Ann Whitney, "A Leaf from an Autobiography," *Woman's Exponent* 7 [September 1, 1878]: 51.) While yet in New York, Joseph had seen Newel and Elizabeth Whitney in a vision, kneeling in prayer, asking the Lord to send the Prophet to Kirtland. (See Orson F. Whitney, in Conference Report, April 1912, p. 50.) Elizabeth Ann, Newel's wife, related this experience that occurred about the time of their conversion: "One night—it was midnight—as my husband and I, in our house at Kirtland, were praying to the father to be shown the way, the spirit rested upon us and a *cloud* overshadowed the house. . . . We were wrapped in the cloud. A solemn awe pervaded us. We saw the cloud and we felt the spirit of the Lord. Then we heard a voice out of the cloud saying: 'Prepare to receive the word of the Lord, for it is coming!' At first we marveled greatly; but from that moment we knew that the word of the Lord was coming to Kirtland." (Quoted in Edward W. Tullidge, *The Women of Mormondom* [New York, 1877], pp. 41–42.) Sister Whitney later described the arrival of Joseph as the fulfillment of the vision they had seen in their home. Newel was born February 5, 1795, at Marlborough, Windham County,

Vermont. He and Elizabeth Ann had eleven children. He remained true to the gospel, and died in Salt Lake City on September 23, 1850.

19. Jesse Gause is a fairly mysterious character in Church history. Though he held high office (member of the Presidency of the High Priesthood—like a counselor in the First Presidency) and is mentioned in the Doctrine and Covenants, he had a short association with the Church. He joined the Church sometime after October 22, 1831, went on a mission to Pennsylvania in August 1832, parted company with his companion, Zebedee Coltrin, and left the Church by the end of that year. Little is known of him after his excommunication on December 3, 1832.

20. This was Tuesday, April 24, 1832. Two days later Joseph received what is now section 82 of the Doctrine and Covenants. While in Jackson County, Joseph was sustained as the President of the High Priesthood by a general council of the Church. (See *History of the Church* I: 267–69.)

21. Daniel P. Porter (1794–1866) was a merchant, tavern keeper, and postmaster. He was one of the early settlers of Greenville, Indiana, and was followed by his brothers, including James W., a physician, who is evidently the doctor who attended to Brother Whitney. (See *Papers*, p. 382.)

22. Joseph Smith III was born on Tuesday, November 6, 1832, in the upper (northwest) bedroom of the Gilbert and Whitney store in Kirtland.

23. See D&C 88: 118–141.

24. John 13:14.

25. This room is located in the northeast corner of the upper story of the store.

26. Edward Partridge reported: "I was taken from my house by the mob, George Simpson being their leader, who escorted me about half a mile, to the court house, on the public square in Independence; and then and there, a few rods from said court house, surrounded by hundreds of the mob, I was stripped of my hat, coat and vest and daubed with tar from head to foot, and then had a quantity of feathers put upon me; and all this because I would not agree to leave the county, and my home where I had lived two years.

"Before tarring and feathering me I was permitted to speak. I told them that the Saints had suffered persecution in all ages of the world; that I had done nothing which ought to offend anyone; that if they abused me, they would abuse an innocent person; that I was willing to suffer for the sake of Christ; but, to leave the country, I was not then willing to consent to it. By this time the multitude made so much noise that I could not be heard: some were cursing and swearing, saying, 'call upon your Jesus,' etc.; others were equally noisy in trying to still the rest, that they might be enabled to hear what I was saying.

"Until after I had spoken, I knew not what they intended to do with me, whether to kill me, to whip me, or what else I knew not. I bore my abuse with so much resignation and meekness, that it appeared to astound the multitude, who permitted me to retire in silence, many looking very solemn, their sympathies having been touched as I thought; and as to myself, I was so filled with the Spirit and love of God, that I had no hatred towards my persecutors or anyone else."

The *History of the Church* goes on to record: "Charles Allen was next stripped and tarred and feathered, because he would not agree to leave the county, or deny the Book of Mormon. Others were brought up to be served likewise or whipped." (*History of the Church* I:390–91.)

27. Parley P. Pratt recorded: "In the battle brother Philo Dibble, of Ohio, was shot in the body through his waistband; the ball remained in him. He bled much inwardly, and, in a day or two his bowels were so filled with blood and so inflamed that he was about to die. . . . At length Elder Newel Knight administered to him, by the laying on of hands, in the name of Jesus; his hands had scarcely touched his head when he felt an operation penetrating his whole system as if it had been a purifying fire. He immediately discharged several quarts of blood and corruption, among which was the ball with which he had been wounded. He was instantly healed, and went to work chopping wood." (Pratt, *Autobiography*, pp. 80–81.)

28. This is the porch of the Newel K. Whitney store. It appears that Joseph and Emma lived here in the store from September 12, 1832, until about two years later. The terrible mobbing and outrages in Jackson County, Missouri, started on July 20, 1833.

29. Further details of that horrible day in Missouri, July 20, 1833, are as follows: "After the mob had retired, and while evening was spreading her dark mantle over the scene, as if to hide it from the gaze of day, men, women, and children, who had been driven or frightened from their homes, by yells and threats, began to return from their hiding places in thickets, corn-fields, woods, and groves, and view with heavy hearts the scene of desolation and wo: and while they mourned over fallen man, they rejoiced with joy unspeakable that they were accounted worthy to suffer in the glorious cause of their Divine Master. There lay the printing office a heap of ruins; Elder Phelps's furniture strewed over the garden as common plunder; the revelations, book works, papers, and press in the hands of the mob, as the booty of highway robbers; there was Bishop Partridge, in the midst of his family, with a few friends, endeavoring to scrape off the tar which, from its eating his flesh, seemed to have been prepared with lime, pearl-ash, acid, or some flesh-eating substance, to destroy him; and there was Charles Allen in the same awful condition. The heart sickens at the recital, how much more at the picture! More than once, those people, in this boasted land of liberty, were brought into jeopardy, and threatened with expulsion or death, because they desired to worship God according to the revelations of heaven, the constitution of their country, and the dictates of their own consciences. Oh, liberty, how art thou fallen! Alas, clergymen, where is your charity!" (*History of the Church* I:393.)

30. George A. Smith notes that this nephew, Jesse, is Jesse Johnson Smith, son of Asael, and then indicates in the left margin of his Edited 1853 version, "The whole statement so far as it relates to Jesse J. Smith is an error" (George A. Smith, Edited 1853, p. 198).

31. A revelation had been received (see D&C 101) December 16, 1833, in the which the Lord commanded the Saints to importune for redress of grievances in Jackson County. Section 103 of the Doctrine and Covenants outlined further instructions, including a commandment to gather an army together. The little army that gathered to "redeem Zion" consisted of 204 men, 11 women, and 7 children.

CHAPTER 42

Lucy recounts her involvement and management of building a new school-house in Kirtland. Joseph and Hyrum return from Zion's Camp. They relate details to their mother about the journey, including the terrible outbreak of cholera, Hyrum's vision of Mother Smith praying for them while they were attacked by the disease, and their healing.

April 1834 to August 1834

Previous to their leaving for Missouri,[1] the brethren had commenced a small building which was designed for a meetinghouse and a school. Brother Reynolds Cahoon was left to finish this house, in order that it might be in readiness to hold meetings in the ensuing winter. When the brethren were gone, we that were left at home held meetings in the schoolhouse, although it merely served as a shelter from the sun. But it seemed as if the prince of the power of the air was permitted greatly to prevail against us, for several successive Sabbaths before meeting was closed, we were overtaken by dreadful storms. This troubled us greatly, as we were unusually anxious to meet together, in order to unite our faith in behalf of our brethren who were either settled in Missouri or were journeying thither at the peril of their lives.

With winter coming, we accordingly began to rather urge upon Brother Cahoon the necessity of hurrying the building, but he said he could do nothing about it, for he had neither means nor time. This made me feel very sorrowful, for we much needed a house of worship where we could hold meetings without being interrupted, as we must be in a dwelling where a family resided. I studied some time upon it, and at last I told my husband that I thought that I could collect the means for finishing the house myself, and if he would consent to it, I would try and see what I could do. My husband told me he should not hinder me in anything of that kind, and he would be glad if I could raise anything toward helping the work along.

I then wrote a subscription paper in which I agreed to refund all the money that should be given, in case it could not be appropriated to the purpose for which it should be subscribed. When I had written this subscription paper, I took it to each one of my daughters and my boarders, two of whom were Mary[2] (who was afterwards married to Hyrum, my oldest son) and Agnes[3] (who was married to my youngest son, Carlos). They all gave me what pocket money they had by them. I then went to Brother Bosley's and received something from each of his family.

As I was leaving Brother Bosley's house, I met Brother Cahoon and informed him of what I was about. He told me to go on and prosper. And it was even so, I did prosper, for in about two weeks I had everything in fine order for commencing the work. I employed a man to case and make the doors at a reduced price and engaged the sash and casing for the windows of one Mr. Bar, who agreed to make the sash for four cents a light.[4] This man went immediately to the house and began to take the measurement of the windows, but in consequence of some misunderstanding, Brother Cahoon forbade his doing the work. Accordingly, Mr. Bar came to my husband to get some explanation of the affair. A council was called, and after a three-hour sitting, it was voted that Mother Smith should go ahead and finish the house as she thought proper. I then proceeded to collect means, employ hands, and get together the necessary materials, until I had the house entirely completed, and there was but six dollars left unpaid. This debt Mr. Smith paid by selling produce, and the house was thoroughly finished, for there was not a door fastening which was wanting.[5]

Late in the fall, Joseph and Hyrum returned.[6] Their joy at meeting us again in health was exceeding great, above measure, because of the perils which they had passed through during their absence. They sat down one on each side of me, Joseph holding one of my hands and Hyrum the other, and related the following sketch of their journey:

"When we got started on our journey, we made arrangements so that the company should be made as comfortable as possible, but the sufferings which are incident to such an excursion soon made some of the brethren discontented, and they began to murmur against us, saying that the Lord never required them to take such a tiresome journey, and that it was folly for them to suffer the fatigue and inconvenience which they underwent just to gratify a foolish fancy.[7] We warned them in the name of the Lord to stop their murmuring or the displeasure of the Almighty would visit them in judgment, but many of them persisted in complaining, until one morning, when they came to harness their horses, they found them so lame as to be unable to travel. This gave

Zion's Camp marched a thousand miles through the areas of
Ohio, Indiana, Illinois, and Missouri.[8]

them great uneasiness, and said Joseph, 'I called them together and told them if they would repent and humble themselves before the Lord, the curse would be removed, but if they did not, a greater curse would come upon them.' This had a good effect with all save one, who was more turbulent than the rest. When he brought up his horse, he found that it would not be possible for him to travel, and after a little delay, the animal died. Soon the spirit of dissension arose again and was not quelled, so that we had any degree of good feeling, until we arrived in Missouri.

"Soon after arriving at the point of destination, the cholera broke out among us, and the brethren were so violently attacked that it seemed impossible to render them any assistance. They immediately sent for us to lay hands on them, but we soon discovered that this also was the judgment of the Almighty, for when we laid our hands upon them in the name of the Lord in order that they might be healed, the disease instantly fastened itself upon us. And in a few minutes we were in awful distress. We made mute signals to each other and left the house for the purpose of going into some secluded place to join in prayer that God would deliver us from this awful influence; but before we could get a sufficient distance to be secure from interruption, we were scarcely able to stand upon our feet and we were greatly alarmed, fearing that we should die in this western wilderness so far from our families, without even the privilege of blessing our children or giving them one word of parting counsel. Hyrum cried out, 'Joseph, what shall we do? Must we be cut off from the face of the earth by this horrid curse?'

"'Let us,' said Joseph, 'get down upon our knees and pray to God to remove the cramp and other distress and restore us to health, that we may return to our families.' We did so but without receiving any benefit, but still grew worse. We concluded, however, to make a second effort, and when we kneeled again, the cramp seized the calves of Joseph's legs, gathering the cords into bunches, and then the operation extended in like manner all over his system. He cried heartily unto God, but the heavens seemed sealed against us and every power that could render us any assistance shut within its gates. The universe was still. 'When we arose again,' said Joseph, 'I found Hyrum was in the same situation with myself.'

"We soon came to the resolution of appealing again to God for mercy, and not to rise from our knees until one or the other got a testimony that we should be healed, and he who received the first intimation from the Spirit should inform the other of the same. We prayed some time, first one and then the other, and soon perceived that the cramp began to loose its hold. In a short time Hyrum sprang to his feet and exclaimed, 'Joseph, we shall return, for I have seen an open vision in which I saw Mother on her knees under an apple tree praying for us, and she is even now asking God, in tears, to spare our lives, that she may behold us again in the flesh. The Spirit testifies to me that her prayers and ours shall be heard'—and from that moment we were healed and went on our way rejoicing."

"Oh, my mother," said Joseph, "how often have your prayers been a means of assisting us when the shadows of death encompassed us!"

"William had the same symptoms, but was not so severely affected as we had been and a sister took him home with her. She was extremely kind and attentive to him, insomuch that in a short time he was well again.

"But our poor cousin Jesse was taken so severely, that we could not render him any assistance, and he died in a short time. Brother Thayre[9] was also taken and called upon us at first to lay hands upon him, but he afterwards said, 'No, you need not do so. I will go into the river.' And he commenced dipping himself in the water until he was better. His example was followed by others, and those who did this recovered."[10]

After hearing this recital, I related to Joseph and Hyrum the circumstances of building the schoolhouse. They highly approved of my zeal and blessed me for what I had done. We all had a time of great rejoicing.

Notes

1. Mother Smith is referring here to Zion's Camp, which, as stated earlier, left Kirtland on Monday, May 5, 1834.

2. Mary Fielding, born the daughter of John and Rachel Ibatson Fielding on July 21, 1801, in Honidon, Bedfordshire, England, came into the Church through the missionary efforts of Parley P. Pratt in Canada in 1836. She married Hyrum Smith December 24, 1837, and immediately became the caring stepmother for Hyrum's five children. Hyrum and Mary had a son, Joseph Fielding Smith (November 13, 1838), who would become the sixth prophet of the Church; and a daughter, Martha Ann Smith (May 14, 1841). After her husband was martyred at Carthage Jail, she continued faithful with the Saints, made the trek west, lived strong and healthy, then was taken suddenly ill and died September 21, 1852, in Salt Lake City.

3. Agnes Coolbrith, born July 11, 1811, in Scarsborough, Cumberland County, Maine, married Don Carlos Smith on July 30, 1835, in Kirtland. Together they had three daughters: Agnes Charlotte (August 1, 1836); Sophronia C. (1838); and Josephine Donna (March 10, 1841).

4. The price was four cents per individual pane of glass.

5. The details of Mother Smith's completing the house were not included in the 1902 publication of her history, as some of them were disputed. George A. Smith added this note in the space between chapters 43 and 44: "The house referred to was not completed for some time after Joseph's return. Most of the carpenter work was done by Brigham Young." (George A. Smith, Edited 1853, p. 202.)

6. It appears from Joseph's history that he and Hyrum returned to Kirtland sometime around August 1, 1834.

7. Of course, not everyone felt this way. Wilford Woodruff recorded: "The Prophet gave us our instructions every day. We were nearly all young men brought together from all parts of the country, and were therefore strangers to each other. We soon became acquainted and had a happy time in each other's association. It was a great school for us to be led by a Prophet of God a thousand miles through cities, towns, villages, and through the wilderness." (Quoted in Matthias F. Cowley, *Wilford Woodruff: History of His Life and Labors* [Salt Lake City: Bookcraft, 1964], p. 40.)

8. This photograph was taken along the Zion's Camp trail in Putnam County, Indiana, not far from Greencastle.

9. Ezra Thayre was born October 14, 1791, married Polly Wales in 1810, was baptized by Parley P. Pratt in October 1830, and served in many callings in the early Church. He did not support the leadership of the Twelve Apostles after Joseph's death and moved to Michigan.

10. Sixty-eight of the men and women were taken sick with the deadly cholera, fourteen of whom died. The bodies were rolled into blankets and they were buried in shallow graves along the banks of Brush Creek in Clay County, Missouri. Joseph Young wrote of a meeting he and Brigham Young had with Joseph Smith on February 8, 1835, six months after the Zion's Camp experience: "[The Prophet] said, 'Brethren, I have seen those men who died of the cholera in our camp; and the Lord knows, if I get a mansion as bright as theirs, I ask no more.' At this relation he wept, and for some time could not speak. When he had relieved himself of his feelings, in describing the vision, he resumed the conversation." (*History of the Church* 2:181.)

CHAPTER 43

A council is called to discuss the matter of building the house of the Lord. Joseph gives the plan of the Lord. Account of the struggles to build the temple in poverty and guarding it against the mob. Sophronia taken very sick and healed by the power of the priesthood. Letter from Joseph the Prophet to his uncle Silas Smith outlining the reasons for modern-day revelation. Joseph Sr. and Lucy Mack Smith move into Joseph and Emma's home. Lucy falls down the stairs, receives a severe injury, later catches a cold and loses her eyesight. She is healed by the blessing of the priesthood and never uses glasses again.

Summer 1833 to spring 1835

The ensuing summer after Joseph's return from Missouri,[1] the brethren called a council to discuss the subject of building another meetinghouse, as the first was now rather small to afford room for the increased congregation.

In this council Joseph requested each of the brethren to rise and give his views, and when they were through, he would give his opinion concerning the matter. They all spoke. Some thought that it would be better to build a frame house. Others said that a frame house was too costly, and the majority concluded upon putting up a log house and made their calculations about what they could do towards building it. Joseph rose and reminded them that they were not making a house for themselves or any other man, but a house for God. "And shall we, brethren, build a house for our God of logs? No, I have a better plan than that. I have the plan of the house of the Lord, given by himself. You will see by this the difference between our calculations and his idea of things."

He then gave them the full plan of the house of the Lord at Kirtland, with which the brethren were highly delighted, particularly Hyrum, who was twice as much animated as if it were designed for himself, and declared that he would strike the first blow towards building the house.[2]

Before the meeting closed, they resolved upon laying the cornerstone one week from the succeeding Wednesday. "Now, brethren," said Joseph, "let us go select a place for the building." They all went out, and when they came to a certain field of wheat, which my sons had sown the fall before, they chose a spot in the northwest corner. Hyrum ran to the house and caught the scythe and was about returning to the place without giving any explanation, but I stopped him and asked him where he was going with the scythe. He said, "We are preparing to build a house for the Lord, and I am determined to be the first at the work."

In a few minutes, the fence was removed, the young wheat cut, and the ground in order for the foundation of the wall, and Hyrum com-

Joseph would say,
"Come, brethren, let us go into the stone-quarry and work for the Lord."[3]

menced digging away the earth where the stones were to be laid. This was Saturday night. Early Monday morning, the brethren were out with their teams, laboring with great ambition at digging a trench for the wall, quarrying stone and hauling it to the place where they were to be used. Although there were but thirty families in Kirtland at that time (as many of the brethren had gone to Jackson County), the work never stopped nor stood still for the want of means or laborers. But they suffered much pain, fatigue, and uneasiness, for as soon as the work was commenced, our enemies began to swear that we should not finish it. Still, the brethren were faithful to their charge, and they took turns keeping guard upon the walls every night.[4] My sons also took their turns, standing upon the walls as often as three nights in the week. How many of those affectionate brethren spent days and nights watching for the enemy, lest they should steal into the town unawares and murder the Prophet and his council and tear down the foundation! But they clung fast by the walls and "gave no quiet sleep to their eyes, nor peaceful slumber to their eyelids, until they found a place for the Lord, an habitation for the mighty God of Jacob."[5]

Many of those who once stood guard lie full low, and their bodies are moldering to dust, but their spirits have returned to God, and their works have followed them, for they did not turn therefrom, but continued faithful to the end; while others, alas, are buried in far more gross and dreadful darkness, for they have forsaken the truth and taken to themselves the god of this world and given heed to vanity and lies, things wherein there is no profit. The Savior said, "If the light that is in thee be darkness, how great is that darkness!"[6]

Mary Bailey[7] and Agnes Coolbrith were then boarding with me. They devoted their whole time to making and mending clothes for the brethren who worked on the house. There was but one mainspring to all our thoughts, and that was building the Lord's house.

I often wonder to hear brethren and sisters murmur at the trifling inconveniences which they have to encounter in living in a little less stylish establishment than they have been accustomed to, and I think to myself, salvation is worth as much now as it was in the beginning of the work. But I find that "all like the purchase, few the price will pay." And although they all speak frequently of being of that people whom the Lord will try in all things, yet when they find by experience that they have been preaching a doctrine which is literally true, they feel as though those who carried them the message of eternal life had injured them, and reflect on those who brought them into the Church as though they had acted the part of an enemy. I often find that even those who have been with us from almost the outset are, some of them, still clinging to their property as if life depended upon close economy.

How often I have, with my daughters and daughters-in-law, parted every bed in the house for the accommodation of the brethren, and then laid a single blanket on the floor for my husband and myself, while Joseph slept upon the same hard floor, with nothing but a cloak for both bed and bedding, Emma placing herself by his side to share his comfort—and this was our rest for two weeks together, while we labored hard every day.

But those who were accommodated by our privations did not know how we fared, for neither Emma nor I suffered them to know that we took unwearied pains for them, and when the Lord's house was being built, how our brethren at Kirtland watched and toiled.

A short time after the work on the temple was commenced, my husband's brother John Smith, who had been lying very low with the consumption, determined to be baptized, notwithstanding he was unable to walk into the water. He was baptized and soon healed. Shortly after, he came to Kirtland with his family in order to assist in the work to which they had been called.[8] Not long after Brother John arrived, my daughter Sophronia Stoddard was taken very sick, and her symptoms soon became so alarming that her husband started for a physician, who, after attending upon her some time, pronounced her beyond the reach of medicine and discontinued his visits, because he said that he could be of no service to her. In a short time, she became so weak that she could not speak nor turn herself in bed for several days, and many thought that she was dying. About this time Jared Carter[9] returned from a preaching mission. He was a man of great faith, and I thought that if I could get him to administer to her with my husband and our sons, by their united faith she might be healed. I mentioned this to Mr. Smith and he called our sons and Brother Carter together, and they laid hands on her, and in one-half an hour she spoke to me and said, "Mother, I shall get well— not suddenly, but the Lord will heal me gradually." The same day she sat up for an hour, and in three days she walked across the street.

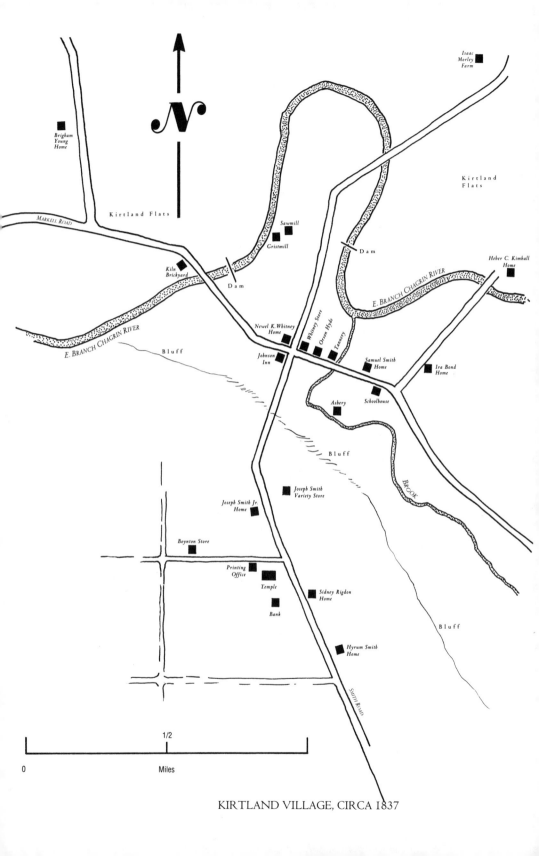

KIRTLAND VILLAGE, CIRCA 1837

After Brother John moved to Kirtland, Joseph wrote a letter to his Uncle Silas which I think would be interesting to my readers, and shall therefore give it insertion in this place:

Kirtland Mills, Ohio, September 26, 1833.

RESPECTED UNCLE SILAS:—It is with feelings of deep interest for the welfare of mankind, which fill my mind on the reflection that all were formed by the hand of Him who will call the same to give an impartial account of all their works on that great day to which you and myself, in common with them, are bound, that I take up my pen and seat myself in an attitude to address a few, though imperfect, lines to you for your perusal.

I have no doubt but that you will agree with me, that men will be held accountable for the things they have done, and not for the things they have not done. Or that all the light and intelligence communicated to them from their beneficent Creator, whether it is much or little, by the same they, in justice, will be judged. And that they are required to yield obedience, and improve upon that, and that only, which is given, for man is not to live by bread alone, but by every word that proceeds out of the mouth of the Lord.

Seeing that the Lord has never given the world to understand, by anything heretofore revealed, that he had ceased forever to speak to his creatures, when sought unto in a proper manner, why should it be thought a thing incredible that he should be pleased to speak again in these last days for their salvation? Perhaps you may be surprised at this assertion, that I should say for the salvation of his creatures in these last days, since we have already in our possession a vast volume of his word, which he has previously given. But you will admit that the word spoken to Noah was not sufficient for Abraham, or it was not required of Abraham to leave the land of his nativity, and seek an inheritance in a strange country upon the word spoken to Noah, but for himself he obtained promises at the hand of the Lord, and walked in that perfection, that he was called the friend of God. Isaac, the promised seed, was not required to rest his hope alone upon the promises made to his father Abraham, but was privileged with the assurance of his approbation, in the sight of Heaven, by the direct voice of the Lord to him. If one man can live upon the revelations given to another, might I not with propriety ask, why the necessity, then, of the Lord's speaking to Isaac as he did, as is recorded in the twenty-sixth chapter of Genesis? For the Lord there repeats, or rather, promises again to perform the oath which he had previously sworn to Abraham; and why this repetition to Isaac? Why was not the first promise as sure for Isaac as it was for Abraham? Was not Isaac Abraham's son? and could he not place implicit confidence in the veracity of his father as being a man of God? Perhaps you may say that he was a very peculiar man, and different from men in these last days, consequently, the Lord favored him with blessings, peculiar and different, as he was different from men of this age. I admit that he was a peculiar man, and was not only peculiarly blessed, but greatly blessed. But all the peculiarity that I can discover in the man, or all the difference between him and men in this age, is, that he was more holy and more perfect before God, and came to him with a purer heart, and more faith than men in this day.

This same might be said on the subject of Jacob's history. Why was it that the Lord spake to him concerning the same promise, after he had made it once to Abraham, and renewed it to Isaac? Why could not Jacob rest contented upon the word spoken to his fathers? When the time of the promise drew nigh for the deliverance of the children of Israel from the land of Egypt, why was it necessary that the Lord should begin to speak to them? The promise or word to Abraham, was, that his seed should serve in bondage, and be afflicted, four hundred years, and after that they should come out with great substance. Why did they not rely upon this promise, and when they had remained in Egypt, in bondage, four hundred years, come out, without waiting for further revelations, but act entirely upon the promise given to Abraham, that they should come out?

Paul said to his Hebrew brethren, that God being more abundantly willing to show unto the heirs of promise the immutability of his counsel, he confirmed it by an oath. He also exhorts them, who, through faith and patience inherit the promises.

Notwithstanding, we (said Paul) have fled for refuge to lay hold upon the hope set before us, which hope we have as an anchor of the soul, both sure and steadfast and which entereth into that within the veil, yet he was careful to press upon them the necessity of continuing on until they, as well as those who then inherited the promises, might have the assurance of their salvation confirmed to them by an oath from the mouth of him who could not lie; for that seemed to be the example anciently, and Paul holds it out to his Hebrew brethren as an object attainable in his day. And why not? I admit that by reading the Scriptures of truth, the saints, in the days of Paul, could learn, beyond the power of contradiction, that Abraham, Isaac, and Jacob had the promise of eternal life confirmed to them by an oath of the Lord, but that promise or oath was no assurance to them of their salvation; but they could, by walking in the footsteps, continuing in the faith of their fathers, obtain, for themselves, an oath for confirmation that they were meet to be partakers of the inheritance with the saints in light.

If the saints, in the days of the apostles, were privileged to take the saints for example, and lay hold of the same promises, and attain to the same exalted privileges of knowing that their names were written in the Lamb's Book of Life, and that they were sealed there as a perpetual memorial before the face of the Most High, will not the same faithfulness, the same purity of heart, and the faith, bring the same assurance of eternal life, and that in the same manner to the children of men now, in this age of the world? I have no doubt, but that the holy prophets, and apostles, and saints in ancient days were saved in the kingdom of God; neither do I doubt but that they held converse and communion with him while they were in the flesh, as Paul said to his Corinthian brethren, that the Lord Jesus showed himself to above five hundred saints at one time after his resurrection. Job said that he knew that his Redeemer lived, and that he should see him in the flesh in the latter days. I may believe that Enoch walked with God, and by faith was translated. I may believe that Noah was a perfect man in his generation, and also walked with God. I may believe that Abraham communed with God, and conversed with angels. I may believe that Isaac obtained a renewal of the covenant made to Abraham by the direct voice of the Lord. I may believe that Jacob conversed with holy angels, and heard the word of his Maker, that he wrestled with the angel until he prevailed, and obtained a blessing. I may believe that Elijah was taken to heaven in a chariot of fire with fiery horses. I may believe that the saints saw the Lord, and conversed with him face to face after his resurrection. I may believe that the Hebrew church came to Mount Zion, and unto the city of the living God, the heavenly Jerusalem, and to an innumerable company of angels. I may believe that they looked into eternity, and saw the Judge of all, and Jesus the Mediator of the New Covenant. But will all this purchase an assurance for me, and waft me to the regions of eternal day, with my garments spotless, pure and white? Or, must I not rather obtain for myself, by my own faith and diligence in keeping the commandments of the Lord, an assurance of salvation for myself? And have I not an equal privilege with the ancient saints? And will not the Lord hear my prayers, and listen to my cries as soon as he ever did theirs, if I come to him in the manner they did? Or, is he a respecter of persons?

I must now close this subject for the want of time; and, I may say, with propriety, at the beginning. We would be pleased to see you in Kirtland; and more pleased to have you embrace the New Covenant.

I remain, yours affectionately,

JOSEPH SMITH, JUN.[10]

In 1835 we were still living on the farm and working with our might to make comfortable the droves of company which were constantly coming in from the country, both those who were in and out of the Church. But when Joseph saw how crowded we were, and that we were breaking ourselves down with hard work, he told us that it would not answer for us to carry on a public house at free cost any longer, and by his request, we moved into an upper room of his house, where we lived very comfortably for a season.

I thought as my time had been so taken up with business, I now devoted the principal part of it to reading, and I studied the Bible and Book of Mormon and the recent revelations constantly until a circumstance

*Not only Joseph and Emma lived in this Kirtland home,
but many of the Smith family as well.*[11]

occurred which deprived me of the privilege. One day upon going downstairs to my dinner, I incautiously set my foot upon a round stick which lay near the top of the stairs. This, rolling under my foot, pitched me forward down the steps, and I bruised my head sadly, for my right arm was lame at the time and I could not use it to any advantage. I was much hurt, but thinking I should be better soon, I said nothing about it at that time.

Brother Cahoon came in the afternoon and requested Mr. Smith to go to his house and give a patriarchal blessing to some of his friends who had just arrived from the East. My husband invited me to accompany him, but I told him that I was afraid that I should take a cold that would affect me seriously on account of my fall. But, as he refused to go without me, after much persuasion on the part of Brother Cahoon, I went. In spite of all the care which I could take, I took cold, and an inflammation settled in my eyes which increased until I was not able to open them. The distress which I suffered for a length of time surpasses all description.

Everything that was supposed to help in the least degree was faithfully tried by my daughters and daughters-in-law, but in vain. I called upon my husband, sons, and other elders to administer to me by prayer and the laying on of hands. I desired that I might receive my sight, even that I might be able to read without ever putting on spectacles again. They did pray for this with fervent spirit, and when they took their hands off of my head, I opened my eyes and read two lines in the Book of Mormon. I am now sixty-nine[12] and I have not worn glasses since. This was done by the special power of God, and I felt to adore his name for the same.

NOTES

1. This was sometime after Joseph's 1832 trip to Missouri and would actually mean the summer of 1833.

2. Joseph and his counselors were given a vision of the yet-to-be-designed temple. "We went upon our knees," said Frederick G. Williams, "called on the Lord, and the building appeared within viewing distance. . . . Then all of us viewed it together. After we had taken a good look at the exterior, the building seemed to come right over us, and the makeup of this hall [standing in the then completed temple as he said this] seemed to coincide with what I there saw to a minutia." (Quoted in Truman O. Angell, Journal, Manuscript, Harold B. Lee Library Special Collections, Brigham Young University, p. 4.)

3. Quoted by Heber C. Kimball, in *JD* 10:165. The Stannard Stone Quarry is

located about two miles south of the Kirtland Temple site. It provided most of the stone for the building of the house of the Lord. The site for the temple was selected in March 1833 and the hauling of the stone began June 5, 1833.

4. Brigham Young described work on the Kirtland Temple as "a mere handful of men, living on air, and a little hominy and milk, and often salt or no salt when milk could not be had; the great Prophet Joseph, in the stone quarry, quarrying rock with his own hands; and the few then in the Church, following his example of obedience and diligence wherever most needed; with laborers on the walls, holding the sword in one hand to protect themselves from the mob, while they placed the stone and moved the trowel with the other" (in *JD* 2:31).

5. See Psalm 132:4–5.

6. See Matthew 6:23.

7. Mary Bailey, daughter of Joshua and Hannah Boutwell Bailey, was born December 20, 1808, in Bedford, Hillsborough County, New Hampshire. She was baptized on June 26, 1832, and married Samuel Harrison Smith on August 13, 1834. Together they had four children: Susanna (October 27, 1835); Mary (March 27, 1837); Samuel Harrison (August 1, 1838); and Lucy (January 1841). Mary Bailey died on January 25, 1841, from health complications in consequence of the expulsion from Missouri.

8. John Smith was baptized January 9, 1832, and arrived in Kirtland on May 25, 1833, about the time of the commencement of the building of the temple (see Cook, *Revelations*, p. 208).

9. Jared Carter, born June 14, 1801, served a mission in the East, during part of which he labored with Sophronia Smith Stoddard's husband, Calvin (see Cook, *Revelations*, pp. 73–74). Clearly his closeness with Sophronia's husband from their mission together was one reason why Mother Smith called Brother Carter to give the blessing.

10. Lucy recorded in her Early Notebook that sometime in 1836 (after this letter from Joseph to Silas) "the Lord gave Hyrum Smith a revelation commanding him to visit his Uncle Silas, for he was ready to be baptized. . . . When he found him he said, 'Uncle Silas . . . the Lord has sent me to baptize you, for the Lord has seen the integrity of your heart but knows your fears with regard to your family, but you need not suffer any anxiety about them, for if you embrace the gospel it will be the means of saving them.' He answered that he had no doubt of the truth of the work and the only thing that hindered him from embracing it was that he was afraid that his family would be so much opposed to it that it would ruin his peace. However, upon receiving this message he was baptized, but through much tribulation, being much opposed by his neighbors as well as his own family." (Early Notebook, pp. 41–42.)

11. This home is located just one block north of the Kirtland Temple and was Joseph and Emma's home for at least two years of their stay in Kirtland. The old cemetery sits on the lot between this home and the temple.

12. Lucy would turn seventy years old on July 8, 1845, not many months after the first dictation of her history.

CHAPTER 44

The completion of the Kirtland Temple. Joseph takes a journey to the East. A vision is given to Joseph as he passes through Palmyra which he finds difficult to look upon. Joseph returns to Kirtland, meets with the Saints, and prophesies about the apostasy of one-third of those present. His words are fulfilled and many turn violently against the Prophet. A woman of Kirtland begins receiving revelations through a black stone. Many are deceived, including David Whitmer and Frederick G. Williams. Lucy describes Sidney Rigdon.

End of March 1836 to late fall 1837

The house of the Lord progressed steadily forward notwithstanding all the threats of the mob. When it was completed, there was much rejoicing in the Church, and great blessings were poured out upon the elders; but as I was not present at the endowment, I shall say but little about it.[1]

Soon after the house was finished, Joseph and Martin Harris took a short tour into the eastern country.[2] As they were returning and were in Palmyra, Joseph had a vision which lasted until he besought the Lord to take it from him, for it showed him things which were very painful for him to contemplate. But it returned immediately and remained before his eyes until the middle of the forenoon.

The Church manifested great joy at his return. The news of his arrival was soon circulated among the brethren, and there was nothing to be heard but, "Brother Joseph has come back," and "We shall hear Brother Joseph preach tomorrow."

The Kirtland Temple was dedicated on Sunday, March 27, 1836.
Over a thousand people attended.

When we met the brethren the next day, he appeared unusually solemn, which caused them to wonder much, but he preached as he was accustomed to do. He told the congregation that had assembled that he was rejoiced to see them, and they no doubt were glad to meet him again. "We are now," said he, "nearly as happy as we can be on earth, for we have accomplished more than we had any reason to anticipate when we began. Our lovely and beautiful house is finished, and the Lord has acknowledged it by pouring out his Spirit upon us here and revealing to us much concerning his purposes in regard to the work which he is about to perform. Furthermore, we have plenty of everything necessary to our comfort and convenience, and judging from appearances, one would not suppose that anything could occur that would break up our friendship for each other or distress us in the least. But, brethren, beware, for I tell you in the name of the Lord that there is an evil in this very congregation, which, if it is not repented of, will result in making one-third of you who are here this day so much my enemies that you will have a desire to take my life; and you even would do so, if God permitted the deed. But, brethren, I call upon you now to repent, while there is room for repentance, and cease all your hardness and turn from these principles of dishonesty and death which you are harboring in your bosoms, before it is eternally too late, for there is yet room for repentance."

He continued to labor in this way with them, appealing to them in the most feeling and solemn manner, until the exertion of his mind and the fatigue of speaking quite exhausted him, and he sat down, leaving almost everyone in the house in tears.

The following week was much given to surmises and speculations as to who would be the traitors and why they should be, etc., etc.

In a short time, a difficulty broke out about the bank which the brethren had established in Kirtland.[3] It seemed that a quantity of money had been taken away by fraud. When Joseph discovered this, he demanded a search warrant of Esquire Frederick G. Williams. This was flatly refused by said Williams, to which Joseph said, "If you will give me a warrant, I can get the money, but if you do not, I will break you of your office."

"Well, break it is, then," said Williams, "and we will strike hands upon it."

"Very well," said Joseph, "from henceforth I drop you from my quorum in the name of the Lord," and Williams in wrath replied, "Amen."[4]

Joseph entered a complaint against him for neglect of duty as an officer of justice, on which account his ministry was taken from him and given to Oliver Cowdery.

Joseph then went to Cleveland in order to transact some business pertaining to the bank; and as he was absent the ensuing Sunday, my husband preached to the people. In speaking of the bank affair, he reflected somewhat sharply upon Brother Warren Parrish.[5] Although the reflection was just, this incensed Mr. Parrish, and he made an attempt to go onto the stand. Mr. Smith told him that he would not be interrupted, and seeing that Parrish intended to force his way, my husband called upon Oliver Cowdery, who was justice of the peace, to have him brought to order. But Oliver paid no attention,[6] and Parrish made a move to pull Mr. Smith out of the stand. At this, William, who was the oldest one of my sons who was present, sprang from his seat, caught Parrish in his arm, and carried him halfway across the house. He would have put him out of the room entirely had not John Boynton[7] stepped forward and, drawing the sword from his cane, presented it to William's breast and said, "If you advance one step further, I will run you through." Before William had time to turn, several gathered around him, threatening to handle him severely if he laid hands upon Parrish again. At this juncture I left the house, sick and grieved of heart, and more distressed as I found that, although a great number did not take active part against the Church, yet many were undecided.[8] This plainly showed me that the seeds of the apostasy were already sown in the breasts of a greater number than I imagined before, just as Joseph had prophesied.[9]

The same week, a young woman who lived with David Whitmer and pretended to be able to discover hidden things and to prophesy by looking through a certain black stone which she had found, revealed to Brother Whitmer and others some facts which gave them a new idea of things altogether.[10] David Whitmer requested her to look through this stone and tell him what Joseph meant by saying one-third of the Church would turn against him. Her answer was that he would fall from his office because of transgression, and either David Whitmer or Martin Harris would be appointed in his place, and the one who did not succeed Joseph in his office would be a counselor to the one who did.

Joseph's study above the Whitneys' store was the Church's headquarters for over two years.[11]

Those persons who were disaffected towards Joseph began collecting together around this girl. Soon, as this news came to his ears, Dr. Williams, the ex-justice of the peace, also became one of the dissenters, and he wrote down the revelations that were given to this girl. Jared Carter, who had always been before a good and faithful brother, lived in the same house with David Whitmer and soon invited the same spirit.

Not long after Brother Carter became one of their party, I was made acquainted with the fact, and having a great regard for him,[12] I improved the first opportunity of talking with him to dissuade him from continuing to associate with persons who would be the means of his destruction. As I had been informed that he had declared in one of their meetings that he possessed power to raise "Joe Smith" to the highest heaven or cast him down to the lowest hell, I questioned him about the matter in the presence of my husband. Mr. Smith, not knowing what I was talking of, began to reason with Brother Carter upon the impurity of his course and warned him to speedily repent and to confess his sins to the Church, or the judgments of God would overtake him. He remained with us until midnight, acknowledged his fault, and said he would confess to the Brethren.

The next morning he was taken with a violent pain in his eyes, and continued in great distress for two days. On the evening of the second day, he rose from his bed, and kneeling down, he besought the Lord to heal him, covenanting that if he were healed, he would make a full confession to the Church the next Sabbath.

The next Sunday when the Brethren were about to open the meeting, he arose and, saying that he had done wrong, asked the forgiveness of the Church, begging to be received again into their confidence. He did not, however, state what he had done that was wrong, but his confession was received and he was forgiven.

The rest of his party were still in opposition, and they continued to meet secretly at Mr. Whitmer's. When the young woman, who was their instructress, was through giving revelations in an evening, she would jump and hop over the floor and dance with all her might, boasting of her great power until she was perfectly exhausted. Her proselytes would also, in the most vehement manner, proclaim how pure and holy they were, and how mighty, great, and powerful they were going to be.

When we held our next prayer meeting, they took no part with us, but after meeting was dismissed, they arose and made a standing appointment for meetings to be held every Thursday by the "pure church," which title they claimed. They circulated a paper to ascertain how many would follow them, and it was ascertained that a great proportion of those whom we considered good members were decidedly in favor of the new party. In this spirit they went to Missouri and contaminated the minds of some of the brethren there against Joseph, in order to destroy his influence with them. This schism in the Church, and the rage of the mob, whom we had contended with from the first, made it necessary to keep a more strict guard than ever at the houses of those who were their chief objects of vengeance.[13]

The brethren would take their stations as a watch and stand night after night through all weather on guard to protect the lives of the Presidency, one of whom was Sidney Rigdon.[14] He was always as faint-hearted as any woman, and far more so than his own wife—for had his faith, patience, and courage been as genuine as Sister Rigdon's, he would not have been where he is now.[15] The Twelve, many of whom were then cheerful to take the brunt of danger and hardship that he recoiled from, are now shining as much brighter in comparison to him as the light of the sun is brighter than the stroke of a tar bill.

NOTES

1. Eliza R. Snow recorded: "The ceremonies of that dedication may be rehearsed, but no mortal language can describe the heavenly manifestations of that memorable day. Angels appeared to some, while a sense of divine presence was realized by all present, and each heart was filled with 'joy inexpressible and full of glory.'" (In Edward W. Tullidge, *The Women of Mormondom* [New York, 1877], p. 95.) George A. Smith described the spiritual outpourings that took place that evening: "There were great manifestations of power, such as speaking in tongues, seeing visions, administration of angels. . . . David Whitmer bore testimony that he saw three angels passing up the south aisle, and there came a shock on the house like the sound of a

mighty rushing wind, and almost every man in the house arose, and hundreds of them were speaking in tongues, prophesying or declaring visions, almost with one voice." (In *JD* 11:10.) Joseph the Prophet wrote: "All the congregation simultaneously arose, being moved upon by an invisible power; many began to speak in tongues and prophesy; others saw glorious visions; and I beheld the Temple was filled with angels, which fact I declared to the congregation. The people of the neighborhood came running together (hearing an unusual sound within, and seeing a bright light like a pillar of fire resting upon the Temple), and were astonished at what was taking place." (*History of the Church* 2:428.)

2. It appears that this trip was to Salem, Massachusetts. By the time the Kirtland Temple was completed the Church still owed an estimated sixteen thousand dollars on construction costs. Rendering aid to the Saints in Missouri and paying for Zion's Camp had also taxed the members' resources to an extreme. According to Ebenezer Robinson's recollection, Jonathan Burgess, a Church member from Massachusetts, informed the brethren that "a large amount of money had been secreted in the cellar of a certain house in Salem, Massachusetts, which had belonged to a widow, and he thought he was the only person now living who had a knowledge of it, or to the location of the house. . . . Steps were taken to try and secure the treasure." (Quoted in Donald Q. Cannon, "Joseph Smith in Salem," in Robert L. Millet and Kent P. Jackson, eds., *Studies in Scripture, Volume 1: The Doctrine and Covenants* [Sandy, Utah: Randall Book, 1984], p. 432.) Joseph, Hyrum, Oliver Cowdery, and Sidney Rigdon (it does not appear from Joseph's history that Martin Harris was with them) left on July 25, 1836, in hopes of finding the treasure and alleviating this terrible burden of debt . The treasure was never discovered, but the Lord explained that there were other treasures in the city of Salem to be found (see D&C 111). The brethren returned from their trip in September 1836.

3. The "Kirtland Safety Society Bank" was the full title of the banking institution of the Saints. The articles of agreement for the bank were drawn up on November 2, 1836.

4. Frederick Granger Williams was dropped from the First Presidency (where he had served as Second Counselor) on November 7, 1837.

5. Warren Parrish (1803–1887), the brother-in-law of Apostle David Patten, was baptized in May 1833 by Brigham Young. He served a mission with Wilford Woodruff (1835–1836) in Kentucky and Tennessee, was a member of the First Quorum of Seventy, did clerical work for Joseph Smith, and was the treasurer of the Kirtland Safety Society. He renounced his membership in the Church in the fall of 1837 and turned violently against the Prophet. By 1870, he was insane, and died seventeen years later in Emporia, Kansas. (See *Papers*, p. 504.)

6. It can been seen here how far Oliver Cowdery had drifted from the mainstream of the Church by his lack of response to Father Smith, whom he had referred to as "Father," and Lucy Mack Smith as "Mother," many times. Oliver Cowdery was excommunicated just a few months later on April 12, 1838. Nine charges were

leveled against Oliver Cowdery, including "persecuting the brethren by urging on vexatious law suits against them, and thus distressing the innocent." Also, "for seeking to destroy the character of President Joseph Smith, Jun., by falsely insinuating that he was guilty of adultery . . . for treating the Church with contempt by not attending meetings . . . for leaving his calling to which God had appointed him by revelation, for the sake of filthy lucre, and turning to the practice of law." (*History of the Church* 3:16.) It seems that after the glorious manifestations at the dedication of the temple, Satan was actively pursuing the Saints in Kirtland, and even Oliver Cowdery had been deceived. Oliver, who would not return to the Church for ten years, was finally rebaptized and passed away fifteen months later at age forty-three (1850).

7. John Farnham Boynton (1811–1890) had a short stay in the Church, yet was one of the original Twelve Apostles, serving from 1835–1837. He became involved with the speculation and financial problems of 1837, turned against the Prophet, and never rejoined with the Saints. (See *Papers*, p. 476.) The conditions in Kirtland at this time were a great contrast to those of a few months earlier when so many spiritual experiences were enjoyed by the Saints. Eliza R. Snow recorded: "A spirit of speculation had crept into the hearts of some of the Twelve, and nearly, if not every quorum was more or less infected. Most of the Saints were poor, and now prosperity was dawning upon them—the Temple was completed, and in it they had been recipients of marvelous blessings, and many who had been humble and faithful to the performance of every duty—ready to go and come at every call of the Priesthood, were getting haughty in their spirits, and lifted up in the pride of their hearts. As the Saints drank in the love and spirit of the world, the Spirit of the Lord withdrew from their hearts, and they were filled with pride and hatred toward those who maintained their integrity. They linked themselves together in an opposing party—pretended that they constituted the Church, and claimed that the Temple belonged to them, and even attempted to hold it." (*History of the Church* 2:487–88.)

8. Apostle Parley P. Pratt was also tempted by the rampant apostasy in Kirtland: "About this time, after I had returned from Canada, there were jarrings and discords in the Church at Kirtland, and many fell away and became enemies and apostates. There were also envyings, lyings, strifes and divisions, which caused much trouble and sorrow. By such spirits I was also accused, misrepresented and abused. And at one time, I also was overcome by the same spirit in a great measure, and it seemed as if the very powers of darkness which war against the Saints were let loose upon me. But the Lord knew my faith, my zeal, my integrity of purpose, and he gave me the victory.

"I went to brother Joseph Smith in tears, and, with a broken heart and contrite spirit, confessed wherein I had erred in spirit, murmured, or done or said amiss. He frankly forgave me, prayed for me and blessed me. Thus, by experience, I learned more fully to discern and to contrast the two spirits, and to resist the one and cleave to the other. And, being tempted in all points, even as others, I learned how to bear with, and excuse, and succor those who are tempted." (Pratt, *Autobiography*, p. 144.)

9. During the raging apostasy in Kirtland, Joseph recorded the following: "In this state of things . . . God revealed to me that something new must be done for the salvation of His Church." Heber C. Kimball recorded: "On Sunday, the 4th day of June, 1837, the Prophet Joseph came to me . . . and whispering to me, said, 'Brother Heber, the Spirit of the Lord has whispered to me: Let my servant Heber go to England and proclaim my Gospel, and open the door of salvation to that nation.'" (*History of the Church* 2:489, 490.) Thus, at the very time when the Church was racked with apostasy, Joseph was shown clearly by the Lord what course should be taken—to take the gospel to England.

10. The Lord had prepared his people for something like this. In one revelation he said: "But, behold, verily, verily, I say unto thee, no one shall be appointed to receive commandments and revelations in this church excepting my servant Joseph Smith, Jun., for he receiveth them even as Moses" (D&C 28:2).

11. It appears that at least seventeen revelations were received in this room that later were canonized in the Doctrine and Covenants.

12. It is to be remembered that Jared Carter had administered a blessing to Lucy's daughter Sophronia and she had been healed.

13. Hepzibah Richards wrote to her brother Willard Richards concerning this time: "A large number have dissented from the body of the Church and are very violent in their opposition to the Presidency and all who uphold them. They have organized a church and appointed a meeting in the house [Kirtland Temple] next Sabbath. Say they will have it, if it is by the shedding of blood." (Hepzibah Richards to Willard Richards, January 18, 1838, in Kenneth W. Godfrey, Audrey M. Godfrey, and Jill Mulvay Derr, *Women's Voices: An Untold History of the Latter-day Saints, 1830–1900* [Salt Lake City: Deseret Book Co., 1982], p. 71.)

14. Hepzibah Richards also wrote concerning the hostility and dangers at this time: "A dreadful spirit reigns in the breasts of those who are opposed to this Church. They are above law and beneath whatever is laudable. Their leading object seems to be to get all the property of the Church for little or nothing, and drive them out of the place. The house of our nearest neighbor has been entered by a mob and ransacked from the top to the bottom under pretense of finding goods which it is thought they had stolen themselves. An attempt has since been made to set the same house on fire while the family were sleeping in bed." (Hepzibah Richards to Dear Friends, March 23, 1838, in Godfrey, Godfrey, and Derr, *Women's Voices*, p. 76.)

15. At the time of Mother Smith's dictation, Sidney Rigdon had recently been excommunicated from the Church. He would never return to the Church. He passed away nearly thirty-two years after his excommunication.

CHAPTER 45

Mary Duty Smith, grandmother of the Prophet Joseph, arrives in Kirtland and dies ten days later. Joseph Smith Sr. and John Smith perform a mission to the East, visiting many of their extended family and trying to further convince them of the Restoration. Hyrum's wife, Jerusha, passes away in Kirtland.

May 10, 1836 to October 13, 1837

In the year 1836, my husband and his brother John were sent on a short mission to New Portage. While there they administered patriarchal blessings and baptized sixteen persons.

Soon after they left for New Portage, their aged mother arrived in Kirtland from New York, after traveling the distance of five hundred miles.[1] We sent immediately for my husband and his brother, who returned as speedily as possible and found the old lady in good health and excellent spirits. She rejoiced to meet so many of her children, grandchildren, and great-grandchildren, whom she expected never to see.

In two days after her sons John and Joseph arrived, she was taken sick and survived but one week, at the end of which she died, firm in the faith of the gospel, although she had never yielded obedience to any of its ordinances. Her age was ninety-three years.[2]

In a short time after her death, my husband and his brother John took a journey to visit branches of the Church in the East, and the following is a sketch from the journal of John Smith of this tour:[3]

"We traveled through New Hampshire, and on our way we visited

Many of the Smith family were buried in this cemetery in Kirtland,
including Mary Duty Smith.[4]

Daniel Mack, who was Joseph's brother-in-law. He treated us very
kindly but was unwilling to hear the gospel. We traveled thence up the
Connecticut River to Grafton. Here we found our sister Mary, whom
we had not seen for twenty years. The prejudice of her husband had become so strong against Mormonism, that she was unwilling to treat us
even decently. From this place we went to Vermont, through Windsor
and Orange Counties, and found many of our relatives, who treated us
kindly, but would not receive the gospel. We next crossed the Green
Mountains to Middlebury. Here we found our oldest sister, Priscilla,
who was very much pleased to see us and received our testimony. We
stayed with her overnight, and the next day set out for St. Lawrence
County, New York, where we had one brother and a sister. Having
arrived at his brother's (who was Jesse Smith), we spent one day with
him. He treated us very ill. Leaving him, we went to see our sister
Susan. I had business about ten miles on one side, and during my absence, Jesse pursued Joseph to Potsdam, with a warrant, on a pretended
debt of twelve dollars, and took him back to Stockholm. Not satisfied

with this, he abused him most shamefully, in the presence of strangers; and he exacted fifty dollars of him, which Joseph borrowed of brother Silas, who happened to be there just at that time from Kirtland, and paid Jesse this sum, in order to save further trouble.

"The meekness manifested by brother Joseph upon this occasion won the feelings of many, who said that Jesse had disgraced himself so much that he would never be able to redeem his character.

"From Potsdam we went to Ogdensburg, when to our joy we found Heber C. Kimball, who had raised up a small branch in that place. These were the first Latter-day Saints we had seen in traveling three hundred miles. On the tenth of October, we returned home."

About one year after my husband returned from this mission, a calamity happened to our family that wrung our hearts with more than common grief. Jerusha, Hyrum's wife, was taken sick and, after an illness of perhaps two weeks, died while her husband was absent on a mission to Missouri.[5] She was a woman whom everybody loved who was acquainted with her, for she was in every way worthy. The family were so warmly attached to her that had she been our own sister they could not have been more afflicted by her death.

NOTES

1. In Joseph Smith's record, dated May 17, 1836, he states: "I went in company with my brother Hyrum, in a carriage to Fairport, and brought home my grandmother, Mary Smith, aged ninety-three years. She had not been baptized, on account of the opposition of Jesse Smith, her eldest son, who has always been an enemy to the work. She had come five hundred miles to see her children, and knew all of us she had ever seen. She was much pleased at being introduced to her great grand-children, and expressed much pleasure and gratification on seeing me.

"My grandfather, Asael Smith, long ago predicted that there would be a prophet raised up in his family, and my grandmother was fully satisfied that it was fulfilled in me. My grandfather Asael died in East Stockholm, St. Lawrence county, New York, after having received the Book of Mormon, and read it nearly through; and he declared that I was the very Prophet that he had long known would come in his family.

"On the 18th, my uncle Silas Smith and family arrived from the east. My father, three of his brothers, and their mother, met the first time for many years. It was a happy day, for we had long prayed to see our grandmother and uncles in the Church." (*History of the Church* 2:442–43.) In Lucy's Early Notebook she noted Mary Duty's move to Kirtland: "When she arrived there, she said to Lucy, 'I am going to have your Joseph baptize me, but I will have my blessing from my Joseph.' But in twenty days after she got there, she was taken sick and died." (Early Notebook, pp. 44–45.)

2. Joseph's record continues: "On May 27 [1836], after a few days' visit with her children, which she enjoyed extremely well, my grandmother fell asleep without sickness, pain or regret. She breathed her last about sunset, and was buried in the burial ground near the Temple, after a funeral address had been delivered by Sidney Rigdon. She had buried one daughter, Sarah; two sons, Stephen and Samuel; and her husband, who died October 30, 1830, and left five sons and three daughters still living. At the death of my grandfather, who had kept a record, there were one hundred and ten children, grand children and great grand children." (*History of the Church* 2:443.) Lucy spoke of her father-in-law, Asael Smith, in her Early Notebook, saying that he, "on his deathbed, declared his full and firm belief in the everlasting gospel, and also regretted that he was not baptized when Joseph, his son, was there, and acknowledged that the doctrine of Universalism which he had so long advocated was not true, for although he had lived this religion fifty years, yet he now renounced it as insufficient to comfort him in death" (Early Notebook, pp. 43–44).

3. Joseph, age sixty-four, and John, age fifty-four, set out on their mission just days after burying their aged mother. This mission would take them by foot and by wagon over twenty-four hundred miles and last four months. "They baptized many, conferred blessings upon many hundreds, and preached the Gospel to many thousands" (*History of the Church* 2:467). This mission would last from about the first week of June until October 2, 1836.

4. Others of the Smith family buried here include Joseph and Emma's little twins, Thaddeus and Louisa; Mary Smith (three-year-old daughter of Hyrum and Jerusha Smith); Sophronia's husband, Calvin Stoddard; and Hyrum's wife, Jerusha.

5. Jerusha Barden Smith passed away on Friday, October 13, 1837.

PART 5

The Missouri
Persecutions

CHAPTER 46

Mob action increases in Kirtland; apostasy is rampant. Mob threatens to burn the Egyptian mummies. Joseph prophesies of the Lord's promise of protection on his life. Joseph flees Kirtland to Missouri. Constable Luke Johnson arrests Joseph Smith Sr., then allows him to escape with son Hyrum. Most of the Smiths move temporarily to New Portage, Ohio, to await removal to Missouri.

Summer 1837 to spring 1838

I will now return to the mob, for we have said little of their proceedings for some time, principally because they were not of sufficient importance to demand attention. They had become discouraged and ceased their operations, when they found that despite their best endeavors, we had built the house of the Lord, and that we had seen prosperity in everything to which we had set our hands. But suddenly, seeing that there was a division in our midst, they began to renew their diligence to effect the desire of their hearts, which was our overthrow.[1]

Their first movement was to sue my son Joseph for debt and, with this pretense, seize upon every piece of property which they could have the least pretext to lay hold upon.[2] They considered it quite sufficient if the article in question belonged to any member of the family. Joseph then had in his possession four Egyptian mummies, with some ancient records that accompanied them. These, the mob swore, they would fetch from the Mormon meetinghouse and burn. They devised every invention to get these things into their possession, hoping to destroy the only then existing evidence in writing of the Book of Mormon[3] which was accessible to the world. Accordingly they levied an execution upon them, claiming that they belonged to Joseph, and that he owed them a debt of fifty dollars. This was an unjust demand, for we did not owe any man out of the Church anything, but by various stratagems, we were able to keep them out of the hands of the rabble, who were joined by the apostates.

The persecution became so hot, that Joseph regarded it as unsafe to remain any longer in Kirtland and began making arrangements to move to Missouri.[4] He was preparing for his journey when the first effort was made to get the mummies and their attendant records.

One evening he was at our house, speaking with the brethren of various things he wished to have them do in case he left. When it was quite late, he rose to go home, but as he was about leaving, he turned to the company and said, "Well, brethren, one thing more. I do not want you to be concerned about me, for I shall see you again, let what will happen, for I have a lease of my life for five years anyway, and they will not kill me till after that time is expired."[5]

That night he was warned by the Spirit of immediate danger and to make his escape as speedily as possible. Therefore, he set out in the night with his family, beds and bedding, and sufficient clothing to make them comfortable.[6] When we came to hear from his house the next morning, he had gone on his journey. Emma's oldest son was then only five years old.[7]

Soon after Joseph left, the constable, Luke Johnson[8] (who had formerly been a member of the Church), came to our house and served a summons on Mr. Smith which requested him to go to the magistrate's office. Johnson said that no mischief was intended, and that it was of a peaceable nature.

Mr. Smith was then sick, and I begged Johnson not to take him away among our enemies, for I knew by experience that their design was generally false imprisonment, and that their civil writs too often proved to be very uncivil. Johnson paid no attention to what I said. Indeed, nothing else would satisfy those very "civil" men but his going into a crowd of apostates and mobocrats and running the risk of what treatment he might receive at their hands.

After Mr. Smith arrived at the office, he was soon informed of the cause of his being arrested, and what would be necessary to escape from imprisonment. He was taken before Esquire Cowdery for marrying a couple. As the apostates and the mob did not consider him a minister of the gospel, they contested his right to perform such a ceremony, and he was fined the sum of three thousand dollars, and in case he should default of paying this, he was sentenced to the penitentiary. Luke Johnson bustled about and seemed to be very much engaged, preparing to draw writings for the money and making other arrangements such as were required of him by the party to which he belonged. But at the first opportunity, he went to Hyrum (who had not yet set out for Missouri) and told him to take his father into a room which he pointed out to him. Luke said, "I will manage to get the window out, and he will be at liberty to jump out and go when or where he pleases."

Joseph the Prophet left Kirtland on Friday, January 12, 1838.
He would never see it again.

Hyrum and Mr. Smith left the company, and Luke told the mob that they had gone to consult together about raising the money. By deceiving them in this way, he kept them still until Mr. Smith crept out of the window, with the help of Hyrum and John Boynton (who said he was our friend at this time).

He traveled about four miles and stopped with Brother Snow,[9] who is the father of Miss Eliza Snow, the poetess. The old man said he would secrete him and forbade his family from saying to anyone that Father Smith was there.

When Luke supposed that my husband was out of their reach, he started up and ran into the room where he had left him, saying that he must see after the prisoner. Upon finding that the prisoner had fled, he made a great parade, calling out that he was gone and hunting in every direction for the fugitive. He came to me and inquired if Mr. Smith was at home. This frightened me very much and I exclaimed, "Luke, you have taken my husband away and given him into the hands of the mob and they have killed him." This he denied but gave me no explanation. In a short time, however, I found out where my husband was and sent him money and clothes to travel with. He started in a few days for New Portage with Carlos, my youngest son, and Brother Wilber. By this time handbills were stuck up on every public or private road, giving a description of his person, and no means which ingenuity could invent was left untried to prevent his escape. Runners were sent through the country to watch for him with authority to bring him back in case they found him. But despite their utmost exertions, he eluded them and succeeded in getting to New Portage, where he remained with Brother Taylor. Don Carlos, having accompanied his father to the above-named place, returned home again to his family; but immediately discovering that the mob contemplated taking him for the same offense, he moved with his family to New Portage, and was there with his father, until the rest of the family were ready to remove to Missouri. Hyrum had already moved there with his family.

Shortly after they left, a man by the name of Edward Woolley came to Kirtland to see Mr. Smith, and not finding him there, he went to New Portage and persuaded my husband to accompany him home.

After Mr. Smith had remained with Mr. Woolley about two weeks, we became very uneasy about him, not having received any intelligence of him since he left us. Accordingly, William resolved to go in pursuit of him to see how he was situated; whether he had met with friends and was comfortably provided for, or had fallen into the hands of his enemies and been murdered by them, for we had as much cause to fear the latter as to hope for the former.

When William arrived at New Portage, now called Norton, it was some time before he could learn exactly where his father had gone. But as soon as he obtained the necessary intelligence, he went immediately to him and had the pleasure of finding him in good health, although in great anxiety about the family, for he did not know how we were situated, nor where we were, since we had designed moving to Missouri soon after he left us.

As soon as it was known that William was in the place, a part of the inhabitants were very anxious that he should preach, and he agreed to do so.[10] But there were a few that declared that if he did preach, they would tar and feather him. One of these was Mr. Bear, a man of extraordinary size and strength. Besides him were three others, no less than he. As these men came in, William was just taking his text, which was, "The Poor Deluded Mormons." The singularity of this text excited their curiosity so much that they stopped in the door, saying, "Wait, let's see what he will do with his text," and they waited so long that they either forgot what they came for, or they changed their minds, for they made no further move towards making use of tar or feathers, and when he got through preaching, Mr. Bear frankly confessed his conviction of the truth and was baptized soon afterwards.[11]

William told his father that we should set out for Missouri soon, and we wished him to be ready to go with us. William then returned home and his father went again to New Portage. Here he remained with Don Carlos until we were ready to go to Missouri.[12]

Notes

1. Benjamin F. Johnson gave a detailed description of these precarious days in Kirtland: "At this time, town property and real estate went up to almost fabulous

prices, and a general rush was made into business of all kinds. Members of the Quorum of the Twelve and Elders on missions hastened home, bringing merchandise and means for general trade, while the Kirtland Bank issued its paper apparently with full confidence in the future. Goods were sold upon credit with great hope of better times; and 'Why be deprived of luxury and fashion today,' seemed to be the spirit of the hour. But when goods bought on credit were to be paid for, and notes became due for lands bought at great prices, then began a reaction. Disappointment engendered feelings which reacted upon fellowship, and men in high places began to complain of and reproach each other, and brotherly love was found smothered by the love of the world. The Bank having issued its currency in the same confidence now began to comprehend that its specie vaults were empty, with no possibility to realize upon collateral to replenish them. The spirit of charity was not invoked, and brethren who had borne the highest priesthood and who had for years labored, traveled, ministered and suffered together, and even placed their lives upon the same altar, now were governed by a feeling of hate and a spirit to accuse each other, and all for the love of *Accursed Mammon.* All their former companionship in the holy anointing in the Temple of the Lord, where filled with the Holy Ghost, the heavens were opened, and in view of the glories before them they had together shouted 'Hosanna to God and the Lamb,' all was now forgotten by many, who were like Judas, ready to sell or destroy the Prophet Joseph and his followers. And it almost seemed to me that the brightest stars in our firmament had fallen. Many to whom I had in the past most loved to listen, their voices seemed now the most discordant and hateful to me. From the Quorum of the Twelve fell four of the brightest: Wm. E. McLellin, Luke and Lyman Johnson and John Boynton; of the First Presidency, F. G. Williams; the three Witnesses to the Book of Mormon, Oliver Cowdery, David Whitmer and Martin Harris. Of other very prominent elders were Sylvester Smith, Warren Cowdery, Warren Parrish, Joseph Coe and many others who apostatized or became enemies to the Prophet. I was then nineteen years of age, and as I now look back through more than fifty years of subsequent experience, to that first great Apostasy, I regard it as the greatest sorrow, disappointment and test through which I have ever passed; the first real experience among false brethren, the greatest sorrow and test for the faithful. But with all my faults I did not forget the Lord nor His chosen servants. And in this day of great affliction and separation by apostasy, I felt to call mightily upon His name, that He would never leave me to follow these examples, but that He would keep me humble, even though in poverty and affliction, so only that I fail not. This prayer of my youth I have never forgotten, neither do I feel that it is forgotten by Him to whom it was made." (*My Life's Review* [Independence, Mo.: Zion's Printing and Publishing, 1947], pp. 27–29.)

    2. Mary Fielding Smith, sister-in-law to Joseph the Prophet, described the conditions in Kirtland in the summer of 1837: "I do thank my Heavenly Father for the comfort and peace of mind I now enjoy in the midst of all the confusion and perplexity, and raging of the devil against the work of God in this place. For although here is a great number of faithful, precious souls, yea, the salt of the earth is here, yet

it may be truly called a place where Satan has his seat. He is frequently stirring up some of the people to strife and contention and dissatisfaction with things they do not understand. . . . I pray God to have mercy upon us all and preserve us from the power of the great enemy, who knows he has but a short time to work in. . . . I believe the voice of prayer has sounded in the house of the Lord some days from morning till night, and it has been by these means that we have hitherto prevailed, and it is by this means only that I for one expect to prevail." (Mary Fielding Smith to her sister Mercy, September 1, 1837, in Kenneth W. Godfrey, Audrey M. Godfrey, and Jill Mulvay Derr, *Women's Voices: An Untold History of the Latter-day Saints, 1830–1900* [Salt Lake City: Deseret Book Co., 1982], pp. 63–64.)

3. This statement comes from the Preliminary Manuscript and could have been referring to the fact that with the mummies were not only the writings of Abraham but also some of the writings of Joseph of Egypt (some of his prophecies are included in the Book of Mormon). Concerning the mummies that had been purchased from Mr. Michael Chandler, and some scrolls that were with them, Joseph recorded: "I commenced the translation of some of the characters or hieroglyphics, and much to our joy found that one of the rolls contained the writings of Abraham, another the writings of Joseph of Egypt, etc.,—a more full account of which will appear in its place, as I proceed to examine or unfold them. Truly we can say, the Lord is beginning to reveal the abundance of peace and truth." (*History of the Church* 2:236.)

4. Brigham Young, whose heart never wavered, attended a meeting in the midst of this terrible time in Kirtland. Many of the apostates had gathered and were criticizing the Prophet. Brigham recorded: "I rose up, and in a plain and forcible manner told them that Joseph was a Prophet, and I knew it, and that they might rail and slander him as much as they pleased, they could not destroy the appointment of the Prophet of God, they could only destroy their own authority, cut the thread that bound them to the Prophet and to God and sink themselves to hell. Many were highly enraged at my decided opposition to their measures, and Jacob Bump (an old pugilist) was so exasperated that he could not be still. Some of the brethren near him put their hands on him, and requested him to be quiet; but he writhed and twisted his arms and body saying, 'How can I keep my hands off that man?' I told him if he thought it would give him any relief he might lay them on. . . . This was a crisis when earth and hell seemed leagued to overthrow the Prophet and Church of God. The knees of many of the strongest men in the Church faltered. During this siege of darkness I stood close by Joseph, and, with all the wisdom and power God bestowed upon me, put forth my utmost energies to sustain the servant of God and unite the quorums of the Church." (*Manuscript History of Brigham Young, 1801–1844*, ed. Elden Jay Watson [Salt Lake City: Elden Jay Watson, 1968], pp. 16–17.)

5. This would be from January 1838 until January 1843.

6. Joseph fled on the night of Friday, January 12, 1838.

7. Joseph Smith III was born Tuesday, November 6, 1832. By this time, Joseph and Emma had lost four children (Alvin, Thaddeus, Louisa, and adopted Joseph Murdock Smith). In addition to Joseph III, eighteen-month-old Frederick Granger

Williams Smith, born Monday, June 20, 1836, and six-year-old Julia would travel to Missouri with them.

8. Luke Johnson had been one of the original Twelve Apostles. In May 1837 he filed a charge against the Prophet Joseph for speaking reproachfully against the brethren. He was disfellowshipped on September 3, 1837, and excommunicated in December 1838. He was rebaptized on March 8, 1846, by Orson Hyde, married Orson Hyde's sister-in-law, had eight children, came west with the Saints, and died in Salt Lake City, December 9, 1861. (See Cook, *Revelations,* pp. 110–11.)

9. Oliver Snow was the father of Eliza and also Lorenzo Snow (who would become the fifth prophet of the Church).

10. It should be remembered that William Smith, younger brother of the Prophet Joseph, was one of the original Twelve Apostles called and ordained in February 1835.

11. This story about Mr. Bear is not included in the 1902 *Improvement Era* series, nor in any later editions of Lucy's history. George A. Smith and Elias Smith may have edited it out because it portrays William Smith in such a favorable light, or because they questioned its authenticity. George A. Smith wrote in the left margin of his 1853 edition: "Bear says this is a mistake" (George A. Smith, Edited 1853, p. 218). A handwritten note at the bottom of the page in the 1845 manuscript edited by the Corays reads, "John Bear story stricken at his request."

12. Lucy also tells us in the Preliminary Manuscript that here in New Portage, while they were waiting to move to Missouri, Don Carlos's second child, Sophronia, was born.

CHAPTER 47

Joseph Smith Sr. and Lucy Mack Smith with twenty-two family members are driven from Ohio and take the nearly one-thousand-mile journey to Far West, Missouri. An account of their terrible suffering and trials along the way. Lucy catches a cold that persists and threatens her life. Catharine Smith Salisbury gives birth to a son on the journey. Mother Smith hobbles into the woods at Huntsville, Missouri, prays for three hours, and is completely healed. Lucy recounts the mob action at the election in Gallatin, Missouri. Eight mobsters enter the Smith home in Far West to murder Joseph the Prophet. Lucy withstands them and Joseph softens their hearts. The Missouri militia surround the city of Far West to lay it to ashes.

May 1838 to October 1838

When we were ready to set out for Missouri, I went to New Portage[1] with a conveyance to bring my husband to the rest of his family, and we were shortly on our way together, right glad to meet again, alive and in good health, after so many perilous adventures.

Almost as soon as we were well on our way, my sons began to have calls to preach, and they soon found that if they would yield to every solicitation, our journey would have been a preaching mission of very great length, which was quite inconsistent with the number and situation of our family.[2] They were obliged to notify the people where we stopped that they could not preach to them at all, as if they did, we would not have means sufficient to take us through. They, however, sowed the seeds of the gospel in many places and were the means in the hands of God of doing much good.

We traveled on through many trials and difficulties. Sometimes we lay in our tents through a driving storm. At other times we traveled on foot through marshes and quagmires, exposing ourselves to wet and cold. Once we lay all night in the rain, which descended in torrents, and I, being more exposed than the other females, suffered much with the cold, and upon getting up in the morning, I found that a quilted skirt which I had worn the day before was wringing wet, but I could not mend the matter by changing that for another, for the rain was still falling. I wore it in this situation for three days. In consequence of this, I took a severe cold and was very sick, so that when we arrived at the Mississippi I was unable to sit up at any length and could not walk without assistance. After we crossed this river, we stopped at a Negro hut, a most unlovely place, but we could go no farther. Here my daughter Catharine gave birth to a fine son named Alvin.[3]

The next morning we set out to find a more comfortable situation for her and succeeded in getting a place about four miles ahead, and my poor child was carried from the loathsome hut to this house in a double wagon. The same day it was agreed that my oldest daughter, Sophronia, and her husband, McLeary, should stay with Catharine, and that Mr. Smith and the remainder of the party would take me with what speed they could to Huntsville.[4]

I was no longer able to ride in a sitting posture, but lay on a bedstead carefully covered, as the fresh air kept me coughing continually. My husband did not much expect me to live to the end of the journey, for I could not travel sometimes more than four miles a day. But as soon as we arrived at Huntsville, he sought a place where we might stop for some time, so that all that nursing could do for me could be done.

Going as far as Huntsville was my own request, but they did not know why I urged the matter. The fact was, I had an impression that if I could get there and be able to find a place where I could be secluded and uninterrupted in calling upon the Lord, I might be healed. Accordingly, I seized upon a time when they were engaged, and by the aid of staffs I reached a fence, and then followed the fence some distance till I came to a dense hazel thicket. Here I threw myself on the ground and thought it was no matter how far I was from the house, for if the Lord would not hear me and I must die, I might as well die here as anywhere. When I was a little rested, I commenced calling upon the Lord to beseech his mercy, praying for my health and the life of my daughter Catharine. I urged every claim which the scriptures give us and was as humble as I knew how to be, and I continued praying near three hours. At last I was entirely relieved from pain, my cough left me, and I was well. Moreover, I received an assurance that I should hear from my sick daughter about the middle of the same day. I arose and went to the house in as good health as I ever enjoyed.

At one o'clock, Wilkins J. Salisbury[5] came to Huntsville and said that Catharine was better and thought if she had a carriage to ride in, she could proceed on her journey.

The next morning Salisbury returned to his wife, who was forty miles from Huntsville. The first day she rode thirty miles, and the day after ten miles, which brought her to Huntsville. When she got there, we were holding a meeting and did not expect her, as the rain had been pouring down in torrents all the forenoon. Although they had driven with great speed through the rain, she was cold, and her bed was very wet. As soon as she was put into a dry bed, she had a dreadful ague fit, and we called the elders to lay hands upon her. This helped her, but she continued weak and inclined to chills and fever for a long time.

The day after she came, I washed a very large quantity of clothes with as much ease as though I had not been out of health at all. When the company was all gathered together, we started on our journey again and arrived at Far West without any further difficulty.[6] Here we met Joseph[7] and Hyrum in good health. They had heard by William and Carlos, who went into Far West before us, of my sickness and were surprised to see me in such good health as well.

We moved into a small log house, having but one room, a very inconvenient place for so large a family. When Joseph saw how we were situated, he proposed that we should take a large tavern house, which he had recently purchased from Brother Gilbert, and we did so. Samuel, previous to this, had moved to a place called Marrowbone, Daviess County. William had moved thirty miles in another direction. We were all now quite comfortable.

Nothing of importance occurred from this time until the first of August[8] when an election took place at Gallatin, the county seat of

Far West was on the frontier of northwestern Missouri and swelled to six thousand citizens.

Daviess County. At this election the Mormon brethren went to the polls as usual for the purpose of voting, but a party of men were collected there who were determined to prevent them from exercising their franchise and forbid them from putting in a vote.[9] Without paying any attention to them, one of the brethren, named John Butler,[10] stepped up to the polls and voted, whereupon a man belonging to the adverse party struck him a severe blow. John Butler was a very high-spirited man and could not brook such treatment; consequently, the blow was returned with a force that brought his antagonist to the ground. Four others of the same party came to the assistance of the fallen man and shared his fate, for Mr. Butler was a man of extraordinary strength and, when excited, was not easily overcome. When the mob party saw the discomfiture of their champions, they were much enraged, and that night procured the assistance of the judge of the election, who wrote a number of letters in their behalf. These letters, which were sent in every direction to all the adjoining counties, stated that Joseph Smith had killed seven men at that place, and that the inhabitants had every reason to expect that he would collect his people together and exterminate all who did not belong to his church. They therefore begged the assistance of their neighbors against the Mormons.

These letters were extensively circulated and as widely believed.

We, who were living at Far West, heard nothing of this until a few days after when Joseph was at our house writing a letter. I was standing at the door of the room where he was sitting, and upon casting my eyes toward the prairie, I saw a large company of armed men advancing toward the city, but, supposing it to be a training day, I said nothing about it to anyone.

Joseph laid out a city here at Adam-ondi-Ahman, about thirty-five miles north of Far West.

I soon observed that the main body of men came to a halt. The officers dismounted and eight of them came up to the house. Thinking that they wanted refreshment or something of that sort, I set chairs. But instead, they entered and placed themselves in a menacing line like a rank of soldiers across the room. When I requested them to sit down they replied, "We do not choose to sit. We have come here to kill Joe Smith and all the Mormons."

"Oh," said I, "what has Joseph Smith done that you should want to kill him?"

"He has killed seven men in Daviess County," replied the foremost, "and we have come to kill him, and all his church."

"He has not been in Daviess County," I answered, "consequently the report must be false. Furthermore, if you should see him, you would not want to kill him."

"There is no doubt that the report is perfectly correct," rejoined the officer; "it came straight to us, and I believe it; and we were sent to kill the Prophet and all who believe him, and I'll be d———d if I don't execute my orders."

"Then you are going to kill me with the rest, I suppose," said I.

"Yes, we will," he replied.

"Very well," I answered, "but I want you to act like a gentleman about it and do the job quick. Just shoot me down at once, for then it will be but a moment till I shall be perfectly happy. But I would hate to be murdered by any slow process, and I do not see the need of it either, for you can just as well dispatch the work at once as for it to be ever so long a time."

"There it is again," said he. "That is always their plea. You tell a Mormon that you'll shoot him, and all the good it does is to hear them answer, 'Well, that's nothing. If you kill me, we shall be happy.' D———, seems that's all the satisfaction you can get from them anyway."

Joseph had continued writing till now, but having finished his letter, he asked me for a wafer to seal it. Seeing that he was at liberty, I said, "Gentlemen, suffer me to make you acquainted with Joseph Smith the Prophet." He looked upon them with a very pleasant smile and, stepping up to them, gave each of them his hand in a manner which convinced them that he was neither a guilty criminal nor yet a cowering hypocrite. They stopped and stared as though a spectre had crossed their path.

Joseph sat down and entered into conversation with them and explained the views and feelings of the people called "Mormons," what their course had been, and the treatment which they had received from their enemies since the first. He told them that malice and detraction had pursued them ever since they entered Missouri, but they were a people who had never broken the laws to his knowledge. They stood ready to be tried by the law—and if anything contrary to the law had been done by any of the brethren at Daviess, it would certainly be just to call them to an account, before molesting or murdering others that knew nothing of these transactions at Gallatin.

After this he rose and said, "Mother, I believe I will go home. Emma will be expecting me." At this, two of the men sprang to their feet, saying, "You shall not go alone, for it is not safe. We will go with you and guard you." Joseph thanked them and they left with him.

While they were absent, the remainder of the officers stood by the door, and I overheard the following conversation between them:

First Officer: "Did you not feel something strange when Smith took you by the hand? I never felt so in my life."

Second Officer: "I felt as though I could not move. I would not harm one hair of that man's head for the whole world."

Third Officer: "This is the last time you will ever catch me coming to kill Joe Smith or the Mormons either."

First Officer: "I guess this is my last expedition against this place. I never saw a more harmless, innocent-appearing man than the Mormon Prophet."

Second Officer: "That story about his killing them men is all a d——d lie. There is no doubt of that, and we have had all this trouble for nothing. It's the last time I'll be fooled in this way."

Those men who went home with my son promised to disband the militia under them and go home. They said that if Joseph had any use for them, they would come back and follow him anywhere. Thus, we considered that hostilities were no longer to be feared from the citizens. Joseph and Hyrum thought it proper, however, to go to Daviess County and ascertain the cause of the difficulty. They did so, and after receiving the strongest assurance of the future good attentions of the civil officers to administer equal rights and privileges among all the citizens, Mormons and anti-Mormons alike, they returned, hoping all would be well.

Joseph and Emma lived here in Far West in a cabin located just a few feet from this barn.[11]

Soon after this we heard that William and his wife, Caroline,[12] who lived twenty miles distant, were very sick. Samuel was at Far West at the time and set out immediately for William's house with a carriage in order to bring them to our house. In a few days they arrived, feeling very low, and seemed more likely to die of the disease than to recover from it when they got there. But with close attention and great care, they soon began to show signs of recovery.

During the time when I was taking care of my son William and his wife, many things transpired that would probably be of interest to my readers, which I know nothing about, as I was so engaged with the care of my house and the sickness of my family, that I did not know, nor yet inquire or hear, what was going on.[13]

In a little while after Samuel brought William and Caroline to our house, there was born unto Samuel a son, whom he called by his own name.[14] When he was but three days old,[15] his father was compelled to leave home. Samuel's family was, at this time, living in a desolate, lonely place about thirty miles from Far West then called Marrowbone, afterwards named Shady Grove. Samuel had not been gone long when a number of the men who lived near him went to his wife and told her that the mob was coming there to drive all the Mormons from the country into Far West and perhaps they would kill them. They accordingly advised her to go immediately to Far West at all hazards and proffered to find her a wagon and boy to drive the horses. She consented, and they brought an open lumber wagon and put her into it on a bed with a very little clothing for herself and her children. In this way, she started for Far West with no one but a small boy to take care of her, the children and the team, and nothing to eat by the way. When they had traveled for some miles they stopped for the night, and in the latter part of the night it began to rain. The water fell upon her in torrents, for she had no shelter for herself or her infant. The bedding was soon completely saturated as the rain continued falling for some time with great violence.

The next day Samuel started from Far West to go to his own house, but met his wife along the way in this situation. He returned with her to Far West, where she arrived about thirty-six hours after she had left Marrowbone without having taken any nourishment. Every garment upon her body, as well as her bed and bedding, was so wet with the rain that the water might have been wrung from them. She was speechless and almost stiff with the cold and effects of her exposure. We laid her on a bed, and my husband and my sons administered to her by the laying on of hands. We then changed her clothing, put her into a bed covered with warm blankets, and after pouring a little rice water into her mouth, she was administered to again. This time she raised her eyes and seemed to revive a little. I continued to employ every means that lay in my power for her benefit and that of my other sick children. In this I was much assisted by Emma and my daughters.

We soon reaped the reward of our labor, for in a short time they began to mend, and I now congratulated myself on the pleasure I should feel in seeing my children all well and enjoying each other's society again.

After William began to sit up a little, he told me that he had a vision during his sickness, in which he saw a tremendous army of men coming into Far West, and that it was his impression that the time would not be long before he should see it fulfilled. I was soon convinced by the circumstances which afterwards transpired that he was not mistaken in his opinion.[16]

I felt concerned about this, for I feared that some evil was hanging over us, but I knew nothing of the operations of the mob party, until one day Joseph rode up and told me to be not at all frightened, but the mob was coming, and we must all keep perfectly quiet. He wished the sisters to stay indoors and not suffer themselves to be seen in the streets. He could not stay with us, for he wanted to see the brethren and have them keep their families quiet and at home. He rode off, but I soon learned who the mob were. This was the state mob[17] that was sent by the governor,[18] a company of ten thousand men[19] that stationed themselves on Salt Creek.

My son-in-law Mr. McLeary went out with some others to meet the mob and ascertain what their business was. They gave the messengers to understand that they would soon commence an indiscriminate butchery of men, women, and children, that their orders were to convert Far West into a human slaughter pen and never quit it while there was a lisping babe or a decrepit old woman breathing within its bounds. There were, however, three persons that they wished brought forth before they began their operations. They desired to preserve their lives, as some of them were related to one of the mob officers. These were Adam Lightner, John Cleminson and his wife, but after a short interview, John Cleminson, who was not a member of the Church, replied that they had lived with the Mormons and knew them to be an innocent people, "and if," said he, "you are determined to destroy them, and lay the city in ashes, you must destroy me also, for I will die with them."

Notes

1. New Portage, Ohio, was about fifty miles southwest of Kirtland.

2. It is noteworthy and poignant to look carefully at those of the Smith family in this party now being driven from their homes in Ohio. They numbered about twenty-four, and included Joseph Smith Sr., sixty-six years old, Lucy Mack Smith, sixty-two, and ten other adults: Sophronia and husband William McLeary; Samuel Harrison and wife Mary; William and wife Caroline; Catharine and husband Wilkins J. Salisbury; and Don Carlos and wife Agnes. Sixteen-year-old Lucy was along, as well as eleven

children eight years old and under: Eunice Stoddard, eight; Maria Stoddard, six; Elizabeth Salisbury, six; Lucy Salisbury, three; Mary Jane Smith, three; Solomon Salisbury, two; Susanna Smith, two; Agnes Smith, twenty-two months; Caroline Smith, twenty-two months; Mary Smith, one; and Sophronia Smith, a few days or weeks old. One more baby, Alvin Salisbury, would be born on the banks of the Mississippi River, June 7, 1838. Mary, Samuel's wife, was seven months pregnant. Agnes, Don Carlos's wife, gave birth in New Portage on the trip; and Catharine was nine months pregnant and gave birth at the Mississippi. Joseph's and Hyrum's families had already moved to Missouri some weeks or months earlier. It must be noted that Sophronia's first husband, Calvin Stoddard, passed away in Kirtland, May 19, 1836.

3. In the Preliminary Manuscript, Lucy incorrectly stated that in the hut Catharine gave birth to a daughter. Alvin was born, as stated, Friday, June 7, 1838.

4. Huntsville, Missouri, was about eighty miles west of the crossing of the Mississippi River.

5. This was Catharine's husband.

6. The journey from Kirtland, Ohio, to Far West, Missouri, was approximately one thousand miles.

7. Joseph and his family arrived in Far West on March 14, 1838.

8. This was the first week of August. The election was held on Monday, August 6, 1838.

9. It is recorded in the *History of the Church* that Colonel William P. Peniston, who had led the mob in Clay County, gave an inflammatory speech on the occasion of this election to those gathered at the polls "for the purpose of exciting them against the 'Mormons,' saying, 'The Mormon leaders are a set of horse thieves, liars, counterfeiters, and you know they profess to heal the sick, and cast out devils, and you all know that is a lie.' He further said that the members of the Church were dupes, and not too good to take a false oath on any common occasion; that they would steal, and he did not consider property safe where they were; that he was opposed to their settling in Daviess county; and if they suffered the 'Mormons' to vote, the people would soon lose their suffrage; 'and,' said he, addressing the Saints, 'I headed a mob to drive you out of Clay county, and would not prevent your being mobbed now.'" (*History of the Church* 3:57.)

10. The name of John Butler was edited out by George A. Smith (see George A. Smith, Edited 1853, p. 221). George A. had desired a "note" to be arranged here explaining the change, but no note was added in the 1902 or later versions.

11. This barn is modern and marks, within a few feet, the site of the home of Joseph and Emma during their brief stay in Far West. Alexander Hale Smith was born here on Saturday, June 2, 1838. No structures exist at the Far West, Missouri, site, having all been burned or disintegrated with time. Four large stones are all that remain in Far West, marking the corners of the temple that was never built.

12. William Smith married Caroline Amanda (or Amelia) Grant on February 14, 1833, in Kirtland. Together they had two daughters, Mary Jane (January 1835) and Caroline (August 1836). William's wife, Caroline, died in Nauvoo, May 22, 1845.

13. This statement, left out of all previous editions, gives us an interesting insight into Lucy's everyday life. Even for one like Lucy, who was at the very center of the events of the Restoration, life's everyday cares sometimes swallowed up her attention to the point that she was oblivious to some of the dramatic events that led to the Missouri expulsion.

14. Samuel Harrison Bailey Smith was born on Wednesday, August 1, 1838, at Shady Grove, Polk County, Missouri.

15. In the 1853 and later editions, "three days" is changed to "three weeks." This would change Samuel's departure from August 4, 1838, to sometime around August 22, 1838.

16. This account describing William's vision was included in the 1853 edition, but cut from all subsequent editions.

17. Lucy refers to this group as "the state mob." It was the Missouri state militia.

18. Governor Lilburn W. Boggs.

19. Lucy's estimate is high. It is more likely that the militia consisted of up to three thousand men.

CHAPTER 48

Hyrum Smith gives sworn statement of the trials, tribulations, abuses, and privations of the Saints in Missouri. Mob action at Far West, Diahman, DeWitt, and Haun's Mill. Missouri militia marches on Far West to lay siege to the city. Joseph, Hyrum, and others are taken prisoner and marched to Independence, Richmond, and Liberty. Sufferings and privations of these leaders and the Saints in general are enumerated. Joseph and others spend six months under guard and in prison. Sufferings of the brethren in Liberty Jail. More than twelve thousand Saints are driven from Missouri. Brethren are aided in escaping.

March 1838 to April 1839

Here I shall introduce a brief history of our troubles in Missouri, given by my son Hyrum when Joseph was before the municipal court at Nauvoo, June 30, 1843, on a writ of habeas corpus:

Hyrum Smith, sworn, said that the defendant now in court is his brother, and that his name is not Joseph Smith Jr., but his name is Joseph Smith Sr.[1] and has been for more than two years past.

"I have been acquainted with him ever since he was born, which was thirty-seven years in December last, and I have not been absent from him at any one time, not even the space of six months, since his birth, to my recollection, and have been intimately acquainted with all his sayings, doings, business transactions, and movements, as much as any one man could be acquainted with any other man's business, up to the present time, and do know that he has not committed treason against any state in the Union, by any overt act, or by levying war, or by aiding and abetting, or assisting an enemy, in any state of the Union. And that the said Joseph Smith has not committed treason in the state of Missouri, nor violated any law or rule of said state, I being personally acquainted with the transactions and doings of said Smith, whilst he resided in said state, which was for about six months in the year 1838; I being also a resident in said state, during the same period of time. And I do know that said Joseph Smith never was subject to military duty in any state, neither was he in the state of Missouri, he being exempt by the amputation or extraction of a bone from his leg, and by his having a license to preach the gospel, or being in other words, a minister of the gospel. And I do know that said Smith never bore arms as a military man, in any capacity whatever, whilst in the state of Missouri, or previous to that time; neither has he given any orders, or assumed any command in any capacity whatever.

"But I do know that whilst he was in the state of Missouri, that the people commonly called 'Mormons,' were threatened with violence and extermination; and on or about the first Monday in August, 1838,[2] at the election at Gallatin, the county seat in Daviess County, the citizens who were commonly called 'Mormons' were forbidden to exercise the rights of franchise, and from that unhallowed circumstance an affray commenced, and a fight ensued among the citizens of that place, and from that time a mob commenced gathering in that county, threatening the extermination of the 'Mormons.' The said Smith, and myself, upon hearing that mobs were collecting together, and that they had also murdered two of the citizens of the same place, and would not suffer them to be buried, the said Smith and myself went over to Daviess County to learn the particulars of the affray; but upon our arrival at Diahman,[3] we learned that none were killed, but several were wounded.

"We tarried all night at Colonel Lyman Wight's. The next morning, the weather being very warm, and having been very dry for some time previous, the springs and wells in that region were dried up. On mounting our horses to return, we rode up to Mr. Black's, who was then an acting justice of the peace, to obtain some water for ourselves and horses. Some few of the citizens accompanied us there, and after obtaining the refreshment of water, Mr. Black was asked by said Joseph Smith if he would use his influence to see that the laws were faithfully

*Lyman Wight's home was located here on the southwestern slope
of Tower Hill at Adam-ondi-Ahman.*

executed and to put down mob violence, and he gave us a paper written
by his own hand, stating that he would do so. He [Joseph Smith] also
requested him to call together the most influential men of the county
the next day, that we might have an interview with them. To this he ac-
quiesced, and accordingly, the next day they assembled at the house of
Colonel Wight and entered into a mutual covenant of peace to put
down mob violence and to protect each other in the enjoyment of their
rights. After this, we all parted with the best of feelings, and each man
returned to his own home.

"This mutual agreement of peace, however, did not last long; for, a
few days afterwards, the mob began to collect again, until several hundreds rendezvoused at Millport, a few miles distant from Diahman.
They immediately commenced making aggressions upon the citizens
called 'Mormons,' taking away their hogs and cattle, and threatening
them with extermination, or utter extinction, saying that they had a
cannon, and there should be no compromise only at its mouth. They
frequently took men, women, and children prisoners, whipping them
and lacerating their bodies with hickory withes, and tying them to trees,
and depriving them of food until they were compelled to gnaw the bark
from the trees to which they were bound in order to sustain life, treating
them in the most cruel manner they could invent or think of, and doing

everything they could to excite the indignation of the 'Mormon' people to rescue them, in order that they might make that a pretext for an accusation for the breach of the law, and that they might the better excite the prejudice of the populace, and thereby get aid and assistance to carry out their hellish purposes of extermination.

"Immediately on the authentication of these facts, messengers were dispatched from Far West to Austin A. King, judge of the fifth judicial district of the state of Missouri, and also to Major-General Atchison, commander-in-chief of that division, and Brigadier-General Doniphan,[4] giving them information of the existing facts and demanding immediate assistance.

"General Atchison returned with the messengers and went immediately to Diahman and from thence to Millport, and he found the facts were true as reported to him; that the citizens of that county were assembled together in a hostile attitude, to the amount of two to three hundred men, threatening the utter extermination of the 'Mormons.' He immediately returned to Clay County and ordered out a sufficient military force to quell the mob.

"Immediately after they were dispersed and the army returned, the mob commenced collecting again. Soon after, we again applied for military aid, when General Doniphan came out with a force of sixty armed men to Far West; but they were in such a state of insubordination, that he said he could not control them, and it was thought advisable by Colonel Hinckle, Mr. Rigdon, and others, that they should return home. General Doniphan ordered Colonel Hinckle to call out the militia of Caldwell, and defend the town against the mob, for, said he, 'you have great reason to be alarmed,' for, he said, Neil Gilliam, from Platte County, had come down with two hundred armed men, and had taken up their station at Hunter's Mill, a place distant about seventeen or eighteen miles northwest of the town of Far West, and, also, that an armed force had collected again at Millport, in Daviess County, consisting of several hundred men, and that another armed force had collected at DeWitt, in Carroll County, about fifty miles southeast of Far West, where about seventy families of the 'Mormon' people had settled, upon the bank of the Missouri River, at a little town called DeWitt.

"Immediately, whilst he was yet talking, a messenger came in from DeWitt, stating that three or four hundred men had assembled together at that place, armed *cap-a-pie*,[5] and that they threatened the utter extinction of the citizens of that place if they did not leave the place immediately; and that they also surrounded the town and cut off all supplies of food, so that many of them were suffering with hunger.

"General Doniphan seemed to be very much alarmed, and appeared to be willing to do all he could to assist and to relieve the sufferings of the 'Mormon' people. He advised that a petition be immediately got up and sent to the governor. A petition was accordingly prepared, and a messenger immediately dispatched to the governor,[6] and another petition was sent to Judge King.

"The 'Mormon' people throughout the country were in a great state of alarm, and also in great distress. They saw themselves completely surrounded with armed forces on the north, and on the northwest, and

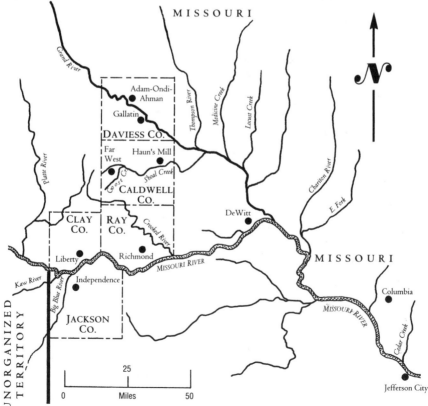

WESTERN MISSOURI FRONTIER

on the south. Bogart, who was a Methodist preacher and who was then a captain over a militia company of fifty soldiers, but who had added to his number out of the surrounding counties about a hundred more, which made his force about one hundred and fifty strong, was stationed at Crooked Creek, sending out his scouting parties, taking men, women, and children prisoners, driving off cattle, hogs, and horses, entering into every house on Log and Long Creeks, rifling their houses of their most precious articles, such as money, bedding, and clothing, taking all their old muskets and their rifles or military implements, threatening the people with instant death if they did not deliver up all their precious things and enter into a covenant to leave the state or go into the city of Far West by the next morning, saying that they 'calculated to drive the people into Far West, and then drive them to hell.' Gilliam also was doing the same on the northwest side of Far West; and Sashiel Woods, a Presbyterian minister, was the leader of the mob in Daviess County; and a very noted man of the same society was the leader of the mob in Carroll County; and they were also sending out their scouting parties, robbing and pillaging houses, driving away hogs, horses, and cattle, taking men, women and children, and carrying them off, threatening their lives, and subjecting them to all manner of abuses that they could invent or think of.

"Under this state of alarm, excitement and distress, the messengers returned from the governor, and from the other authorities, bringing the fatal news that the 'Mormons' could have no assistance. They stated that the governor said that the 'Mormons' had got into a difficulty with the citizens, and they might fight it out for all what he cared. He could not render them any assistance.

"The people of DeWitt were obliged to leave their homes and go into Far West; but did not do so until many of them had starved to death for want of proper sustenance, and several died on the road there and were buried by the wayside without a coffin or a funeral ceremony. The distress, sufferings, and privations of the people cannot be expressed.

"All the scattered families of the 'Mormon' people, in all the counties except Daviess were driven into Far West, with but few exceptions. This only increased their distress, for many thousands who were driven there had no habitations or houses to shelter them and were huddled together, some in tents, and others under blankets, while others had no shelter from the inclemency of the weather. Nearly two months the people had been in this awful state of consternation, many of them had been killed, whilst others had been whipped until they had to swathe up their bowels to prevent them from falling out.

"About this time General Parks, who was one of the commissioned officers, came out from Richmond, Ray County, to Diahman, and I, myself, and my brother Joseph Smith went out at the same time.

"On the evening that General Parks arrived at Diahman, the wife of the late Don Carlos Smith,[7] my brother, came into Colonel Wight's about eleven o'clock at night, bringing her two children along with her, one about two and a half years old, the other a babe in her arms.[8] She came in on foot, a distance of three miles, and waded Grand River, and the water was then about waist deep, and the snow about three inches deep. She stated that a party of the mob, a gang of ruffians, had turned her out of doors, had taken her household goods, and had burnt up her house, and she had escaped by the skin of her teeth. Her husband at that time was in Virginia,[9] and she was living alone.

Agnes Smith and her babies waded the Grand River
after the mob burned her house to the ground.

"This cruel transaction excited the feelings of the people of Diahman, especially of Colonel Wight, and he asked General Parks in my hearing how long we had got to suffer such base treatment. General Parks said he did not know how long. Colonel Wight then asked him what should be done. General Parks told him he 'should take a company of men, well armed, and go and disperse the mob wherever he should find any collected together, and take away their arms.' Colonel Wight did so precisely, according to the orders of General Parks, and my brother, Joseph Smith, made no order about it.

"And after Colonel Wight had dispersed the mob, and put a stop to their burning houses belonging to the 'Mormon' people and turning women and children out of doors, which they had done up to that time, to the amount of eight or ten houses, which were consumed to ashes, after being cut short in their intended designs, the mob started up a new plan. They went to work and moved their families out of the county, and set fire to their houses, and not being able to incense the 'Mormons' to commit crimes, they had recourse to this stratagem—to set their houses on fire and send runners into all the counties adjacent to declare to the people, that the 'Mormons' had burned up their houses and destroyed their fields; and if the people would not believe them, they would tell them to go and see if what they had said was not true. Many people came to see—they saw the houses burning; and being filled with prejudice, they could not be made to believe, but that the 'Mormons' set them on fire; which deed was most diabolical and of the blackest kind; for indeed the 'Mormons' did not set them on fire nor meddle with their houses or their fields.   ·

"And the houses that were burnt, together with the pre-emption rights, and the corn in the fields, had all been previously purchased by the 'Mormons' of the people, and paid for in money, and with wagons and horses, and with other property about two weeks before; but they had not taken possession of the premises. This wicked transaction was for the purpose of clandestinely exciting the minds of a prejudiced populace and the executive, that they might get an order, that they could the more easily carry out their hellish purposes in expulsion or extermination or utter extinction of the 'Mormon' people.

"After witnessing the distressed situation of the people in Diahman, my brother, Joseph Smith, and myself, returned back to the city of Far West and immediately dispatched a messenger with written documents to General Atchison, stating the facts as they did then exist, praying for assistance if possible, and requesting the editor of the *Far West* to insert the same in his newspaper, but he utterly refused to do so.

"We still believed that we should get assistance from the governor and again petitioned him, praying for assistance, setting forth our distressed situation. And in the meantime, the presiding judge of the county court issued orders, upon affidavits made to him by citizens, to the sheriff of the county to order out the militia of the county to stand in constant readiness night and day to prevent the citizens from being massacred, which fearful situation they were exposed to every moment.

"Everything was very portentous and alarming. Notwithstanding all this, there was a ray of hope yet existing in the minds of the people that the governor would render us assistance. And whilst the people were waiting anxiously for deliverance—men, women, and children frightened, praying and weeping—we beheld at a distance, crossing the prairies and approaching the town, a large army in military array, brandishing their glittering swords in the sunshine; and we would not but feel joyful for a moment, thinking that probably the governor had sent an armed force to our relief, notwithstanding the awful forebodings that pervaded our breasts.

"But to our great surprise when the army arrived, they came up and formed a line in double file within one-half mile on the east[10] of the city of Far West, and dispatched three messengers with a white flag to come to the city. They were met by Captain Morey with a few other individuals, whose names I do not now recollect. I was, myself, standing close by, and could very distinctly hear every word they said.

"Being filled with anxiety, I rushed forward to the spot, expecting to hear good news, but, alas! and heart-thrilling to every soul that heard them—they demanded three persons to be brought out of the city, before they should massacre the rest. The names of the persons they demanded were Adam Lightner, John Cleminson, and his wife. Immediately the three persons were brought forth to hold an interview with the officers who had made the demand, and the officers told them they had now a chance to save their lives, for they calculated to destroy the people, and lay the city in ashes. They replied to the officers, and said, 'If the people must be destroyed, and the city burned to ashes, we

Four large cornerstones, laid on July 4, 1838,
still mark the site of the Far West Temple.

will remain in the city and die with them.' The officers immediately returned, and the army retreated and encamped about a mile and a half from the city.

"A messenger was immediately dispatched with a white flag, from the colonel of the militia of Far West requesting an interview with General Atchison and General Doniphan; but, as the messenger approached the camp, he was shot at by Bogart, the Methodist preacher. The name of the messenger was Charles C. Rich,[11] who is now brigadier-general of the Nauvoo Legion. However, he gained permission to see General Doniphan. He also requested an interview with General Atchison. General Doniphan said, that General Atchison had been dismounted by a special order of the governor, a few miles back, and had been sent back to Liberty, Clay County. He also stated, that the reason was, that he (Atchison) was too merciful unto the 'Mormons' and Boggs would not let him have the command, but had given it to General Lucas,[12] who was from Jackson County, and whose heart had become hardened by his former acts of rapine and bloodshed, he being one of the leaders in murdering, driving, plundering, and burning some two or three hundred houses belonging to the 'Mormon' people in that county, in the years 1833 and 1834.

"Mr. Rich requested General Doniphan to spare the people and not suffer them to be massacred until the next morning, it then being evening. He coolly agreed that he would not and also said, that he had not as yet received the governor's order, but expected it every hour and should not make any further move until he had received it; but he would not make any promises so far as regards Neil Gilliam's army, (he having arrived a few minutes previously, and joined the main body of the army, he knowing well at what hour to form a junction with the main body).

"Mr. Rich then returned to the city, giving this information. The colonel [G. M. Hinckle] immediately dispatched a second messenger with a white flag to request another interview with General Doniphan in order to touch his sympathy and compassion, and if it were possible for him to use his best endeavors to preserve the lives of the people. On the return of this messenger, we learned that several persons had been killed by some of the soldiers, who were under the command of General Lucas.

"One Mr. Carey had his brains knocked out by the breech of a gun, and he lay bleeding several hours, but his family were not permitted to approach him, nor any one else allowed to administer relief to him whilst he lay upon the ground in the agonies of death. Mr. Carey had just arrived in the country, from the state of Ohio, only a few hours previous to the arrival of the army. He had a family consisting of a wife and several small children. He was buried by Lucius N. Scovil, who is now the senior warden of the Nauvoo Legion.

"Another man, of the name of John Tanner, was knocked on the head at the same time, and his skull laid bare the width of a man's hand, and he lay, to all appearance, in the agonies of death for several hours; but by the permission of General Doniphan, his friends brought him out of the camp, and with good nursing he slowly recovered, and is now living.

"There was another man, whose name is Powell, who was beaten on the head with the breech of a gun until his skull was fractured. He is now alive, and resides in this [Hancock] county, but has lost the use of his senses. Several persons of his family were also left for dead, but have since recovered.

"These acts of barbarity were also committed by the soldiers under

the command of General Lucas, previous to having received the governor's order of extermination.[13]

"It was on the evening of the thirtieth of October, according to the
best of my recollection, that the army arrived at Far West, the sun about
half an hour high. In a few moments afterwards, Cornelius Gilliam arrived with his army and formed a junction. This Gilliam had been stationed at Hunter's Mill for about two months previous to that time—
committing depredations upon the inhabitants, capturing men, women
and children, and carrying them off as prisoners, lacerating their bodies
with hickory withes.

"The army of Gilliam were painted like Indians, some of them
were more conspicuous than others, designated by red spots, and he
also was painted in a similar manner, with red spots marked on his face,
and styled himself the 'Delaware Chief.' They would whoop, and halloo,
and yell, as nearly like Indians as they could, and continued to do so all
that night.

"In the morning early the colonel of the militia [G. M. Hinckle]
sent a messenger into the camp, with a white flag, to have another interview with General Doniphan. On his return, he informed us that the
governor's order had arrived. General Doniphan said that the order of
the governor was to exterminate the 'Mormons,' but he would be d——d
if he would obey that order, but General Lucas might do as he pleased.

"We immediately learned from General Doniphan, that the governor's order that had arrived was only a copy of the original, and that the
original order was in the hands of Major-General Clark,[14] who was on
his way to Far West, with an additional army of six thousand men.

"Immediately after this there came into the city a messenger from
Haun's Mill, bringing the intelligence of an awful massacre of the
people who were residing in that place, and that a force of two or three
hundred, detached from the main body of the army, under the superior
command of Colonel Ashley, but under the immediate command of
Captain Nehemiah Comstock, who, the day previous, had promised
them peace and protection, but on receiving a copy of the governor's
order, 'to exterminate or expel,' from the hands of Colonel Ashley, he
returned upon them the following day, and surprised and massacred the
whole population of the town, and then came on to the town of Far
West, and entered into conjunction with the main body of the army.[15]

Sixteen hundred balls were fired upon the people here at Haun's Mill.
Nineteen were massacred.

"The messenger informed us that he, himself, with a few others, fled into the thickets which preserved them from the massacre, and on the following morning they returned and collected the dead bodies of the people, and cast them into a well; and there were upwards of twenty who were dead or mortally wounded, and there are several of the wounded, who are now living in this city. One, by the name of Yocum, has lately had his leg amputated, in consequence of wounds he then received. He had a ball shot through his head, which entered near his eye and came out at the back part of his head, and another ball passed through one of his arms.

"The army during all the while they had been encamped in Far West, continued to lay waste fields of corn, making hogs, sheep and cattle common plunder, and shooting them down for sport.

"One man shot a cow and took a strip of her skin the width of his hand, from her head to her tail, and tied it around a tree to slip his halter into to tie his horse to.

"The city was surrounded with a strong guard, and no man, woman, or child was permitted to go out or come in under the penalty of death. Many of the citizens were shot, in attempting to get out to obtain sustenance for themselves and families. There was one field fenced in, consisting of twelve hundred acres, mostly covered with corn. It was entirely laid waste by the horses of the army.

"The next day after the arrival of the army, towards evening, Col. Hinckle came up from the camp, requesting to see my brother Joseph, Parley P. Pratt, Sidney Rigdon, Lyman Wight, and George W. Robinson, stating that the officers of the army wanted a mutual consultation with those men. Hinckle also assured them that these Generals Doniphan, Lucas, Wilson and Graham, (however, General Graham is an honorable exception; he did all he could to preserve the lives of the people, contrary to the order of the governor,) had pledged their sacred honor, that they should not be abused or insulted; but should be guarded back in safety in the morning, or so soon as the consultation was over.

"My brother Joseph replied that he did not know what good he could do in any consultation, as he was only a private individual. However, he said that he was always willing to do all the good he could and would obey every law of the land, and then leave the event with God.

"They immediately started with Colonel Hinckle to go down into the camp. As they were going down, about halfway to the camp, they met General Lucas with a phalanx of men, with a wing to the right and to the left and a four-pounder in the center. They supposed he was coming with his strong force to guard them into the camp in safety; but, to their surprise, when they came up to General Lucas, he ordered his men to surround them, and Hinckle stepped up to the general and said, 'These are the prisoners I agreed to deliver up.'

"General Lucas drew his sword, and said, 'Gentlemen, you are my prisoners,' and about that time the main army were on their march to meet them.

"They came up in two divisions and opened to the right and left, and my brother and his friends were marched down through their lines with a strong guard in front and the cannon in the rear to the camp, amidst the whoopings, howlings, yellings, and shoutings of the army, which were so horrid and terrific, that they frightened the inhabitants of the city. It is impossible to describe the feelings of horror and distress of the people.

"After being thus betrayed, they were placed under a strong guard of thirty men, armed *cap-a-pie*, which were relieved every two hours. There they were compelled to lie on the cold ground that night and were told in plain language that they need never expect their liberties again.[16] So far for their honors pledged! However, this was as much as could be expected from a mob under the garb of military and executive authority in the state of Missouri.

"On the next day, the soldiers were permitted to patrol the streets, to abuse and insult the people at their leisure, and enter into the houses and pillage them and ravish the women, taking away every gun and every other kind of arms or military implements. About twelve o'clock that day, Colonel Hinckle came to my house with an armed force, opened the door and called me out of doors and delivered me up as a prisoner unto that force. They surrounded me and commanded me to march into the camp. I told them that I could not go; my family were sick, and I was sick myself, and could not leave home. They said they did not care for that—I must and should go. I asked when they would permit me to return. They made me no answer, but forced me along with the point of the bayonet into the camp, and put me under the same guard with my brother Joseph; and within about half an hour afterwards, Amasa Lyman was also brought and placed under the same guard. There we were compelled to stay all that night and lie on the ground. But some time in the same night, Colonel Hinckle came to me and told me that he had been pleading my case before the court-martial, but he was afraid he would not succeed.

"He said there was a court-martial then in session, consisting of thirteen or fourteen officers; Circuit Judge Austin A. King, and Mr. Birch, district attorney; also Sashiel Woods, Presbyterian priest, and about twenty other priests of the different religious denominations in that country. He said they were determined to shoot us on the next morning in the public square in Far West. I made him no reply.

"On the next morning about sunrise, General Doniphan ordered his brigade to take up the line of march and leave the camp. He came to us where we were under guard to shake hands with us and bid us farewell. His first salutation was, 'By G———d, you have been sentenced by the court-martial to be shot this morning; but I will be d——d if I will have any of the honor of it, or any of the disgrace of it, therefore I have ordered my brigade to take up the line of march and to leave the camp, for I consider it to be cold-blooded murder, and I bid you farewell,' and he went away.

"This movement of General Doniphan made considerable excitement in the army, and there was considerable whisperings amongst the officers. We listened very attentively and frequently heard it mentioned by the guard that 'the d——d Mormons would not be shot this time.'

"In a few moments the guard was relieved by a new set. One of those new guards said that 'the d——d Mormons would not be shot this time,' for the movement of General Doniphan had frustrated the whole plan, and that the officers had called another court-martial and had ordered us to be taken to Jackson County and there to be executed; and in a few moments two large wagons drove up, and we were ordered to get into them; and while we were getting into them, there came up four or five men armed with guns, who drew up and snapped their guns at us in order to kill us. Some flashed in the pan, and others only snapped, but none of their guns went off. They were immediately arrested by several officers, and their guns taken from them, and the drivers drove off.

"We requested General Lucas to let us go to our houses and get some clothing. In order to do this, we had to be driven up into the city. It was with much difficulty that we could get his permission to go and see our families and get some clothing; but, after considerable consultation, we were permitted to go under a strong guard of five or six men to each of us, and we were not permitted to speak to any one of our families, under the pain of death. The guard that went with me ordered my wife to get me some clothes immediately, within two minutes; and if she did not do it, I should go off without them.

"I was obliged to submit to their tyrannical orders, however painful it was, with my wife and children clinging to my arms and to the skirts of my garments, and was not permitted to utter to them a word of consolation, and in a moment was hurried away from them at the point of the bayonet.[17]

"We were hurried back to the wagons and ordered into them, all in about the same space of time. In the meanwhile, our father, and mother, and sister had forced their way to the wagons to get permission to see us, but were forbidden to speak to us and we were immediately driven off for Jackson County. We traveled about twelve miles that evening, and encamped for the night.[18]

"The same strong guard was kept around us and was relieved every two hours, and we were permitted to sleep on the ground. The nights were then cold with considerable snow on the ground, and for the want of covering and clothing, we suffered extremely with the cold. That night was the commencement of a fit of sickness from which I have not wholly recovered unto this day,[19] in consequence of my exposure to the inclemency of the weather.

"Our provision was fresh beef, roasted in the fire on a stick; the army having no bread, in consequence of the want of mills to grind the grain.

"In the morning, at the dawn of day, we were forced on our journey, and were exhibited to the inhabitants along the road, the same as they exhibit a caravan of elephants or camels. We were examined from head to foot by men, women, and children, only I believe they did not make us open our mouths to look at our teeth.[20] This treatment was continued incessantly until we arrived at Independence, in Jackson County.

"After our arrival at Independence, we were driven all through the town for inspection, and then we were ordered into an old log house and there kept under guard as usual until supper, which was served up to us as we sat upon the floor or on billets of wood, and we were compelled to stay in that house all that night and the next day.

"They continued to exhibit us to the public by letting the people come in and examine us, and then go away and give place for others alternately, all that day and the next night. But on the morning of the following day we were all permitted to go to the tavern to eat and sleep; but afterwards they made us pay our own expenses for board, lodging, and attendance, and for which they made a most exorbitant charge.

"We remained in the tavern about two days and two nights, when an officer arrived with authority from General Clark to take us back to Richmond, Ray County, where the general had arrived with his army, to await our arrival. But on the morning of our start for Richmond, we were informed by General Wilson that it was expected by the soldiers that we would be hung up by the necks on the road while on the march to that place, and that it was prevented by a demand made for us by General Clark, who had the command in consequence of authority; and that it was his prerogative to execute us himself.

"During our stay at Independence, the officers informed us that there were eight or ten horses in the place belonging to the 'Mormon' people, which had been stolen by the soldiers, and that we might have two of them to ride upon if we would cause them to be sent back to the owners after our arrival at Richmond. We accepted of them and they were ridden to Richmond, and the owners came there and got them.

"We started in the morning under our new officer, Colonel Price, of Keytsville, Chariton County, Missouri, with several other men to guard us. We arrived there on Friday evening, the ninth day of November, and were thrust into an old log house with a strong guard placed over us. After we had been there for the space of half an hour, there came in a man who was said to have some notoriety in the penitentiary, bringing in his hands a quantity of chains and padlocks. He said he was commanded by General Clark to put us in chains.

"Immediately the soldiers rose up, and pointing their guns at us, placed their thumb on the cock and their finger on the trigger, and the state's prison keeper went to work putting a chain around the leg of each man and fastening it on with a padlock, until we were all chained together, seven of us.[21]

"In a few moments General Clark came in. We requested to know of him what was the cause of all this harsh and cruel treatment. He refused to give us any information at that time, but said he would in a few days; so we were compelled to continue in that situation—camping on the floor, all chained together, without any chance or means to be made comfortable, having to eat our victuals as they were served up to us, using our fingers and teeth instead of knives and forks.[22]

"Whilst we were in this situation, a young man of the name of Jedediah M. Grant,[23] brother-in-law to my brother, William Smith, came to see us and put up at the tavern where General Clark made his quarters. He happened to come in time to see General Clark make choice of his men to shoot us on Monday morning, the twelfth day of November. He saw them make choice of their rifles and load them with two balls in each; and after they had prepared their guns, General Clark saluted them by saying, 'Gentlemen, you shall have the honor of shooting the "Mormon" leaders on Monday morning at eight o'clock!'

"But in consequence of the influence of our friend, the inhuman general was intimidated so that he durst not carry his murderous design into execution, and sent a messenger immediately to Fort Leavenworth to obtain the military code of laws.

"After the messenger's return, the general was employed nearly a whole week examining the laws, so Monday passed away without our being shot. However, it seemed like foolishness to me for so great a man as General Clark pretended to be, should have to search the military law to find out whether preachers of the gospel, who never did military duty, could be subjected to court-martial.

"However, the general seemed to learn the fact after searching the military code, and came into the old log cabin, where we were under guard and in chains, and told us he had concluded to deliver us over to the civil authorities, as persons guilty of treason, murder, arson, larceny, theft, and stealing. The poor, deluded general did not know the difference between theft, larceny, and stealing.

"Accordingly, we were handed over to the pretended civil authorities, and the next morning our chains were taken off, and we were guarded to the courthouse where there was a pretended court in session; Austin A. King being the judge and Mr. Birch the district attorney, the two extremely, and very honorable gentlemen, who sat on the court-martial when we were sentenced to be shot!

"Witnesses were called up and sworn, at the point of the bayonet, and if they would not swear to the things they were told to do, they were threatened with instant death; and I do know, positively, that the evidence given in by those men, whilst under duress, was false.

"This state of things was continued twelve or fourteen days, and after that we were ordered by the judge to introduce some rebutting evidence, saying if we did not do it, we would be thrust into prison. I could hardly understand what the judge meant, for I considered we were in prison already and could not think of anything but the persecutions of the days of Nero, knowing that it was a religious persecution and the court an inquisition; however, we gave him the names of forty persons who were acquainted with all the persecutions and sufferings of the people.

"The judge made out a subpoena and inserted the names of those men and caused it to be placed in the hands of Bogart, the notorious Methodist minister; and he took fifty armed soldiers and started for Far West. I saw the subpoena given to him and his company, when they started.

"In the course of a few days, they returned with most of all those forty men, whose names were inserted in the subpoena, and thrust them into jail, and we were not permitted to bring one of them before the court; but the judge turned upon us, with an air of indignation, and said, 'Gentlemen, you must get your witnesses, or you shall be committed to jail immediately, for we are not going to hold the court open, on expense, much longer for you, anyhow.'

"We felt very much distressed and oppressed at that time. Colonel Wight said, 'What shall we do? Our witnesses are all thrust into prison, and probably will be, and we have no power to do anything; of course we must submit to this tyranny and oppression; we cannot help ourselves.'

"Several others made similar expressions, in the agony of their souls, but my brother Joseph did not say anything, he being sick at that time with the toothache, and pain in his face, in consequence of a severe cold brought on by being exposed to the severity of the weather. However, it was considered best by General Doniphan and Lawyer Reese that we should try to get some witnesses, before the pretended court.

"Accordingly, I myself gave the names of about twenty other persons; the judge inserted them in a subpoena, and caused it to be placed in the hands of Bogart, the Methodist priest, and he again started off with his fifty soldiers, to take those men prisoners, as he had done to the forty others.

"The judge sat and laughed at the good opportunity of getting the names, that they might the more easily capture them, and so bring them down to be thrust into prison in order to prevent us from getting the truth before the pretended court, of which himself was the chief inquisitor or conspirator. Bogart returned from his second expedition, with one witness only, whom he also thrust into prison.

"The people at Far West had learned the intrigue and had left the state, having been made acquainted with the treatment of the former witnesses. But we, on learning that we could not obtain witnesses, whilst privately consulting with each other what we should do, discovered a Mr. Allen, standing by the window on the outside of the house. We beckoned to him as though we would have him come in. He immediately came in.

"At that time Judge King retorted upon us again, saying, 'Gentlemen, are you not going to introduce some witnesses?'—also saying it was the last day he should hold the testimony open for us, and if we did not rebut the testimony that had been given against us, he should have to commit us to jail.

"I had then got Mr. Allen into the house, and before the court (so called) I told the judge we had one witness, if he would be so good as to put him under oath. He seemed unwilling to do so, but after a few moments' consultation, the state's attorney arose and said, he should object to that witness being sworn, and that he should object to that witness giving his evidence at all, stating that this was not a court to try the case, but only a court of investigation on the part of the state.

"Upon this, General Doniphan arose, and said he would be G——d d——d, if the witness should not be sworn, and that it was a d——d shame, that these defendants should be treated in this manner, that they could not be permitted to get one witness before the court, whilst all their witnesses, even forty at a time, have been taken by force of arms and thrust into the 'bull pen,' in order to prevent them from giving their testimony.

"After Doniphan sat down, the judge permitted the witness to be sworn and enter upon his testimony. But as soon as he began to speak, a man by the name of Cook, who was a brother-in-law to priest Bogart, the Methodist, and who was a lieutenant [in the state militia], and whose place at that time was to superintend the guard, stepped in before the pretended court, and took him by the nape of his neck and jammed his head down under the pole or log of wood that was placed up around the place where the inquisition was sitting, to keep the bystanders from intruding upon the majesty of the inquisitors, and jammed him along to the door, and kicked him out of doors. He instantly turned to some soldiers, who were standing by him, and said to them, 'Go and shoot him, d——n him, shoot him, d——n him.'

"The soldiers ran after the man to shoot him. He fled for his life, and with great difficulty made his escape. The pretended court immediately arose, and we were ordered to be carried to Liberty, Clay County, and there to be thrust into jail. We endeavored to find out for what cause, but, all that we could learn was, because we were 'Mormons.'

"The next morning a large wagon drove up to the door, and a blacksmith came into the house with some chains and handcuffs. He said his orders from the judge were to handcuff us and chain us together. He informed us that the judge had made out a mittimus, and sentenced us to jail for treason. He also said the judge had done this, that we might not get bail. He also said the judge stated his intention to keep us in jail until all the 'Mormons' were driven out of the state. He also said that the judge had further stated, that if he let us out before the 'Mormons' had left the state, that we would not let them leave, and there would be another d———d fuss kicked up. I also heard the judge say myself, whilst he was sitting in his pretended court, that there was no law for us nor the 'Mormons' in the state of Missouri; that he had sworn to see them exterminated and to see the governor's order executed to the very letter, and that he would do so. However, the blacksmith proceeded and put the irons upon us, and we were ordered into the wagon, and were driven off for Clay County. As we journeyed along on the road, we were exhibited to the inhabitants, and this course was adopted all the way, thus making a public exhibition of us until we arrived at Liberty, Clay County.

"There we were thrust into prison again and locked up and were held there in close confinement for the space of six months, and our place of lodging was the square side of a hewed white oak log, and our food was anything but good and decent. Poison was administered to us three or four times. The effect it had upon our system was that it vomited us almost to death, and then we would lay some two or three days in a torpid, stupid state, not even caring or wishing for life—the poison being administered in too large doses, or it would inevitably have proved fatal, had not the power of Jehovah interposed on our behalf to save us from their wicked purpose.

"We were also subjected to the necessity of eating human flesh for the space of five days or go without food, except a little coffee or a little corn bread. The latter I chose in preference to the former. We none of

Liberty Jail, where Joseph and his brethren remained from the beginning of December until April.[24]

us partook of the flesh, except Lyman Wight. We also heard the guard which was placed over us making sport of us, saying they had fed us on 'Mormon' beef.[25] I have described the appearance of this flesh to several experienced physicians and they have decided that it was human flesh. We learned afterwards, by one of the guard, that it was supposed that that act of savage cannibalism in feeding us with human flesh would be considered a popular deed of notoriety: but the people, on learning that it would not take, tried to keep it secret; but the fact was noised abroad before they took that precaution.

"Whilst we were incarcerated in prison, we petitioned the supreme court of the state of Missouri twice for habeas corpus but were refused both times, by Judge Reynolds, who is now the governor of that state. We also petitioned one of the county judges for a writ of habeas corpus, which was granted in about three weeks afterwards, but we were not permitted to have any trial. We were only taken out of jail and kept out for a few hours, and then remanded back again.[26]

"In the course of three or four days after that time, Judge Turnham came into the jail in the evening and said he had permitted Mr. Rigdon to get bail, but said he had to do it in the night and unknown to any of the citizens or they would kill him, for they had sworn to kill him if they could find him.[27] And as to the rest of us, he dared not let us go, for fear of his own life as well as ours. He said it was d——d hard to be confined under such circumstances; for he knew we were innocent men, and he said the people also knew it; and that it was only a persecution and treachery, and the scenes of Jackson County acted over again for fear that we would become too numerous in that upper country. He said the plan was concocted from the governor down to the lowest judge, and that that Baptist priest, Riley, was riding into town every day to watch the people, stirring up the mind of the people against us all he could, exciting them and stirring up their religious prejudices against us for fear they would let us go. Mr. Rigdon, however, got bail, and made his escape to Illinois.

"The jailer, Samuel Tillery, Esq., told us also that the whole plan was concocted by the governor, down to the lowest judge, in that upper country early in the previous spring, and that the plan was more fully carried out at the time that General Atchison went down to Jefferson City with Generals Wilson, Lucas, and Gilliam, the self-styled 'Delaware Chief.' This was sometime in the month of September, when

The lower floor of Liberty Jail, where the prisoners spent much time, was only six feet high.[28]

the mob were collected at DeWitt in Carroll County. He also told us that the governor was now ashamed of the whole transaction, and would be glad to set us at liberty if he dared to do it. 'But,' said he, 'you need not be concerned, for the governor has laid a plan for your release.' He also said that Esquire Birch, the state's attorney, was appointed to be circuit judge, on the circuit passing through Daviess County, and that he (Birch) was instructed to fix the papers, so that we would be sure to be clear of any incumbrance in a very short time.

"Sometime in April we were taken to Daviess County,[29] as they said, to have a trial. But when we arrived at that place, instead of finding a court or jury, we found another inquisition, and Birch, who was the district attorney—the same man who was the one of the court-martial when we were sentenced to death—was now the circuit judge of that pretended court, and the grand jury that was empaneled were all at the massacre at Haun's Mill, and lively actors in that awful, solemn, disgraceful, cool-blooded murder; and all the pretense they made of excuse was, they had done it because the governor ordered them to do it.

"The same men sat as a jury in the daytime and were placed over us as a guard in the nighttime. They tantalized us and boasted of their great achievements at Haun's Mill and at other places, telling us how many houses they had burned, and how many sheep, cattle, and hogs they had driven off belonging to the 'Mormons,' and how many rapes they had committed, and what kicking and squealing there was . . . , saying that they lashed one woman upon one of the d——d 'Mormon' meeting benches, tying her hands and her feet fast, and sixteen of them abused her as much as they had a mind to, and then left her bound and exposed in that distressed condition. These fiends of the lower regions boasted of these acts of barbarity and tantalized our feelings with them for ten days. We had heard of these acts of cruelty previous to this time, but we were slow to believe that such acts had been perpetrated. The lady who was the subject of this brutality did not recover her health to be able to help herself for more than three months afterwards.

"This grand jury constantly celebrated their achievements with grog and glass in hand like the Indian warriors at their war dances, singing and telling each other of their exploits in murdering the 'Mormons,' in plundering their houses and carrying off their property. At the end of every song they would bring in the chorus, '. . . [30] Mormons! we have sent them to hell.' Then they would slap their hands and shout, 'Hosanna! Hosanna! Glory to God!' and fall down on their backs and kick with their feet a few moments. Then they would pretend to have swooned away into a glorious trance, in order to imitate some of the transactions at camp meetings. Then they would pretend to come out of the trance, and would shout and again slap their hands and jump up, while one would take a bottle of whiskey and a tumbler and turn it out full of whisky and pour down each other's necks, crying, '. . . Take it; you must take it!' And if anyone refused to drink the whiskey, others would clinch him and hold him, whilst another poured it down his neck; and what did not go down the inside went down the outside.

"This is a part of the farce acted out by the grand jury of Daviess County, whilst they stood over us as guards for ten nights successively. And all this in the presence of the great Judge Birch, who had previously said, in our hearing, that there was no law for the 'Mormons' in the state of Missouri. His brother was there acting as district attorney in that circuit, and if anything, was a greater ruffian than the judge.

"After all their ten days of drunkenness, we were informed that we were indicted for 'treason, murder, arson, larceny, theft, and stealing.' We asked for a change of venue from the county to Marion County, but they would not grant it, but they gave us a change of venue from Daviess to Boone County, and a mittimus was made out by the pretended Judge Birch, without date, name, or place.

"They fitted us out with a two-horse wagon and horses, and four men, besides the sheriff, to be our guard. There were five of us. We started from Gallatin in the afternoon, the sun about two hours high, and went as far as Diahman that evening, and stayed till morning. There we bought two horses of the guard, and paid for one of them in our clothing which we had with us, and for the other we gave our note.[31]

"We went down that day as far as Judge Morin's, a distance of some four or five miles. There we stayed until the morning when we started on our journey to Boone County, and traveled on the road about twenty miles distance. There we bought a jug of whiskey, with which we treated the company, and while there the sheriff showed us the mittimus before referred to, without date or signature, and said that Judge Birch told him never to carry us to Boone County, and never to show the mittimus 'and,' said he, 'I shall take a good drink of grog, and go to bed, you may do as you have a mind to.' Three others of the guard drank pretty freely of whiskey, sweetened with honey; they also went to bed, and were soon asleep, and the other guard went along with us and helped to saddle the horses.

"Two of us mounted the horses, and the other three started on foot, and we took our change of venue for the state of Illinois, and, in the course of nine or ten days, we arrived in Quincy, Adams County, Illinois, where we found our families in a state of poverty, although in good health, they having been driven out of the state previously, by the murderous militia, under the exterminating order of the executive of Missouri. And now the people of that state, a portion of them, would be glad to make the people of this state believe that my brother Joseph has committed treason, for the purpose of keeping up their murderous and hellish persecution; and they seem to be unrelenting and thirsting for the blood of innocence, for I do know, most positively, that my brother Joseph has not committed treason, nor violated one solitary item of law or rule in the state of Missouri.

"But I do know that the 'Mormon' people, en masse, were driven out of that state after being robbed of all they had, and they barely escaped with their lives, as well as my brother Joseph, who barely escaped with his life. His family also were robbed of all they had, and barely escaped with the skin of their teeth, and all of this in consequence of the exterminating order of Governor Boggs, the same being confirmed by the legislature of that state.

"And I do know, so does this court, and every rational man who is acquainted with the circumstances, and every man who shall hereafter become acquainted with the particulars thereof will know, that Governor Boggs, and Generals Clark, Lucas, Wilson, and Gilliam, also Austin A. King, have committed treason upon the citizens of Missouri and did violate the Constitution of the United States and also the constitution and laws of the state of Missouri and did exile and expel, at the point of bayonet, some twelve or fourteen thousand inhabitants from the state and did murder some three or four hundreds of men, women, and children in cold blood, and in the most horrid and cruel manner possible; and the whole of it was caused by religious bigotry and persecution, because the 'Mormons' dared to worship Almighty God according to the dictates of their own consciences, and agreeable to his divine will, as revealed in the scriptures of eternal truth, and had turned away from following the vain traditions of their fathers and would not worship according to the dogmas and commandments of those men who preach for hire and divine for money and teach for doctrine the precepts of men, expecting that the Constitution of the United States would have protected them therein.

"But notwithstanding the 'Mormon' people had purchased upwards of two hundred thousand dollars' worth of land, most of which was entered and paid for at the land office of the United States in the state of Missouri; and although the President of the United States has been made acquainted with these facts and the particulars of our persecutions and oppressions by petition to him and to Congress, yet they have not even attempted to restore the 'Mormons' to their rights, or given any assurance that we may hereafter expect redress from them. And I do also know most positively and assuredly, that my brother Joseph Smith, has not been in the state of Missouri since the spring of the year 1839. And further this deponent saith not."

HYRUM SMITH

NOTES

1. Hyrum gave this report to the court after his father, Joseph Smith Sr., had died, meaning that the Prophet, Joseph Smith Jr., who now also had a son by the name of Joseph, had then become Joseph Smith Sr., according to the custom of the time. To avoid confusion, however, in this book, throughout Hyrum's report the "Sr." has been dropped from Joseph's name altogether. This sworn statement of Hyrum's was first published in full in *Times and Seasons* 4 (July 1, 1843): 246–56.

2. It was Monday, August 6, 1838.

3. The early Saints referred to Adam-ondi-Ahman as "Diahman." On May 19, 1838, Joseph received a revelation that states: "Spring Hill is named by the Lord Adam-ondi-Ahman, because, said he, it is the place where Adam shall come to visit his people, or the Ancient of Days shall sit, as spoken of by Daniel the prophet" (D&C 116).

4. Alexander William Doniphan (1808–1887) proved to be a true friend to the Saints in Missouri. He was a prominent lawyer in Liberty, Missouri, in 1833. He was elected to the Missouri state legislature in 1836, 1840, and 1854. He was instrumental in helping establish Caldwell and Daviess Counties as a refuge for the Saints. He refused to carry out his commanding officer's order against the Mormon leaders at Far West. He later refused a general's commission in both the Union and the Confederate armies during the Civil War. He died at Richmond, Missouri, a hero to the Saints.

5. That is, "from head to foot."

6. Governor Lilburn W. Boggs had been one of the large landowners in Jackson County and had helped instigate the driving out of the Mormons from there in 1833. Now, as governor, he took up residence in Jefferson City (on the Missouri River) in the center of the state about 175 miles from Far West.

7. Agnes Coolbrith Smith was widowed on August 7, 1841. Don Carlos apparently died of pneumonia.

8. These daughters were Agnes and Sophronia.

9. The *Times and Seasons* stated that Don Carlos was on a mission in Tennessee.

10. The account in the *Times and Seasons* states "on the south of the city."

11. Charles Coulson Rich, baptized April 1, 1832, proved to be a great leader in the Church. He stood by the Prophet and the Brethren in all trials; was ordained an Apostle on February 12, 1849; lived "the principle," having six wives and fifty-one children; and died true to the faith on November 17, 1883. (See Cook, *Revelations,* pp. 271–72.)

12. General Samuel D. Lucas, born 1799, was an early settler in Independence, Missouri, where he was a store owner. He was major-general of the fourth division of the Missouri militia. When General Atchison was dismissed from his post, Lucas became senior officer of the actions against the Saints and presided at the surrender at Far West. (See *Papers,* p. 498.)

13. The infamous "extermination order" was issued Saturday, October 27, 1838, in the form of a letter to Major-general John Clark, commanding officer of the Missouri militia (superior to Samuel Lucas), from Governor and Commander-in-Chief Lilburn W. Boggs. It stated, in part: "The Mormons must be treated as enemies and *must be exterminated* or driven from the state, if necessary for the public good. Their outrages are beyond all description. If you can increase your force, you are authorized to do so, to any extent you may think necessary." (*History of the Church* 3:175.)

14. John B. Clark (1802–1885) was born in Madison County, Kentucky, and moved to Howard County, Missouri, in 1818. A lawyer by trade, he was appointed major-general in the Missouri militia in 1836. Beginning in 1854 he served three terms in the U.S. Congress and later became a Confederate brigadier-general during the Civil War. Clark was given supreme command over the militia forces operating against the Saints in the summer of 1838 and, although not in Far West when the Prophet Joseph and companions surrendered to General Lucas, presided over the dismantling of the community. (See *Papers*, pp. 479–80.)

15. Joseph Young, brother of Brigham Young, was an eyewitness to the massacre at Haun's Mill and gave this account: "On Tuesday, the 30th, that bloody tragedy was acted, the scene of which I shall never forget. More than three-fourths of the day had passed in tranquility, as smiling as the preceding one. I think there was no individual of our company that was apprised of the sudden and awful fate that hung over our heads like an overwhelming torrent, which was to change the prospects, the feelings and the circumstances of about thirty families. The banks of Shoal creek on either side teemed with children sporting and playing, while their mothers were engaged in domestic employments, and their fathers employed in guarding the mills and other property, while others were engaged in gathering in their crops for their winter consumption. The weather was very pleasant, the sun shone clear, all was tranquil, and no one expressed any apprehension of the awful crisis that was near us—even at our doors.

"It was about four o'clock, while sitting in my cabin with my babe in my arms, and my wife standing by my side, the door being open, I cast my eyes on the opposite bank of Shoal creek and saw a large company of armed men, on horses, directing their course towards the mills with all possible speed. As they advanced through the scattering trees that stood on the edge of the prairie they seemed to form themselves into a three square position, forming a vanguard in front.

"At this moment, David Evans, seeing the superiority of their numbers, (there being two hundred and forty of them, according to their own account), swung his hat, and cried for peace. This not being heeded, they continued to advance, and their leader, Mr. Nehemiah Comstock, fired a gun, which was followed by a solemn pause of ten or twelve seconds, when, all at once, they discharged about one hundred rifles, aiming at a blacksmith shop into which our friends had fled for safety; and charged up to the shop, the cracks of which between the logs were sufficiently large to enable them to aim directly at the bodies of those who had there fled for refuge from the fire of their murderers. There were several families tented in the rear of the shop, whose lives were exposed, and amidst a shower of bullets fled to the woods in different directions.

"After standing and gazing on this bloody scene for a few minutes, and finding myself in the uttermost danger, the bullets having reached the house where I was living, I committed my family to the protection of heaven, and leaving the house on the opposite side, I took a path which led up the hill, following in the trail of three of my brethren that had fled from the shop. While ascending the hill we were discovered by the mob, who immediately fired at us, and continued so to do till we reached the summit. In descending the hill, I secreted myself in a thicket of bushes, where I lay till eight o'clock in the evening, at which time I heard a female voice calling my name in an under tone, telling me that the mob had gone and there was no danger. I immediately left the thicket, and went to the house of Benjamin Lewis, where I found my family (who had fled there) in safety, and two of my friends mortally wounded, one of whom died before morning. Here we passed the painful night in deep and awful reflections on the scenes of the preceding evening." (*History of the Church* 3:184–85.)

16. Parley P. Pratt, one of the Brethren taken prisoner, recorded: "In camp we were placed under a strong guard, and were without shelter during the night, lying on the ground in the open air, in the midst of a great rain. The guards during the whole night kept up a constant tirade of mockery, and the most obscene blackguardism and abuse. They blasphemed God; mocked Jesus Christ; swore the most dreadful oaths; taunted brother Joseph and others; demanded miracles. . . . Thus passed this dreadful night, and before morning several other captives were added to our number. . . . We were informed that the general officers held a secret council during most of the night; . . . we were all sentenced to be shot. The day and hour was also appointed for execution of this sentence, viz: next morning at 8 o'clock, in the public square at Far West. . . . It was the common talk, and even the boast in the camp, that individuals lay here and there unburied, where they had shot them down for sport. The females they had ravished; the plunder they had taken; the houses they had burned; the horses they had stolen; the fields of grain they had laid waste, were common topics; and were dwelt on for mere amusement." Parley goes on to describe the night before their planned execution: "No pen need undertake to describe our feelings during that terrible night, while there confined—not knowing the fate of our wives and children, or of our fellow Saints, and seeing no way for our lives to be saved except by the miraculous power of God. But, notwithstanding all earthly hopes were gone, still we felt a calmness indescribable. A secret whispering in our inmost soul seemed to say: 'Peace, my sons, be of good cheer, your work is not yet done; therefore I will restrain your enemies, that they shall not have power to take your lives.'" (Pratt, *Autobiography*, pp. 160, 161.)

17. Parley Pratt added further witness to this: "This was the most trying scene of all. I went to my house, being guarded by two or three soldiers; the cold rain was pouring down without, and on entering my little cottage, there lay my wife sick of a fever, with which she had been for some time confined. At her breast was our son Nathan, an infant of three months, and by her side a little girl of five years. On the foot of the same bed lay a woman in travail, who had been driven from her house in the night, and had taken momentary shelter in my hut of ten feet square—my larger house having been torn down. I stepped to the bed; my wife burst into tears; I spoke a

few words of comfort, telling her to try to live for my sake and the children's; and expressing a hope that we should meet again though years might separate us. She promised to try to live. I then embraced and kissed the little babes and departed.

"Till now I had refrained from weeping; but, to be forced from so helpless a family, who were destitute of provisions and fuel, and deprived almost of shelter in a bleak prairie, with none to assist them, exposed to a lawless banditti who were utter strangers to humanity, and this at the approach of winter, was more than nature could well endure.

"I went to Gen. Moses Wilson in tears, and stated the circumstances of my sick, heart-broken and destitute family in terms which would have moved any heart that had a latent spark of humanity yet remaining. But I was only answered with an exultant laugh, and a taunt of reproach by this hardened murderer." (Pratt, *Autobiography*, p. 162.)

18. Parley Pratt related a comforting episode here: "As we arose and commenced our march on the morning of the 3d of November, Joseph Smith spoke to me and the other prisoners, in a low, but cheerful and confidential tone; said he: *'Be of good cheer, brethren; the word of the Lord came to me last night that our lives should be given us, and that whatever we may suffer during this captivity, not one of our lives should be taken'* " (Pratt, *Autobiography*, p. 164).

19. Fifty-six months had passed since this "fit of sickness" began.

20. Parley Pratt recorded that at the Missouri River "one of the ladies came up and very candidly inquired of the troops which of the prisoners the 'Mormons' worshipped? One of the guards pointing to Mr. Smith with a significant smile, said, 'This is he.' The woman, then turning to Mr. Smith, inquired whether he professed to be the Lord and Saviour?

"Do not smile, gentle reader, at the ignorance of these poor innocent creatures, who, by the exertions of a corrupt press and pulpit, are kept in ignorance and made to believe in every possible absurdity in relation to the Church of the Saints. Mr. Smith replied, that he professed to be nothing but a man, and a minister of salvation, sent by Jesus Christ to preach the gospel. After expressing some surprise, the lady inquired what was the peculiar nature of the gospel, as held by himself and his Church? At this the visitors and soldiers gathered around, and Mr. Smith preached to them faith in the Lord Jesus Christ, repentance towards God, reformation of life, immersion in water, in the name of Jesus Christ, for remission of sins, and the gift of the Holy Ghost by the laying on of hands.

"All seemed surprised, and the lady, in tears, went her way, praising God for the truth, and praying aloud that the Lord would bless and deliver the prisoners." (Pratt, *Autobiography*, pp. 164–65.)

21. From correspondence of the Prophet to his wife we learn who these seven were: "Brother Robison [George W. Robinson, son-in-law of Sidney Rigdon] is chained next to me. He has a true heart and a firm mind. Brother Wight [Lyman Wight] is next. Br. Rigdon, next; Hyrum, next; Parley, next; Amasa [Amasa Lyman], next; and thus we are bound together in chains as well as the cords of everlasting love. We are in good spirits and rejoice that we are counted worthy to be persecuted for Christ's sake." (*The Personal Writings of Joseph Smith*, ed. Dean C. Jessee [Salt Lake City:

Deseret Book Co., 1984], p. 368.) Others who were at this time imprisoned include: Alexander McRae, Caleb Baldwin, Morris Phelps, Luman Gibbs, Darwin Chase, and Norman Shearer.

22. Parley Pratt's account of the Richmond imprisonment gives a view of this horrific situation: "In one of those tedious nights we had lain as if in sleep till the hour of midnight had passed, and our ears and hearts had been pained, while we had listened for hours to the obscene jests, the horrid oaths, the dreadful blasphemies and filthy language of our guards, Colonel Price at their head, as they recounted to each other their deeds of rapine, murder, robbery, etc., which they had committed among the 'Mormons' while at Far West and vicinity. They even boasted of defiling by force wives, daughters and virgins, and of shooting or dashing out the brains of men, women and children.

"I had listened till I became so disgusted, shocked, horrified, and so filled with the spirit of indignant justice that I could scarcely refrain from rising upon my feet and rebuking the guards; but had said nothing to Joseph, or any one else, although I lay next to him and knew he was awake. On a sudden he arose to his feet, and spoke in a voice of thunder, or as the roaring lion, uttering, as near as I can recollect, the following words:

"'*SILENCE, ye fiends of the infernal pit. In the name of Jesus Christ I rebuke you, and command you to be still; I will not live another minute and bear such language. Cease such talk, or you or I die THIS INSTANT!*'

"He ceased to speak. He stood erect in terrible majesty. Chained, and without a weapon; calm, unruffled and dignified as an angel, he looked upon the quailing guards, whose weapons were lowered or dropped to the ground; whose knees smote together, and who, shrinking into a corner, or crouching at his feet, begged his pardon, and remained quiet till a change of guards.

"I have seen the ministers of justice, clothed in magisterial robes, and criminals arraigned before them, while life was suspended on a breath, in the Courts of England; I have witnessed a Congress in solemn session to give laws to nations; I have tried to conceive of kings, of royal courts, of thrones and crowns; and of emperors assembled to decide the fate of kingdoms; but dignity and majesty have I seen but *once*, as it stood in chains, at midnight, in a dungeon in an obscure village of Missouri." (Pratt, *Autobiography*, pp. 179–80.)

23. Jedediah Morgan Grant, born February 21, 1816, would be ordained an Apostle at age thirty-eight and become a counselor to Brigham Young in the First Presidency in 1854. He passed away on December 1, 1856, just nine days after his wife, Rachel, had given birth to a son, Heber Jeddy Grant, who later would become the seventh President of the Church.

24. It appears that the actual confinement in the jail at Liberty, Clay County, Missouri, started on Saturday, December 1, 1838, and lasted until Saturday, April 6, 1839, when the brethren were removed to be taken to Daviess County. Their stay in Liberty Jail, then, lasted 127 days.

25. George A. Smith reported: "Joseph and Hyrum Smith, Alexander McRae,

Lyman Wight and others were for several months thrust into prison, and in one instance, while there, were fed on human flesh and tantalized with the inquiry, 'How
they liked Mormon beef'—it being the flesh of some of their murdered brethren" (in
JD 13:108). A history of Lyman Wight indicates that he testified "of the sufferings
of Joseph Smith and his fellow prisoners, concerning which he said, 'We were committed to Liberty jail, under the care of Samuel Tillery, Jailor; we were received with a
shout of indignation and scorn by the populace. The jailor sent for a mittimus some
days after. His *tender mercies* were intolerable; he fed us on a scanty allowance of filthy
and unpalatable food, and for five days on human flesh; from extreme hunger I was
compelled to eat it.' The guards inquired, 'How do you like Mormon beef?'"
("History of Lyman Wight," *Millennial Star* 27 [July 29, 1865]: 471.)

26. For Tuesday, January 1, 1839, Joseph recorded: "The day dawned upon us as
prisoners of hope, but not as sons of liberty. O Columbia, Columbia! How thou art
fallen! 'The land of the free, the home of the brave!' 'The asylum of the oppressed'—
oppressing thy noblest sons, in a loathsome dungeon, without any provocation, only
that they have claimed to worship the God of their fathers according to His own
word, and the dictates of their own consciences." (*History of the Church* 3:245.)

27. Sometime around the end of January, 1839, Sidney Rigdon was let out of jail
on habeas corpus. The mob had sworn that if any of them got out of the jail they
would be killed. It appears that the intention of the mob was to kill Sidney, yet, as
Joseph recorded, "through the friendship of the sheriff, Mr. Samuel Hadley, and the
jailor, Mr. Samuel Tillery, he was let out of the jail secretly in the night . . . ; and
being solemnly warned by them to be out of the state with as little delay as possible,
he made his escape. Being pursued by a body of armed men, it was through the direction of a kind Providence that he escaped out of their hands, and safely arrived in
Quincy, Illinois." (*History of the Church* 3:264.)

28. This is a modern depiction of those imprisoned in the jail, representing
Joseph, Hyrum, Sidney, Lyman Wight, Alexander McRae, and Caleb Baldwin.

29. The prisoners were removed from Liberty Jail, as noted, on Saturday, April 6,
1839.

30. The "drinking song" was so full of profanity, and the use of God's name
taken so many times in vain, much of the text has been deleted from the original so as
not to take away from the spirit of the reading of the text.

31. William Bowman, ex-sheriff of Daviess County, was one of the guards of the
Prophet and his companions in their change of venue. Bowman was later charged with
complicity in the escape of the brethren (by providing them with horses), and "was
dragged over the square by the hair of the head" and evidently, at this or a later time,
was ridden on an iron rail until he was dead. Apparently the man who headed the
mob that killed William Bowman was Obadiah Jennings, the same who, with
Nehemiah Comstock, led the slaughter at Haun's Mill. (See *History of the Church*
3:321–22; *Manuscript History of Brigham Young, 1846–1847*, ed. Elden Jay Watson [Salt
Lake City: Elden Jay Watson, 1971], pp. 558–59.)

PART 6

Nauvoo and
the Martyrdom

CHAPTER 49

Joseph, Hyrum, and others are taken prisoner in Far West. His parents think Joseph has been murdered. Lucy describes the scenes of Joseph and Hyrum being taken prisoner and their parting emotions. The Spirit whispers peace to the mind and heart of Mother Smith. Merciless conditions in Far West are beyond description. The Smiths leave for Illinois. Lucy describes the deplorable conditions of their journey east. The Saints, as destitute refugees, gather at Quincy, Illinois.

October 31, 1838 to late February 1839

At the time when Joseph went into the enemy's camp,[1] Mr. Smith and myself stood in the door of the house in which we were then living, and could distinctly hear their horrid yellings. Not knowing the cause, we supposed they were murdering him. Soon after the screaming commenced, five or six guns were discharged. At this Mr. Smith, folding his arms tight over his breast and grasping his sides, cried, groaning with mental agony, "Oh, my God! my God! they have murdered my son and I must die, for I cannot live without him!"

I was unable to answer him. In all our other troubles I had been able to speak a word of consolation to him, but now I could do nothing but mingle my cries and groans with his. Still, the shrieking and screaming continued. No tongue can ever express the sound that was conveyed to our ears nor the sensations that were produced in our hearts. It was like the screeching of a hundred owls mingled with the howling of an army of bloodhounds and the screaming of a thousand panthers all famishing for the prey which was being torn piecemeal among them.

My husband was immediately taken sick and never regained his health afterwards, although he lived two more years.[2]

It will be seen by the testimony of Hyrum that he was taken by the officers the next day after he arrived at the camp, and that he was seated with Joseph on a log. The soldiers began to crowd around, raging and swearing that they would shoot them. Several guns were snapped at them before anyone interfered.

"Protect them," Captain Martin ordered his men. "Surround the prisoners instantly with drawn swords and loaded muskets. Now, I swear by God, if one of you attempts to harm a hair of the head of one of the prisoners, I will cut his d———d head off in a minute. Do protect them, and if any man attempts to lift a gun to his face to shoot the prisoners, cut him down instantly, for they are innocent men. I know they are innocent. Just look at them. They show the fact in their very faces."[3]

This man was but a captain, but he stood there on guard and kept his men at their places two nights and a day. He neither slept himself, nor suffered his company to rest until Joseph and Hyrum were taken from this place.

When our sons were to be taken away, a messenger came and told us that if we ever were to see our sons alive again, we would have to go immediately to them, as they were in the wagon to be driven to Independence and would be gone in a few minutes. My husband was then too ill to be able to go, but Lucy[4] and I started alone, for we were the only well ones of the family.

When we came within about four hundred yards of the wagon, we could go no farther because they were surrounded by men. "I am the mother of the Prophet," I cried, "and is there not a gentleman here who will assist me through this crowd to that wagon that I may take a last look at my children and speak to them once more before they die?" One individual volunteered to make a pathway through the army, and we went on through the midst of swords, muskets, pistols, and bayonets, threatened with death at every step, until at last we arrived at the wagon. The man who accompanied me spoke to Hyrum, who was sitting in the front, and told him his mother was there and wished him to reach his hand to her. He did so, but I was not permitted to see him, for the cover of the wagon was made of very heavy cloth and tied closely down in front and nailed fast at the sides.

We merely shook hands with him and the other prisoners who sat in the forepart of the wagon, before several of the men in the mob exclaimed, "Drive over them," calling to us to get out of the way, swearing at us and threatening us in the most dreadful manner.

Our friend then conducted us to the hinder part of the wagon where Joseph was, and said, "Mr. Smith, your mother and sister are here and wish to shake hands with you." Joseph crowded his hand through between the wagon and cover where it was nailed down to the end board. We caught hold of his hand, but he did not speak to us. I could not bear to leave him without hearing his voice. "Oh, Joseph," said I. "Do speak to your poor mother once more. I cannot go until I hear you speak."

"God bless you, Mother," he sobbed out. Then a cry was raised and the wagon dashed off, tearing my son from us just as Lucy was pressing his hand to her lips to bestow upon it a sister's last kiss—for we knew that they were sentenced to be shot.[5]

We succeeded in getting to the house again, although we were scarcely able to support ourselves. Before this final moment, the wagon had been driven through Far West and my sons had been allowed to see their families, but not permitted to speak to them nor to visit me.

To describe this scene is impossible. You have read something of how they were rushed from their wives and children amid their sobs and screams. Little Joseph clung to his father and exclaimed, "Oh, my Father. Why can you not stay with us?" They answered his question by pushing the child from his father with their swords, but there is a day when that question will be repeated, "Why did you tear the servant of God from his family and from his home and treat him thus cruelly?"[6] If any of you who did this deed are living, let me warn you to prepare yourselves to answer that question before the bar of God, for I testify to you in the name of Jesus, you will have it to do. Repent, therefore, and be converted, that your sins may be blotted out when the times of refreshment shall come from the presence of the Lord.

I will now return to my family at home. For some time nothing was heard in the house but sighs and groans, as we thought we had seen Joseph and Hyrum for the last time. But in the midst of my grief, I found consolation that surpassed all earthly comfort. I was filled with the Spirit of God and received the following by the gift of prophecy: "Let your heart be comforted concerning your children, for they shall not harm a hair of their heads, and before four years, Joseph shall speak before the judges and great men of the land and his voice shall be heard in their councils. And in five years from this time he will have power over all his enemies."

This relieved my mind, and I was prepared to comfort my children. "My children," said I, "do not cry anymore. The mob will not kill them, for the Lord has signified to me that he will deliver them out of the hands of their enemies." This was a great comfort to us all, and we were not so much distressed afterwards as to their lives being taken.

As soon as William was able to stir about a little, he besought his father to leave the place and move to Illinois, but Mr. Smith would not consent to do this, for he was in hopes that our sons would be liberated and peace be settled again. William still expostulated with him, but to no effect. At last Mr. Smith declared that he would not go away from Far West unless he was called upon to do so by revelation. "Very well, Father," said William, "I can give you revelation, then," and he rehearsed the vision which he had related to me.[7] Mr. Smith answered this by saying that the family might get ready to start, and then if we were obliged to go, there would be nothing to hinder us.

Our business in Far West had been trading in corn and wheat, as well as keeping a public boardinghouse. When the state mob came in, we had some corn and wheat on hand but very little flour or meal, therefore we had sent a young man that lived with us to mill with fourteen bags of grain to be ground. But he had been obliged to leave because the mob was so near at hand that the miller declared it unsafe for the brethren to remain about his mill lest the mob militia should burn his premises. We were therefore obliged for a long time to pound our corn in a samp-mortar[8] to make bread. It was all the breadstuff we had for a length of time, but there were many who subsisted on parched corn.

The people were all driven in from the country, and there was more than an acre of land in front of our house completely covered with beds, lying in the open sun, where men, women, and children were compelled to sleep in all weather. These were the last who had got into the city, and the houses were so full that there was no room for them. It was enough to make the heart ache to see children in the open sun and wind, sick with colds and very hungry, crying around their mothers for food and their parents destitute of the means of making them comfortable, while their houses, which lay a short distance from the city, were pillaged of everything, their fields thrown open for the horses belonging to the mob to lay waste and destroy, and their fat cattle shot down and turning to carrion before their eyes, while a strong guard, which was set over us for the purpose, prevented us from making use of a particle of the stock that was killed on every side of us.

It may be said that this evil certainly might have been provided against if Joseph Smith had the spirit of prophecy. To this I reply that he did all in his power to get the brethren to move into the city before they heard of the mob, but they did not hearken to counsel. Let this be an everlasting warning to the Saints not to reject the counsel of the authorities of the Church because they do not understand the reason of its being given. If the brethren at Haun's Mill had observed to do what they were advised repeatedly to do, their lives would no doubt have been preserved, for they would have been at Far West with the rest of the brethren. I shall not attempt here to give a detail of facts which are already published. My mind is loathe to dwell on these days of sorrow more than is necessary.

When William began to be able to walk, he went to the stable to see after his horse, and not finding him, he inquired of one of the mob officers where his horse was. The officers replied that he had sent a messenger on him with a dispatch to another part of the county. William told him that the horse must be returned, for he would not have him used in any such way. In a little while the dispatch came up, and William took the horse by the bridle and ordered the rider to dismount, with the officer seconding the order. It was obeyed and the horse was led to the stable.

Soon after this the brethren were compelled to lay down their arms and sign away their property. It was done immediately in front of our house, and I could hear General Clark's speech distinctly in which he declared that my sons must die, that "their die was cast, their doom was fixed, their fate was sealed," and also that if he could invoke the spirit of the unknown God to rest upon us, he would advise us to scatter abroad.[9] I thought of the words of Paul to the Athenians and of the scripture which saith, "Ye know not God. I speak this to your shame."[10]

For General Clark did not know that he could not measure arms with the Almighty, or he would not have said so positively what was to befall my imprisoned children.

Soon after Hyrum left home, his youngest son was born.[11] This was Mary's first child.[12] Mary's confinement was considered rather premature, being probably brought on by her extreme anxiety about her husband. She never saw him but once afterwards before she left the state in which he was held a prisoner. Mary suffered in her sickness beyond description, but in her affliction, her sister, Mrs. Thompson,[13] stood by her and devoted her whole time to nursing and comforting her as they were equally alone, for one of their husbands was imprisoned and the other flying for his life. However, she gained sufficient strength to accompany Emma to the prison once before she left the state.

At this time, my husband sent to Joseph to know if it was the will of the Lord that we should leave the state. Whereupon Joseph sent him a revelation which he had received while in prison, which satisfied my husband's mind, and he was willing to remove to Illinois as soon as possible.

After this, William made his arrangements as soon as possible to remove his family to Illinois, and in a short time had them comfortably situated in the town of Plymouth[14] and sent back his team for his father's family.

We loaded the wagon with our goods, but just before we were ready to start, word came that Sidney Rigdon's family were ready to start and they must have the wagon. Thus, we were compelled to remain a season longer until William sent the team again. The wagon was again loaded and again unloaded, for another messenger came, saying that Emma, my son's wife, was ready, and she must have the wagon.[15] However, after a long time, we succeeded in getting one wagon in which to convey beds, clothing, and provisions for our own family and two of our sons-in-law and their families.[16] Don Carlos, my youngest son, was in company with us. He rode with his wife and children in a one-horse buggy, and the greatest part of their baggage was also in our wagon.

In consequence of our crowded situation, we left a large stock of provisions and most of our pursuit[17] in boxes and barrels in the house. But that was not the worst, for our horses were what is termed windbroken, and every hill which we came to, we were obliged to get out and walk, which was both tiresome to the patience and the body.

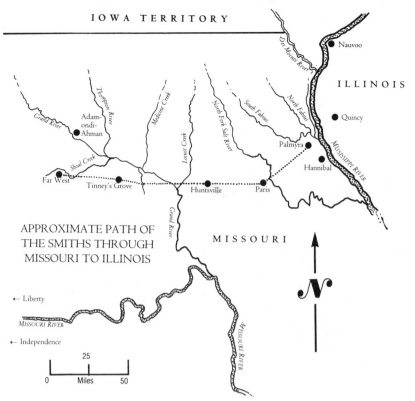

APPROXIMATE PATH OF
THE SMITHS THROUGH
MISSOURI TO ILLINOIS

The first day we arrived at a place called Tinney's Grove,[18] where we lodged in an old log house, spending a rather uncomfortable time. The day after, I traveled on foot half the day, and at night came to the house of one Mr. Thomas, who was then a member of the Church. My husband was very much out of health, as he had not recovered from the shock occasioned by the capture of Hyrum and Joseph, and he suffered much with a severe cough.

The third day in the afternoon, it commenced raining. When night arrived, we stopped at a house and asked permission to stay over. The man of the house showed us a miserable outhouse,[19] filthy enough to sicken the stomach, even to look at, and told us if we would clean this place out and haul our own wood, we might lodge there. We cleaned out the place so as to be able to lay our beds down, and here we spent the night without a fire. The next morning the landlord charged us seventy-five cents for the use of this shed, and we went on in the pouring rain. We asked for shelter at many places but were refused admittance until near night. We traveled through the rain and mud without finding anyone who was willing to take us in. At last we came to one other place very much like where we had spent the night before. Here we stayed all night, again without a fire.

Lucy and Joseph and family came through this area of Missouri in the bitter winter of 1839.[20]

The day after, which was the fifth from the time we started, just before we got to Palmyra, Missouri, Don Carlos called to us and said, "Father, this exposure is too bad and I will not bear it any longer. And the first place I come to that looks comfortable, I shall drive up to the house and go in, and do follow me."

We soon came to a handsome, neat-looking farmhouse which was surrounded with every appearance of comfort. The house stood a short distance from the road, but there was a large gate which opened into the field in front of it. Don Carlos opened the gate, drove into the field, and then, after he had assisted us through, he started to see the landlord, who met him before he came to the house. "Landlord," said Don Carlos, "I do not know but that I am trespassing, but I have with me an aged father, who is sick, besides my mother and a number of women with small children. We have now traveled two days and a half in the rain, and we shall die if we are compelled to go much further. If you will allow us to stay with you overnight, we will pay you any price for our accommodations."

"Why, what do you mean, sir?" said the gentleman. "Do you not consider us human beings? Do you think that we would turn anything that was flesh and blood away from our doors in such a time as this? Where are your parents? Drive your wagons to the door and help your wife and children out. I will attend to the others." He then assisted Mr. Smith and myself into the room where his lady was sitting, but as she was not well and he was afraid the dampness of the room might cause her to take cold, he ordered a black servant to make her a fire in another room. He then helped each one of the family into the house and hung their cloaks and shawls up to dry, saying he never in his life saw a family so uncomfortable from the effects of rainy weather.

At this house we had everything that could conduce to our comfort as this gentleman, whose name was Esquire Mann, did all that he could do to assist us. He brought us milk for our children, hauled us water to wash with, furnished good beds to sleep in, and more. In short, he left nothing undone.

In the evening he remarked that he had been sent by the people of his county the year before to be a member of the House of Representatives, where he met one Mr. Carroll, who was sent from the county where the Mormons resided. "And," said Esquire Mann, "if I ever felt like fighting any man it was him, for he never raised his hand nor his voice in behalf of that abused people once while the House was in session. My blood boiled to hear how they were treated, but I never was a member of the House before and had not sufficient confidence to take a stand in their behalf upon the floor as I would have done if I had been a man of a little more experience."

After spending the night here with this good man, we set out again the next morning, although it continued raining, for we were obliged to travel in order to avoid being detained by high water. We went on through mud and rain until we arrived within six miles of the Mississippi River. Here the ground was low and swampy, so much so that a person on foot would sink in above his ankles at every step. The weather grew colder and it began snowing and hailing, but still we were compelled to go on foot as the horses were not able to draw us. As we were crossing this place, Lucy lost her shoes several times, and her father had to thrust his cane into the mud to ascertain where they were, because they were so completely covered with mud and water.

The Smiths crossed the Mississippi River near here
and spent the rest of the winter in Quincy.

When we came to the Mississippi River, we could not cross nor yet find a place of shelter, for there were many Saints there waiting to go over into Quincy. The snow was now six inches deep and still falling, but we were very tired, and we made up our beds on the snow and went to rest with what comfort we might under such circumstances. The next morning, our beds were covered with snow, but we rose and after considerable pains succeeded in folding up our frozen bedding. We tried to light a fire, but finding it impossible, we resigned ourselves to our situation and waited patiently for some opportunity to cross the river.

Soon after, Samuel came over from Quincy, and he, with Seymour Brunson's[21] assistance, obtained permission of the ferryman to have us cross that day. About sunset we landed in Quincy, where Samuel had hired a house into which we moved. Our household included five other families, namely, Mr. Smith and myself with our daughter, Henry and Hyrum Hoit, also the families of Samuel Smith, Jenkins Salisbury, William McLeary, and Brother Graves.

NOTES

1. This was on Wednesday, October 31, 1838 (at Far West).

2. Joseph Smith Sr. died on September 14, 1840, in Nauvoo.

3. George A. Smith commented about this man in the left margin of his marked copy of the 1853 version: "This is merely Martin's braggadocio to Mother Smith with the design to lead astray her daughter Lucy" (George A. Smith, Edited 1853, p. 250).

4. Young Lucy was seventeen years old.

5. Hyrum Smith gave his testimony of this time period: "I have endeavored to give you a short account of my sufferings while in the state of Missouri, but how inadequate is language to express the feelings of my mind, while under them: knowing that I was innocent of crime, and that I had been dragged from my family at a time, when my assistance was most needed; that I had been abused and thrust into a dungeon, and confined for months on account of my faith, and the 'testimony of Jesus Christ.' However I thank God that I felt a determination to die, rather than deny the things which my eyes had seen, which my hands had handled, and which I had borne testimony to, wherever my lot had been cast; and I can assure my beloved brethren that I was enabled to bear as strong a testimony, when nothing but death presented itself, as ever I did in my life. My confidence in God, was likewise unshaken. I knew that he who suffered me, along with my brethren, to be thus tried, that he could and that he would deliver us out of the hands of our enemies; and in his own due time he did so, for which I desire to bless and praise his holy name. From my close and long confinement, as well as from the sufferings of my mind, I feel my body greatly broke down and debilitated, my frame has received a shock from which it will take a long time to recover; yet, I am happy to say that my zeal for the cause of God, and my courage in defence of the truth, are as great as ever. 'My heart is fixed,' and I yet feel a determination to do the will of God, in spite of persecutions, imprisonments or death; I can say with Paul 'none of these things move me so that I may finish my course with joy.'" (*Times and Seasons* I [December 1839]: 23.)

6. In a revelation received in Liberty Jail nearly six months later, the Lord said to Joseph: "If thou art accused with all manner of false accusations; if thine enemies fall upon thee; if they tear thee from the society of thy father and mother and brethren and sisters; and if with a drawn sword thine enemies tear thee from the bosom of thy wife, and of thine offspring, and thine elder son, although but six years of age, shall cling to thy garments, and shall say, My father, my father, why can't you stay with us? O, my father, what are the men going to do with you? and if then he shall be thrust from thee by the sword, and thou be dragged to prison, and thine enemies prowl around thee like wolves for the blood of the lamb; and if thou shouldst be cast into the pit, or into the hands of murderers, and the sentence of death passed upon thee; if thou be cast into the deep; if the billowing surge conspire against thee; if fierce winds become thine enemy; if the heavens gather blackness, and all the elements

combine to hedge up the way; and above all, if the very jaws of hell shall gape open the mouth wide after thee, know thou, my son, that all these things shall give thee experience, and shall be for thy good." (D&C 122:6–7.)

7. The whole concept of William having had a vision or any kind of revelation was edited out of the 1902 and later versions of the history.

8. A bowl with coarsely ground or parched corn.

9. Lyman Wight testified that, upon their being taken prisoner, "night came on and under the dark shadows of the night, General Wilson, subaltern of General Lucas, took me to one side, and said, 'We do not wish to hurt you nor kill you, neither shall you be, by G—— d——, but we have one thing against you, and that is you are too friendly to Joe Smith, and we believe him to be a G——d d——d rascal! and Wight, you know all about his character.' I said, 'I do, sir.' 'Will you swear all you know concerning him?' said Wilson. 'I will, sir,' was the answer I gave. 'Give us the outlines,' said Wilson. I then told said Wilson I believed said Joseph Smith to be the most philanthropic man he ever saw and possessed of the most pure and republican principles, a friend to mankind, a maker of peace, and 'Sir, had it not been that I had given heed to his counsel I would have given you hell before this time with all your mob forces.' He then observed: 'Wight, I fear your life is in danger, for there is no end to the prejudice against Joe Smith.' 'Kill and be d——d, sir,' was my answer. He answered and said, 'There is to be a court-martial held this night, and will you attend sir?' 'I will not, unless compelled by force,' was my reply. He returned about 11 o'clock that night and took me aside, and said, 'I regret to tell you your die is cast, your doom is fixed, you are sentenced to be shot tomorrow morning on the public square in Far West, at 8 o'clock.' I answered, 'Shoot, and be d——d.'" (*Times and Seasons* 4 [July 15, 1843]: 267.)

10. This is likely a paraphrase of I Corinthians 15:34.

11. Joseph Fielding Smith was born on Tuesday, November 13, 1838. He would become the sixth President of the Church.

12. Hyrum and Jerusha Barden Smith had had six children, five of whom were then living. Mary Fielding Smith, Hyrum's second wife, would bear two children: Joseph Fielding and Martha Ann Smith.

13. Mercy Fielding, sister to Mary, married Robert B. Thompson on June 4, 1837, in Kirtland. The Thompsons were living with Hyrum's family in Far West.

14. Plymouth, Hancock County, Illinois, was located about fifty miles northeast of Quincy, where the main body of the Saints was gathering.

15. Emma and her four children (Julia, Joseph, Frederick, and Alexander) left Far West on February 7, 1839. On this same date, the brethren had contemplated an escape from Liberty Jail. Alexander McRae, a fellow prisoner, later reported: "After we had been there some time, and had tried every means we could to obtain our liberty by the law . . . , and also having heard, from a reliable source, that it had been stated in the public street, by the most influential men in that part of the country, that 'the Mormon prisoners would have to be condemned or the character of the state would have to go down,' we came to the conclusion that we would try other means to effect it.

"Accordingly, on the 7th day of February, 1839, after counseling together on the subject, we concluded to try to go that evening when the jailor came with our supper;

but Brother Hyrum, before deciding fully, and to make it more sure, asked Brother Joseph to inquire of the Lord as to the propriety of the move. He did so, and received answer to this effect—that if we were all agreed, we could go clear that evening; and if we would ask, we should have a testimony for ourselves. I immediately asked, and had not no more than asked, until I received as clear a testimony as ever I did of anything in my life, that it was true. Brother Hyrum Smith and Caleb Baldwin bore testimony to the same: but Lyman Wight said we might go if we chose, but he would not. After talking with him for some time, he said, 'if we would wait until the next day, he would go with us.' Without thinking we had no promise of success on any other day than the one above stated, we agreed to wait.

"When night came, the jailor came alone with our supper, threw the door wide open, put our supper on the table, and went to the back part of the room, where a pile of books lay, took up a book, and went to reading, leaving us between him and the door, thereby giving us every chance to go if we had been ready. As the next day was agreed upon, we made no attempt to go that evening.

"When the next evening came, the case was very different; the jailer brought a double guard with him, and with them six of our brethren, to-wit.: Erastus Snow, William D. Huntington, Cyrus Daniels, David Holeman, Alanson Ripley and Watson Barlow. I was afterwards informed that they were sent by the Church. The jailer seemed to be badly scared; he had the door locked and everything made secure. It looked like a bad chance to get away, but we were determined to try it; so when the jailer started out, we started too. Brother Hyrum took hold of the door, and the rest followed; but before we were able to render him the assistance he needed, the jailer and guard succeeded in closing the door, shutting the brethren in with us. . . .

"The scene that followed this defies description. I should judge, from the number, that all the town, and many from the country, gathered around the jail, and every mode of torture and death that their imagination could fancy, was proposed for us, such as blowing up the jail, taking us out and whipping us to death, shooting us, burning us to death, tearing us to pieces with horses, etc. But they were so divided among themselves that they could not carry out any of their plans." (*History of the Church* 3:257–58.)

16. It appears that this party of the Smiths left sometime in the third or fourth week of February, 1839.

17. "Pursuit" likely refers to those things which they had gathered from and used for their trade business in Far West.

18. Tinney's (or Tenny's) Grove is about twenty-five miles east of Far West (see *History of the Church* 3:319).

19. This is an outbuilding such as a barn or shed and is not a privy.

20. The photograph was taken in Marion County, Missouri, about fifteen miles west of Palmyra along the approximate path the Smiths would have taken.

21. Seymour Brunson, born in 1799, joined the Church in January 1831, served two missions, served on the Missouri and Nauvoo high councils, and died at Nauvoo on August 10, 1840. At his funeral the Prophet Joseph Smith first publicly announced the doctrine of baptism for the dead. (See Cook, *Revelations*, p. 153.)

CHAPTER 50

Lucy and Joseph Sr. gather with members of their family and share their experiences of the expulsion from Missouri. Samuel and party nearly starve to death, but are saved by direction from the Lord. Young Lucy becomes very ill. Mother Smith contracts cholera. Both finally receive their health. Mother Smith sees Joseph and Hyrum in vision as they make their way painfully across Missouri. She prophesies of their arrival. They are reunited in Quincy and rejoice together.

Late February 1839 to May 1839

We spent the evening after we arrived in Quincy[1] relating our adventures in escaping from the hands of our enemies. Samuel's story was very interesting, for he was compelled to fly for his life with a company of others and leave his family behind.

He said that they suffered very much with hunger on their route, as they were pursued by their enemies, and they considered it unsafe to be seen by the inhabitants of the country. Game being very scarce, they soon lacked for provisions and finally ran out altogether, yet they pursued their journey, until they became so faint that they were almost in despair. After counseling together a short time, they concluded to appoint Samuel to receive the word of the Lord, and they united in prayer that the Lord would communicate to them his will concerning what he would have them to do.

After continuing in prayer for some time, it was signified to Samuel that in one-half hour they might obtain some refreshment by traveling in a certain direction. He made this known to the company, and he set out with two others in quest of the promised food. After traveling several miles, they came to an Indian wigwam, and told the Indians by signs that they were hungry. Upon this, the squaw, with all possible speed, made some cakes, baked them in a pan over the fire, and gave each one of them two. They then told her that more of their friends were in the woods far off, and in a trice she made a quantity more of her wheat cakes and gave them to the brethren on a piece of birch bark. She also gave them to understand by signs that she would send more, but she had but little flour and her papooses would be hungry.

After this the brethren traveled on and succeeded in getting sufficient food to sustain them so that none of the company perished. In a short time they separated and took different routes through the country for Quincy, where Samuel arrived some time before we got there.

After we came, it was but a few days before Samuel moved his family into another house, leaving rather more room for those who remained. We soon found that we had many kind neighbors. In fact, they were all kind. One in particular I would mention who lived across the street from us by the name of Messer. This man and his wife seemed to seek every opportunity to oblige us, and while we were there they took care that we were accommodated with everything that we needed which was at their command.

We had not been in Quincy one week when Lucy, my youngest daughter, was taken very sick with a pain in her head and dreadful distress in her limbs, occasioned by her exposure in coming from Missouri. She utterly refused from the first to take any nourishment whatever. I took care of her myself several days, until I was taken in a similar manner myself. The day on which I was taken, Mr. Milliken,[2] a young man to whom she was engaged to be married, came to see her, and he watched with her all that day, for my disease proved to be a very severe case of cholera. Although I suffered dreadfully with the cramp which usually attends that complaint, yet that was nothing in comparison to another pain which operated upon the marrow of my bones and sometimes seemed to me to be almost bursting the bones themselves asunder.

Everything that could be obtained that was known to be good for such diseases was administered in my case, but without effect. Supposing that I could not live any length of time, Lucy wanted to see me, but she was unable to stand on her feet, and Samuel carried her down the stairs in his arms several times before I got any better. At last a young man who was a botanic physician was brought, who gave me a kind of herb tea that relieved me immediately, so that I went to sleep very soon after. I took it and continued from that time getting better until I recovered.

During our sickness, the ladies of Quincy sent us every delicacy which could be obtained, with the hopes of pleasing our appetites, particularly Lucy's, as she was not inclined to take any kind of food into her stomach. When I got better, I found that since she had been sick, she had taken nothing but ice water, but her fever was broken, and by careful nursing, she was soon able to walk about a little.

Previous to our sickness, Mr. Smith had sent one Brother Lamoreaux to Missouri to see if any intelligence could be obtained concerning the prisoners. This man received strict injunctions from the brethren not to return until he saw my sons or knew where they were. He had now been gone a long time, and no intelligence had come of him or the prisoners.

About the time that Lucy began to go about on her feet a little, Brother Partridge and Brother Morley came to our house from Lima[3] to see if Lamoreaux had written or returned. Upon learning that he had not been heard of, Brother Partridge was in despair. He said that he never would consent to having another messenger sent on such business, that he would go himself, for, said he, "you cannot get anybody to do as they ought to do."

Just then news came that Lamoreaux had come back, but had not seen Joseph or Hyrum. Upon this Brother Partridge felt worse than ever, and blamed Lamoreaux very much for non-performance of duty. I listened to him some time. At last an assurance entered my heart that my sons would be at home by the following night, and it filled my soul with such joy that I exclaimed aloud with tears, "Brother Partridge, I shall see my sons again before tomorrow night."

"No," said he, "Mother Smith, I am perfectly discouraged. I don't know as we shall ever see them again in the world. At any rate do not flatter yourself that they will be here as soon as that, for I tell you, you will be disappointed. I have always believed everything you told me before, but I have no faith in what you say, for I cannot see any prospect of your prophecy being fulfilled; but if it proves to be true, I will never dispute you again while I live." I asked him if he would stay in town long enough to see if I told him the truth, and he did so.

That night upon lying down on my bed to go to sleep, I saw my sons in vision on the prairie in Missouri. They appeared to be very tired and hungry. They had but one horse, and I saw them stop and tie him to the burnt stub of a sapling, after which they lay down on the ground to rest themselves. Oh, how pale and faint they looked! I sprang up in bed. "Oh, Father," I said, "I see Joseph and Hyrum, and they are so weak they can scarcely stand, and now they are lying on the cold ground asleep. Oh, how I want to give them something to eat!"

Mr. Smith begged me to be quiet, saying that I was nervous, but it was impossible to rest, for they were still before my eyes and I saw them until they had lain there nearly two hours. Then one of them went away to try to get something to eat, but did not succeed, and they traveled on. This time Hyrum rode and Joseph walked by his side, holding himself up by the stirrup leather. I saw him almost reel with weakness, and yet I could not help him. My soul was grieved, and I could not sleep, so I arose from my bed and spent the night walking the floor.

The next day I commenced making preparations for their reception as confidently as though I had received word that they would be there for supper, but the day was so long and so tedious that in the afternoon near sunset, I went upstairs to consult with Lucy about my cooking. As we came down, she was before me, and when she came to the bottom of the stairs, she screamed out, "There is Elder Baldwin. Oh, my brothers," said she, "where are they?" This was Caleb Baldwin, who had been in prison with my sons. He told us that Hyrum and Joseph were then on their way over the river and would soon be in Quincy. Lucy caught her bonnet and started for Hyrum's house as hard as she could run, but the excitement was not sufficient to keep up her strength, and when she got to the door, she fell prostrate on the floor. After she had communicated the happy news to them, she returned to assist me.

Hyrum and Joseph landed soon after and went immediately to see their families.[4] They, with their wives and the rest of our connections, spent the next day with us. When the news went abroad that the Smiths had been liberated and were now at home, the Quincy Grays came down to our house and saluted them in the most polite manner. Our friends swarmed around us, and we spent the day in eating and drinking and making merry. During the afternoon, I asked Joseph in the presence of the company if they were not on the prairie the night previous in the situation that I saw them in vision. They replied that they were. I then asked Brother Partridge if he now believed what I had told him the evening before. He said he would forever after that time acknowledge me a true prophet. The day passed very pleasantly, and my sons returned to their homes as happy as it was possible for them to be.

A short time after this, we were visited by a man by the name of George Miller[5] from McDonough County, who showed a very friendly disposition and informed us that he had a quantity of land and also a number of log houses that were somewhat out of repair, but if the brethren were disposed to settle on his premises, they might have the use of the houses by repairing them. We were much pleased with the disposition which he manifested, and before he left, my sons Samuel, Don Carlos, and Jenkins Salisbury, my son-in-law, agreed with him for a piece of land sufficient for them to work that season. Samuel returned with him, and after making preparations for their families they removed them to that place.

NOTES

1. Quincy, Illinois, at this time had about 1,800 inhabitants.

2. Arthur Milliken (or Millikin), born May 9, 1817, in Saco, York County, Maine, married Lucy Smith on June 4, 1840, in Nauvoo, Illinois. The couple was married by Joseph the Prophet, Lucy's brother. Arthur and Lucy had one son, Don Carlos Milliken. Arthur died April 23, 1882.

3. Lima, Illinois, is eighteen miles north of Quincy.

4. Joseph and Hyrum arrived at Quincy, Illinois, on Monday, April 22, 1839.

5. George Miller, born November 25, 1794, owned three hundred acres near Macomb, Illinois (about forty-five miles east of Nauvoo). He offered the farm to the exiled Saints from Missouri, as well as hogs and cattle to feed them in their deprived circumstances. He was baptized August 12, 1839, by John Taylor; became "Second Bishop" (like the Presiding Bishop) of the Church in Nauvoo; served missions; helped to build the Nauvoo Temple; but later rejected Brigham Young's leadership and was excommunicated. He followed Lyman Wight in Texas for some time, then James Strang in Wisconsin. He died in 1856 in Illinois. (See Cook, *Revelations*, pp. 268–69.)

CHAPTER 51

Large tracts of land are purchased at Commerce, Illinois. The Smiths move from Quincy to a log cabin in what will later be called Nauvoo. Sickness reigns in Nauvoo and the Smiths' household. Don Carlos's tender letter to his wife. Joseph the Prophet with Sidney Rigdon and others go to Washington, D.C., and visit with President Martin Van Buren to no avail. Mother Smith comments on her love for the Constitution and her sorrow for the nation's departing from the Founding Fathers' ideas. Joseph Smith Sr. gives patriarchal blessings to a number of Saints. Father Smith's health worsens; he gathers his family around him, gives his dying blessings, and passes on. Lucy's sorrow and reflections after forty-four years of marriage.

April 1839 to September 1840

In the spring of 1839 Joseph and Hyrum came to this place, which was then called Commerce,[1] to look at the situation and make a purchase of land in order to gather the Saints together again. They succeeded in buying a large tract of land from Mr. White, who was one of the proprietors of Commerce, and returned for their families.[2] After they left, we remained a short time in Quincy, as we were not ready to leave at that time. But in a few days my sons sent a team after us to bring us to Commerce, for my husband's health was so poor that he was unable to attend to any kind of business, and they wanted to have their father near them. Jacob Bigler came after us, but when he saw how poor my husband's health was, he thought it best to leave the heavy wagon he had brought and get a carriage that would be more pleasant to travel in.

The morning before we started, Mr. Messer came and said that he could not go to work, for he wanted to stay with us while we remained. "This, " said Mr. Messer, "is the first time I ever left my work on account of a neighbor leaving the place." He remained with us all the forenoon, and in the afternoon returned with his wife and stayed till near dark. I have always had the warmest attachment for this family, and I pray God that his choicest blessings may rest upon them.

The next morning we set out for Commerce and proceeded about twenty miles when our carriage broke down, leaving us in the middle of the prairie unable to proceed on our journey. My husband and I sat in the burning sun nearly three hours before the necessary aid could be obtained. Brother Bigler went some distance and got another wagon. We then started on and soon arrived at Bear Creek below Lima. This stream was very high and very dangerous for strangers to cross it at all, but providentially we took the right course and, with much difficulty, got across at Sister Lawrence's house near Lima just after dark. Here we stayed overnight, and the next day came to Commerce, where we found those of our family who were there in good health.

We moved into a small log room attached to the house in which Joseph was living. Here we might have enjoyed ourselves in quiet retirement, but my husband's health still failed, he was fast sinking into the consumption, and medicines were of but little benefit.

As the season advanced, the brethren who had settled here began to feel the effects of the hardships which they had endured, joined with the unhealthiness of the climate in which we were then situated. They came down with agues and bilious fevers to such an extent that there were some whole families in which there was not one who was able to give another a drink of cold water or even to help themselves. Hyrum's family was mostly sick. My youngest daughter, Lucy, was also very sick, and there was, in fact, but few of the inhabitants of the place who were well.

Joseph and Emma had the sick brought to their house and took care of them there. They continued to have them brought as fast as they were taken down, until their house, which consisted of four rooms, was so crowded that they had to spread a tent in the yard for that part of the family who were still on their feet. Joseph and Emma devoted their whole time and attention to the care of the sick during this time of distress.

Joseph Sr., Lucy, and young Lucy moved into this home with Joseph and Emma in May 1839.

Silas Smith, my husband's brother, came up from Pike County to consult my husband upon some Church business and returned with the intention of bringing his family here, but before he could accomplish it, he was taken sick and died, and we never saw him again.[3]

About this time William came from Plymouth and informed us that he had sent to Missouri for our furniture and provisions and that nothing remained of all that we had left, as they had been destroyed by the mob. When William returned, he took Hyrum's oldest daughter, Lovina,[4] who had been sick, with him to Plymouth, thinking that the ride and change of atmosphere would be a benefit to her. Instead she grew much worse, and in a little while she was supposed to be on her deathbed. Her uncle sent word to us that he was afraid that she would not live until we could get there. Her father was not able to sit up when the news came, but Lucy and I started, although Lucy was quite sick and I, myself, would have been unable to go had it not been in a case of extremity. On our arrival at Plymouth, we found her very low, but some better than we expected, for she had revived a little since the messenger had left. She continued to get better from this time until she got quite well, but the ague seemed to take a fresh hold upon Lucy. The journey over the prairie in the hot sun in the dry season of the year, when it was almost impossible to get a drink of cold water to cool her fever, had been a great disadvantage to her health. She remained completely under the power of the disease until the sickness in Commerce had so abated that Joseph could leave home long enough to make a visit to Plymouth.[5]

When he arrived, Lucy was lying on the bed upstairs in a high fever. Upon hearing her brother's voice below, before he even had time to get up the steps, she flew down as though she had been perfectly well. She was so overjoyed to see her brother and hear that her relatives were all alive and through with the dreadful siege of sickness, that the excitement performed an entire cure so that she did not have the ague again and soon got back her strength.

During the summer, in the commencement of the sickness, Don Carlos came from McDonough County to make preparations to establish a printing press, as the press and type had been buried during the Missouri troubles to keep them out of the hands of our enemies. They had gathered so much dampness that the type was considerably injured, and it was necessary to get it into use as soon as possible. He found one room at liberty, and that was an underground room through which a spring was constantly flowing. It needed a great deal of cleaning out before it could be made to answer his purpose at all. He worked alone in this cellar some time, and together the dampness of the place and his labor caused him to take a severe cold with which he was sick for some time. But he continued his work until he had got his press started, and a few numbers of the paper printed.[6] He went to McDonough to see his family, and after this, returned to Commerce, but found the distress so great that no business could be done. After his arrival in Commerce, he wrote the following letter to his wife, which shows pretty clearly the situation of the Church at the time as well as his affectionate disposition, which was always breathed in every word and stamped on every line he wrote to his family.

Commerce, July 29, 1839.

Beloved companion,

I am in tolerable health and have just risen from imploring the throne of grace in your behalf and that of our family—that God would preserve your health and give you every blessing and protect you by day and by night. When I arrived here, there had been nothing done in the office, as Brother Robinson has been sick every day since I left and is sick yet. I have done but little labor since I returned, for I have been striving against the destroyer and attending upon the sick continually. There are not well ones enough to take care of the sick. There has been but one death, however, since I returned, and that was of a child, but one week old. McLeary and Sophronia are both sick. Brother Robinson's wife has been nigh unto death. Father is better. Last Tuesday I administered to sixteen souls and have since administered to a great many in company with George A. Smith, and some notable miracles were wrought with our hands. I never had so great power over disease as I have had this week, for this let God be glorified. The devil is determined to destroy the Saints here. There is between 50 and 100 that are sick, but they are generally on the gain and I do not know of more than two or three who are dangerously sick.

I send you five dollars so that you may not be destitute in case you should be sick or in want of money. My dear, you shall be made happy by me, the Lord being my helper. Hereafter you shall not want. Elijah's God will bless you and I will bless you. You are entwined round my heart with ties that are stronger than death, and time cannot sever them. Yes, deprived of your society and that of my prattling babes,[7] life would be irksome to me. Oh, that you might live till the coming of the Son of Man and I also for your sakes, that I might comfort you and you might comfort me, and we might comfort our babes and instill into their tender and noble minds principles of virtue that God may bless us all that we may be happy. I shall come home as soon as we can get through with our present hurry.

I am as ever your most true and faithful earthly friend both in time and in eternity.

Don C. Smith[8]

We returned to Commerce, and when the weather became cold the sallow faces of the community began to assume a more fresh and ready hue, and all was bustle and business—some building, some fencing, some hauling wood, and indeed all hands were as active in gathering around them the comforts of life as though they had never been disturbed from their possessions, and had no reason to distrust the lasting friendship of those who professed to be their friends.

How often have I looked upon the innocent, cheerful countenances of our brethren and wondered at the difference between them and the dark, lowering, wicked look of the persecutors who thronged our lovely city at the time when Joseph was taken prisoner. The fact is our brethren, when they have the spirit of the gospel upon them, meditate no evil, and consequently, they fear no evil, until they are taught to fear as the sheep is taught to fear the fierce wolf or tiger. But now they have had sufficient experience to make them more wary than they once were, so that they will be likely for the future to calculate both ways and not lick the hand just raised to shed their blood.

It now became a duty for Joseph to fulfill a commandment which he received while in prison to go as soon as he could leave home to the city of Washington and petition Congress for redress. He said that if

The center for the Smith family was here until August 1843,
when the Mansion House was done.

there was any virtue in the government that they might not fail to do justice for want of a correct understanding of the facts. Accordingly, Joseph set off with Sidney Rigdon, Dr. Foster, Elias Higbee, and Porter Rockwell for the seat of government.[9]

After arriving in Washington, Joseph and Sidney waited upon his excellency Martin Van Buren[10] for some time. They had no opportunity to lay their grievances before him, as rather than lend an ear to the complaints of a distressed people, he chose to give his attention to the frivolous chat of visitors, who had no other business but to compliment him upon his fine circumstances. At length, however, he concluded to listen to them, and heard the entire history of our oppression, and the abuse we had received from our existence as a people until the slaughter of our brethren at Haun's Mill, and our final expulsion from our homes. They concluded with an appeal to him as the principal officer of this great, mighty republic for his assistance.

Has not everyone read our tale of woe? If you have not, I beseech you to take the trouble to do so. I've not told the half, but if you will peruse a pamphlet entitled "Missouri Persecutions," you will then be able to appreciate the magnanimous reply of this mighty ruler of a mighty republic when his heart was under the fresh influence of the story of his people's grief. "Hear it ye nations. Hear it, oh ye dead." Martin Van Buren said, *"Gentlemen, your cause is just, but I can do nothing for you."*[11]

You, that at the peril of your lives, your fortunes, and your sacred honor stepped forth and placed your names upon the list attached to the Declaration of Independence, and nobly stood targets for the vengeance of the oppressor, willing to sacrifice your own lives to save your countrymen—look down upon your children, spirit of our departed. Washington, but little did you expect that sacred seat which you so lately occupied,[12] and from which you dealt out evenhanded justice to all, would be so very soon filled by one who can do nothing for your own fellow soldiers, when they are murdered upon the soil that you and they defended breast to breast.

But we are your children. We love the Constitution and the law and we will abide the same. We love those hearts from whose pure depths that Constitution emanated. We love the many that fought for us in our infant years. We have your brethren in our midst, some who battled by your side. We honor and we cherish and we love them. The scheme of our national salvation we dearly love, but oh, the hands in which it is placed! They will not take thee for an example. Therefore, we go mourning all the day long, and the chain of the oppressor lays heavy on our necks. Our feet are fettered, our hands are shackled, and behold we are cast into prison, for is this all? We are even murdered, and yet no one has raised the yoke, but still we bow down and bear our grief.

The matter was, however, laid before Congress. They too concluded that our cause was just, but that they could do nothing for us, as Missouri was a sovereign, independent state; and that the "Mormons" might appeal to her for redress, for, in their opinion, she neither wanted the power nor lacked the disposition to redress the wrongs of her own citizens.

Joseph remained with his brethren in Washington until a decision was had upon the subject. While he was absent, his father was very feeble. His cough increased, and he became so weak, that I was often under the necessity of lifting him from his bed. One night I was raising him and he said, "Mother, I don't know but I shall die here alone with you, and perhaps in your arms while lifting me."

"Oh, no, Father," said I, "you will not; for when you die, you will have all your children round you."

"Well," said he, "if you say so in real earnest, I believe it will be so." I told him that it was impressed upon my mind that such would be the case. He was much comforted by this, for he had been very anxious to live until Joseph returned, that he might bless him again before he died.

This was in the winter of 1840. Before spring he got some better so that he walked around the neighborhood and even attended to blessing some few of the brethren, among whom was Elder John E. Page[13] and his wife, Mary. On this occasion he stood upon his feet three hours, and when he got through blessing and preaching, he laid hands on Brother Page, who was terribly afflicted with the black canker, but was healed very suddenly, for there was a great manifestation of the Spirit of God at this meeting.

He gave one person a blessing whom he had never seen before that day, and who had not been in the Church a fortnight. When he blessed her, he repeated a prophecy word for word that had been pronounced upon her head by Brother Page and said that the Spirit testified that she had been told these things in her confirmation. This surprised her, for she had just arrived in Nauvoo with Brother and Sister Page, and she knew that not one word had passed between him and my husband upon the subject.

In March of 1840, Mr. Smith had a relapse and was confined again to his bed, not able to help himself out of it. I was standing by the window and saw Joseph coming, for he had just arrived from Washington.[14] I told Mr. Smith that Joseph was coming and he cried for joy at the thought that he had been spared to see Joseph's face again. Joseph came immediately into the room, and before he left, he laid hands on him and assisted him out of bed.

Joseph's family were rejoiced to see him again, for they had heard many reports of danger which had threatened him, and Emma had suffered much uneasiness on the account. The Church was also much rejoiced to meet him, but had they yielded their feelings to the influence of circumstances, their joy would have been mingled with grief, for the Senate of the United States sent back our brethren with documents saying that as Missouri was the place where our difficulties occurred, she alone could exercise jurisdiction in the affair of our trouble, and that

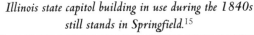

Illinois state capitol building in use during the 1840s still stands in Springfield.[15]

whatever might be the outrages committed upon us by the inveterate state of Missouri, we had no hopes of redress. We plainly discovered that murder was licensed and *every outrage upon us permitted.* However, we did not lose all hopes of resting from persecution for a season. At least the authorities of Illinois had been very forward to give us every assurance of their honor, and it is our motto ever to trust our friends until they betray our trust, and so we acted in this instance, resting perfectly secure upon the laws which were then, and for some time after, promptly executed.

After Joseph's arrival, he had a house erected for his father, and we were soon very comfortably situated. My husband seemed to revive a little in the spring, but when the heat of the ensuing summer came on, he began to fail again. This was perhaps partially because Missouri again renewed her persecutions against us and sent officers with writs demanding sixty of our brethren, my sons with the rest considered as fugitives from *justice* (as they chose to call their proceedings just). The brethren concluded at this time to fly from such justice and were obliged to leave the city and absent themselves from their families for some time before the writs were returned.

About this time, General John C. Bennett[16] came into the city and undertook to devise a scheme that would result in the security of our persecuted brethren, that they might remain at home in peace. I do not know what he did. I only know that he seemed to be very much engaged about law as well as the gospel. My heart was then too full of anxiety about my husband to inquire much into matters which I did not understand; however, the result was, Joseph returned from Iowa.

On the evening of his return, his father was taken with vomiting blood. This was the first time that I had allowed myself to doubt but that he would sooner or later recover from his illness, but I now concluded that he was appointed unto death. I sent for Joseph and Hyrum, who, when they came, gave him something to relieve his distress, and he became more easy. This was on Saturday night.[17]

On Sunday, Joseph came in and said, "Now, Father, I am at liberty and I can stay with you as much as you wish. Bennett is here and he will fix things so that we will not be in danger of being disturbed by the Missourians." His father was delighted to hear it, for he knew that he could live but a short time and he wished Joseph to remain with him.

After which Joseph informed his father, that it was then the privilege of the Saints to be baptized for the dead, and Mr. Smith requested that Joseph should be baptized for Alvin immediately.

We had sent for the children who did not live in the city and they had all got here save Catharine, who was detained by a sick husband and sick children. Mr. Smith, being apprised of this, sent Arthur Milliken, who, but a short time previous, was married to our youngest daughter,[18] after Catharine and her children. Mr. Milliken made all haste to get a team and to make the necessary preparations for his journey. Before he went, however, my husband blessed him, as he feared that it might be too late when he returned. He took him by the hand and said:

"Arthur, my son, I have given you my darling, my youngest child, and will you be kind to her?"

"Yes, Father," he replied, "I will."

"Arthur," he continued, "you shall be blessed, and you shall be great in the eyes of the Lord, and if you will be faithful, you shall have all the desires of your heart in righteousness. Now, I want you to go after my daughter Catharine, for I know the faithfulness of your heart, that you will not come back without her."

Arthur then left. After he was gone, he called us all around his bed and addressed me first.[19]

"Mother," said he, "do you not know that you are the mother of the greatest family that ever lived upon the earth?[20] The world loves its own, but it does not love us. It hates us because we are not of the world; therefore, all their malice is poured out upon us, and they seek to take away our lives. When I look upon my children and realize that although they were raised up to do the Lord's work, yet they must pass through scenes of trouble and affliction as long as they live upon the earth, my heart is pained and I dread to leave you so surrounded by enemies."

At this Hyrum bent over his father and said, "Father, if you are taken away, will you not intercede for us at the throne of grace, that our enemies may not have so much power over us to distress and harass us?" His father laid his hands upon Hyrum's head[21] and said:

"My son, Hyrum, I seal upon your head your patriarchal blessing which I placed on your head before, for that shall be verified. In addition, I now give you my dying blessing. You shall have a season of peace, so that you shall have sufficient rest to accomplish the work which God has given you to do. You shall be as firm as the pillars of heaven unto the end of your days. I seal upon your head the patriarchal power, and you shall bless the people. This is my dying blessing upon your head in the name of Jesus. Amen."

To Joseph he said:

"Joseph, my son, you are called to a high and holy calling. You are called to do the work of the Lord. Now, hold out faithful and you will be blessed, and your family shall be blessed, and your children after you. You shall live to finish your work."

At this Joseph cried out, "Oh, Father, shall I?"

"Yes," said his father, "you shall. You shall live to lay out all the plan of all the work that God requires at your hand.[22] Be faithful to the end. This is my dying blessing on your head in the name of Jesus. I also confirm your former blessing upon you, for it shall be fulfilled. Even so. Amen."

To Don Carlos he said:

"Carlos, my darling son, you remember that when I blessed you, your blessing never was written, and I could not get it done, but now I want you to get my book, which contains the blessings of my family. I want you to take your pen and fill out those parts of your blessing that were not written. You shall have the Spirit of the Lord and shall be able to fill up all the vacancies which were left by Oliver when he wrote it. You shall be great in the sight of the Lord, for he sees and knows the integrity of your heart, and you shall be blessed; and all that know you shall bless you. Your wife and your children shall also be blessed, and you shall live to fulfill all the Lord has sent you to do.[23] Even so. Amen."

To Samuel he said:

"Samuel, you have been a faithful and obedient child. By your faithfulness, you have brought many into the Church. The Lord has seen your faithfulness and you are blessed in that the Lord has never chastised you, but has called you home to rest; and there is a crown laid up for you which shall grow brighter and brighter until the perfect day.[24]

"When the Lord called you, he said, 'Samuel, I have seen thy sufferings, have heard thy cries, seen thy faithfulness, and your skirts are clear of the blood of this generation.' This is my dying blessing, and all the blessings which I have before pronounced upon you I now seal upon you again. Even so. Amen."

To William he said:

"William, my son, thou hast been faithful in declaring the word, even before the Church was organized. Thou hast been sick, yet thou hast traveled to warn the people. And when thou couldst not walk, thou didst sit by the wayside and call upon the Lord, until he did provide a way for thee to be carried. Thou wast sick and afflicted, when thou wast away from thy father's house, and no one knew it to assist thee in thy afflictions; but the Lord did see the honesty of thy heart, and thou wast blessed in thy mission. William, thou shalt be blessed, and thy voice shall be heard in distant lands, from place to place, and they shall regard thy teachings and thy voice. Thou shalt be like a roaring lion in the forest, for they shall hearken and hear thee. And thou shalt be the means of bringing many sheaves to Zion, and thou shalt be great in the eyes of many people, and they shall call thee blessed, and I will bless thee and thy children after thee. And the blessings which I sealed upon thy head before I now confirm again, and thy days shall be many[25] and thou shall do a great work and live as long as thou desire life. Even so. Amen."

To Sophronia he said:

"Sophronia, my oldest daughter, thou hadst sickness when thou wast young.[26] Thy mother and thy father did cry over thee to have the Lord spare thy life. Thou didst see trouble and sorrow,[27] but thy trouble shall be lessened, for thou hast been faithful in helping thy father and thy mother in the work of the Lord. And thou shalt be blessed, and the blessings of heaven shall rest down upon you and your last days shall be your best days. Although thou shalt see trouble and sorrow and mourning, thou shalt be comforted and the Lord will lift you up and the blessings of the Lord will rest upon you and upon your family. Thou shalt live as long as thou desirest life.[28] I pronounce this dying blessing with your other blessings I seal upon your head. Even so. Amen."

After this he rested some time and then said:

"Catharine has been a sorrowful child. Trouble has she seen, and the Lord has looked down upon her and seen her patience[29] and has heard her cries. She shall be comforted when her days of sorrow are ended. Then shall the Lord look down upon her, and she shall have the comforts of life and the good things of the world, and then shall she rise up and defend her cause. And she shall live to raise up her family and in time her suffering shall be over, for the day is coming when the patient shall receive their reward. She shall rise over her enemies, and she shall have houses and land and things around her to make her heart glad. I, in this dying blessing, confirm her patriarchal blessing upon her head,[30] and she shall receive eternal life. Even so. Amen."

To Lucy he said:

"Lucy, thou art my youngest child, thou art my darling. And the Lord gave you unto us to be a comfort to us in our old age, and thou must take good care of thy mother.[31] Thou art innocent and thy heart is right before the Lord. Thou hast been through all the persecution and hast seen nothing but persecution, trouble, and sickness except when the Lord would cheer our hearts. If thou wilt continue and hold out faithful, thou shalt be blessed with a house and land, and thou shalt have food and raiment and no more be persecuted and driven as thou hast hitherto been. And continue faithful and you shall receive a reward in heaven and you shall live long and be blessed, and thou shalt receive a reward in heaven. And now I seal this dying blessing and your patriarchal blessing upon your head. Even so. Amen."

He then called to me again. "Mother," said he, "where are you?" I was standing at his back, but went immediately to his head. "Do you not know that you are one of the most singular women in the world?"

I said, "No, I do not."

"Well," said he, "I do. You have brought up my children for me by the fireside, and when I was gone from home, you comforted them. You have brought up all my children and could always comfort them when I could not. We have often wished that we might both die at the same time, but you must not desire to die when I do. You must stay to comfort the children when I am gone.[32] So do not mourn, but try to be comforted. Your last days shall be your best days, as to being driven, for you shall have more power over your enemies than you have had. Now, be comforted."

He paused and then said, "Why, I can see and hear as well as ever I could." (A pause.) "And I have my senses perfectly well." (A pause of some minutes.) "I see Alvin." (Another pause.) "I shall live seven or eight minutes." He then straightened himself, laid his hands together, and began to breathe shorter and shorter until at last his breath stopped without a struggle or even a sigh.[33] He departed so calmly that we could not believe for some time but that he would breathe again.

I am convinced that no one but a widow can imagine the feelings of a widow, but my situation was not such as is common in similar cases. My beloved companion who had shared my joy and grief for forty-four years lay before me, a cold, lifeless corpse, and the cold hand which I held in mine returned the pressure of my own no longer. My fatherless children stood around me, gazing in agony upon those eyes which had, until a few minutes ago, always beamed upon them with the tenderest gaze. I then thought that there was no evil for me to fear upon the earth more than what I had experienced in the death of my beloved husband. It was all the grief which my nature was able to bear, and I thought that I could never again be called to suffer so great an affliction as this. I reflected upon the many years of happiness which I had spent with him, and that the one with whom I had spent my life was now buried beneath the cold clods, and that portion of my life which lay before seemed desolate indeed. I thought that the greatest sorrow of which it was possible for me to experience had fallen upon me.

My children were all there save Catharine, who did not arrive until the evening of the second day.[34] We were compelled to attend his obsequies the day following his death or run the risk of seeing Hyrum and Joseph torn from their father's corpse and carried to prison and perhaps to Missouri by our enemies, for they had obtained another writ which they were hurrying to the city in order to serve it upon my sons.

My own heart was broken, and I had but one reason to desire life, which was, as Mr. Smith said in his dying moments, that I might comfort my children. All that has transpired since that period, except the calamities which have befallen my own family, is like a shadow or a dream. From this time I shall enumerate the events of my life as rapidly as possible and shall endeavor to suppress my feelings altogether, until I have related the remainder of what I have to tell.[35]

The evening after my husband was buried, Catharine arrived at our house, bringing her husband upon a bed, sick with the ague. She remained with me some time and comforted me what she could.

NOTES

1. Later known as Nauvoo, Hancock County, Illinois.

2. For Wednesday, May 1, 1839, Joseph Smith recorded: "I this day purchased, in connection with others of the committee, a farm of Hugh White, consisting of one hundred and thirty-five acres, for the sum of five thousand dollars; also a farm of Dr. Isaac Galland, lying west of the White purchase, for the sum of nine thousand dollars" (*History of the Church* 3:342).

3. In her Early Notebook, Lucy recorded about her brother-in-law Silas Smith: "During his last sickness he saw many important visions which I would be glad to relate but cannot remember them clearly enough to do so" (Early Notebook, p. 49).

4. Lovina was nearly twelve years old at this time.

5. Joseph the Prophet had also been sick with the malarial fevers that were rampant around the mosquito-infested swamps of the Mississippi bottomlands. Wilford Woodruff wrote about what happened on July 22, 1839: "[Joseph] arose from his bed and commenced to administer to the sick in his own house and door-yard, and he commanded them in the name of the Lord Jesus Christ to arise and be made whole; and the sick were healed upon every side of him. Many lay sick along the bank of the river; Joseph walked along up to the lower stone house, occupied by Sidney Rigdon, and he healed all the sick that lay in his path. . . . He called upon Elder Kimball and some others to accompany him across the river to visit the sick at Montrose. . . . The first house he visited was that occupied by Elder Brigham Young . . . , who lay sick. Joseph healed him, then he arose and accompanied the Prophet on his visit to others who were in the same condition. . . . The next place they visited was the home of Elijah Fordham, who was supposed to be about breathing his last. . . . The Prophet of God walked up to the dying man and took hold of his right hand and spoke to him; but Brother Fordham was unable to speak, his eyes were set in his head like glass, and he seemed entirely unconscious of all around him. . . . Joseph asked him if he had faith to be healed. He answered, 'I fear it is too late; if you had come sooner I think I would have been healed.' The Prophet said, 'Do you believe in Jesus Christ?' He answered in a feeble voice, 'I do.' Joseph then stood erect, still holding his hand in silence several moments; then he spoke in a very loud voice, saying, 'Brother Fordham, I command you, in the name of Jesus Christ, to arise from this bed and be made whole.' . . . It seemed as though the house shook to its very foundations. Brother Fordham arose from his bed, and was immediately made whole. His feet were bound in poultices which he kicked off; then putting on his clothes he ate a bowl of bread and milk and followed the Prophet into the street." (*History of the Church* 4:3–4.)

6. For November 1839, *History of the Church* records: "Some time this month the first number of the *Times and Seasons*, a monthly religious paper, in pamphlet form, was published at Commerce, Hancock County, Illinois, by my brother Don Carlos Smith and Ebenezer Robinson, under the firm name of Robinson & Smith, Publishers" (*History of the Church* 4:23).

7. At this time Don Carlos and Agnes had two daughters—Agnes, three, and Sophronia, fourteen months. They would have one more daughter, Josephine, who would be born five months before Don Carlos's death.

8. In the Preliminary Manuscript, the paragraph preceding the letter from Don Carlos (beginning with "During the summer, in the commencement of the sickness . . .") through and including the letter to his wife were placed by Mother Smith in the midst of her story about Joseph leaving for Washington, D.C. (specifically following the line which reads: "Accordingly, Joseph set off with Sidney Rigdon, Dr. Foster, Elias Higbee, and Porter Rockwell for the seat of government"). The paragraph preceding the letter was not included in any edition. The letter from Don Carlos to Agnes was added to the appendix of the 1853 edition.

9. Joseph recorded: "While on the mountains some distance from Washington, our coachman stepped into a public house to take his grog, when the horses took fright and ran down the hill at full speed. I persuaded my fellow travelers to be quiet and retain their seats, but had to hold one woman to prevent her throwing her infant out of the coach. The passengers were extremely agitated, but I used every persuasion to calm their feelings; and opening the door, I secured my hold on the side of the coach the best way I could, and succeeded in placing myself in the coachman's seat, and reining up the horses, after they had run some two or three miles, and neither coach, horses, or passengers received any injury. My course was spoken of in the highest terms of commendation, as being one of the most daring and heroic deeds, and no language could express the gratitude of the passengers, when they found themselves safe, and the horses quiet. There were some members of Congress with us, who proposed naming the incident to that body, believing they would reward such conduct by some public act; but on inquiring my name, to mention as the author of their safety, and finding it to be Joseph Smith the 'Mormon Prophet,' as they called me, I heard no more of their praise, gratitude, or reward." (*History of the Church* 4:23–24.)

10. Martin Van Buren was the eighth president of the United States and served from 1837 to 1841. The economic crash of 1837 came during his administration (the same that had caused the spirit of speculation to run wild in Kirtland) and led to about five years of depression and economic disaster in the nation, with hundreds of banks and businesses failing and thousands of people losing their lands.

11. Joseph recorded that Van Buren also said, "*If I take up for you I shall lose the vote of Missouri.*" Joseph's history goes on to say of Van Buren, "His whole course went to show that he was an office-seeker, that self-aggrandizement was his ruling passion, and that justice and righteousness were no part of his composition." On his way home Joseph said about this president, "May he never be elected again to any office of trust or power." And indeed Van Buren never was. (*History of the Church* 4:80, 89.) Wilford Woodruff later reported in an 1877 discourse a vision he had in the St. George Temple: "I will here say, before closing, that two weeks before I left St. George, the spirits of the dead gathered around me, wanting to know why we did not redeem them. Said they, 'You have had the use of the Endowment House for a number of years, and yet nothing has ever been done for us. We laid the foundation of the

government you now enjoy, and we never apostatized from it, but we remained true to it and were faithful to God.' These were the signers of the Declaration of Independence, and they waited on me for two days and two nights. I thought it very singular, that notwithstanding so much work had been done, and yet nothing had been done for them. The thought never entered my heart, from the fact, I suppose, that heretofore our minds were reaching after our more immediate friends and relatives. I straightway went into the baptismal font and called upon brother McCallister to baptize me for the signers of the Declaration of Independence, and fifty other eminent men, making one hundred in all, including John Wesley, Columbus, and others; *I then baptized him for every President of the United States, except three; and when their cause is just, somebody will do the work for them.*" (In *JD* 19:229—September 16, 1877; emphasis added.)

12. President George Washington was still president when Lucy Mack and Joseph Smith married in Tunbridge, Vermont (having served from the time Lucy Mack was nearly fourteen years old until she was nearly twenty-two).

13. John Edward Page, born February 25, 1799, was baptized by Emer Harris on August 18, 1833. He was ordained an Apostle on December 19, 1838. After the death of his first wife, Lorain Stevens, he married Mary Judd in January 1839. He failed to go with the Twelve to England in 1839 as called. He was also assigned to go with Orson Hyde to Jerusalem in 1840 and did not complete the mission. He did not support Brigham Young and the Twelve in their leadership after Joseph's death, was excommunicated June 26, 1846, and decided to follow James Strang. He later helped the Hedrickites in gaining possession of the Independence Temple lot. He died near Sycamore, Illinois, on October 14, 1867. (See Cook, *Revelations*, pp. 232–33.)

14. Joseph the Prophet arrived safely from Washington on Wednesday, March 4, 1840 (see *History of the Church* 4:89).

15. This building is now used only for state offices and is no longer used as the capitol.

16. John Cook Bennett, born August 4, 1804, was a trained and skilled medical doctor and did extensive research in this field, publishing many articles in the medical journals of the day. He was appointed brigadier general of the Illinois militia by Governor Thomas Carlin on February 20, 1839. He moved to Nauvoo in early September 1840 and was baptized soon thereafter. He was instrumental in obtaining the city charter, and charters for the Nauvoo Legion and the University of Nauvoo. He was elected the first mayor of Nauvoo, and appointed Assistant President to Joseph Smith. He resigned as mayor on May 17, 1842, and was excommunicated eight days later for adultery and teaching that illicit sexual relations were condoned by Church leaders. He published an anti-Mormon book in 1842, associated with James Strang, practiced medicine, and finally died on August 5, 1867, never returning to the Church. (See Cook, *Revelations*, p. 253.)

17. It appears that this was Saturday, September 12, 1840.

18. Arthur Milliken and Lucy Smith were married (as noted, on June 4, 1840) just 102 days before Joseph Smith Sr. passed away.

19. This tender scene must have taken place late in the evening on Sunday, September 13, 1840, and into the early hours of the next morning. Patriarch Joseph Smith Sr. passed away on Monday, September 14, 1840.

20. In all versions after the Preliminary Manuscript, Father Smith is quoted as saying, "Mother, do you not know, that you are the mother of as great a family as ever lived upon the earth?"

21. In this dying blessing of Father Smith's upon the head of Hyrum, the pattern is seen for the rest of the blessings that would be given that night, namely, by the laying on of hands.

22. Joseph and Hyrum would be killed just three years and nine months after the death of their father.

23. This is poignant in that Don Carlos passed away just eleven months later.

24. Samuel would pass away three years and ten months after his father.

25. William Smith's days were long, as he lived to be eighty-two years old, passing away November 13, 1893.

26. Likely referring to the typhoid fever she had for ninety days, nearly dying when she was about ten years old.

27. In Sophronia's patriarchal blessing given in Kirtland, her father said that she had suffered "much sickness and much sorrow because of the conduct of thy husband." Calvin Stoddard had at one time surrendered his preaching license for inactivity and transgression.

28. Sophronia passed away in late summer or early fall 1876.

29. Catharine (or Katharine, as she later spelled it) struggled with her husband's liquor problems and with his occasionally deserting her family. Her husband, Wilkins Jenkins Salisbury, passed away October 28, 1853 (according to his gravestone in old Webster Cemetery near Fountain Green, Illinois).

30. In her 1834 blessing from her father she was told she would "live to a good old age." She died February 2, 1900 (according to her gravestone), at age eighty-seven. She was the oldest survivor of the Smith family.

31. Lucy cared for her mother for seven years, until Mother Smith moved in with Emma for her remaining years.

32. Mother Smith would be a widow for nearly sixteen years.

33. Patriarch Joseph Smith Sr.'s age at death was sixty-nine years, two months, and two days.

34. Catharine arrived on Wednesday evening, September 16, 1840. Her father had been buried on Tuesday, the day before she arrived. That the family could not wait for Catharine to arrive shows their great fear of Joseph and Hyrum's being arrested and taken back to Missouri on the false charges still leveled against them there.

35. Though more than four years of events would pass from the death of Father Smith until the writing of her history, Mother Smith records only a few short pages, the greatest portion of which would give her feelings about the martyrdom of her sons. Truly her heart had been broken.

CHAPTER 52

City of Nauvoo established. Lucy's severe illness. Death of a number of the Smith family, including Samuel's wife, Mary; Don Carlos; Hyrum's brother-in-law Robert Thompson; Joseph's toddler son, Don Carlos; Hyrum's son Hyrum; and Don Carlos's daughter Sophronia. Joseph the Prophet put on trial in Monmouth, Illinois. Assassination attempt on ex-Governor Lilburn Boggs of Missouri. Joseph and Orrin Porter Rockwell are accused. To avoid false arrest, Joseph goes into hiding. Joseph is tried and acquitted in Springfield. Joseph is arrested in Dixon, Illinois. He is tried in Nauvoo, Hyrum gives sworn testimony, and Joseph is acquitted.

December 1840 to October 1843

In the month of December, 1840, we received for Nauvoo a city charter with extensive privileges; and in February of the same winter, charters were also received for the Nauvoo Legion and for the University of the City of Nauvoo. Not long after this the office of lieutenant-general was conferred upon Joseph by the vote of the people and a commission from the governor of the state.[1]

In the early part of the same winter, I made Brother Knowlton a visit on Bear Creek. When I arrived there it was dark and I was very cold, and in getting out of the wagon, I stepped upon some round substance which, rolling under my foot, brought me round so suddenly, that in trying to save myself from falling, I injured my right knee. The cold settled in the injured part and the rheumatism set in. I suffered considerable while there, but I only remained about one week. After I returned home, my sickness increased. This, with other sickness produced by the same

Nauvoo arose from the mosquito-infested swamps and became, like its name, "a beautiful place."

cause, kept me very low all winter, and for six weeks I had watchers every night. Sophronia and Lucy took care of me and faithfully did they watch over me. Never was a disconsolate widow more blessed in her children than I was in them. By their faithful care I was enabled, after a long season of helplessness, to stand upon my feet again.

The same winter, on the twenty-fifth of January, 1841, Mary Smith, Samuel's wife, was taken suddenly away to meet my husband where parting shall be no more.[2] She had never been well since she was driven with her infant by the Missouri mob into Far West, and that was the cause of her death.

On the fifth of June the same year, Joseph went, in company with several others, on a visit to Quincy. As he was returning, Governor Carlin sent one of the Missouri writs after him and had him arrested for murder, treason, etc., etc. Joseph, choosing to be tried at Monmouth,[3] Warren County, returned the next day with the officers to Nauvoo and, after procuring witnesses, proceeded to Monmouth. Esquire Browning spoke in Joseph's defense, and was moved upon by the spirit that was given him, in answer to the prayers of the Saints; and, of course, he gained the case. The opposing attorney tried his utmost to convict Joseph of the crimes mentioned in the writ, but before he had spoken many minutes, he turned sick and vomited at the feet of the judge; which, joined to the circumstance of his advocating the case of the Missourians, who are called pukes by their countrymen, obtained for him the same appellation, and was a source of much amusement to the court.

The Church was much rejoiced when Joseph returned, and many besought him never again to leave the city.

About the first of August, Don Carlos came to me and told me that for a long time he had suffered such distress in his side, that he thought the same disease had fastened upon him as his father had, and he feared it would sooner or later take him away. He was taken bedfast the same day, and on the seventh day of August, he died, and on the eighth he was buried under the honors of war.[4]

On the first day of September, Robert B. Thompson,[5] who was Hyrum's brother-in-law and associate editor with Don Carlos of the *Times and Seasons*, died of the same disease which carried Carlos out of the world—supposed to be quick consumption.

On the fifteenth of September, Joseph's youngest son, who was named after Don Carlos, died after a long season of sickness and distress.[6]

On the twenty-eighth of September, Hyrum's second son, named Hyrum, died of a fever.[7]

The succeeding winter we were left to mourn over the ravages which death had made in our family, without interruption; but sickness ceased from among us, and the mob retired to their homes.

On the sixth of May, 1842, some assassin attempted to shoot Lilburn W. Boggs, ex-governor of Missouri, and in a trice[8] the cry went forth that "Joe Smith" had shot Governor Boggs. But, as Joseph was on that day at an officer's drill in Nauvoo, several hundred miles from

Joseph was no longer safe on the streets of Nauvoo after the attempted assassination of Boggs.

where Boggs resided, and was seen by hundreds, and, on the day following, at a public training, where thousands of witnesses beheld him, we supposed that the crime being charged upon him was such an outrage upon common sense that when his persecutors became apprised of these facts, they would cease to accuse him. But in this we were disappointed, for when they found it impossible to sustain the charge in this shape, they preferred it in another, in order to make it more probable. They now accused my son of sending O. P. Rockwell into Missouri with orders to shoot the ex-governor, and from this time they pursued both Joseph and Porter with all diligence, till they succeeded in getting the latter into jail in Missouri.

Joseph, not choosing to fall into their hands, fled from the city and secreted himself sometimes in one place, sometimes in another. He generally kept some friends with him, in whom he had confidence, who came frequently to the city. Thus communication was kept up between Joseph, his family, and the Church. At this time Brother John Taylor lay very sick of the fever and was so reduced that he was not able to stand upon his feet. Joseph visited him and, after telling him that he wished to start that night on a journey of fifty miles, requested Brother Taylor to accompany him, saying if he would do so he would be able to ride the whole way. Brother Taylor believing this, they set out together and performed the journey with ease.

This time Joseph remained away two weeks, then made his family and myself a short visit, after which he again left us. In this way he lived, hiding first in one place and then in another,[9] until the sitting of the legislature when Governor Ford wrote Joseph a letter advising him to come to Springfield, with a guard sufficient to secure himself against molestation, and suffer himself to be tried for the crimes alleged against him, namely, that of being accessory to the attempted assassination of ex-Governor Boggs. Joseph went and was tried before Judge Pope and honorably acquitted. When he returned home, there was a jubilee held throughout the city. The remainder of the winter, and the next spring, we spent in peace.

About the middle of June, 1843, Joseph went with his wife to visit Mrs. Wasson, who was his wife's sister.[10] While he was there, an attempt was made to kidnap him and take him into Missouri, by J. H. Reynolds

Joseph's trial here in this Springfield courtroom has become famous in Illinois's legal history.[11]

of that state and Harmon Wilson of Carthage, Hancock County, Illinois, who was a Missourian in principle. You have read Hyrum's testimony and can judge of the treatment which Joseph received at their hands. Suffice to say he was shamefully abused. Wilson had authority from the governor of Illinois to take Joseph Smith Jr. and deliver him into the hands of the before-named Reynolds; but as neither of them showed any authority save a brace of pistols, Joseph took them for false imprisonment. He then obtained a writ of habeas corpus of the master in chancery of Lee County, returnable before the nearest court authorized to determine upon such writs; and the Municipal Court of Nauvoo being the nearest one invested with this power, an examination was had before said court, when it was made to appear that the writ was defective and void; furthermore, that he was innocent of the charges therein alleged against him. It was in this case that Hyrum's testimony was given, which is rehearsed in a preceding chapter.[12]

Not long after this I broke up housekeeping, and at Joseph's request, I took up my residence at his house. Soon after which I was taken very sick and was brought nigh unto death. For five nights Emma never left me, but stood at my bedside all the night long, at the end of which time she was overcome with fatigue and taken sick herself. Joseph then

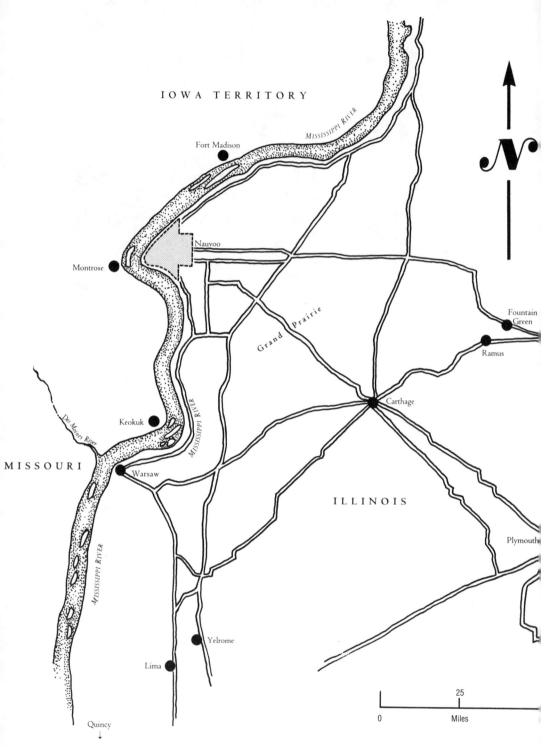

IOWA TERRITORY

Fort Madison

Nauvoo

Montrose

MISSISSIPPI RIVER

Grand Prairie

Fountain
Green

Ramus

Carthage

Keokuk

MISSISSIPPI RIVER

Des Moines River

MISSOURI

Warsaw

ILLINOIS

Plymouth

MISSISSIPPI RIVER

Yelrome

Lima

Quincy

25

0   Miles

HANCOCK COUNTY, CIRCA 1843

Joseph and Emma moved into the Mansion House in August 1843.
Joseph lived here ten months.

took her place and watched with me the five succeeding nights, as faithfully as Emma had done. About this time I began to recover, and, in the course of a few weeks, I was able to walk about the house a little and sit up during the day. I have hardly been able to go on foot further than across the street since.

On the third day of October, 1843, Sophronia, second daughter of Don Carlos, died of the scarlet fever, leaving her widowed mother doubly desolate.[13]

NOTES

1. The commission was issued by Governor Carlin of Illinois: "Know ye that Joseph Smith, having been duly elected to the office of lieutenant-general, Nauvoo Legion, of the militia of the State of Illinois, I, Thomas Carlin, governor of said state, do commission him lieutenant-general of the Nauvoo Legion, to take rank from the fifth day of February, 1841. He is, therefore, carefully and diligently to discharge the duties of said office, by doing and performing all manner of things thereunto belonging; and I do strictly require all officers and soldiers under his command to be obedient to his orders: and he is to obey such orders and directions as he shall receive, from time to time, from the commander-in-chief or his superior officer." (*History of the Church* 4:309–10.)

2. Mary Bailey Smith died on Monday, January 25, 1841, at the age of thirty-two.

3. Monmouth, Illinois, is sixty-five miles northeast of Nauvoo.

4. Don Carlos Smith died Saturday, August 7, 1841, at his residence in Nauvoo. He was twenty-five years old. The particulars of his death are given in the 1853 edition of Mother Smith's history: "While Don Carlos was at work in the before mentioned cellar, he took a severe pain in his side, which was never altogether removed. About a fortnight prior to his death, his family were very sick; and in taking care of them, he caught a violent cold—a fever set in, and the pain in his side increased, and with all our exertions, we were unable to arrest the disease, which I have no doubt was consumption, brought on by working in a damp room, in which he printed his paper." (*Biographical Sketches*, p. 291.) From Joseph's eulogy of his younger brother Don Carlos we read: "[Don Carlos] . . . was one of the first to receive my testimony, and was ordained to the Priesthood when only 14 years of age. . . . He was one of the 24 Elders who laid the corner stones of the Kirtland Temple. . . . Don Carlos visited us several times while we were in Liberty jail, and brought our wives to see us, and some money and articles to relieve our necessities. . . . He was six feet four inches high, was very straight and well made, had light hair, and was very strong and active. His usual weight when in health was 200 pounds. He was universally beloved by the Saints." (See *History of the Church* 4:393–99.)

5. It will be remembered that Robert B. Thompson was married to Mercy Fielding, who was the sister of Mary Fielding, wife of Hyrum Smith. Robert Thompson's actual date of death was August 27, 1841 (see Cook, *Revelations*, p. 278).

6. Don Carlos Smith, son of Joseph and Emma Smith, was born June 13, 1840, and passed away, according to *History of the Church*, on Sunday, August 15, 1841, aged fourteen months and two days (see *History of the Church* 4:402). Joseph and Emma had now lost four sons (Alvin, Thaddeus, Joseph Murdock, and Don Carlos) and one daughter (Louisa). Emma would yet have a stillborn baby in 1842. A few days before Emma's death, nearly thirty-five years after the Martyrdom, she told her nurse, Elizabeth Revel, that Joseph had come to her in a vision and said, "Emma, come with

me, it is time for you to come with me." "As Emma related it, she said, 'I put on my bonnet and my shawl and went with him; I did not think that it was anything unusual. I went with him into a mansion, and he showed me through the different apartments of that beautiful mansion.' And one room was the nursery. In that nursery was a babe in the cradle. She said, 'I knew my babe, my Don Carlos that was taken from me.' She sprang forward, caught the child up in her arms, and wept with joy over the child. When Emma recovered herself sufficient she turned to Joseph and said, 'Joseph, where are the rest of my children.' He said to her, 'Emma, be patient and you shall have all of your children.' Then she saw standing by his side a personage of light, even the Lord Jesus Christ." (Alexander Hale Smith, sermon given I July 1903, Bottlineau, North Dakota, as quoted in Gracia N. Jones, "My Great-Great-Grandmother, Emma Hale Smith," *Ensign*, August 1992, p. 38.)

7. Hyrum Smith, son of Hyrum and Jerusha Barden Smith, was born on April 27, 1834, and passed away on Saturday, September 25, 1841, aged seven years, four months, and twenty-eight days (see *History of the Church* 4:418).

8. In an instant.

9. One of Joseph's hiding places was Edward Hunter's home in Nauvoo. Edward Hunter later became a Presiding Bishop, and, as Truman Madsen relates, Bishop Hunter later recorded how he and Joseph "would hide in the little attic in his house. . . . I say 'little' because they couldn't even stand up there. They went up through a trapdoor, but by then they were over the rafters and under the roof, so they had to double down and sit. They were often many hours in that exact setting." (*Joseph Smith the Prophet* [Salt Lake City: Bookcraft, 1989], p. 63.) In those conditions Joseph wrote: "Shall we not go on in so great a cause? Go forward and not backward. Courage, . . . and on, on to the victory! Let your hearts rejoice, and be exceedingly glad." (D&C 128:22.)

10. She was living in Dixon, Illinois, about 165 miles northeast of Nauvoo.

11. This courtroom is located across the street from the old Illinois state capitol building in Springfield, Illinois. The trapdoor that can be seen above the courtroom bench led to an office on the next floor, where two young attorneys had their practice. One of them would later become the president of the United States—Abraham Lincoln.

12. As noted, Hyrum's testimony was given in Nauvoo on June 30, 1843.

13. Sophronia was five years old at the time of her death.

CHAPTER 53

William Law identified as an enemy of the Church. Joseph Jackson wants Hyrum's daughter for a wife, is refused, begins to plot the murders of all the Smith family. The Nauvoo Expositor *affair. Governor Thomas Ford arrives in Carthage, Illinois. Joseph and Hyrum are arrested, taken to Carthage Jail, and murdered by a mob of between one and two hundred men. Samuel Smith chased by the mob, receives injury, dies thirty-three days after the Martyrdom. Tremendous scene of sorrow at the family viewing of their murdered sons, husbands, and fathers. Church leadership set in order after Joseph's death. Mother Smith ends her history with a soliloquy and a testimony of warning to her persecutors.*

May 17, 1842 to July 1845

About the time that John C. Bennett left Nauvoo, an election was held for the office of mayor, and Joseph, being one of the candidates, was elected to that office.[1] I mention this fact in order to explain a circumstance that took place in the winter of 1843 and 1844, which was as follows. Joseph, in organizing the city police, remarked that "were it not for enemies within the city, there would be no danger from foes without," adding, "If it were not for a Brutus, I might live as long as Caesar would have lived."

Someone who suspected that Joseph alluded to William Law[2] went to the latter and informed him that Joseph regarded him as a Brutus; and that it was his own opinion that he (Law) was in imminent danger. Law, on hearing this tale, went immediately to Joseph, who straightway called a council and had all that knew anything concerning the matter brought together and thus succeeded in satisfying Law that he intended no evil in what he had said.

About this time a man by the name of Joseph Jackson, who had been in the city several months, asked Hyrum for his daughter Lovina,[3] for he wished to make a wife of her. Hyrum, not choosing to have his daughter marry a man who did not belong to the Church, refused for this and other reasons. Jackson then asked Joseph to use his influence with Hyrum to get the girl for him. As Joseph refused to do that, he next applied to Law, who was our secret enemy, for assistance in stealing Lovina from her father. Hyrum heard of this and came to me several times for advice. He said he was alarmed about her, that he felt worse than he did when he was in prison. Jackson went from one to another, wherever he could learn that anyone had any feeling against our family, till finally he succeeded in getting a number to join in a conspiracy to murder the whole Smith family. They commenced holding secret meetings, one of which was attended by a man named Eaton, who was our friend, and he exposed the plot.

This man declared that the Higbees, Laws, and Fosters were all connected with Jackson in his operations.[4] There was also another individual, named Augustine Spencer, a dissolute character who, I believe, was concerned in this conspiracy (although his brother Orson, formerly a Baptist minister, was one of Joseph's warmest friends). About the time of Eaton's disclosures, this man went to the house of his brother Orson, and abused my sons and the Church at such a rate that Orson finally told him that he must either stop or leave the house. Augustine refused and they grappled. In the contest Orson was considerably injured. He went immediately to Joseph and, stating the case, asked for a warrant. Joseph advised him to go to Dr. Foster, who was a justice of the peace. Accordingly, he went and demanded a warrant of Foster, but was refused. On account of this refusal, Foster was brought before Esquire Wells, and tried for non-performance of duty. At this trial Joseph met Charles Foster, the doctor's brother, who attempted to shoot him as soon as they met, but Joseph caught his hands and prevented him, and he was compelled to hold the man in this way above an hour in order to preserve his own life. Jackson and the apostates continued to gather strength, till, finally, they established a printing press in our midst.[5] Through this organ they belched forth the most intolerable and the blackest lies that were ever palmed upon a community.[6] Being advised by men of influence and standing to have this scandalous press removed, the city council took the matter into consideration, and finding that the law would allow them to do so, they declared it a nuisance and had it treated accordingly.[7]

At this the apostates left the city in a great rage, swearing vengeance upon Joseph, the council, and the city.[8] They went forthwith to Carthage and got out writs for Joseph and all those who were in any wise concerned in the destruction of the press. But, having no hope of justice in that place, the brethren took out a writ of habeas corpus and were tried before Esquire Wells at Nauvoo. With this the apostates were not satisfied. They then called upon one Levi Williams, who was a bitter enemy to us, whenever he was sufficiently sober to know his own sentiments, for he was a drunken, ignorant, illiterate brute that never had a particle of character or influence until he began to call mob meetings and placed himself at the head of a rabble like unto himself, to drive the "Mormons," at which time he was joined by certain unmentionable ones in Warsaw and Carthage; and for his zeal in promoting mobocracy he became the intimate acquaintance and confidential friend of some certain preachers, lawyers, and representatives, and, finally, of Joseph Jackson and the apostates.[9]

He, as Colonel Levi Williams, commands the militia (alias mob) of Hancock County. On this man, I say, they called for assistance to drag Joseph and Hyrum, with the rest of the council, to Carthage. Williams swore it should be done and gathered his band together. Joseph, not wishing to fall into the hands of wolves or tigers, called upon the Legion to be in readiness to defend the city and its chartered rights.[10] Just at this crisis, Governor Ford arrived in Carthage. The apostates then appealed from the mob to the governor. At this time he came into the midst of the mob and asked them if they would stand by him in executing and defending the law. They said they would, and so organized them into militia and then demanded the brethren for trial upon the warrant issued by Smith (as he did not choose to recognize the right of habeas corpus granted us in the city charter). At the same time he pledged the faith of the state that the brethren should be protected from mob violence.[11] Those called for in the warrant made their appearance at Carthage, June 24, 1844. On the morning of the twenty-fifth, Joseph and Hyrum were arrested for treason, by a warrant found upon the oaths of A. O. Norton and Augustine Spencer. I will not dwell upon the awful scene which succeeded. My heart is filled with grief and indignation, and my blood curdles in my veins whenever I speak of it.

My sons were thrown into jail, where they remained three days in company with Brothers Richards, Taylor, and Markham. At the end of this time, the governor disbanded most of the men, but left a guard of eight of our bitterest enemies over the jail and sixty more of the same character about a hundred yards distant.[12] He then came into Nauvoo with a guard of fifty or sixty men, made a short speech, and returned immediately.

Joseph, Hyrum, Willard Richards, and John Taylor
were in Carthage Jail until June 27, 1844.

Joseph and Hyrum were killed by a ruthless mob in this upper room of the Carthage Jail.

During his absence from Carthage, the guard rushed Brother Markham out of the place at the point of the bayonet. Soon after this two hundred of those discharged in the morning rushed into Carthage, armed and painted black, red, and yellow, and in ten minutes fled again, leaving my sons murdered and mangled corpses![13]

In leaving the place, a few of them found Samuel coming into Carthage, alone, on horseback, and, finding that he was one of our family, they attempted to shoot him, but he escaped out of their hands, although they pursued him at the top of their speed for more than two hours. He succeeded the next day in getting to Nauvoo in season to go out and meet the procession with the bodies of Hyrum and Joseph, as the mob had the *kindness* to allow us the privilege of bringing them home and burying them in Nauvoo, notwithstanding the immense reward which was offered by the Missourians for Joseph's head.[14]

Their bodies were attended home by only two persons, save those that went from this place. These were Brother Willard Richards and a Mr. Hamilton; Brother John Taylor having been shot in prison, and nearly killed, he could not be moved until some time afterwards.

After the corpses were washed and dressed in their burial clothes, we were allowed to see them. I had for a long time braced every nerve, roused every energy of my soul, and called upon God to strengthen me, but when I entered the room and saw my murdered sons extended both at once before my eyes and heard the sobs and groans of my family and the cries of "Father! Husband! Brothers!" from the lips of their wives, children, brothers, and sisters, it was too much; I sank back, crying to the Lord in the agony of my soul, "My God, my God, why hast thou forsaken this family!" A voice replied, "I have taken them to myself, that they might have rest." Emma was carried back to her room almost in a state of insensibility.

Her oldest son approached the corpse and dropped upon his knees and, laying his cheek against his father's and kissing him, exclaimed, "Oh, my father! my father!" As for myself, I was swallowed up in the depths of my afflictions, and though my soul was filled with horror past imagination, yet I was dumb until I arose again to contemplate the spectacle before me. Oh! at the moment how my mind flew through every scene of sorrow and distress which we had passed, together, in which they had shown the innocence and sympathy which filled their guileless

Joseph and Hyrum stand side by side as the heads of the dispensation of the fulness of times.

hearts. As I looked upon their peaceful, smiling countenances, I seemed almost to hear them say, "Mother, weep not for us, we have overcome the world by love; we carried to them the gospel, that their souls might be saved; they slew us for our testimony, and thus placed us beyond their power; their ascendancy is for a moment, ours is an eternal triumph."

I then thought upon the promise which I had received in Missouri, that in five years Joseph should have power over all his enemies. The time had elapsed and the promise was fulfilled.

I left the scene and returned to my room, to ponder upon the calamities of my family. Soon after this, Samuel said, "Mother, I have had a dreadful distress in my side ever since I was chased by the mob, and I think I have received some injury which is going to make me sick." And indeed he was then not able to sit up, as he had been broken of his rest, besides being dreadfully fatigued in the chase, which, joined to the shock occasioned by the death of his brothers, brought on a disease that never was removed.

On the following day the funeral rites of the murdered ones were attended to, in the midst of terror and alarm, for the mob had made their arrangements to burn the city that night, but by the diligence of the brethren, they were kept at bay until they became discouraged and returned to their homes.

In a short time Samuel, who continued unwell, was confined to his bed, and lingering until the thirtieth of July, his spirit forsook its earthly tabernacle and went to join his brothers, and the ancient martyrs,[15] in the Paradise of God.[16]

At this time William was absent on a mission to the eastern states. And he had taken his family with him in consequence of his wife being afflicted with the dropsy, hoping that the journey might be a benefit to her. Thus was I left desolate in my distress. I had reared six sons to manhood, and of them all, one only remained, and he was far too distant to speak one consoling word to me in this trying hour. It would have been some satisfaction to me if I had expected his immediate return, but his wife was lying at the point of death, which compelled him to remain where he was. His case was, if it were possible, worse than mine, for he had to bear all his grief alone in a land of strangers, confined to the side of his dying wife, and absent from those who felt the deepest interest in his welfare; whilst I was surrounded with friends, being in the midst of the Church; my daughters, too, were with me, and from their society I derived great comfort.

The Church at this time was in a state of gloomy suspense. Not knowing who was to take the place of Joseph, the people were greatly wrought upon with anxiety, lest an imposter should arise and deceive many. Suddenly, Sidney Rigdon made his appearance from Pittsburgh, and rather insinuated that the Church ought to make choice of him, not as President, but as guardian; for "Joseph," said he, "is still President, and the Church must be built up unto him." But before he could carry his measures into effect, the Twelve, who had also been absent, arrived and assuming their proper places, all was set to rights.[17]

William, however, did not return till the spring of 1845, when, with great difficulty, he got his wife to Nauvoo. She survived but a short time after her arrival, for in about two weeks, to complete the sum of William's afflictions, he followed her to the grave. Her disease was brought on by her exposures in Missouri, so that she was what might be termed an indirect martyr to the cause of Christ, which makes the sum of martyrs in our family no less than six in number.[18]

Shortly after William's return from the East, he was ordained Patriarch of the Church, in the place of Hyrum, who held the keys of that priesthood previous to his death.[19]

I have now given a history of my life as far as I intended carrying it at this time. I leave the world at liberty to pass judgment upon what I have written as seemeth it good. But this much I will say, that all that I have written is true and will stand forever. Yes, it will stand before God at that hour when small and great shall appear to answer at his bar for the deeds done in the body, whether they be good or evil, and there will I meet the persecutors of my family who are the enemies of the Church and declare with a voice that shall penetrate the ears of every intelligence which shall be present on that momentous occasion—when the spirits of the just and the unjust, the beggars and lords, the princes and potentates, the kings and emperors, the angels and seraphs, the cherubims and gods be called before him who is the God of gods and Lord of lords.

Yes, in the presence of all these will I declare concerning our persecutors, that for eighteen years they hunted us like wild beasts who were thirsting for the blood of their prey; that without any just cause they drove me and my family from our home in New York; that they maliciously cast my husband into prison and despitefully used him; that they, while he was there, plundered my house and sought my son Hyrum that they might slay him; that in consequence of their abuse, we fled again before them and went to the state of Ohio. Here they dragged my son Joseph out of his bed at midnight and beat him until life for a season departed from his body, and after he recovered, they still continued to persecute him and the rest of my family so sorely that we were compelled to flee to Missouri, where they again renewed their hostilities against my household, and tore my sons from their wives, from their little ones, and from me; that they were thrown into prison, bound in chains, and sentenced to be shot, and all this when my sons were guilty of no sin and had committed no crime or offense against the law.

I will testify to our Lord that after my sons had been in the hands of their adversaries for six months, they were compelled to fly from the state of Missouri into the state of Illinois in order to save their lives, for Governor Boggs had decreed that all Saints found within his jurisdiction after a certain time should be slain by the sword; that in Illinois, we were promised protection from murders and from mobs and we bought us homes and lived with them for a short time like brothers of one family. They were kind to us and we loved them, but the spoiler came, and certain who were not of our faith, joined themselves with the rabble of Warsaw, Carthage, and Green Plains, and they lied about us and scandalized us unto our friends, which caused our friends to become lukewarm and our enemies to increase, until at last they again seized my sons and cast them into prison and slew them.

Furthermore, I will testify before him who was slain in like manner that in consequence of all these wrongs, the gray hairs of my aged companion were brought down in sorrow to the grave, and he was caused to weep over his children when he was even dying because of the wickedness of their enemies; that the cries of widows and orphans have gone up to the councils of the great men of the land and the rulers of the nation, but they laughed at our calamities; and the hands of murderers were upon us, and we were threatened, oppressed, and despoiled by our enemies. We appealed to lawyers, judges, governors, and presidents, but they heeded not our cry, their pledges were broken, the laws were trampled upon, and the statutes and ordinances of the land were tarnished to gratify murderers, thieves, and robbers.

This shall be my testimony in the day of God Almighty, and if it be true, what will Lilburn W. Boggs, Thomas Carlin, Martin Van Buren, and Governor Ford answer me when I shall appear where the prayers of the Saints and the complaints of the widow and orphan come up before a just and righteous judge, who is not only our judge but the judge of the *whole* earth?

Say unto those who have suffered us to be thus abused, "Ye have not bound up that which was broken, neither brought again that which was driven away, neither have ye sought that which was lost, but with force and cruelty have ye ruled my people; therefore, because ye ruled in unrighteousness, because you have robbers to devour my people, and murderers to steal and pierce the hearts of the defenseless in prison chambers and didst suffer fierce demons to rush upon them with fire and with sword to demolish their dwellings and destroy their substance; because ye had power to preserve the innocent and did not—you cannot answer because you did not take your future destiny to heart."[20]

You suffered my husband and children to be robbed, imprisoned, and murdered until the cries of five widows and twenty-four orphan children were lifted to you in vain, and we are still chased before a lawless band from one kingdom to another.

Although I am now seventy years of age[21] and a citizen of the United States, and although my father and my brothers fought hard and struggled to establish a government of liberty and equal rights upon this home of my birth, and although I violated no law, yet in common with many thousands equally innocent, we were commanded by a mob to leave a country or stay there at the peril of our lives.

Last of all and most to be deplored, those who are chosen to enforce and execute the law declare that the proceedings are outrageous but we must of necessity submit to them, for our countrymen have all become so corrupt that there are none to defend and maintain the sacredness of the law.

If this be so, well may I say with the poet: Oh, for a lodge in some vast wilderness, some boundless contiguity of shade, where rumor of oppression and deceit might never reach me more.

Let me leave the bones of my fathers and brothers, and the bones of the martyred children, and go to a land where never man dwelt.

Farewell, my country, thou that killest the prophets and hath exiled those that were sent unto thee. Once thou wert fair, once thou wert pure and lovely, when thy legislators were just men and the lawgivers sought the good of the people like unto themselves. But now thou art fallen.

Mother Smith's riding bonnet on display in Nauvoo, Illinois.
Lucy passed away on Wednesday, May 14, 1856.

The halls where wisdom and justice once dwelt, debauchery and despotism reign. Thy tables are filled with vomit and filthiness, and the hearts of the people with rottenness and deceit; but, oh, if there is left one in the midst of this sink of corruption in whose breast flows one feeling that warmed the heart of Washington, come forth, I pray you, declare yourself men, and spurn a spot which is so polluted that nothing can cleanse it but the judgments of him who is a consuming fire.

I bid farewell until I shall appear before him who is the judge of both quick and dead; to whom I solemnly appeal in the name of Jesus Christ. Amen.

NOTES

1. John C. Bennett resigned the office of mayor of Nauvoo on Tuesday, May 17, 1842. Joseph Smith Jr. was elected mayor of Nauvoo on Thursday, May 19, 1842, with Hyrum Smith as vice-mayor. (See *History of the Church* 5:12.)

2. William Law, born September 8, 1809, in Tyrone County, Northern Ireland, was a controversial character in the early history of the Church. Converted to the Church in 1836, he seemed destined to be a leader. He wrote to his friend Issac Russell in 1837: "Although trials, persecutions, privations and sorrows await the Saints, yet God will not forsake them; yea in the hour of their greatest need, he will stand by them to deliver. . . . Bro Joseph is truly a wonderful man he is all we could wish a prophet to be—and Bro. Sidney what Eloquence is his, and think how he has sacrificed for the Truth. . . . I am aware we must endure affliction, but I won't shrink from my calling though I should have to sacrifice all things." (William Law to Isaac Russell, November 10, 1837, as quoted in Lyndon W. Cook, *William Law* [Orem, Utah: Grandin Book Company, 1994], p. 7.) Three years after that statement Law would write Russell again concerning Joseph in Nauvoo (Russell had now apostatized): "I have carefully watched his movements since I have been here, and I assure you I have found him honest and honorable in all our transactions which have been very considerable. I believe he is an honest, upright man, and as to his follies let who ever is guiltless throw the first stone at him, I shant do it." (Quoted in Cook, *William Law*, p. 11.) Soon thereafter William and his brother Wilson Law were in real estate competition with Joseph the Prophet in Nauvoo. The reasons for Law's turning against Joseph were: feeling like Joseph had unfair advantage in control and influence of the sale of lots in Nauvoo, feeling like Joseph had introduced false doctrines and corrupt practices, and likely because Law's father and daughter, Helen, died after the brethren had prayed for their recovery. (See Cook, *William Law*, pp. 20–22.) Though he was in the First Presidency, Law turned violently against Joseph and was excommunicated; and partly through Law's actions and schemes, by and by, Joseph was killed. William Law died in Wisconsin on January 12, 1892.

3. Lovina was only sixteen years old at this time.

4. John P. Greene swore an affidavit on June 21, 1844, to city recorder Willard Richards: "Personally appeared John P. Greene before me, Willard Richards, recorder . . . ; and after being duly sworn, deposeth and saith that on or about the 27th day of May, 1844, while at Hamilton's tavern, in Carthage . . . , in company with Joseph Smith and others, Robert D. Foster called deponent into a private room, and there and then said, 'For God's sake, don't suffer that man, Joseph Smith, to go out of doors; for if he steps outside of the door his blood will be spilt;' to which statement deponent replied he had no such fears; when said Foster confirmed said statements with considerable emotion, and said he knew that Smith could not go out of doors, but his blood would be spilt. Deponent asked Foster who would do it. Foster said he would not tell; but he knew the proud spirit of Jackson, that he would not be in-

sulted, and that he would kill Joseph Smith if he had to die on the spot; and there were many others in Carthage who would assist to do the same thing. . . . Deponent heard Joseph H. Jackson say that Joseph Smith was the damnedest rascal in the world, and he would be damned if he did not take vengeance on him, if he had to follow him to the Rocky Mountains; and said Jackson made many more such like threats against Joseph Smith and Hyrum Smith." (*History of the Church* 6:522–23.)

5. The first and only number of the *Nauvoo Expositor* was published on Friday, June 7, 1844, twenty days before the Martyrdom.

6. In the prospectus of the *Nauvoo Expositor* its explosive and divisive purpose was stated: "A part of its columns will be devoted to a few primary objects, which the publishers deem of vital importance to the public welfare. Their particular locality gives them a knowledge of the many *gross abuses exercised under the 'pretended' authorities of the Charter of the City of Nauvoo,* by the legislative authorities of said city and the *insupportable oppression* of the *Ministerial powers in carrying out the unjust, illegal and unconstitutional ordinances of the same.* The publishers therefore deem it a sacred duty they owe to their country and their fellow-citizens to advocate through the columns of the *Expositor* THE UNCONDITIONAL REPEAL OF THE NAUVOO CITY CHARTER, to restrain and correct the abuses of the UNIT POWER, to ward off the iron rod which is held over the devoted heads of the citizens of Nauvoo and the surrounding country, to advocate unmitigated DISOBEDIENCE TO POLITICAL REVELATIONS, and to censure and decry gross moral imperfections wherever found, either in the plebeian, patrician or SELF-CONSTITUTED MONARCH." (*History of the Church* 6:443.)

7. The meetings were held on Saturday, June 8, 1844, lasting over six hours, and on Monday, June 10, 1844, for another nearly seven hours. Based on the power of the charter for the city of Nauvoo, and based on the precedents of twenty other presses having been destroyed for similar reasons in the state of Illinois in the twenty years previous to the *Expositor,* the city council declared the *Nauvoo Expositor* a nuisance and issued an order to abate the nuisance. Joseph Smith, as mayor, ordered the marshal to destroy it without delay. Marshal John P. Greene carried out the orders of the mayor and the council, reporting by eight P.M. on that same Monday that "he had removed the press, type, printed paper, and fixtures into the street, and destroyed them." (*History of the Church* 6:432.)

8. The press, type, and fixtures were the property of apostates William Law, Wilson Law, Charles Ivins, Francis M. Higbee, Chauncey L. Higbee, Robert D. Foster, and Charles A. Foster (see *History of the Church* 6:453). Francis Higbee had warned openly concerning the press: "If they [the citizens of Nauvoo] lay their hands upon it, or break it, they may date their downfall from that very hour, and in ten days there will not be a Mormon left in Nauvoo" (quoted in B. H. Roberts, *A Comprehensive History of The Church of Jesus Christ of Latter-day Saints,* 6 vols. [Provo, Utah: Brigham Young University Press, 1965], 2:230).

9. Inflammatory editor Thomas Sharp of the anti-Mormon newspaper the *Warsaw Signal* published on June 12, 1844, his response to the *Expositor* action at Nauvoo: "War and extermination is inevitable! *Citizens* ARISE, ONE and ALL!!!—

Can you *stand* by, and suffer such INFERNAL DEVILS! to ROB men of their property and RIGHTS, without avenging them. We have no time for comment, every man will make his own. LET IT BE MADE WITH POWDER AND BALL!!!" (*Warsaw Signal,* June 12, 1844, p. 2.)

10. On Saturday, June 22, 1844, the brethren read a letter from Governor Ford concerning Joseph and his safety. According to Abraham C. Hodge, upon hearing it "Joseph remarked, 'There is no mercy—no mercy here.' Hyrum said, 'No; just as sure as we fall into their hands we are dead men.' Joseph replied, 'Yes; what shall we do, Brother Hyrum?' He replied, 'I don't know.' All at once Joseph's countenance brightened up and he said, 'The way is open. It is clear to my mind what to do. All they want is Hyrum and myself; then tell everybody to go about their business, and not to collect in groups, but to scatter about. There is no doubt they will come here and search for us. Let them search; they will not harm you in person or property, and not even a hair of your head. We will cross the river tonight, and go away to the West.'" The last of the direct narrative in Joseph's history reads: "I told Stephen Markham that if I and Hyrum were ever taken again we should be massacred, or I was not a prophet of God. I want Hyrum to live to avenge my blood, but he is determined not to leave me." Joseph, Hyrum, and Willard Richards, with O. P. Rockwell at the oars, took a leaky skiff across the Mississippi at about two A.M. to put the plan in action. (See *History of the Church* 6:545–48.) Word immediately started coming across the river to these Brethren calling for them to return. To these messages Joseph replied: "If my life is of no value to my friends it is of none to myself" (*History of the Church* 6:549). Joseph and Hyrum returned during the evening of Sunday, June 23, 1844.

11. Though Governor Ford had given his personal pledge of executive protection to Joseph and Hyrum, there is great irony in his speech in Nauvoo about the time of the Martyrdom: "A great crime has been done by destroying the *Expositor* press and placing the city under martial law, and a severe atonement must be made, so prepare your minds for the emergency" (*History of the Church* 6:623).

12. When Dan Jones left the jail at 5:30 A.M., June 27, he passed the officer of the guard, Frank Worrell (one of the Carthage Greys), and in a very bitter spirit Worrell said, "We have had too much trouble to bring Old Joe here to let him ever escape alive, and unless you want to die with him you had better leave before sundown; and you are not a damned bit better than him for taking his part, and you'll see that I can prophesy better than Old Joe, for neither he nor his brother, nor anyone who will remain with them will see the sun set today" (*History of the Church* 6:602).

13. The deed was done in an instant. A ball blasted through the door hitting Hyrum in the left bridge of the nose between his eyes, and he fell to the floor. He landed on his back, saying, "I am a dead man!" He received three more balls. John Taylor tried to escape through the window and was hurled back in the room by a ball striking him in the chest against his pocket watch, pulverizing the glass and stopping the watch at sixteen minutes and twenty-six seconds after the hour of five o'clock P.M. He rolled under the bed and was hit with another ball in the hip (having received a total of four balls). Joseph sprang to the window, surely to draw fire away from his

friends, and was hit in the right breast from outside; and as he fell forward, he exclaimed, "O Lord, my God!" then fell to the ground. Willard Richards escaped unharmed. (See *History of the Church* 6:617–19.) Willard Richards sent a restrained and powerful message by courier to Nauvoo: "Carthage Jail, 8:05 o'clock, p.m., June 27th, 1844. Joseph and Hyrum are dead. Taylor wounded, not very badly [this message was understated at Brother Taylor's request so as to not frighten his family]. I am well. Our guard was forced, as we believe, by a band of Missourians from 100 to 200. The job was done in an instant, and the party fled towards Nauvoo instantly. This is as I believe it. The citizens here are afraid of the Mormons attacking them. I promise them no! W. Richards. John Taylor." (*History of the Church* 6:621–22.) At the time of his death Hyrum was forty-four years, four months, and eighteen days old. Joseph was thirty-eight years, six months, and four days old.

14. It appears that Samuel came to Carthage to help his brothers but arrived after the slaughter. He assisted Willard Richards in preparing the bodies and getting them safely back to Nauvoo.

15. In the Early Notebook Lucy dwells upon the ancient martyrs (such as Paul, James, Jude, Peter, etc.), filling four pages, namely, 5–8 inclusive.

16. Samuel Harrison Smith died on Tuesday, July 30, 1844, just thirty-three days after his brothers had been killed. He was thirty-six years, four months, and seventeen days old.

17. Members of the Twelve scattered about the East all recorded feeling darkness in their souls on the afternoon of the twenty-seventh of June. By August 6, 1844, most of the Twelve had arrived back in Nauvoo, and a meeting was planned to determine who should take the leadership of the Church. Two days later, the Saints met to decide by common consent whom they would support as their leader. Sidney Rigdon stood first and spoke for an hour and a half about his desires to be guardian of the Church and to build the Church up to Joseph. Then Brigham Young arose. As he gave his brief remarks, he was miraculously transfigured before the people. Benjamin Johnson jumped to his feet, "for in every possible degree it was Joseph's voice, and his person, in look, attitude, dress and appearance was Joseph himself, personified; and I knew in a moment the spirit and mantle of Joseph was upon him" (*My Life's Review* [Independence, Mo.: Zion's Printing and Publishing, 1947], p. 104). Zina D. Huntington Young wrote: "I closed my eyes. I could have exclaimed, I know that is Joseph Smith's voice! Yet I knew he had gone. But the same spirit was with the people." (As quoted in Edward W. Tullidge, *The Women of Mormondom* [New York, 1877], p. 327.)

18. Caroline Grant Smith, wife of William, passed away May 22, 1845. Clearly Mother Smith's list of Smith martyrs included her husband, Joseph Smith Sr.; Samuel's wife, Mary Bailey Smith; Joseph; Hyrum; Samuel; and Caroline.

19. William Smith was ordained Patriarch to the Church on May 24, 1845, by the Quorum of the Twelve. William was later rejected by the membership at the general conference held October 6, 1845, and excommunicated October 12, 1845. He later associated with James Strang (1846–47). He was rebaptized in early 1860 but

subsequently withdrew from the Church. He joined the Reorganized LDS Church in 1878, and died in Osterdock, Clayton County, Iowa, November 13, 1893, aged eighty-two years, eight months. (See Cook, *Revelations*, pp. 276–77.)

20. Lucy is paraphrasing from Ezekiel 34:4: "The diseased have ye not strengthened, neither have ye healed that which was sick, neither have ye bound up that which was broken, neither have ye brought again that which was driven away, neither have ye sought that which was lost; but with force and with cruelty have ye ruled them."

21. Lucy Mack Smith turned seventy years old on July 8, 1845.

Appendix I

Genealogy of the Smith and Mack Families as Given by Lucy Mack Smith

[*Editors' Note:* The following information is taken from chapter 9 of the 1853 edition of Mother Smith's history, and incorporates all of the changes made by George A. Smith for the 1902 version of the history. Numbering of children, correction of spellings, and corrected entries of children have been added.]

Here I would like to give the early history of my husband, for many facts might be mentioned that doubtless would be highly interesting, but as I am not able to give them in order, I shall decline making the attempt, and in the place thereof shall insert a transcript from the record of his family, beginning with Samuel Smith, who was the son of Robert and Mary French Smith, who came from England.

The above Samuel Smith was born January 26, 1666, in Topsfield, Essex County, Massachusetts, and was married to Rebecca Curtis, daughter of John Curtis, January 25, 1707.

* * *

Children of Samuel (died July 12, 1748) and Rebecca Curtis Smith (died March 2, 1753).
1) Phebe, born Jan. 8, 1708; married to Stephen Averel.
2) First Mary, born Aug. 14, 1711; married to Amos Towne.
3) Second Samuel, born Jan. 26, 1714; married to Priscilla Gould; died Nov. 11, 1785.

4) Rebecca, born Oct. 1, 1715; married to John Balch.

5) Elizabeth, born July 8, 1718; married to Eliezer Gould; died March 15, 1753.

6) Hephzibah, born May 12, 1722; married to William Gallop; died Nov. 15, 1774.

7) Robert, born April 25, 1724.

8) Susanna, born May 2, 1726; died May 5, 1741.

9) Hannah, born April 5, 1729; married to John Peabody; died Aug. 17, 1764.

* * *

Children of second Samuel (child no. 3 above), and first Priscilla Gould Smith, which Samuel was the son of first Samuel and Rebecca Smith.

1) Priscilla, born Sept. 26, 1735; married to Jacob Kimball, Sept. 15, 1755.

2) Third Samuel, born Oct. 28, 1737; married to Rebecca Towne, Jan. 2, 1760.

3) Vashti (or Vasta), born Oct. 5, 1739; married to Solomon Curtis, Sept. 15, 1763; married second time to Jacob Hobbs, 1767.

4) Susanna, born Jan. 24, 1742; married to Isaac Hobbs, 1767.

5) First Asael, born March 7, 1744; married to Mary Duty, Feb. 12, 1767.

* * *

Children of first Asael (child no. 5 above—died Oct. 31, 1830) and Mary Duty Smith (died May 27, 1836); which Asael was the son of second Samuel and Priscilla Smith.

1) First Jesse, born April 20, 1768; married to Hannah Peabody, Jan. 20, 1792.

2) Priscilla, born Oct. 21, 1769; married to John C. Waller, Aug. 24, 1796.

3) First Joseph, born July 12, 1771; married to Lucy Mack, Jan. 24, 1796; died Sept. 14, 1840.

4) Second Asael, born May 21, 1773; married to Betsy Schellenger March 21, 1802. 1809, St. Lawrence Co., N.Y.

5) Mary, born June 4, 1775; married to Isaac Pierce, Dec. 22, 1796.

6) Fourth Samuel, born Sept. 15, 1777; married Frances Wilcox, Feb., 1816; died April 1, 1830.

7) First Silas, born Oct 1, 1779; married to Ruth Stevens, Jan. 29, 1806; second time to Mary Aikens, March 4, 1828.

8) First John, born July 16, 1781; married to Clarissa Lyman, Sept. 11, 1815.

9) Third Susannah, born May 18, 1783.

10) Stephen, born April 23, 1785; died July 25, 1802.

11) Sarah, born May 16, 1789; married to Joseph Sanford, Oct. 15, 1809; died May 27, 1824.

* * *

Children of fourth Samuel (child no. 6 above) and Frances Wilcox.

1)	Charles	Born Potsdam, St. Lawrence Co., N.Y.
2)	Laura	Born Potsdam, St. Lawrence Co., N.Y.
3)	Horace Jay	Born Potsdam, St. Lawrence Co., N.Y.
4)	Elizabeth	Born Potsdam, St. Lawrence Co., N.Y.
5)	Sarah	Born Potsdam, St. Lawrence Co., N.Y.

* * *

Children of first Jesse and Hannah Smith, which Jesse was the son of first Asael and Mary Smith.

1)	Benjamin P.	Born May 2, 1793
2)	Eliza	Born March 9, 1795
3)	Ira	Born Jan. 30, 1797
4)	Harvey	Born April 1, 1799
5)	Harriet	Born April 8, 1801
6)	Stephen	Born May 2, 1803
7)	Mary	Born May 4, 1805
8)	Catherine	Born July 13, 1807

| 9) Royal | Born July 2, 1809 |
| 10) Sarah | Born Dec. 16, 1810 |

* * *

Children of John C. and Priscilla Waller, which Priscilla was the daughter of first Asael Smith.

1) Calvin C.	Born June 6, 1797
2) Polly	Born Oct. 16, 1799; died July 20, 1800
3) Marshall	Born March 18,1801
4) Royal H.	Born Nov. 29, 1802; died Sept. 29, 1866
5) Dudley C.	Born Sept. 29, 1804
6) Bushrod W.	Born Oct. 18, 1806
7) Silas B.	Born Jan. 1, 1809; died June 12, 1866
8) Sally P.	Born Oct. 31, 1810; died Aug. 15, 1874
9) John H.	Born Sept. 9, 1812; died Nov. 5, 1812

* * *

Children of first Joseph and Lucy Smith, which Joseph was the son of first Asael and Mary Smith.

1) Unnamed son, born 1796/97.
2) Alvin, born Feb. 11, 1798, Tunbridge, Vermont; died Nov. 19, 1823.
3) Hyrum, born Feb. 9, 1800, Tunbridge, Vermont; married to Jerusha Barden, Nov. 2, 1826, Manchester, N. Y.; to Mary Fielding, December 24, 1837; murdered by a mob, June 27, 1844, in Carthage Jail, Hancock County, Illinois, while under the protection of Governor Thomas Ford.
4) Sophronia, born May 17, 1803, Tunbridge, Vermont; married to Calvin Stoddard, Dec. 2, 1828, Palmyra, N. Y.; to William McCleary, Feb. 11, 1838, Ohio; died in Hancock County, Illinois, 1876.
5) Second Joseph, born Dec. 23, 1805, Sharon, Windsor County, Vermont; married to Emma Hale, daughter of Isaac and Elizabeth Hale, in South Bainbridge, Chenango County, N. Y.,

Jan. 18, 1827; murdered by a mob, June 27, 1844, in Carthage Jail, Hancock County, Illinois, while under the protection of Governor Thomas Ford.

6) Fifth Samuel Harrison, born March 13, 1808, Tunbridge, Vermont; married to Mary Bailey, Aug. 13, 1834; later to Levira Clark, May 30, 1841 (Levira Clark born July 30, 1815, daughter of Gardner and Delicta); died July 30, 1844, of a fever occasioned by overexertion in getting away from a mob when his brothers were killed.

7) Ephraim, born March 13, 1810; died March 24, 1810.

8) William, born March 13, 1811, Royalton, Vermont; married to Caroline Grant, daughter of Joshua Grant, Feb. 14, 1833; died Nov. 13, 1893.

9) Catharine, born July 28, 1812, Lebanon, New Hampshire; married to Wilkins J. Salisbury, Jan. 8, 1831; died Feb. 1, 1900.

10) Don Carlos, born March 25, 1816; married to Agnes Coolbrith, July 30, 1835, Kirtland, Ohio; died Aug. 7, 1841.

11) Lucy, born July 18, 1821; married to Arthur Milliken, June 4, 1840, Nauvoo; died Dec. 9, 1882.

* * *

Children of second Asael (died July 21, 1844) and Betsy Smith, which Asael was the son of first Asael and Mary Smith.

1) Elias	Born Sept. 6, 1804; died June 24, 1888
2) Emily	Born Sept. 1, 1806; died Aug. 11, 1893
3) Jesse J.	Born Oct. 6, 1808; died July 1, 1834
4) Esther	Born Sept. 20, 1810; died Oct. 31, 1856
5) Mary J.	Born April 29, 1813; died March 1, 1878
6) Julia P.	Born March 6, 1815
7) Martha	Born June 9, 1817
8) Second Silas	Born June 6, 1822; died June 6, 1892

* * *

Children of Isaac and Mary Pierce, which Mary was the daughter of first Asael and Mary Smith.

1)	Eunice	Born April 29, 1799
2)	Miranda	Born June 17, 1803
3)	Horace	Born June 8, 1805
4)	John S.	Born March 6, 1807
5)	Susan	Born June 20, 1809
6)	Mary	Born April 25, 1811
7)	Laura	Born Feb. 8, 1814
8)	Elise A.	Born Sept. 2, 1817

* * *

Children of first Silas (died Sept. 13, 1839) and Ruth Smith (died March 14, 1826), which Silas was the son of first Asael and Mary Smith.

1)	Charles	Born Nov. 11, 1806; died May 7, 1809
2)	Charity	Born April 1, 1808; died June 2, 1888
3)	Curtis S.	Born Oct. 29, 1809; died Sept. 23, 1861
4)	Sixth Samuel	Born Oct. 3, 1811; died March 7, 1826
5)	Stephen	Born June 8, 1815; died Feb. 20, 1891
6)	Susan	Born Oct. 19, 1817; died Nov., 1846
7)	Third Asael	Born Oct. 12, 1819; died May 15, 1834

* * *

Children of his second wife, Mary Aikens Smith (died April 27, 1877).

1)	Silas L.	Born Oct. 26, 1830
2)	John A.	Born July 6, 1832; died Nov. 27, 1834
3)	Jesse Nathaniel	Born Dec. 2, 1834

* * *

Children of first John (died May 23, 1854) and Clarissa Smith (died Feb. 14, 1854), which John was the son of first Asael and Mary Smith.

1)	George A.	Born June 26, 1817; died Sept. 1, 1875
2)	Caroline	Born June 6, 1820
3)	Second John L.	Born Nov. 17, 1828

* * *

Children of Hyrum Smith and Jerusha Barden Smith (died Oct. 13, 1837, at Kirtland, Ohio), which Hyrum was the son of first Joseph and Lucy Smith.

1) Lovina	Born Sept. 16, 1827; died Oct. 8, 1876
2) Mary	Born June 27, 1829; died May 29, 1832
3) John	Born Sept. 22, 1832
4) Second Hyrum	Born April 27, 1834; died Sept. 21, 1841
5) Jerusha	Born Jan. 13, 1836
6) Sarah	Born Oct. 2, 1837; died Nov. 6, 1876

Children of Hyrum and Mary Fielding Smith, his second wife.

1) Fourth Joseph F.	Born Nov. 13, 1838
2) Martha Ann	Born May 14, 1841

* * *

Children of second Joseph, the Prophet, and Emma Smith, which Joseph was the son of first Joseph and Lucy Smith.

1) Alvin Smith	Born June 15, 1828; died same day
2) Thaddeus Smith	Born April 30, 1831; died same day (twin)
3) Louisa Smith	Born April 30, 1831; died same day (twin)
4) Julia Murdock Smith, adopted daughter	Born April 30, 1831 (twin); died 1880
5) Joseph Murdock Smith, adopted son	Born April 30, 1831 (twin); died March 30, 1832, from exposure caused by the mob at Hiram, Ohio
6) Third Joseph	Born Nov. 6, 1832; died Dec. 10, 1914
7) Frederick G. W.	Born June 20, 1836; died Apr. 13, 1862
8) Alexander H.	Born June 2, 1838; died Aug. 12, 1909
9) Don Carlos	Born June 13, 1840; died Aug. 15, 1841
10) Stillborn son	Born 1842
11) David Hyrum	Born Nov. 17, 1844; died Aug. 29, 1904

* * *

Children of fifth Samuel Smith and Mary Bailey Smith, his first wife (died Jan. 25, 1841); which Samuel was the son of first Joseph and Lucy Smith.

    1) Susanna B.   Born Oct. 27, 1835
    2) Mary B.   Born March 27, 1837
    3) Samuel H. B.   Born Aug. 1, 1838
    4) Lucy B.   Born Jan., 1841

Children of Samuel Smith and Levira Clark Smith, his second wife.

    1) Levira A. C.   Born April 29, 1842
    2) Lovisa C.   Born Aug. 28, 1843
    3) Lucy J. C.   Born Aug. 20, 1844

* * *

Children of William Smith and Caroline Grant Smith (died May 22, 1845), which William was the son of first Joseph and Lucy Smith.

    1) Mary Jane   Born Jan., 1835
    2) Caroline L.   Born Aug., 1836

* * *

Children of Don Carlos and Agnes Coolbrith Smith, which Don Carlos was the son of first Joseph and Lucy Smith.

    1) Agnes C.   Born Aug. 1, 1836
    2) Sophronia C.   Born 1838
    3) Josephine D.   Born March 10, 1841

* * *

Children of Calvin and Sophronia Smith Stoddard, which Sophronia was the daughter of first Joseph and Lucy Smith.

    1) Eunice   Born March 22, 1830
    2) Maria   Born April 12, 1832

* * *

Children of Wilkins J. and Catharine Salisbury, which Catharine was the daughter of first Joseph and Lucy Smith.

1)	Elizabeth	Born April 12, 1832
2)	Lucy	Born Oct. 3, 1834
3)	Solomon J.	Born Sept. 18, 1835
4)	Alvin	Born June 7, 1838
5)	Don C.	Born Oct. 25, 1841
6)	Emma C.	Born March 25, 1844

* * *

Arthur and Lucy Milliken have one son, named Don Carlos Milliken.

* * *

George A. Smith, son of first John Smith, was married to Bathsheba W. Bigler, July 25, 1841.

Children of George A. and Bathsheba W. Smith.

1)	George Albert	Born July 7, 1842; died Nov. 2, 1860
2)	Bathsheba	Born Aug. 14, 1844

* * *

Having now given all the names belonging to the family of Smith, I shall take up another lineage, namely, that of the Mack family, commencing with my grandfather, Ebenezer Mack. Ebenezer Mack had three sons, Elisha, Samuel, and Solomon, and one daughter named Hypsebeth. His son Solomon was born in the town of Lyme, state of Connecticut, Sept. 15, 1732; was married to a young woman by the name of Lydia Gates, in the year 1759. This Lydia Gates was born in East Haddam, state of Connecticut, Sept. 3, 1732.

❉ ❉ ❉

The following are the names of the children of first Solomon and Lydia Mack, which Solomon was the son of Ebenezer and Hannah Mack.

1)	Jason	Born 1760
2)	Lovisa	Born 1761
3)	Lovina	Born 1762
4)	Lydia	Born 1764
5)	Stephen	Born June 15, 1766
6)	Daniel	Born 1770
7)	Second Solomon	Born Jan. 28, 1773
8)	Lucy	Born July 8, 1775.

❉ ❉ ❉

Children of second Solomon Mack, which Solomon was the son of first Solomon Mack.

1)	Calvin	Born Nov. 28, 1797
2)	Orlando	Born Sept. 23, 1799
3)	Chilon	Born July 26, 1802
4)	Third Solomon	Born May 23, 1805
5)	Amos	Born May 1, 1807
6)	Dennis	Born Oct. 18, 1809
7)	Merrill	Born Sept. 14, 1812
8)	Esther	Born April 2, 1815
9)	Rizpah	Born June 5, 1818

Appendix 2

SIMPLIFIED GENEALOGY CHART FOR THE FAMILY OF JOSEPH SMITH

Joseph Smith's Grandparents	Joseph Smith's Parents, Aunts, Uncles	Joseph Smith and His Brothers and Sisters (Spouses Shown in Italics)	Joseph Smith's Children
	Jesse Smith (1768–1853)	Unnamed son (about 1797)	Alvin Smith (1828–1828)
	Priscilla Smith (1769–1867)	Alvin Smith (1798–1823)	Louisa Smith (1831–1831)
	Joseph Smith Sr. (1771–1840)	Hyrum Smith (1800–1844) *Jerusha Barden* *Mary Fielding*	Thaddeus Smith (1831–1831)
	Asael Smith (1773–1848)	Sophronia Smith (1803–1876) *Calvin Stoddard* *William McCleary*	Julia Murdock Smith (adopted twin) (1831–1880)
Asael Smith (1744–1830)	Mary Smith (1775–1844)	Joseph Smith Jr. (1805–1844) *Emma Hale*	Joseph Murdock Smith (adopted twin) (1831–1832)
Mary Duty (1743–1836)	Samuel Smith (1777–1830)	Samuel Harrison Smith (1808–1844) *Mary Bailey* *Levira Clark*	Joseph Smith III (1832–1914)
	Silas Smith (1779–1839)	Ephraim Smith (1810–1810)	Frederick Granger Williams Smith (1836–1862)
	John Smith (1781–1854)	William Smith (1811–1893) *Caroline Amanda Grant* *Roxy Ann Grant* *Eliza Elsie Sanborn* *Rosa Surprise*	Alexander Hale Smith (1838–1909)
	Susan Smith (1783–1849)	Catharine Smith (1812–1900) *Jenkins Salisbury* *Joseph Younger*	Don Carlos Smith (1840–1841)
	Stephen Smith (1785–1802)	Don Carlos Smith (1816–1841) *Agnes Coolbrith*	Unnamed son (1842–1842)
	Sarah Smith (1789–1824)	Lucy Smith (1821–1882) *Arthur Milliken*	David Hyrum Smith (1844–1904)
	Jason Mack (1760–?)		
	Lovisa Mack (1761–1794)		
	Lovina Mack (1762–1794)		
Solomon Mack (1732–1820)	Lydia Mack (1764–1826)		
Lydia Gates (1732–1818)	Stephen Mack (1766–1826)		
	Daniel Mack (1770–?)		
	Solomon Mack (1773–1851)		
	Lucy Mack (1775–1856)		

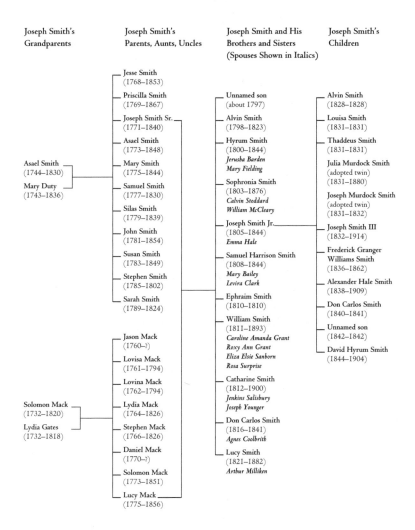

479

Appendix 3

BRIEF CHRONOLOGY OF THE
JOSEPH AND LUCY MACK SMITH FAMILY
(EMPHASIS ON JOSEPH SMITH JR.'S LIFE)

1771–1856

New England

1771	July 12	Joseph Smith Sr. born in Topsfield, Mass.
1775	July 8	Lucy Mack born in Gilsum, N.H.
1796	Jan 24	Joseph Smith and Lucy Mack married at Tunbridge, Vt.
1797		Loss of firstborn son of the Smiths.
1798	Feb 11	Birth of Alvin.
1800	Feb 9	Birth of Hyrum.
1802	Spring	Move to Randolph, Vt.
1803	Winter	Move back to the Tunbridge farm (early in the year).
1803	May 17	Birth of Sophronia.
1803	Spring	Loss of the Tunbridge farm.
1803	Summer	Move to Royalton, Vt.
1803	Fall	Move to Sharon, Vt. Rent farm from Solomon Mack.
1804	July 10	Birth of Emma Hale at Harmony, Pa.
1805	Dec 23	Birth of Joseph Jr.
1806/7		Move to Tunbridge.
1808	Mar 13	Birth of Samuel Harrison.
1808/9		Move to Royalton, Vt.
1810	Mar 13	Birth of Ephraim.
1810	Mar 24	Death of Ephraim.
1811	Mar 13	Birth of William.
1811	Apr	First in series of seven visions received by Joseph Smith Sr. (1811–19).
1811	Summer	Move to Lebanon, N.H.
1812	July 28	Birth of Catharine.

1812/13		Typhoid fever epidemic. All Smith children contract the disease.
1813		Joseph Jr.'s leg operation.
1814		Move from Lebanon, N.H., to Norwich, Vt.
1814	Fall	Complete crop failures for the Smiths in Norwich.
1815		Complete crop failures for the Smiths in Norwich.
1815		Newspaper reports of good land available in western N.Y.
1816	Mar 25	Birth of Don Carlos.
1816	June	Crops are killed by series of untimely ice storms. "Year without a summer."
1816	Fall	Move from New England to Palmyra, N.Y. (could be Jan. 1817).

New York/Pennsylvania

1817		Smiths purchase 100 acres of virgin forest land two miles south of Palmyra.
1818	Fall	Smiths move into small cabin at north end of their Manchester property.
1819	Dec 23	Joseph Jr. turns fourteen years old.
1819/20		Attempted assassination of Joseph Jr.
1820	Spring	Joseph Jr.'s first vision
1821	July 18	Birth of Lucy.
1822		Alvin begins construction on frame house at Manchester farm.
1823	Sept 21	Moroni's first visit to Joseph Jr.
1823	Sept 22	Joseph Jr. views the plates for the first time.
1823	Nov 19	Death of Alvin.
1824	Sept 22	Moroni meets with and teaches Joseph Jr. at Hill Cumorah.
1825	Sept 22	Moroni meets with and teaches Joseph Jr. at Hill Cumorah.
1825	Oct	Joseph Jr. hires with Josiah Stowell and works in Harmony, Pa.
1825	Dec	Smith family loses farm by fraud and become tenants on their own land.
1826		Joseph Jr. works most of the year for Josiah Stowell and Joseph Knight Sr.
1826	Sept 22	Moroni meets with and teaches Joseph Jr. at Hill Cumorah.
1827	Jan 18	Marriage of Joseph Jr. to Emma Hale at S. Bainbridge, N.Y.
1827	Jan	Joseph and Emma move in with the Smiths at the Manchester farm.
1827	Sept 22	Joseph Jr. obtains the plates from the angel Moroni.

1827	Dec	Joseph and Emma move to Harmony. Martin Harris gives them $50.
1828	Feb 27	Martin Harris takes facsimile transcript to New York City.
1828	Apr 12	Martin Harris begins work as scribe for Joseph in translation of plates.
1828	June 14	Martin Harris takes 116 manuscript pages from Harmony to Palmyra.
1828	June 15	Birth and death of Joseph and Emma's first son, Alvin.
1828	June/July	Loss of 116 manuscript pages. Joseph loses privileges of translation.
1828	Sept 22	Joseph receives plates again from angel Moroni. A scribe is promised.
1829	Apr 5	Oliver Cowdery arrives in Harmony, Pa.
1829	Apr 7	Oliver Cowdery begins services as scribe to Joseph in translation process.
1829	May 15	John the Baptist confers Aaronic Priesthood upon Joseph and Oliver.
1829	Late May	Restoration of Melchizedek Priesthood by Peter, James, and John.
1829	June	Joseph and Oliver move to Fayette, N.Y., to Peter Whitmer Sr. home.
1829	June 11	Copyright of Book of Mormon obtained.
1829	June	Three Witnesses see angel, plates, and hear the voice of God.
1829	June	Eight Witnesses view and handle the ancient plates.
1829	Aug 25	Martin Harris signs agreement of mortgage to printer E. B. Grandin.
1829	Sept	Printing process begins for Book of Mormon.
1830	Jan 2	Abner Cole begins illegally publishing parts of the Book of Mormon.
1830	Jan	Cole's illegal activities are put to a stop.
1830	Jan	Palmyra citizens agree not to purchase copies of Book of Mormon.
1830	Mar 26	Book of Mormon goes on sale at Palmyra Bookstore.
1830	Apr 6	Legal organization of the Church at the home of Peter Whitmer Sr.
1830	June	Revelations of Moses given—translation of the Bible begun.
1830	June 30	Samuel Harrison Smith leaves as first official missionary of the Church.
1830	Summer	Joseph Sr. and Don Carlos go on mission to extended Smith family.
1830	Fall	Joseph Sr. goes to debtor's prison for a month.

1830	Fall	Oliver Cowdery, Parley Pratt, and companions leave for Lamanite mission.
1830	Fall	Great numbers join the Church in northern Ohio, including Sidney Rigdon.
1830	Fall	Smith family moves from Manchester cabin to Waterloo, N.Y.
1830	Dec 10	Sidney Rigdon and Edward Partridge arrive in Waterloo.
1830	Dec	Commandment given (D&C 37) to gather to Ohio.

Ohio/Missouri

1831	Feb 1	Joseph and Emma arrive at Kirtland, Ohio. Stay with Whitneys.
1831	Feb 9	Law of the Church given (D&C 42).
1831	Mar	Joseph and Emma move to Isaac Morley farm.
1831	Apr	Lucy Mack Smith and group of eighty Saints depart N.Y. for Ohio.
1831	Apr 30	Joseph and Emma's twins, Thaddeus and Louisa, are born and die.
1831	Apr 30	Julia Murdock passes away in childbirth with twins.
1831	May 9	Joseph and Emma adopt Murdock twins (Joseph Murdock and Julia)
1831	May	Lucy Mack Smith and group arrive in Kirtland.
1831	June	Joseph Jr. and company start for Jackson County, Mo.
1831	Aug 2	Foundation of Zion laid in Kaw Township, Jackson County, Mo.
1831	Aug 3	Place for the temple dedicated by Joseph Jr.
1831	Sept 12	Joseph and Emma move to John Johnson farm in Hiram, Ohio.
1832	Feb 16	Vision of the three degrees of glory given.
1832	Mar 24/25	Joseph and Sidney are mobbed, beaten, tarred, and feathered.
1832	Mar 30	Joseph Murdock Smith, eleven months old, dies from exposure.
1832	Apr 1	Joseph Jr. leaves for Mo.
1832	June	Joseph Jr. arrives back from trip to Mo.
1832	Sept 12	Joseph and Emma and Julia move to Newel K. Whitney store in Kirtland.
1832	Oct	Joseph and Newel Whitney travel to Albany, New York City, and Boston.
1832	Nov 6	Joseph Smith III born at Kirtland.

1832	Dec 25	Revelation on war given (D&C 87).
1832	Dec 27	Beginning of the "Olive Leaf" given (D&C 88). Balance given Jan 1833.
1833	Jan 23	School of the Prophets begins in Kirtland.
1833	Feb 27	Revelation known as the Word of Wisdom given at Kirtland (D&C 89).
1833	Mar 18	First Presidency organized.
1833	July 2	Translation of the Bible "completed."
1833	July 23	Cornerstone for Kirtland Temple laid.
1833	Oct 5	Joseph Jr. leaves on proselyting mission to Canada.
1833	Nov 4	Joseph Jr. returns to Kirtland.
1833	Nov 25	News received in Kirtland of expulsion of the Saints from Jackson County.
1834	Feb 17	High council is organized at Kirtland (D&C 102).
1834	May 5	Joseph Jr. leaves as leader of Zion's Camp.
1834	June 19	Arrival of Zion's Camp in Clay County, Mo.
1834	Aug 1	Joseph Jr. returns to Kirtland.
1835	Feb 14	Organization of the Quorum of the Twelve Apostles.
1835	Feb 28	Organization of the Quorum of the Seventy.
1835	Mar 28	Revelation on priesthood given (D&C 107).
1835	July	Egyptian mummies purchased from Michael Chandler.
1836	Mar 27	Kirtland Temple dedication (D&C 109).
1836	Apr 3	The Savior, Moses, Elias, and Elijah come to the temple (D&C 110).
1836	May 17	Mary Duty Smith, grandmother of the Prophet, arrives in Kirtland.
1836	May 27	Grandmother Mary Duty Smith dies; Sidney Rigdon gives funeral address.
1836	June 20	Joseph and Emma's Frederick G. W. born at Kirtland.
1837	Fall	Apostasy in Kirtland grows rapidly.
1838	Jan 12	Joseph Jr. and Sidney Rigdon ride at midnight to escape danger in Kirtland.
1838	Mar 14	Joseph and Emma arrive in Far West, Mo.
1838	June 2	Joseph and Emma's Alexander Hale born at Far West, Mo.
1838	Aug 6	Election held at Gallatin, Mo.—riot ensues.
1838	Oct 25	David Patten, President of the Twelve, shot and killed at Crooked River.
1838	Oct 27	Extermination order issued by Governor Lilburn W. Boggs.
1838	Oct 30	Haun's Mill massacre.
1838	Oct 31	Joseph, Hyrum, and others surrender to Missouri militia at Far West.
1838	Nov 1	Joseph, Hyrum, and others sentenced to be shot. Doniphan intervenes.

1838	Nov 13	Birth of Joseph Fielding Smith, son of Hyrum and Mary Fielding Smith.
1838	Dec 1	Joseph, Hyrum, and others imprisoned at Liberty Jail.
1839	Feb 7	Emma and the children leave Far West for Ill.
1839	Feb	Joseph Sr., Lucy Mack Smith, and extended family begin trek for Ill.
1839	Mar	Revelations received in Liberty Jail (D&C 121, 122, and 123).
1839	Apr 6	Joseph and other prisoners taken from Liberty Jail to go to Daviess County.
1839	Apr 15	On way to Boone County on change of venue, Joseph and others allowed to escape.
1839	Apr 22	Joseph and Hyrum are reunited with their families at Quincy, Ill.

Nauvoo

1839	May 1	Joseph purchases the first lands for the Church in Ill.
1839	May 10	Move to Commerce, Ill., later called Nauvoo (Hancock County).
1839	July 22	Joseph arises from bed of sickness and gives blessings to the sick.
1839	Oct 29	Joseph leaves for Washington, D.C., to present grievances to the president.
1839	Nov	*Times and Seasons* is published at Nauvoo, Ill.
1839	Nov 28	Joseph arrives in Washington, D.C.
1839	Nov 29	Joseph visits President Martin Van Buren: "Your cause is just . . ."
1839	Dec	Joseph visits Saints in Philadelphia and N.J.
1840	Mar 4	Joseph arrives in Nauvoo from Washington, D.C., trip.
1840	June 13	Joseph and Emma's Don Carlos born at Nauvoo.
1840	Sept 14	Death of Joseph Sr.
1840	Dec 16	Charter for city of Nauvoo, Nauvoo Legion, and university granted.
1841	Feb 4	Joseph commissioned as lieutenant-general of Nauvoo Legion.
1841	Apr 6	Cornerstone laid for the Nauvoo Temple.
1841	June 4	Arrested on old Missouri charges.
1841	June 9	Two-day trial begins at Monmouth, Ill., before Judge Stephen Douglas.
1841	Aug 7	Death of Don Carlos.
1841	Aug 15	Death of Joseph and Emma's Don Carlos.
1841	Nov 8	Dedication of baptismal font in Nauvoo Temple.

1842	Jan 15	Joseph spends time correcting proof for new edition of the Book of Mormon.
1842	Feb 6	Stillborn son of Joseph and Emma.
1842	Mar 15	Joseph becomes editor of *Times and Seasons.*
1842	Mar 17	Female Relief Society of Nauvoo organized with Emma as president.
1842	May 4	Temple endowment is introduced in this dispensation.
1842	May 19	Joseph elected mayor of Nauvoo.
1842	Aug 8	Joseph arrested for alleged complicity in Boggs assassination attempt.
1842	Aug	Joseph goes into hiding.
1842	Fall	Emma and children ill. Emma nearly dies.
1842	Dec 26	Second arrest in Boggs case.
1843	Jan 5	Acquitted in Boggs case.
1843	Jan 18	Joseph and Emma celebrate sixteenth wedding anniversary with guests.
1843	May 28	Sealed to Emma for time and eternity.
1843	June 13	Joseph leaves Nauvoo to visit relatives at Dixon, Ill.
1843	June 23	Arrested by Missouri and Illinois officers disguised as missionaries.
1843	June 30	Arrives back in Nauvoo.
1843	July 1	Discharged by Nauvoo court.
1843	Aug 31	Joseph and Emma move into new residence, Nauvoo Mansion.
1843	Sept 28	Joseph introduces fulness of priesthood ordinances.
1844	Jan 29	Elected candidate for United States presidency.
1844	Feb 20	Instructions given to Twelve to investigate place of refuge for the Saints.
1844	Apr 7	Joseph delivers King Follett discourse.
1844	May 17	Nominated for U.S. presidential candidate at Nauvoo convention.
1844	June 7	*Nauvoo Expositor* published.
1844	June 10	Joseph, as mayor, orders destruction of *Expositor* press.
1844	June 18	Nauvoo placed under martial law.
1844	June 22	Joseph, Hyrum, Willard Richards, O. P. Rockwell cross Mississippi River.
1844	June 25	Joseph and Hyrum surrender at Carthage to face *Expositor* riot charge.
1844	June 27	Death of Hyrum and Joseph Jr. at Carthage Jail.
1844	July 30	Death of Samuel Harrison.
1844	Nov 17	Birth of David Hyrum Smith, son of Joseph and Emma.
1846	Feb 4	Saints begin exodus from Nauvoo to the West.
1847	Dec 23	Emma marries "Major" Lewis C. Bidamon at Nauvoo.
1856	May 14	Lucy Mack Smith dies, having spent her last three years with Emma.

BIBLIOGRAPHY

In the bibliographical entries that follow, "LDS Church Archives" stands for either the Church Library or the Archives Division, Church Historical Department, The Church of Jesus Christ of Latter-day Saints, Salt Lake City, Utah.

Anderson, Karl Ricks. *Joseph Smith's Kirtland: Eyewitness Accounts.* Salt Lake City: Deseret Book Co., 1989.

Anderson, Richard Lloyd. "The Emotional Dimensions of Lucy Smith and Her History." Dedication Colloquiums, Harold B. Lee Library, March 15–17, 1977, Brigham Young University, Provo, Utah, pp. 129–37.

———."His Mother's Manuscript: An Intimate View of Joseph Smith." Brigham Young University Forum address, January 27, 1976.

———. *Investigating the Book of Mormon Witnesses.* Salt Lake City: Deseret Book Co., 1981.

———. *Joseph Smith's New England Heritage.* Salt Lake City: Deseret Book Co., 1971.

———. "The Reliability of the Early History of Lucy and Joseph Smith." *Dialogue* 4 (Summer 1969): 13–28.

Angell, Truman O. Journal. Manuscript. Brigham Young University Special Collections, Provo, Utah.

Arrington, Leonard J., and JoAnn Jolley. "The Faithful Young Family: The Parents, Brothers, and Sisters of Brigham." *Ensign* 10 (August 1980): 52–57.

Backman, Milton V., Jr. *Eyewitness Accounts of the Restoration.* Salt Lake City: Deseret Book Co., 1986.

———. *Joseph Smith's First Vision: Confirming Evidences and Contemporary Accounts.* 2d ed. Salt Lake City: Bookcraft, 1980.

Bennett, Archibald F. "Solomon Mack and His Family." Parts 1–8. *Improvement Era* 58 (1955): 630–32, 663–65, 712–14, 749–51, 906–7, 987; 59 (1956): 34–37, 90–91, 110, 154–55, 190–91, 246–48, 322–23.

The Book of Mormon. Palmyra, New York: Printed by E. B. Grandin, 1830.

The Book of Mormon: Another Testament of Jesus Christ. Translated by Joseph Smith Jr. Salt Lake City: The Church of Jesus Christ of Latter-day Saints, 1981.

Bushman, Richard L. *Joseph Smith and the Beginnings of Mormonism.* Urbana and Chicago: University of Illinois Press, 1984.

Cannon, Donald Q. "Joseph Smith in Salem." In Robert L. Millet and Kent P. Jackson, eds., *Studies in Scripture, Volume 1: The Doctrine and Covenants.* Sandy, Utah: Randall Book, 1984.

Conference Reports of The Church of Jesus Christ of Latter-day Saints. Salt Lake City: The Church of Jesus Christ of Latter-day Saints.

Cook, Lyndon W., ed. *David Whitmer Interviews: A Restoration Witness.* Orem, Utah: Grandin Book Co., 1991.

————. *The Revelations of the Prophet Joseph Smith: A Historical and Biographical Commentary of the Doctrine and Covenants.* Salt Lake City: Deseret Book Co., 1985.

————. *William Law: Biographical Essay, Nauvoo Diary, Correspondence, Interview.* Orem, Utah: Grandin Book Co., 1994.

Cooper, Robert P. "Martha Jane Knowlton Coray and *The History of Joseph Smith by His Mother.*" Typescript. 1965. LDS Church Archives.

Cowley, Matthias F. *Wilford Woodruff: History of His Life and Labors.* Salt Lake City: Bookcraft, 1964.

Deseret Evening News. Salt Lake City, Utah.

The Doctrine and Covenants of The Church of Jesus Christ of Latter-day Saints. Salt Lake City: The Church of Jesus Christ of Latter-day Saints, 1981.

Enders, Donald L. "The Sacred Grove." *Ensign* 20 (April 1990): 14–17.

————. "'A Snug Log House': A Historical Look at the Joseph Smith, Sr., Family Home in Palmyra, New York." *Ensign* 15 (August 1985): 14–23.

Godfrey, Kenneth W., Audrey M. Godfrey, and Jill Mulvay Derr. *Women's Voices: An Untold History of the Latter-day Saints, 1830–1900.* Salt Lake City: Deseret Book Co., 1982.

Hartley, William G. "The Knight Family: Ever Faithful to the Prophet." *Ensign* 19 (January 1989): 43–49.

"History of Lyman Wight." Parts 1 and 2. *Millennial Star* 27 (1865): 455–57, 471–72.

Hyde, Orson. Journal. (Feb-Dec 1832). LDS Church Archives.

Jessee, Dean C. "Joseph Knight's Recollection of Early Mormon History." *BYU Studies* 17 (Autumn 1976): 29–39.

Johnson, Benjamin F. *My Life's Review.* Independence, Mo.: Zion's Printing and Publishing, 1947.

Johnson, Jeffery O. "Martha Jane Knowlton Coray: Masculine in Her Strength of Character." Dedication Colloquiums, Harold B. Lee Library, March 15–17, 1977, Brigham Young University, Provo, Utah, pp. 115–28.

Jones, Gracia N. "My Great-Great-Grandmother Emma Hale Smith." *Ensign* 22 (August 1992): 30–39.

Journal of Discourses. 26 vols. Liverpool, England: Printed and published by Albert Carrington [and others], 1853–1886.

Kirkham, Francis W. *A New Witness for Christ in America: The Book of Mormon.* Vol. I, 4th ed.; vol. 2, rev. ed. Salt Lake City: Utah Printing Co., 1967, 1959.

Knight, Joseph Jr. "Autobiographical Sketch." 1862. LDS Church Archives.

LeBaron, E. Dale. "Benjamin Franklin Johnson: Colonizer, Public Servant, and Church Leader." Master's thesis, Brigham Young University, 1967.

Mack, Solomon. *A Narrative of the Life of Solomon Mack. . . .* Windsor, Vt.: Printed at the expense of the author, 1811.

Madsen, Truman. *Joseph Smith the Prophet.* Salt Lake City: Bookcraft, 1989.

Manuscript History of Brigham Young, 1801–1844. Salt Lake City: Elden Jay Watson, 1968.

Maxfield, Miriam. "A Compiled History of Phineas Howe Young." Unpublished paper. 1970. LDS Church Archives.

Murdock, John. Journal. Typescript. Brigham Young University Archives, Provo, Utah.

The New Grolier Multimedia Encyclopedia. Release 6. The Software Toolworks Inc., 1993.

Nibley, Hugh. *Lehi in the Desert. . . .* Provo, Utah: Deseret Book Co. and Foundation for Ancient Research and Mormon Studies, 1988.

Paine, Thomas. *The Age of Reason. Part the First. Being an Investigation of True and Fabulous Theology.* 3rd ed. London: R. Carlile, 1819.

The Pearl of Great Price. Salt Lake City: The Church of Jesus Christ of Latter-day Saints, 1981.

Perkins, Keith W. "True to the Book of Mormon—the Whitmers." *Ensign* 19 (February 1989): 34–42.

Porter, Larry C. "From a Book Coming Forth." *Ensign* 18 (July 1988): 42–46.

———. "A Study of the Origins of the Church of Jesus Christ of Latter-day Saints in the States of New York and Pennsylvania, 1816–1831." Ph.D. diss., Brigham Young University, 1971.

Pratt, Parley P. *Autobiography of Parley P. Pratt.* Edited by Parley P. Pratt Jr. Classics in Mormon Literature. Salt Lake City: Deseret Book Co., 1985.

Presbyterian Church of Palmyra Session Records, March 10–29, 1830. Microfilm. LDS Church Archives.

Proctor, Scot Facer. *Witness of the Light: A Photographic Journey in the Footsteps of the American Prophet Joseph Smith.* Salt Lake City: Deseret Book Co., 1991.

Rich, Russell R. "The Dogberry Papers and the Book of Mormon." *BYU Studies* 10 (Spring 1970): 315–20.

Roberts, Brigham H. *A Comprehensive History of The Church of Jesus Christ of Latter-day Saints.* 6 Vols. Provo, Utah: Brigham Young University Press, 1965.

Searle, Howard Clair. "Early Mormon Historiography: Writing the History of the Mormons 1830–1858." Ph.D. diss., University of California, Los Angeles, 1979.

Shipps, Jan. *Mormonism: The Story of a New Religious Tradition.* Urbana and Chicago: University of Illinois Press, 1985.

Smith, George A. "Memoirs." Brigham Young University Special Collections, Provo, Utah.

Smith, Joseph. *History of The Church of Jesus Christ of Latter-day Saints.* Edited by Brigham H. Roberts. 7 vols. Salt Lake City: The Church of Jesus Christ of Latter-day Saints, 1932–51.

―――. *The Papers of Joseph Smith, Volume 1: Autobiographical and Historical Writings.* Edited by Dean C. Jessee. Salt Lake City: Deseret Book Co., 1989.

―――. *The Personal Writings of Joseph Smith.* Compiled and edited by Dean C. Jessee. Salt Lake City: Deseret Book Co., 1984.

Smith, Lucy Mack. *Biographical Sketches of Joseph Smith, the Prophet, and His Progenitors for Many Generations.* Liverpool: Published for Orson Pratt by S. W. Richards, 1853; photomechanical reproduction, Orem, Utah: Grandin Book Co., 1995.

―――. *Biographical Sketches of Joseph Smith, the Prophet, and His Progenitors for Many Generations.* Liverpool: Published for Orson Pratt by S. W. Richards, 1853. Personal copy with pencil and ink mark edits and notes by George A. Smith.

―――. *History of Joseph Smith by His Mother.* Edited by Preston Nibley. Salt Lake City: Bookcraft, 1954.

―――. "History of the Prophet Joseph." Parts 1–12. *Improvement Era* 5 (1901): 3–16, 81–102; 5 (1902): 161–71, 241–59, 321–38, 401–21, 481–99, 561–73, 641–60, 737–58, 817–42, 913–38.

―――. Unpublished Early Notebook. 1844–45. Special Collections, Harold B. Lee Library, Brigham Young University.

―――. Unpublished Preliminary Manuscript. 1845. LDS Church Archives.

Times and Seasons. Nauvoo, Illinois.

Tullidge, Edward W. *The Women of Mormondom.* New York, 1877.

Warsaw Signal. Warsaw, Illinois.

Wayne Sentinel. Palmyra, New York.

"Where the Book of Mormon Went to Press." *Ensign* 19 (February 1989): 43–47.

Whitney, Elizabeth Ann. "A Leaf from an Autobiography." *Woman's Exponent* 7 (September 1, 1878): 51.

Whitney, Orson F. *Life of Heber C. Kimball.* Collector's Edition. Salt Lake City: Bookcraft, 1992.

INDEX

Italicized page numbers indicate photographs or maps.